THE FIGURE OF THE TERRORIST IN LITERATURE AND VISUAL CULTURE

THE FIGURE OF THE TERRORIST IN LITERATURE AND VISUAL CULTURE

Edited by Maria Flood and
Michael C. Frank

EDINBURGH
University Press

Edinburgh University Press is one of the leading university presses in the UK. We publish academic books and journals in our selected subject areas across the humanities and social sciences, combining cutting-edge scholarship with high editorial and production values to produce academic works of lasting importance. For more information visit our website: edinburghuniversitypress.com

© editorial matter and organisation Maria Flood and Michael C. Frank, 2023, 2024
© The chapters their several authors, 2023, 2024

Edinburgh University Press Ltd
13 Infirmary Street
Edinburgh, EH1 1LT

First published in hardback by Edinburgh University Press 2023

Typeset in 10/12.5 pt Sabon
by IDSUK (DataConnection) Ltd

A CIP record for this book is available from the British Library

ISBN 978 1 4744 9758 9 (hardback)
ISBN 978 1 4744 9759 6 (paperback)
ISBN 978 1 4744 9760 2 (webready PDF)
ISBN 978 1 4744 9761 9 (epub)

The right of Maria Flood and Michael C. Frank to be identified as editors of this work has been asserted in accordance with the Copyright, Designs and Patents Act 1988 and the Copyright and Related Rights Regulations 2003 (SI No. 2498).

Every effort has been made to trace the copyright holders, but if any have been inadvertently overlooked, the publisher will be pleased to make the necessary arrangements at the first opportunity.

CONTENTS

List of Figures vii
Notes on Contributors ix

1. Introduction: The Figure of the Terrorist in Literature and Visual Culture 1
   Maria Flood and Michael C. Frank

PART ONE HISTORICISING THE FIGURE OF THE TERRORIST: CROSS-MEDIA PERSPECTIVES

2. The Psychology of Post-War Revolutionary Terrorism in Muriel Spark's *The Only Problem* and Doris Lessing's *The Good Terrorist* 29
   Beatriz Lopez

3. Sympathy for the Devil? The Changing Face of the IRA in American Superhero Comics 47
   Shane Walshe

4. Terrorists and Hooligans: Re-politicising a De-politicised Figure in Contemporary Representations of British Football Culture 67
   Cyprian Piskurek

5. Screening Railway Terrorists: Light Modernity, Invisible Threats and the Aesthetics of Concealment in *The 15:17 to Paris* and *Bodyguard* 87
   Johannes Riquet

6. 'Nothing Terroristic About Him': The Figure of the Terrorist in
   Karan Mahajan's *The Association of Small Bombs*   105
   Peter C. Herman

PART TWO   GENDER, IDENTITY AND TERRORISM

7. Militancy, Maternity and Masquerade in Santosh Sivan's
   The Terrorist   125
   Rajeswari Mohan

8. The Female Counter-Strike: Terrorising Patriarchy in Hindi Cinema   143
   Harald Pittel

9. Contrasting Terrorist Figures: Far-Right Extremists and
   Jihadists in Contemporary French Cinema   165
   Sarah Davison

10. 'I Was a Big Girl. I Could Pack My Bags and Leave': ISIS and
    Female Emancipation in Tabish Khair's *Just Another Jihadi Jane*   183
    Zaynab Seedat

PART THREE   INTIMATE ENEMIES: FEELING FOR THE TERRORIST?

11. Circumventing the Condemnation Imperative: The Figure of
    the Female Suicide Bomber in Akin and El Akkad   203
    Tim Gauthier

12. Discomfort and Documentary Film: The Figure of the
    White Extremist in Deeyah Khan's *White Right*   223
    Maria Flood

13. Intimate Conflicts: Rebels, Heroes and Disfigured Terrorists in
    Burmese Anglophone Literature   245
    Pavan Kumar Malreddy

    Afterword   263
    Richard Jackson

Index   275

FIGURES

1.1	Using a child as suicide bomber: the opening scene of *American Sniper*	7
1.2	Becoming a terrorist: the recording of Khaled's martyrdom video in *Paradise Now*	12
3.1	The 'Troubled Terrorist': Alan Cavenaugh's recurring nightmare (Source: *Iron Fist #11*, 1977)	52
3.2	Glorianna defends the 'good people' of the IRA (Source: *Daredevil #217* 1985)	57
5.1	Liquid modernity and high speed: the station of Liège-Guillemins at the beginning of *Gemini Man*	88
5.2	An aesthetics of concealment: the terrorist and the train in *The 15:17 to Paris*	95
5.3	Mediated views, digital communication and multipile screens in *Bodyguard*	100
7.1	A close-up of Malli's face as she is bathing	134
8.1	Domestic violence equals terrorist violence: a parallel montage with flashback shows Neerja hiding from both male aggressors, terrorist and husband	149
8.2	Low-angle shot of Zoya undressing for Bagdawi, seconds before she cuts his throat	153
8.3	Simmba's female police officers beat up Ranade's brothers under the watchful eyes of their male colleagues	156
9.1	*Chez Nous*: a refugee is placed in a cage by Stanko's group	173

9.2	*Made in France*: Hassan is killed by RAID police	177
11.1	*In the Fade*: a closeup of an anguished Katja as she is wrestled to the ground	210
11.2	The defendants sit coldly and unemotionally throughout the court proceedings	211
11.3	Katja, bomb strapped to her back, the moment before she enters the trailer	211
12.1	Filming the 'Enemy': Khan amidst the crowd of NSM supporters at the Charlottesville Rally, 2017	231
12.2	Schoep's emotional and physical discomfort mirrored in the awkward shot composition	233
12.3	Spencer and his friends surrounded by objects that evoke a well-worn iconography of wealth, power and masculinity	239

NOTES ON CONTRIBUTORS

Sarah Davison is a PhD Researcher in the University of Manchester's French Department. She completed a Master's in German and French with dissertations on 'Representations of the Stasi in Post-Millennium German Film' and the 'Phenomenology of the Nude in French Film'. Her doctoral thesis, *Approaching Terrorism on Screen: Contemporary French and Belgian Cinema and Television*, explores contemporary depictions of terrorism through an interdisciplinary framework combining the ethics of representation and critical race theory; it is funded by the Arts and Humanities Research Council.

Maria Flood is Senior Lecturer in World Cinema at the University of Liverpool. A specialist in political violence, ethics, gender and spectatorship, she has published widely on French and Algerian cinemas of conflict, including the monograph *France, Algeria and the Moving Image: Screening Histories of Violence 1963–2010* (2018). She is also the author of *Moonlight: Screening Black Queer Youth* (2022).

Michael C. Frank is Professor of English Literature at the University of Zurich and the author of *The Cultural Imaginary of Terrorism in Public Discourse, Literature, and Film* (2017). His other publications include the co-edited volumes *Literature and Terrorism: Comparative Perspectives* (2012) and *Narratives of the War on Terror: Global Perspectives* (2020) as well as a special issue on *Migrations and Contacts* (SPELL, vol. 41, 2022).

Tim Gauthier is the Director of the Multidisciplinary Studies and Social Science Studies programmes in the Department of Interdisciplinary, Ethnic and Gender Studies at the University of Nevada, Las Vegas (UNLV). He is the author of *9/11 Fiction, Empathy, and Otherness* (2015) and *Narrative Desire and Historical Reparations* (2006). His research focuses on contemporary fiction and spans postcolonial concerns and artistic reactions to social and personal trauma experiences. His current project examines the themes of contagion and empathy in recent pandemic fiction.

Peter C. Herman teaches at San Diego State University. He is the author of *Unspeakable: Literature and Terrorism from the Gunpowder Plot to 9/11* (2020) and the editor of *Cambridge Critical Concepts: Terrorism and Literature* (2018). He has also published numerous books and articles on early modern literature, and the most recent is *Early Modern Others* (forthcoming).

Richard Jackson holds the Leading Thinker Chair in Peace and Conflict Studies at the University of Otago, New Zealand. He is the editor-in-chief of the journal *Critical Studies on Terrorism* and some of his recent publications include the co-edited volumes *Revolutionary Nonviolence: Concepts, Cases and Controversies* (2020) and *Encountering Extremism: Theoretical Issues and Local Challenges* (2020). He is also the author of a terrorism-related novel entitled *Confessions of a Terrorism* (2014).

Beatriz Lopez is Teaching Assistant in English Studies at Durham University. She has recently completed a PhD entitled *Muriel Spark and the Political Warfare Executive: The Legacies of Covert Propaganda in Post-War Fiction* at Durham University. She is the author of 'Muriel Spark and the Art of Deception: Constructing Plausibility with the Methods of WWII Black Propaganda', published in *The Review of English Studies* (2020). Her research interests include post-war British literature, Scottish literature, the cultural history of the Second World War, and Gothic Studies.

Pavan Kumar Malreddy is a Researcher in English Literature at Goethe University Frankfurt. He is the author of *Orientalism, Terrorism, Indigenism: South Asian Readings in Postcolonialism* (2015) and he has co-edited ten special issues and collected volumes, including 'Global Literature and Violence' (special issue of *Postcolonial Text*, in preparation), *Writing Brexit: Colonial Remains* (2021), and *Narratives of the War on Terror: Global Perspectives* (2020). He is currently preparing his second monograph, *Insurgent Cultures: World Literatures and Narratives of Violence from the Global South*, for publication; he is also working on a volume titled *Remapping World Anglophone Studies: English in a World of Strangers*.

NOTES ON CONTRIBUTORS

Rajeswari Mohan is a member of the English Department at Haverford College, where she teaches courses on postcolonial literature, twentieth century and contemporary British literature, literary theory, and gender and sexuality studies. She has published articles on the representation of modernity in Tamil film, female insurgency in Palestine, and the writings of Anita Desai and Michelle Cliff. She is currently working on a manuscript that explores cognitive mapping, gastropolitics, gossip, rioting and nostalgia as practices that assert citizenship and claim space for migrant communities in western metropolitan centres, especially London.

Cyprian Piskurek is Lecturer in British Cultural Studies at TU Dortmund University and the author of *Fictional Representations of English Football and Fan Cultures: Slum Sport, Slum People?* (2018). He has co-edited special issues for several journals, including one on 'Housing in Britain' (*Hard Times*, no. 105, 2021) and one on 'Political Bodies' (*Journal for the Study of British Cultures*, vol. 25, no. 1, 2018).

Harald Pittel teaches British Cultural Studies at Leipzig University. He has published articles on post-Brexit fiction, working-class literature and decadent theory. From 2018 to 2019, he was a visiting scholar at Delhi University. He wrote his PhD thesis on *Romance and Irony: Oscar Wilde and the Political*. His second book (in progress) explores how the crises of the present might shape a new understanding of world literature. His other research interests include political affect studies, comparative film studies, genre theories, and materialist theories of culture.

Johannes Riquet is Professor of English Literature at Tampere University. He is the author of *The Aesthetics of Island Space: Perception, Ideology, Geopoetics* (2019) and *Trains, Interrupted: Railway Fiction and the Accidents of Modernity* (forthcoming) as well as the co-author of *The Mediated Arctic: Poetics and Politics of Contemporary Circumpolar Geographies* (also forthcoming). He has written numerous articles and edited various collections on spatiality, literary geography, phenomenology, ecocriticism, mobility, and visual culture.

Zaynab Seedat is a PhD Researcher at the University of York, where she is working on the thesis *Writing the South Asian Muslim Terrorist: Politics, Religion and 'Terror' through a Postcolonial Lens*. She holds an MA in English Literature from the University of Durham. Her doctoral research is fully funded by the Arts and Humanities Research Council through the White Rose College of the Arts and Humanities. She is a member of the State Violence Research Network and a committee member of the White Rose South Asia Conference.

THE FIGURE OF THE TERRORIST IN LITERATURE AND VISUAL CULTURE

Shane Walshe is a Lecturer in the English Department of the University of Zurich and a co-founder of the Swiss Center for Irish Studies. He was awarded a PhD in English linguistics for his work *Irish English as Represented in Film* (2009) and has published widely on the representation of the Irish in popular culture, particularly in film, television, comics, and joke books. He is currently writing a book on portrayals of the Irish Republican Army and the Northern Ireland conflict in comic books.

1. INTRODUCTION: THE FIGURE OF THE TERRORIST IN LITERATURE AND VISUAL CULTURE

Maria Flood and Michael C. Frank

"Those Hell-Hounds Called Terrorists" – Then and Now

In their pioneering study *Terror and Taboo*, the cultural anthropologists Joseba Zulaika and William Douglass point out a curious paradox in the contemporary preoccupation with terrorism. Whereas the topic of terrorism has been ubiquitous in Western public discourse since the late twentieth century, the voices of terrorists themselves are usually silenced. Zulaika and Douglass suggest that the terrorist is 'the paradigm of inhuman bestiality, the quintessential proscribed or tabooed figure of our times' (1996, 6). To say that there is such a thing as a 'terrorism taboo' (Jackson 2015a, 320) is not to say that terrorism is not talked about. Quite the opposite is true. Quoting Michel Foucault's well-known phrase (which originally refers to the public repression of sexuality in Victorian times), we may speak of a 'veritable discursive explosion' (1978, 17) surrounding the subject of terror, which the events of 11 September 2001 propelled to the forefront of political action and media attention. What is taboo is not the topic of terrorism as such; it is the political subjectivity of the *perpetrator* of terrorism, whose motives cannot be acknowledged, since 'the very attempt to "know" how the terrorist thinks or lives can be deemed an abomination' (Zulaika and Douglass 1996, 149). Zulaika and Douglass maintain that what they term 'terrorism discourse' is caught up in a self-referential tangle; rather than engaging with the actual circumstances and perpetrators of political violence, counterterrorism experts and the media reiterate the same set of assumptions in a posture of 'rhetorical circularity' (ix).

The Figure of the Terrorist in Literature and Visual Culture takes up these ideas within the fields of literary, film, television, and media studies. In what ways, we ask, do media forms such as novels, fiction and nonfiction films, or comic books frame and make sense of the figure of the terrorist? And how do the resulting narratives relate to official, state-led discourses? Do they reinforce the terrorism taboo, or do they find ways of circumventing it? Surprisingly few studies have devoted themselves to narrative representations of *terrorists* rather than *terrorism* as a more abstract concept and phenomenon. As the following sections will demonstrate, moreover, the existing research tends to limit itself to one medium and context. Building and expanding on this scholarship, the present volume takes a cross-media and comparative approach. In doing so, it aims to illustrate the pressures, challenges and restrictions involved in any narrative engagement with the figure of the terrorist. At the same time, we hope to demonstrate that this figure is far from stable. Not only has the terrorist undergone several historical incarnations; narrative representations of this figure also differ according to the medium used, as well as the ethnicity, gender and political orientation of the actors portrayed. Taken together, these factors allow for varying degrees of empathy with the terrorist.

Before we turn to the figure of the terrorist, it is worth remembering that the concept of the terrorist itself has a long history. Its emergence in the English language can be dated to 1795 (see *OED*, s.v. 'terrorist, *n.*', sense 1a). In an unfinished letter begun at the end of that year, the British royalist Edmund Burke expressed his disdain for the then current government of Revolutionary France, the Directory. According to Burke, this new administration was sustained by 'military force and terrour [*sic*]' (1991, 89) rather than popular will. To prove his point, Burke stressed the Directory's reliance on the supporters of the Reign of Terror, who had been freed from incarceration to help the new rulers of France secure their power: 'Thousands of those Hell-hounds called Terrorists, whom they had shut up in Prison on their last Revolution, as the Satellites of Tyranny, are let loose on the people' (89). In this passage, Burke is citing – and translating – a recently invented French term: *terroriste* had been coined in 1794 to distance the Directory from the Jacobin dictatorship of 1793–4 (see Walther 1990, 348). By adding the suffix '–ist' to the word 'terror', representatives of the new regime indicated their rejection of their predecessors' politics of intimidation and surveillance, even if they themselves used some of the same methods.

Ever since its first occurrence, 'terrorist' has preserved this element of self-distanciation. According to the criminologist Sebastian Scheerer, the deployment of the term depends less on the actions of those labelled as 'terrorists' than on the standpoint of those doing the labelling: 'the terrorists are always the others' (2002, 19; our trans.). So-called terrorists invariably describe themselves as fighters in a just cause, and it is this very self-legitimisation that the label 'terrorist' aims to call into question. Like 'terrorism', a term invented in the same year, the 'terrorist' label *delegitimises* those to whom it is attached, and this delegitimisation operates at several levels: 'terrorism' implies that the actions thus described are not only 'illegal from a judicial point of view, but also politically illegitimate', which categorically undermines any attempt at justification; moreover, the term carries overtones of 'moral condemnation' (Daase 2001, 55; our trans.). Contrary to 'war', 'terrorism' is not a designation that can be agreed upon by conflicting parties to describe the nature of their conflict. As a term of condemnation, it is typically applied unilaterally by one party to the other. In 1998, al-Qaeda leader Osama bin Laden told American television network ABC that 'the worst thieves in the world today and the worst terrorists are the Americans' (qtd in *The 9/11 Commission Report* 2004, 47). This accusation demonstrates that the attribution of terrorism is never neutral, as it is inevitably informed by political interests.

Burke's reference to 'those Hell-hounds called Terrorists' serves as a reminder of how long the term 'terrorist' has been in use, and how much the context of its use has changed over time. Originally associated with the mass-executions perpetrated by a totalitarian state, the *Grande Terreur* of June and July 1794, the term is now almost exclusively applied to nonstate actors. Like state terrorism (or terrorism from above), nonstate terrorism (or terrorism from below) can be described as coercion through intimidation. As its name indicates, terrorism in all its guises involves the strategic deployment of 'terror' – that is, the fear of possible future violence – as an instrument of political pressure serving to either forcefully maintain the status quo (state terrorism) or to challenge it (nonstate terrorism). In comparison to state actors like the Jacobin dictatorship and its various historical successors, nonstate actors possess very limited means of inducing a prolonged sense of insecurity within a population. Consequently, the attention created by their acts of violence (or the threat thereof) tends to be disproportionate to their actual capacities. Yet even though they lack the power of state actors, nonstate terrorists are subjected to the same dehumanising rhetoric by their opponents. As Marco Pinfari notes, '"Terrorists" are seldom talked about as humans' (2019, 27), which is why the stereotype of 'terrorists as monsters' – to cite the title of Pinfari's book – has persisted with surprising continuity from the French Revolution to the rise of the Islamic State.

During the last two centuries, the strategy of dehumanisation has been applied to terrorists of all hues. Accordingly, Burke's double gesture of demonisation ('Hell') and bestialisation ('hounds') has remained a fixture of counterterrorism discourse. As such, it became particularly prominent in the wake of the 11 September 2001 attacks on New York City and Washington, DC. In a speech delivered twelve days after the event, the then-US Ambassador to Japan, Howard Baker, spoke of 'a strike against those values that separate us from animals' (2001). After namedropping Enlightenment philosopher Denis Diderot, Baker thus referred to the idea that the capacity for empathy, or feeling with others, is what makes us human. By displaying an utter lack of 'compassion, tolerance, mercy', Baker claimed, the suicide terrorists had proved that they were less than human. Baker's speech goes on to describe terrorism as a 'cancer' to be 'removed . . . from our international body'. Ironically, this kind of rhetoric justifies the very ruthlessness that Baker ascribes to terrorists: being incapable of empathy, terrorists are themselves undeserving of our 'compassion, tolerance, mercy'.

By constructing terrorists as inhuman monsters, counterterrorist discourse legitimises counterterrorism 'as a form of monstrous response to what has been framed as a form of monstrous brutality' (Pinfari 2019, 24). If terrorists are inhuman, then they have no right to be treated like human beings. In a 2005 study, peace and conflict studies scholar Richard Jackson demonstrates that the dehumanisation of terrorists was a common feature of political discourse in the run-up to the war on terror. In a 'public narrative' (Jackson 2005, 1) designed to justify drastic measures in the name of countering terrorism, the Bush administration constructed terrorists as 'fundamentally inhuman' (61). In doing so, the US government pre-empted alternative explanations of terrorism. For a time, George W. Bush's preferred designation for Osama bin Laden was 'the evil one', a biblical term for Satan (66). Not only were terrorists likened to animals, a curse, a scourge, a cancer, spawn, or parasites (73–4); they were also associated with the non-human villains of popular culture. At the end of October 2001, US Attorney General John Ashcroft informed the American public about the creation of a Foreign Terrorist Tracking Task Force. '[A]s September the 11th vividly illustrates', he declared, 'aliens also come to our country with the intent to do great evil' (Ashcroft 2001). While reading Ashcroft's speech, one cannot help noticing that although the phrase used in the title of the task force is 'foreign terrorist', the Attorney General chooses the word 'alien' whenever he speaks of foreigners who threaten domestic security. The word appears no less than 23 times in the short text. 'Terrorist alien' is the latest variation of the legal category of the 'enemy alien', which has a long history in US law. As Jackson emphasises, however, John Ashcroft's scenario of evil-intentioned aliens does more than stir xenophobic fears; it exploits the unavoidable ambiguity of the term 'alien', which denotes space invaders as much as non-citizens (2005, 71).

So dominant was the public narrative established by the Bush administration that it became difficult to counter the dehumanisation of terrorists without raising suspicions about one's loyalties. As Judith Butler remembers in the 2003 preface to *Precarious Life: The Power of Mourning and Violence*, 'anyone who sought to understand the "reasons" for the attack on the United States was regarded as someone who sought to "exonerate" those who conducted that attack' (2004, xiii). Although Butler's observation specifically refers to the post-9/11 situation in the United States, the dilemma described in her collection of essays is a more general feature of the public discourse on terrorism. In an essay written at around the same time as Butler's study, the sociologist

Ghassan Hage discusses the difficulties involved in attempting to understand Palestinian suicide bombers. Hage opens his essay by describing an email that he sent to a group of colleagues to vent his frustration at the Israeli reinvasion of the West Bank in 2002. In the message in question, he criticised the Sharon government for employing the same 'dehumanizing gaze' as suicide bombers, a gaze that fails to differentiate between individuals, seeing only a 'communal Us versus Them' (Hage 2003, 65). As Hage soon realised, any such comparison between counterterrorist and terrorist violence prompts accusations of moral equivocation. In response to his email, he was asked to '"absolutely condemn"' suicide bombers' (66). For Hage, this goes to show that whoever addresses the topic of terrorism 'in the Western public sphere' (67) is expected, or compelled, to categorically denounce terrorism on ethical grounds. Hage speaks of a 'condemnation imperative', which he describes as a 'mode of censoring the attempts to provide a sociological explanation for why [terrorists] act the way they do' (67). Against this background, Hage asks whether it is possible to 'talk about suicide bombers by leaving condemnation aside in order to concentrate on explanation, without this being seen as a form of "justification"' (68).

Frames of Violence: Difficult Empathy

Like Butler, Hage thus emphasises the detrimental effects of equating *understanding* with *sympathy*. The consequences of this equation become obvious in an essay by Richard Jackson, which contains several variations of the sentence: 'I am a terrorist sympathiser because I can understand . . .' (2015b). In each instance, Jackson lists motivational factors of political violence such as the experience of trauma, injustice and humiliation, the lack of prospects, or the feeling of powerlessness. Jackson concludes his essay by naming several reasons as to why 'sympathy for the terrorist . . . is necessary'. Among other things, he states that 'We need sympathy for the terrorist if we are to find . . . more ethical, peaceful and effective ways of responding to terrorism'. As Jackson emphasises, the dehumanisation of terrorists has led to a normalisation of incarcerations without trial in so-called black sites as well as extrajudicial assassinations by killer drones.

Yet 'sympathy' is not, perhaps, quite the right word to describe the 'kind of empathy and understanding' that Jackson (2015b) has in mind. In her book *Empathy and the Novel*, literary scholar Suzanne Keen makes a helpful differentiation between sympathy and empathy. As Keen reminds us, the English word 'empathy' is a relatively recent invention, having been introduced in the early twentieth century to approximate the German term *'Einfühlung'* (see Keen 2009, 6). 'Empathy' denotes the process of feeling one's way into another person in order to understand that person's viewpoint. This process does not necessarily involve a positive identification, or alignment, with the other person's actions, as it is possible to empathise with someone without supporting their decisions. Whereas in the case of empathy 'we feel what we believe to be the emotions of others', sympathy means to have 'feelings *for* another' (5). Keen illustrates this difference as follows: when I feel empathetic, 'I feel what you feel' (for example, '*I feel your pain*'); when I feel sympathetic, on the other hand, 'I feel a supportive emotion about your feelings' (to stay with the previous example, '*I feel pity for your pain*') (5). Sympathy is personal concern and compassion (feeling *for* someone). In that sense it is distinguished from empathy (feeling *with* someone), which entails a different kind of emotional investment.

What scholars like Butler, Hage and Jackson advocate is *empathy* in the sense of 'reaching out toward the other person's situation' (Vetlesen 1994, 225). In *Precarious Life*, Butler characterises the aftermath of 9/11 as a missed 'opportunity' (2004, xi) precisely because it did not involve such a reaching out. The basic premise of Butler's book is that instead of giving way to rage – the desire to strike back at the source of the violence, and to retaliate for the losses suffered by Americans – the grief caused by the suicide bombings could have led to a very different kind of response. In Butler's view, 9/11 brought home the message that all life is precarious because of its dependency on others, and for the United States, to concede this vulnerability would have meant rethinking its role in global politics. What Butler terms 'injurability' (xii) is a universally shared condition and as such, it connects the United States to the rest of the world, raising the question as to how the violence inflicted on Americans on September 11 is related to aggression endured by others.

As Butler goes on to argue, however, the pain of others often remains imperceptible. The essays collected in *Precarious Life* suggest that the perception of human suffering is contingent on framing – an idea that Butler would later take up and develop in *Frames of War: When Is Life Grievable?* (2009). Because the frames established by official discourse and mainstream media tend to focus on only one side of a conflict, the violence suffered by the other side can become 'derealized' (Butler 2004, 38). There are victims whose images are never shown and whose names never uttered, meaning that their existence is never acknowledged. For Butler, this 'derealization of loss' entails a 'dehumanization' (148). Butler's understanding of dehumanisation goes beyond the earlier-mentioned equation of terrorists with devils, animals or aliens. It is less a matter of *mis*-representation than a matter of *non*-representation; certain lives are rendered 'ungrievable' (148) by virtue of not being recognised as lives in the first place. At the beginning of *Frames of War*, Butler sums up this idea as follows: 'specific lives cannot be apprehended as injured or lost if they are not first apprehended as living' (2009, 1).

Butler adds that the 'selective and differential framing of violence' determines the 'affective and ethical dispositions' (1) of the audience. Evidence of this can be found in Hollywood representations of the Global War on Terrorism – a conflict better known under George W. Bush's notorious shorthand 'war on terror'. Nominated for six Oscars and winning one, Clint Eastwood's *American Sniper* was the highest-grossing film of 2014 in the United States. It tells the story of US Navy Seal Chris Kyle, whose bestselling 2012 memoir was marketed as *The Autobiography of the Most Lethal Sniper in U.S. History* on account of his 160 confirmed enemy kills (Kyle, McEwen and DeFelice 2012). At the beginning of Eastwood's film, we witness one such kill. Kyle (played by Bradley Cooper) is lying on a rooftop as he covers an American convoy in an unidentified Iraqi city. In the words of the screenplay, Kyle has his 'dick in the dirt' and his 'eye to the glass of a .300 Win-Mag sniper rifle' (Hall 2014, sc. 3). Initially, he aims at a man with a mobile phone who observes the convoy from the top of a house. Then, a veiled woman and boy – presumably the man's wife and son – step out of the house. Kyle watches them approach the convoy, his index finger on the trigger.

From closeups of the protagonist taking aim at the couple in the street, the film cuts to what Kyle sees through the scope of his rifle: the woman and boy behind crosshairs (Figure 1.1). In this way, the film thrusts viewers into the point of view of the titular American sniper. Significantly, the tension and suspense created in the sequence do not concern the fate of the Iraqi mother and son; they concern the dilemma of the protagonist, who is about to make a terrible

Figure 1.1 Using a child as suicide bomber: the opening scene of *American Sniper*.

choice. It is obvious that the woman is hiding something under her robes. When she pulls out an anti-tank grenade and hands it to the boy, motioning him to hurry along, the intended effect is one of moral consternation and horror. At the same time, we are made to feel for the protagonist, who will have to live with the consciousness of having killed a child. The purpose of the sequence is to illustrate the psychological toll of fighting in a war, a theme that the film goes on to develop during its remaining two hours of runtime. Whereas the protagonist's trauma is explored in some depth, the nameless Iraqis vanish as suddenly as they appeared. The film is not interested in the conditions leading to the deployment of children as suicide bombers, nor does it give viewers time to wonder about the desperation on the part of the boy's parents. Instead, it evokes empathy and sympathy with Chris Kyle, depicting an American sniper as the emotional victim of America's own war.

Rather than exploring the impact of the invasion of Iraq on the local population, Hollywood films on the Iraq War from *The Hurt Locker* (Kathryn Bigelow, 2008) to *The Yellow Birds* (Alexandre Moors, 2017) tend to concentrate on how the country's war-torn environment affects US soldiers, who move through this alienating space like visitors on a strange planet. According to the same narrative logic, the actions of the Iraqi mother and son in the opening sequence of *American Sniper* are isolated from previous events. Butler's concept of framing is quite appropriate here: as viewers of the film, we only see what is shown within the frame. The boy killed by Kyle remains a blank, giving viewers no clue as to his motivations. As a result, his death is 'ungrievable' in the sense that the character in question has never fully come alive to begin with.

For Butler, it is not adequate simply to state that a life is grievable, it must be avowed as such in a public, material, visible realm: 'if there were to be an obituary, there would have been a life, a life worth noting, a life worth valuing and preserving, a life that qualifies for recognition' (2006, 35). Such recognition occurs in and through discourse, including cinematic and fictional representations. The figure of the enemy combatant in the war on terror is occulted to a sphere that is beyond the recognisably human, and such processes of distancing and distinction can also apply to the non-Western victims of terrorist attacks as well. Thus, a film like the French-produced *Des hommes et des dieux* (*Of Gods and Men*, 2010) precludes audiences from understanding the motivations of the Algerian terrorists, as well as the suffering of their Algerian victims, in favour of a detailed focus on a small group of French monks (see Flood 2016). The cultivated invisibility of the victims of Western invasions, occupations and interventions versus the heavily mediated coverage of Euro-American losses has also been pointed out by Jacques Derrida. In the wake of 9/11, Derrida noted that 'one does not count the dead in the same way from one corner of the globe to the other' (2003, 15). By failing to recognise lives lost to Western violence as lives and as losses, an opportunity for self-reflection is missed: we fail to situate our safety in the same space as their suffering.

In the words of Eric Leake (2014), empathy with perpetrators of violence is 'difficult' because it requires us to recognise similarities between ourselves and those we consider to be other. By establishing such a connection, difficult empathy 'pushes us not only to see others differently but to also perhaps . . . see ourselves differently and more expansively through problematic others and their social conditions' (Leake 2014, 184). This has important implications for the representation of the figure of the terrorist, as engaging 'difficult empathy' in this way opens the possibility of viewing the political motivations of extremists, and perhaps ultimately addressing their grievances. In a similar sense, Butler emphasises the importance of asking how anti-American hatred is connected to American politics in the first essay of *Precarious Life* (2004, 1–18). To avoid the recurrence of similar events, Butler insists, Americans need to understand the conditions that made 9/11 possible, and to confront their country's own role in creating these conditions. Throughout the essay, Butler is at pains to underline that this kind of explanation by no means implies an exculpation of the perpetrators, whose responsibility for their deeds Butler never calls into question. To say that 'US imperialism is a necessary *condition* for the attacks on the United States', Butler stresses, is not the same as saying that US foreign policies *caused* the attacks (12; emphasis added). Nor does it imply a justification of terrorism. Yet even if we agree that the acts cannot be condoned, it is imperative to understand their 'prehistory' (6) if we want to break the current cycle of violence rather than perpetuate it (as the wars in Afghanistan and Iraq notoriously did).

With its repeated disclaimers that it does not mean to exonerate terrorists, Butler's book shows how difficult it is to approach terrorism in a way that does not dehumanise the perpetrators. Sentences like 'I condemn on several ethical bases the violence done against the United States' (40) illustrate the workings of the 'condemnation imperative' described by Ghassan Hage (2003, 67). According to Hage, the public discourse on terrorism is marked by a veritable fear of explanation, or 'exighophobia' (87). As Hage points out, gaining an understanding of the social conditions of suicide terrorism means to confront a 'humanized other' (87). It is much easier, however, to wage war on a dehumanised enemy, whose motives remain unexplored.

Previous Studies on Terrorism in Cinema and Literature

Can narrative representations of terrorists work towards a re-humanisation? Or does the condemnation imperative to which terrorism is subjected preclude an empathetic identification with terrorists and their agendas? According to Richard Jackson, the tabooing of terrorists not only affects debates about actual perpetrators of politically motivated violence, but also fictional approaches to the topic in literature and film, where terrorists tend to be 'dehumanized, demonized, and most importantly, depoliticized' (2018, 382; see also Frank 2018). The case of cinema is treated in more detail in book-length studies by Helena Vanhala (2011) and Tony Shaw (2015). Whereas the former focuses on Hollywood blockbusters from the mid-1980s to the late 1990s, the latter takes a geographically and historically broader approach. As Vanhala demonstrates, the cinematic treatment of terrorism in American mainstream films closely correlates with contemporary government views on the issue, which the films tend to mirror back in 'simplified and stereotypical' form (2011, 5). Throughout the Reagan, Bush Senior and Clinton eras, no fewer than sixteen blockbuster films featured international terrorism as their central theme (6). In them, the figure of the terrorist is invariably deployed as a disposable villain, whose elimination at the hands of the white male hero serves to affirm the respective period's political, social and cultural status quo – and, hence, its prevailing power structures (296–8).

The 1994 Schwarzenegger vehicle *True Lies* is a case in point. The third highest-grossing film of its year (behind *The Lion King* and *Forrest Gump*, to give some historical context), *True Lies* was the most expensive film of its time. A spy-thriller action comedy, the film revolves around a terrorist plot involving four thermonuclear warheads that a terrorist organisation by the name of 'Crimson Jihad' threatens to detonate on American soil. The Middle Eastern terrorists of uncertain national origin demand the complete withdrawal of US troops from the Persian Gulf – a demand that anticipates Osama bin Laden's first fatwa of 1996, in which the leader of al-Qaeda warned Americans to leave the Arabian Peninsula. In one scene in *True Lies*, Salim Abu Aziz, the leader of 'Crimson Jihad', records a video message to the American public: 'You have killed our women and our children, bombed our cities from afar like cowards, and dare to call us terrorists.' This passionate criticism of the Gulf War is undercut by a rather blunt form of character and situation comedy. While the vain terrorist leader delivers his speech in a preposterously theatrical manner, dramatically wagging his finger at the camera, we see that the battery is running low. The recording is interrupted before Aziz has the chance to finish his threat and demands.

Even though they are endowed with a political agenda – by no means a given in the action film genre – the terrorists in *True Lies* mainly serve as cannon fodder, appearing in the film for the sole purpose of being dispatched by Schwarzenegger's one-line cracking protagonist. Commenting on the film's mind-boggling body count, Vanhalla notes: 'Schwarzenegger's character kills dozens of nameless and often faceless Arabs in horrific and painful ways. Rather than portraying these Third World characters as human beings, the film uses them as props for a variety of creative and brutally entertaining killings' (2011, 100). The fact that they are dehumanised makes the killing of terrorists uncomplicated in the sense that it does not elicit any moral qualms on the part of either the characters or the audience; on the contrary, it serves as a source of gratification. In one of the film's most striking instances of killing as comedy, a MAC-10 submachine gun accidentally falls down a flight of stairs. On each step, it fires off a round of bullets, which conveniently mow down the terrorists in the room. Avi Nesher, a former Israeli commando working in Hollywood as a consultant, had this to say about the sequence: 'You were supposed to laugh? I fought Arabs and I had Arab friends, but this was completely dehumanizing a group' (qtd in Arjana 2015, 151). In the film's showdown, the protagonist uses a Harrier fighter jet to free his teenage daughter from the clutches of the terrorists, who hold her captive in a Miami skyscraper. During the ensuing battle on the hovering jet, the machine gun-toting Aziz is symbolically castrated when he hits his crotch on the tail fin; shortly after, Schwarzenegger's hypermasculine Harry Tasker fires a phallic missile with the terrorist dangling from it. The terrorist threat gives Harry the chance to prove his worth to his estranged wife and daughter and to redeem himself for his previous failings as a husband and father. Thus, *True Lies* ends with the restoration of a nuclear family in crisis, using the encounter with the terrorist other to reinforce the sense of the white, Euro-American and heteronormative self.

Unsurprisingly, the cinematic engagement with terrorism turns out to be rather more complex and multifaceted if we move beyond the narrow genre of the Hollywood action blockbuster. In his *Global History of Terrorism on Film*, historian Tony Shaw demonstrates that terrorism has been depicted in a 'multitude of ways that cut across the political spectrum' (2015, 284). Once we consider films from different national and historical contexts, we are confronted with a whole range of answers to the questions of 'what terrorism is, who uses it, why and to what effect' (284). Although Hollywood continues to dominate this visual field, with its grand battles between 'Good' versus 'Evil', and Manichean narratives featuring ethnically marked perpetrators and villains, world cinema continues to offer more nuanced portrayals of the figure of the terrorist, depicting extremists as angry and hate-filled, but also as loving, pitiful and confused. Notable examples include the Franco-Moroccan production Nabil Ayouch's *Horses of God* (2012) or Abderrahmane Sissako's *Timbuktu* (2014), a fictional account of the occupation of the eponymous Malian city by the jihadist group Ansar Dine in 2012. These films do not question the humanity of the extremist, but rather take it for granted. They provoke intimate, face-to-face encounters with this problematic figure, drawing on spectator affects such as discomfort, disgust, compassion and fear. Terrorism in these films is not represented as a civilisational menace that arrives from elsewhere, but rather as a social problem, where extremists are not outsiders, but individuals deeply embedded in societies, communities and families.

As a matter of fact, many of the broad pronouncements regarding the impenetrability of the terrorist figure or their inhumanity cease to apply, or have limited relevance, to representations of contexts outside of mainstream Euro-American culture. The notion of the terrorist as a dehumanised outsider only functions in relation to a posited human 'inside' from which they are excluded – echoing Edward Said's critique of the whole Western machine of terrorism discourse as one that does not reflect, but rather creates, notions of interiority and exteriority, 'Us' and 'Them' (1987). Indeed, as Florence Martin and Maria Flood have argued, Francophone cinema from the Maghreb and sub-Saharan Africa, grounded in the realist traditions of European, Soviet and Arab film, frequently presents 'a cinematic process of undoing in relation to the representational codes that have come to be established in Hollywood films' (2019, 176). The 2005 film *Paradise Now* by Palestinian-Dutch writer-director Hany Abu-Assad is another case in point. Shot entirely on location in the West Bank, the film portrays two young men from the city of Nablus who are selected to carry out retaliatory suicide bombings in Tel Aviv. Following the protagonists over two days, *Paradise Now* explores the process of transformation through which ordinary Palestinians are made into terrorists (although the term used by the unnamed organisation responsible for these conversions is, of course, not 'terrorists' but 'resistance fighters' and 'martyrs').

The night before the protagonists are sent on their suicide mission, they are made to hold machine guns on a makeshift stage while reciting scripted speeches for the camera (Figure 1.2). In a brilliant reading of this pivotal sequence, Phoebe Bronstein argues that it shows how closely connected

Figure 1.2 Becoming a terrorist: the recording of Khaled's martyrdom video in *Paradise Now*.

jihadism is to media-enabled 'mechanical reproduction' (2010). By performing for the camera, the two men assume a new identity reflecting a particular 'image of the martyr' (Bronstein 2010). We are made aware of the artificiality of this image – the creation of which requires a conscious effort on the part of everyone involved – when the camera malfunctions in the middle of Khaled's impassioned speech (a possible nod to the corresponding scene in *True Lies*). Forced to interrupt his performance, Khaled immediately shifts back to his old self. Relaxing his rigid posture, he softens his facial expression and overall demeanour. It becomes obvious that his seemingly heart-felt delivery of the scripted martyrdom message has been emotionally exhausting.

During one of the following retakes, Khaled suddenly deviates from the script and addresses a personal message to his mother, informing her where to find cheaper water filters. As Bronstein notes, this aside calls attention to 'the Israeli control of water in the region and the daily challenges and suffering that this particular material oppression causes an individual family' (2010). By including such moments of oscillation between two versions of Khaled – Khaled-the-martyr-to-be and Khaled-the-soon-to-be-dead-son – the sequence illustrates that behind the construction of the martyr, there are actual circumstances, experiences and emotions which may help to explain a particular individual's actions, no matter how misguided these actions may appear to the viewer. In this way, *Paradise Now* avoids the common portrayal of the figure of the terrorist as a *fait accompli*. It shows us the protagonists *before* they have become terrorists or, rather, *in the process of* becoming terrorists – an approach that clearly goes beyond essentialist views of terrorists (see also Frank 2019).

Despite such nuanced and context-sensitive representations, Tony Shaw concludes that the issue of terrorism is ultimately depoliticised in the majority of films (2015, 205). He argues that in cinema, terrorism is predominantly 'looked at . . . from the perspective of individuals rather than wider societal and political conditions', a perspective that reduces the 'complexities of terrorism to simple, often psychological causes' (285). The same appears to be true for literary representations of terrorism. In an essay attempting to cover the whole range of English-language terrorism fiction written between 1970 and 2001, Robert Appelbaum and Alexis Paknadel observe that in these novels, the terrorists' motives tend to be personal – 'money, anger, personal revenge, psychopathy' – rather than political (2008, 410). Moreover, the novels focus on the victims of terrorism much more than on the perpetrators. Instead of inviting 'difficult empathy' with the originators of political violence, terrorism novels rely on 'easy empathy' with those who are on the receiving end of that violence. For Eric Leake, empathy with characters who are victimised is a 'non-threatening form of empathy' as it confirms our positive self-image by reassuring us 'that we are the caring people we consider ourselves to be' (2014, 175). By contrast, empathy with victimisers challenges our self-distanciation from violent others and therefore has a more disturbing effect (177). Not only do the novels considered by Appelbaum and Paknadel overwhelmingly direct their readers' emotional investment towards the victims rather than the perpetrators, they also rarely 'narrate their tales from the point of view of terrorist ideology or the internal psychology of someone devoted to such an ideology' (2008, 408). Appelbaum and Paknadel conclude that 'the cultural work' performed by terrorism novels consists in affirming 'that terrorism is the violence of an Other; it is illegitimate violence perpetrated from an illegitimate position' (427).

In his essay 'Sympathy for the Devil: Evil, Taboo, and the Terrorist Figure in Literature', Richard Jackson draws a similarly pessimistic conclusion. By extending the analysis to novels published after 2001, Jackson provides an important update to the study of Appelbaum and Paknadel. In the period investigated by Appelbaum and Paknadel, the cast of literary terrorists was dominated by Palestinians as well as, to a lesser extent, IRA recruits, post-sixties anarchists in the US and Europe, and Latin American communists (2008, 404). Since 9/11, literary terrorists have tended to be religious extremists, most notably radical Islamists. As Jackson emphasises, such terrorists are supposedly 'motivated by a deep hatred of Americans and American society and culture borne out of fanatical religious devotion, rather than political grievances in relation to US foreign policy in the middle East, for example' (2018, 381). What they have in common with their non-Islamic predecessors is that they are frequently depicted as sexually deviant (Jackson 2018, 382). Jackson contends that literature merely echoes the official discourse. Fictional representations of terrorism, he writes, 'stereotype, dehumanize, and demonize the terrorist figure in ways reflective of dominant social and political rhetoric' (377). In a 2020 study, Peter C. Herman contradicts this view by insisting that literature and cinema have repeatedly found ways of representing terrorism in a manner that does more than reassure 'audiences and readers of their moral superiority and the perfidy of the terrorists' (10). For Herman, the likes of William Shakespeare(!), William James, Joseph Conrad, Don DeLillo, John Updike, and Steven Spielberg have 'confront[ed] the unspeakable by attempting to try to see the world from the terrorist's perspective and examining the roots of terrorist violence' (10).

Herman's survey of terrorism fiction and film also considers several works by writers of non-Western origin, such as Yasmina Khadra (alias Mohammed Moulessehoul) and Nadeem Aslam. Over the last two decades, postcolonial novels like Khadra's *L'attentat* (*The Attack*, 2005) or Aslam's *The Wasted Vigil* (2008) and *The Blind Man's Garden* (2013) have tried to represent the often-silenced views of people on the other side of conflicts such as the Israeli-Palestinian one or the US invasion of Afghanistan. A more recent example is *Home Fire* (2017), a modern retelling of *Antigone* by Karachi-born novelist Kamila Shamsie. Unlike *L'attentat*, which offers the perspective of a bereaved husband attempting to understand what drove his late wife to commit a suicide bombing in Tel Aviv, *Home Fire* gives readers more immediate access to the process of radicalisation. One of the novel's focalisers, nineteen-year-old Parvaiz Pasha, is the son of a British-Pakistani jihadist who fought in Bosnia, Chechnya, Kashmir and Afghanistan before he died in US captivity. Having never met his father and lacking a clear purpose in life, Parvaiz proves susceptible to the manipulations of ISIS recruiter Farooq, who paints his father as a legendary war hero while simultaneously assuming the role of a – homoerotically tinged (see Chambers 2018, 207) – substitute father. Appealing to Parvaiz's male pride, Farooq manages to pry him away from his two sisters by purporting to teach him 'how to be a man' (Shamsie 2018, 129). Together, they re-enact the torture to which Parvaiz's father was subjected in US captivity. Eventually, Parvaiz – who is obsessed with sound and spends his days recording everyday noises – agrees to join the Islamic State's media arm in Raqqa, where he hopes to learn more about his father through the latter's former fellow combatants.

Shamsie's intimate portrayal of the process of radicalisation enables empathy with the figure of the ISIS recruit, whose personal motives are shown to be conditioned by the larger social and political context in which he exists. Parvaiz Pasha is far removed from the stereotype of the '"mad or bad"' terrorist (Jackson 2018, 382). Crucially, however, he never commits acts of violence. In fact, quite the opposite happens in the novel: Parvaiz abhors the brutality he witnesses in Raqqa, which prompts him to flee Syria. This makes him a representative of two subcategories of literary terrorists identified by Jackson: on the one hand, he belongs to the group of characters 'who become involved in terrorism by accident or as a result of naivety or mental weakness' (380–1); on the other hand, he is reminiscent of would-be terrorists who ultimately decide against killing innocents, which redeems them in the eyes of the reader (379–80). As Jackson points out, accidental terrorists and repentant terrorists are rewarded with a relatively sympathetic treatment. In both instances, we see a 'distancing mechanism' (379) at work, which spares readers from a direct confrontation with the horrors of terrorism.

Refiguring the Terrorist: Histories, Identities and Emotions

All in all, then, can it be said that explorations of terrorism in literature and film confirm the tenets of Richard Jackson's somewhat sweeping claim that 'In all the thousands of popular and literary novels, all the newspaper columns and news reports, all the movies and television shows and even in many academic books and articles, terrorists are virtually always depicted in stereotypical terms and as caricatures of what we imagine terrorists to be – fanatical, extremist, aggressive, hateful, dysfunctional, damaged' (2015a, 319)? Using this deliberately provocative statement as a starting point, *The Figure of the Terrorist in Literature and Visual Culture* aims to revisit the notion of the terrorism taboo by seeking out works from a wide range of cultural, linguistic, national and artistic traditions. We suggest that across cultures and time periods, complex artistic representations of the terrorist figure can and do persist, challenging hegemonic discourses and simplistic and damaging stereotypes. The terrorists presented in this book are sometimes 'hateful, dysfunctional, [or] damaged', but they are also confused, pathetic, loving, lost and lonely. In order to effect this re-examination, a key concern of this volume is the re-historicisation of terrorism as a broad transnational and transcultural process, moving beyond the 9/11-centric emphasis of much of the current research with its limited focus on a 'West and the Rest' dichotomy.

As Rudolf Walther points out, across the course of decades and centuries, the concept of 'terrorism' has become so 'dehistoricised' that it can be used 'arbitrarily' to disparage any kind of enemy (1990, 324; our trans.). Yet this process of uncoupling the political motivations of the terrorist from their actions is one that is deliberately provoked by those they oppose – states and governments, for the most part. It is desirable to view one's enemy as entirely removed from the flow of historical and political events, so that they may stand apart from 'normal' human action and motivation. Edward Said identified this trend in 1987, writing about the growing rhetoric in America and Europe around, precisely, the figure of the terrorist. As he notes, 'isolat[ing] your enemy from time, from causality, from prior action' means they can be depicted as having a 'terrorist essence' with no other motivation than 'wreaking havoc for its own sake' (1987, 199). Additionally, the terrorist is frequently depicted as an anachronism, at odds with or in opposition to the forward march of progress and time, in that they seek to return a people, place or nation to an earlier state. The terrorist is also out of time, or out of joint, in the sense that they project an imagined post-revolutionary future. Re-historicising the terrorist allows us to situate them squarely within clearly defined temporal parameters, and to understand the role that histories of colonialism, postcolonial governmentality, occupation and discrimination play in producing political violence.

The chapters presented in the first section of this book, 'Historicising Terrorism: Cross-Media Perspectives', explore various forms of political violence and representations of terrorists from the post-war period to the present across a range of media, including film, television, literature and comic books. In so doing, they chart a connecting line between phenomena such as left-wing revolutionary terrorism and the IRA in the 1970s and 1980s, football hooliganism in the 1990s, and the technologised and globalised post-9/11 counterterrorist context. The section begins with Beatriz Lopez's detailed discussion of terrorist psychology and the left-wing female revolutionary terrorist in two works by post-war British authors, Muriel Spark's *The Only Problem* (1984) and Doris Lessing's *The Good Terrorist* (1985). Lopez examines the interweaving of personal and political grievance in both novels and highlights the ways in which gender and social class influence the formation of both central female characters. In the end, Lopez suggests, Lessing and Spark show their protagonists Effie and Alice to be 'dangerous dreamers of the absolute', highlighting 'the empty rhetoric of revolutionary groups' amid the growing conservatism of the 1980s. Shane Walshe's fascinating contribution also engages with this time period, but instead examines fluctuating representations of the IRA man in the works of two major American comic book publishing companies, Marvel and DC, from the 1970s to the 1980s. Walshe highlights how the figure of the IRA man featured consistently as antagonist or friend to a range of superheroes, including Iron Fist, Daredevil, Spider-Man and Green Arrow. Illustrating the usefulness of a transhistorical perspective on the figure of the terrorist, Walshe shows how this representation changes over time in line with the shifting tactics of the Northern Irish organisation: as the IRA increasingly targets civilians, representations grow less sympathetic and focus instead turns to their victims. Cyprian Piskurek builds on these contexts, elaborating on the policies of Margaret Thatcher, whose right-wing rhetoric frequently sought to unite disparate groups under the banner of 'terrorist': football hooligans, striking miners and the IRA. Importantly, Pisturek shows how this discursive positioning de-politicised these groups and situated them outside of the rationale of legitimate political motivation. Yet, as Pisturek notes, while the figure of the football hooligan has receded as the sport has become increasingly commercialised, the terrorist has instead risen to a position of prominence in the public imagination. Piskurek examines the connection between terrorism and hooliganism across three different texts and forms: Chris Cleave's novel *Incendiary* (2005), Scott Mann's film *Final Score* (2018), and the episode 'To Be a Somebody' from the television series *Cracker* (1994).

Johannes Riquet transports the reader firmly into the twenty first century, while retaining a focus on past representations, examining the historical association between the railroad and political crime. Riquet offers a stimulating analysis of the ways in which the terrorist comes to serve as a metaphor, 'personify[ing] the threats posed by technological modernity'. Honing in on Clint Eastwood's *The 15:17 to Paris* (2018) and the first episode of the British television series *Bodyguard* (2018), he charts an evolution from the 'heavy' technology of twentieth century terrorism and train travel, and its transmutation into the 'lighter' or 'liquid' forms of travel, terrorism, and counterterrorism after 2001. The concluding chapter in this section by Peter C. Herman offers a detailed examination of Indian-American novelist Karan Mahajan's *The Association of Small Bombs* (2016), focusing on the work's nuanced exploration of the motivations of different terrorist figures. Eschewing the dehumanising post-9/11 rhetoric of the othered or even the monstrous terrorist, Mahajan describes how different individuals deal with the impact of violence on their victims, highlighting how the political and the personal are interwoven in the pull towards terrorist violence. Ultimately, Herman argues, the book refuses to give the readers clues in how we are to judge these figures, instead presenting 'multiple and sometimes contradictory perspectives on both terrorists and their victims'.

Gender remains a hugely significant arena for the study of the figure of the terrorist. While it remains true across cultures and time periods that more men than women are drawn to extremist ideologies and to commit acts of violence, women are highly significant actors in violent conflicts. As the chapters in the next section demonstrate, women's roles range from being perpetrators of violence, often chosen and lauded for their apparently greater ability to conceal their violent aims under the guise of feminine stereotypes, to being co-conspirators, victims, opponents of violence and figures of symbolic exaltation. Historically, women's motivations for joining terrorist organizations were often framed in relation to male relatives or counterparts, in accordance with what Laura Sjoberg and Caron E. Gentry (2007) call the 'mother, monster, whore' paradigm common to accounts of women in times of war. This theory shows how frequently political and representational accounts of female participation in war and revolutionary violence situate women as non-agents, buffeted by the forces of male-dominated movements and simply caught up in revolution by virtue of their parenthood (real or symbolic) or a sexual and/or romantic relationship with a male perpetrator. The third part of the equation, the 'monstrosity' component, echoes the dehumanising and depoliticising rhetoric that is sometimes applied to male terrorists: such women are pure and radical evil, perhaps even more than the men who commit similar acts, for they have had to push against an 'innate' feminine desire to nurture and care, in order to kill and maim. Sjoberg and Gentry show how this labelling of female perpetrators and combatants occurs and recurs across regions and time periods, from the Middle East, through Chechnya and Bosnia, to Rwanda, and reduces women's roles in times of war to mere satellites, orbiting the central event of male action. This further results in persistent attempts to situate women's violence in relation to paradigms of maternity or caregiving. One example of this trend is the figure of Zohra Drif, an Algerian revolutionary responsible for the bombing of the Milk Bar in Algiers in 1956 during the Algerian War of Independence. Victims of the bomb attack and the French press have frequently called upon Drif to express sorrow or contrition for her actions, interpolations that were never directed towards her male counterparts like Saadi Yacef (see Hubbell 2018).

This stereotyping of women's political violence results in a privileging of the personal over the political in terms of female motivation. Significantly, then, the opening chapters in this section on 'Gender, Identity and Terrorism' address the figure of the female terrorist and female resistant to violence by interweaving the private sphere with public and politicised incentives. They show how women are implicated in violent histories: they resist, inflict and experience violence in ways that are complex and multi-faceted. The contributions by Rajeswari Mohan and Harald Pittel examine South Asian cinema, an important regional context for the exploration of representations of terrorism and terrorists, given its turbulent histories of colonialism and postcolonial violence in the form of partition and state formations. Mohan's chapter analyses what might be considered one of the most important feature-length fiction films about the figure of the female suicide bomber, Santosh Sivan's *The Terrorist* (1999). Based on the 1991 assassination of Rajiv Gandhi, the erstwhile Prime Minister of India, by a female Sri Lankan suicide bomber, the film seeks to uncover the assassin's motivations while simultaneously retuning these motivations to the sphere of the feminine through a sexualised gaze and an evocation of maternal imagery and allegories. Harald Pittel's intervention in this volume examines terrorism within Hindi popular cinema, and the ways in which it has been used as a metaphor for violence against women, with a concomitant alignment of counterterrorism with female opposition to such violence. Examining three popular films, *Neerja* (2016), *Tiger Zinda Hai* (2017), and *Simmba* (2018), Pittel carefully shows how these narratives work to entrench gendered codes around women's roles as mystical caregivers, while also depicting their resistance as either a copy of spectacular male violence or subject to the patriarchal legal and moral strictures of mainstream Indian society. In the end, Pittel argues, such representations serve to entrench ideologies of saviourism and retaliation, 'veil[ing] the actual social complexities faced by Indian women today'.

Pittel also demonstrates how the male terrorist is often represented in racialised terms as Muslim, and how this contemporary cinematic association of the figure of the terrorist with a Muslim man (and occasionally woman) mushroomed in the wake of the 9/11 attacks, although it certainly existed beforehand (see Shaheen 2015). Addressing such identarian and religiously-based bias and discrimination was almost taboo in the early years of the twenty first century, although works like Mira Nair's short film for the collection *11'09"01* (2002, multiple directors) and Mohsin Hamid's novel *The Reluctant Fundamentalist* (2007) offer early examples of works that engage with the issue of Islamophobia and prejudice. Indeed, if the figure of the terrorist in general is already occluded and excluded from the realm of history and politics, the figure of the jihadist or Islamist extremist may be even more subject to discourses of dehumanisation and discrimination. In 2017, an extensive meta-analysis by Saifuddin Ahmed and Jörg Matthes of 345 academic articles on the media representation of Muslims and Islam globally found that post-9/11, 'media and political debates pertaining to Muslims and Islam have narrowed to an Orientalist discourse . . . there is a dominant antagonistic view against Muslims and Islam across many societies' (2017, 2). Sociologically driven surveys of Islamophobia in France, such as those of Abdellali Hajjat and Marwan Mohammed (2016) and Thomas Delthombe (2007), point to shared issues around media discourse and representation. Furthermore, scholarship has highlighted the unequal opportunities available to young people, particularly young Muslims and young people of colour, who suffer discrimination and disenfranchisement under global capitalism (Esposito and Mogahed 2007).

Importantly, the next set of chapters in the collection seeks to think through the means and motivations of the jihadist, both male and female, within the contexts of British and French society and the prejudice experienced by Muslims in both countries. Both Zaynab Seedat and Sarah Davison show that the figure of the contemporary terrorist is bound to questions of nationhood, belonging, identity and gender. Seedat presents a detailed intersectional examination of the figure of the young female jihadist who joins ISIS in Indian author Tabish Khair's 2016 novel *Just Another Jihadi Jane*. Khair's central protagonist Jamila is a young woman who seeks a double escape: from the oppressive strictures of a private life in which an arranged marriage is threatened, and from the racism and discrimination she lives through on a daily basis in her hometown in the north of England. Seedat carefully considers the 'jihadi girl-power subculture' which proves appealing to many young women who are radicalised and recruited by such groups. She thus argues against widespread media interpretations of their actions as 'naïve romanticism' and highlights how the Caliphate employs a false rhetoric of personal and political emancipation in seeking new female recruits. Next, Davison examines how race and ethnicity are represented in two recent French feature films about terrorism, Lucas Belvaux's *Chez nous* (2017) and Nicolas Boukhrief's *Made in France* (2016). Engaging with some of the specificities of the French context, including French republican ideology, *laïcité* (secularism), and anxieties about terrorism, immigration and integration, Davison importantly draws comparisons between jihadist and right-wing extremists in terms of the compassion viewers are invited to feel for the protagonists. She argues that cinematic techniques like narrative, framing and lighting create disparities between white extremists and jihadists of Arab, Black or Berber origin, producing a 'racially-coded categorisation between "good terrorists" and "bad terrorists"'.

Compassion for the perpetrator, and the ways in which an art form can seek to generate or block this emotion in the reader of viewer, has been a key debate in the field of terrorism and cultural studies, notably since 9/11. In his book *9/11 Fiction, Empathy, and Otherness*, Tim Gauthier suggests that an empathetic identification with terrorists would require an acknowledgment of the terrorist's own sense of victimisation – a perspective that is invariably denied to the reader in American post-9/11 fiction, since writers shy away from framing terrorist violence as 'serving altruistic purposes, . . . a form of extreme communication meant to awaken the world to the injustices suffered by the community' (2015, 164). Such an acknowledgement of the terrorist's own potential sense of victimisation is of course made possible by the work of re-historicisation and re-politicisation outlined in the preceding sections. For, if we can situate the terrorist in concrete spatio-temporal and historical parameters, it may become easier to understand their motivations. Nonetheless, in seeking to evoke audience or reader understanding and even compassion for these problematic figures, works of art raise a number of ethical quandaries. They risk either justifying their membership of these violent groups, tied to Raya Morag's critique of 'perpetrator cinema' (2013), or reducing these complex and diverse personalities to figures of pity. Pity, compassion and empathy, while not interchangeable, have been variously critiqued for the ways in which they can separate the subject who feels pity from the pitiful object: the subject who feels pity is not required to implicate themselves in the suffering of another; rather, the boundary between self and other is maintained, and even reinforced (Ahmed 2014, 31). In documentary film theory, Belinda Smaill (2015, 54) has identified what she calls a 'politics of pity', in which a voyeuristic gaze on minority groups serves to further distance their suffering from the collective majority.

Additionally, the form of the representation matters when it comes to the evocation of sympathetic or empathetic feeling for the terrorist. Carl Boggs and Tom Pollard argue that the blood, guts, and gore of audio-visual spectacles of terrorist acts, prevalent in Hollywood film, radically block pity for the terrorist, who becomes a 'personality type [that] exists beyond history, beyond politics, beyond psychology, a type so irredeemably evil and irrational that no normal mode of interpretation is possible' (2006, 350). This prevalent, mainstream mode of spectacularising political violence distances the viewing subject from the viewed object through a privileging of action over narrative, and fear over compassion. Indeed, Brad Evans and Henry A. Giroux suggest that spectacle and theatricality, mainstays of Hollywood, have come to dominate in the realm of politics, such that they undermine 'more measured and thoughtful commentary on human suffering . . . Representations of fear, panic, vulnerability, and pain increasingly override narratives of justice' (2015, 222). What is at stake, then, in both art and politics is a mode of narrating political violence that not only acknowledges the suffering of victims, but that offers a clear-eyed appraisal of how justice, for all parties, might best be served.

The final section of this book, entitled 'Intimate Enemies: Feeling for the Terrorist?', builds on previous discussions of the problem of empathy with terrorist perpetrators in literature and cinema. It examines works that not only seek to evoke feeling for the terrorist, but that also retain a carefully calibrated critical and affective distance, treading a delicate line between distance and proximity, sameness and difference, certainty and interrogation. Coined by Patrick Rotman to describe the relationship between French and Algerian combatants during the War of Independence in his 2002 film of that name, the phrase 'intimate enemies' captures something of this precarious balancing act between knowledge and difference, antagonism and familiarity (Flood and Martin 2019, 173). Recent discussions on empathy have sought to highlight the power of the feeling not as a pleasant emotion that centres on the similarity of self and other, but rather as one that functions best through an often-uncomfortable acknowledgement of difference. Writing about empathy and the #MeToo movement, Michelle Rodino-Colocino notes the distinction between passive forms of empathy and what she calls active, or transformative empathy. Passive empathy is akin to pity: it allows the viewer or reader to gain the pleasurable feeling of pity for another's suffering (the sense of oneself as a 'good person' who feels pity) without having to actively engage in the work of actively changing society so that such suffering does not occur in the first place. It is, as she aptly summarises, 'the feeling of being in another's shoes without the risk of actually doing so' (Rodino-Colocino 2018, 96). Active or transformative empathy, by contrast, invites the individual to situate themselves in relation to another's suffering, to listen rather than to speak, calling for 'self-reflexivity and potential transformation of one's own assumptions' (96).

The transformation of one's own assumptions in relation to the figure of the terrorist must, in some sense, involve what Tim Gauthier calls a 'circumvention of the condemnation imperative', in the first chapter in this section. Drawing on Hage's work, Gauthier asks whether it is truly possible for writers and directors to present protagonists who commit acts of violence without seeking to condemn them. Examining a film and a novel, Fatih Akin's *In the Fade* (German original: *Aus dem Nichts*, 2017) and Omar El Akkad's *American War* (2017), Gauthier offers a refined account of the notion of 'difficult empathy' which stresses the limitations of the recipient's feeling. Gauthier argues that although both works seek to connect readers or viewers to their protagonists, through narrative contextualisation, gender and strategies of emotional identification, ambivalence remains, 'achieving some balance between forgiveness and condemnation'. Maria Flood's chapter also engages with ideas around forgiveness and condemnation, examining the work of documentary maker Deeyah Khan, whose film *White Right: Meeting the Enemy* (2017) features interviews with white supremacists in the United States. Khan herself was subject to racist abuse as a child and an adult, and the documentary began as a quest for understanding of men whom she feared. Flood offers a novel engagement with the feeling of discomfort, rarely examined in studies of film emotion, identified both as a transformative strategy Khan adopts as she engages with these men, and a reaction that is evoked in the audience. Finally, Flood analyses discomfort's relation to empathy, and both its potential and limitations as a political strategy when confronting an apparently intransigent ideological adversary. The book closes on Pavan Malreddy's thought-provoking discussion of intimacy, conflict and insurgency in Burmese Anglophone literature within the context of the military junta, namely Pascal Khoo Thwe's *From the Land of Green Ghosts* (2002) and Lucy Cruickshanks' *The Road to Rangoon* (2015). Malreddy argues for a refashioning of the concept of the terrorist within the Burmese context, where forms of what he calls 'intimate conflict' and inherited violence mean that 'the figures of terrorism themselves undergo constant transformation; from insurgents, rebels, lovers and neighbours to the victims or agents of state and counterterrorism'. The chapter shows that the very concept of 'the figure of the terrorist' may need revision, as the intensity, duration and intimate spatiality of internecine conflicts in the postcolonial world destabilise the exclusivist categories of terrorist and counterterrorist.

These modes of straddling sameness and difference, and intimacy and enmity, take place through the narrative and the cinematic choices the directors and authors adopt, and they are key to the functioning of empathy, in both the personal and political spheres. Rather than viewing empathy as only a mode of sympathetic feeling for those who we view as *similar* to ourselves, a politically fruitful form of approaching the pain of another might allow spaces of disagreement to emerge, one in which social actors are neither vilified nor lionised, but rather appraised in all their human complexity. Such a mode of apprehending the enemy in times of conflict also allows for a continual appraisal of the slippery nature of the labels assigned to individuals in turbulent times, what Dominick LaCapra calls 'the tragic grid' that 'locks together perpetrator, collaborator, victim, bystander, and resister' (1998, 41). Unlike critics who are cynical about empathy's capacity to inspire social change – such as Paul Bloom (2016), who divorces empathy from rationality – the works discussed in this section show that while empathy may be most effective when grounded in shared emotion, it can also be a profoundly rational choice that could lead to deep social and political change. Empathy, and particularly active or difficult empathy, can thus serve, in the words of Judith Butler, 'to create a sense of the public in which oppositional voices are not feared, degraded, or dismissed, but valued for the instigation to a sensate democracy they occasionally perform' (2010, 151). This book seeks to contribute to such a discussion, not by offering any schematised definitions, humanising tropes or condemnatory gestures, but rather by holding together contradictory impulses and acknowledging the complexity and fallibility of the labels we ascribe to that most protean of figures, the terrorist.

* * *

The editors would like to thank Zoë Achilles for her valuable help in preparing this book for publication.

References

The 9/11 Commission Report: Final Report of the National Commission on Terrorist Attacks upon the United States. Official Government Edition, Washington, DC: US Government Printing Office.

Abu-Assad, Hany, dir. *Paradise Now*, 2005. Warner Home Video, 2006. DVD.

Ahmed, Saifuddin, and Jörg Matthes. 2017. "Media Representation of Muslims and Islam from 2000 to 2015: A Meta-Analysis." *The International Communication Gazette* 79, no. 3: 1–26.

Ahmed, Sara. 2014. *The Cultural Politics of Emotion*. Edinburgh: Edinburgh University Press.

Appelbaum, Robert, and Alexis Paknadel. 2008. "Terrorism and the Novel, 1970–2001." *Poetics Today* 29, no. 3: 387–436.

Arjana, Sophie Rose. 2015. *Muslims in the Western Imagination*. Oxford and New York: Oxford University Press.

Ashcroft, John. 2001. "Attorney General Ashcroft Outlines Foreign Terrorist Tracking Task Force." US Department of Justice. October 31. https://www.justice.gov/archive/ag/speeches/2001/agcrisisremarks10_31.htm.

Baker, Howard H. 2001. "Remarks by U.S. Ambassador Howard H. Baker, Jr. at Japanese Observance Ceremony for Victims of Terrorism in the U.S." US Embassy & Consulates in Japan. September 23. https://japan2.usembassy.gov/e/p/2001/tp-20010923-65.html

Bloom, Paul. 2016. *Against Empathy: The Case for Rational Compassion*. New York: Ecco Press.

Boggs, Carl, and Tom Pollard. 2006. "Hollywood and the Spectacle of Terrorism." *New Political Science* 28, no. 3: 335–51.

Bronstein, Phoebe. 2010. "Man-Made Martyrs in the Age of Mechanical Reproduction: Disturbing Manufactured Martyrdom in Paradise Now." *Jump Cut: A Review of Contemporary Media* 52. https://www.ejumpcut.org/archive/jc52.2010/bronsteinParadiseNow/index.html

Burke, Edmund. [1795] 1991. "Fourth Letter on a Regicide Peace 1795: To the Earl Fitzwilliam." *The Writings and Speeches of Edmund Burke, Vol. 9: I: The Revolutionary War, 1794–1797; II: Ireland*, edited by R. B. McDowell and William B. Todd, 45–119. Oxford: Clarendon Press.

Butler, Judith. 2004. *Precarious Life: The Power of Mourning and Violence*. London and New York: Verso.

—— 2009. *Frames of War: When Is Life Grievable?* London and New York: Verso.

Cameron, James, dir. *True Lies*, 1994. 20th Century Fox, 2010. DVD.

Chambers, Claire. 2018. "Sound and Fury: Kamila Shamsie's *Home Fire*." *The Massachusetts Review* 59, no. 2, 202–19.

Daase, Christoph. 2001. "Terrorismus – Begriffe, Theorien und Gegenstrategien: Ergebnisse und Probleme sozialwissenschaftlicher Forschung." *Die Friedens-Warte* 76, no. 1: 55–79.

Delthombe, Thomas. 2007. *L'islam imaginaire : La construction médiatique de l'islamophobie en France, 1975–2005*. Paris: La Découverte.

Derrida, Jacques. "Autoimmunity: Real and Symbolic Suicides. A Dialogue with Jacques Derrida." In Giovanna Borradori, ed., *Philosophy in a Time of Terror: Dialogues with Jürgen Habermas and Jacques Derrida*, 85–136. Chicago and London: The University of Chicago Press, 2003.

Eastwood, Clint, dir. *American Sniper*, 2014. Warner Home Video, 2016. DVD.

Esposito, John L., and Dalia Mogahed. 2007. *Who Speaks for Islam? What a Billion Muslims Really Think*. New York: Gallup Press.

Evans, Brad, and Henry A. Giroux. 2016. *Disposable Futures: The Seduction of Violence in the Age of Spectacle*. San Francisco: City Lights Books.

Flood, Maria, and Florence Martin. 2019. "Introduction: The terrorist as *ennemi intime* in French and Francophone Cinema." *Studies in French Cinema* 18, no. 2: 171–8.

Flood, Maria. 2016. "Terrorism and Visibility in Algeria's 'Black Decade': *Des Hommes et des dieux* (2010)" *French Cultural Studies* 27, no. 1, pp. 62–72.

Foucault, Michel. 1978. *The History of Sexuality, Volume I: An Introduction*. Trans. Robert Hurley. New York: Pantheon Books.

Frank, Michael C. 2018. "Why Do They Hate Us? Terrorists in American and British Fiction of the Mid-2000s." In *Terrorism and Literature*, ed. Peter C. Herman, 340–60. Cambridge: Cambridge University Press.

———. 2019. "Terrorist Self-Fashioning: Politics, Identity and the Making of 'Martyrdom' Videos – from the 7/7 Bombers to *Four Lions*." In *Imaging Identity: Text, Mediality and Contemporary Visual Culture*, eds Johannes Riquet and Martin Heusser, 237–58. Cham, Switzerland: Palgrave Macmillan.

Gauthier, Tim. 2015. *9/11 Fiction, Empathy, and Otherness*. Lanham, Boulder, New York, and London: Lexington Books.

Gentry, Caron E., and Laura Sjoberg. 2007. *Mother, Monsters, Whores: Women's Violence in Global Politics*. London: Zed Books.

Hage, Ghassan. 2003. "'Comes a Time We Are All Enthusiasm': Understanding Palestinian Suicide Bombers in Times of Exighophobia." *Public Culture* 15, no. 1: 65–89.

Hajjat, Abdellali, and Marwan Mohammed. 2016. *Islamophobie : Comment les élites françaises fabriquent le 'problème musulman'*. Paris: La Découverte.

Hall, Jason. 2014. "American Sniper: Based on the Book by Chris Kyle with Scott McEwen and Jim DeFelice." *The Internet Movie Script Database (IMSDb)*. https://imsdb.com/scripts/American-Sniper.html

Herman, Peter C. 2020. *Unspeakable: Literature and Terrorism from the Gunpowder Plot to 9/11*. New York and London: Routledge.

Hubbell, Amy L. 2018. "Scandalous Memory: Terrorism Testimonial from the Algerian War." *Contemporary French and Francophone Studies* 22, no. 1: 49–57.

Jackson, Richard. 2015a. Afterword to *Confessions of a Terrorist*, 317–22. London: Zed Books.

———. 2015b. "Confessions of a Terrorist Sympathiser." Resources from the National Centre for Peace and Conflict Studies, University of Otago, New Zealand, December 2015. https://www.otago.ac.nz/ncpacs/otago370201.pdf

———. 2018. "Sympathy for the Devil: Evil, Taboo, and the Terrorist Figure in Literature." In *Terrorism and Literature*, ed. Peter C. Herman, 377–94. Cambridge: Cambridge University Press.

Keen, Suzanne. 2009. *Empathy and the Novel*. Oxford and New York: Oxford University Press.

LaCapra, Dominick. 1998. *History and Memory after Auschwitz*. Ithaca, NY: Cornell University Press.

Leake, Eric. 2014. "Humanizing the Inhumane: The Value of Difficult Empathy." *Rethinking Empathy through Literature*, eds Meghan Marie Hammond and Sue J. Kim, 175–85. New York and London: Routledge.

Morag, Raya. 2013. *Waltzing with Bashir: Perpetrator Trauma Cinema*. London and New York: I. B. Tauris.

Khadra, Yasmina. 2005. *L'attentat*. Paris: Éditions Julliard, 2005.

Kyle, Chris, with Scott McEwen and Jim DeFelice. 2012. *American Sniper: The Autobiography of the Most Lethal Sniper in U.S. Military History*. New York: HarperCollins.

Pinfari, Marco. 2019. *Terrorists as Monsters: The Unmanageable Other from the French Revolution to the Islamic State*. Oxford and New York: Oxford University Press.

Razack, Sharene H. 2008. *Casting Out: The Eviction of Muslims from Western Law and Politics*. Toronto: University of Toronto Press.

Rodino-Colocino, Michelle. 2018. "Me Too, #MeToo: Countering Cruelty with Empathy." *Communication and Critical/Cultural Studies* 15, no. 1: 96–100.

Said, Edward W. 1987. "The Essential Terrorist." *Arab Studies Quarterly* 9, no. 2: 195–203.

Scheerer, Sebastian. 2002. *Die Zukunft des Terrorismus: Drei Szenarien*. Lüneburg, Germany: Zu Klampen.

Shaheen, Jack G. 2009. *Reel Bad Arabs: How Hollywood Vilifies a People*. Northampton, MA: Olive Branch Press.

Shamsie, Kamila. 2018. *Home Fire*. London: Bloomsbury.

Shaw, Tony. 2015. *Cinematic Terror: A Global History of Terrorism on Film*. New York: Bloomsbury.

Smaill, Belinda. 2015. *The Documentary: Politics, Emotion, Culture*. London: Palgrave Macmillan.

Vanhala, Helena. 2011. *The Depiction of Terrorists in Blockbuster Hollywood Films, 1980–2001: An Analytical Study*. Jefferson, NC: McFarland & Company.

Vetlesen, Arne Johan. 1994. *Perception, Empathy, and Judgment: An Inquiry into the Preconditions of Moral Performance*. University Park, PA: The Pennsylvania State University Press.

Walther, Rudolf. 1990. "Terror/Terrorismus." *Geschichtliche Grundbegriffe: Historisches Lexikon zur politisch-sozialen Sprache in Deutschland, Band 6*, eds Otto Brunner, Werner Conze, and Reinhart Koselleck, 323–444. Stuttgart, Germany: Klett-Cotta.

PART ONE

HISTORICISING THE FIGURE OF THE TERRORIST: CROSS-MEDIA PERSPECTIVES

2. THE PSYCHOLOGY OF POST-WAR REVOLUTIONARY TERRORISM IN MURIEL SPARK'S *THE ONLY PROBLEM* AND DORIS LESSING'S *THE GOOD TERRORIST*[1]

Beatriz Lopez

Introduction

In the 1980s, the waning of communism led to sub-state terrorism becoming 'public enemy number one' in the Western world (Said 1988, 149). The early post-war idealism that had fostered social welfare vanished in the wake of decolonisation struggles, Cold War polarisation and economic decline, leading individuals to feel alienated from political institutions and incapable of shaping historical events (Zulaika and Douglass 1996, 17–19). In this context, a generation of mostly middle-class, educated young people embraced left-wing activism such as the civil rights, anti-colonial and anti-capitalist movements in search for 'a meaningful cause' which, paired with a willingness to use violence for the achievement of their political ends, gave rise to a new revolutionary terrorist tradition (Zulaika and Douglass 1996, 19–20). Inspired by the late nineteenth-century anarchist principle of 'propaganda by the deed', which adopted violence as the most effective weapon to encourage workers to revolt, many post-war revolutionary movements such as the Red Brigades (Italy) and the Angry Brigades (Britain) exhibited a similar disenchantment with the power of words to bring about socio-political change and turned to a reliance on acts of terrorism to communicate their views. Influenced by the rise of mass communications, the decline of conventional warfare and the spread of modern liberal democratic values such as freedom and self-determination, post-war revolutionary terrorists discarded mere propaganda as futile, adopting instead the shock of violent action to manipulate public opinion and coerce states into accepting their demands (Ganor 2004, 34–5).

Terrorism can be defined as 'the deliberate creation and exploitation of fear through violence or the threat of violence in the pursuit of political change' (Hoffman 2006, 40).[2] Terrorism does not primarily seek material damage and human fatalities; instead, a '*physical* act affecting a limited group of immediate victims serves the greater aim of producing *psychological* reactions among a larger audience, namely fear', which is exploited to achieve the '*political* aim' of 'exercis[ing] pressure on power holders, who must respond to the disruptive and destabilising effects of the violence' (Frank 2015, 92). To accomplish this goal, terrorists often employ the methods of state-sanctioned psychological warfare, which seeks 'to influence attitudes and behaviour affecting the achievement of political or military objectives' (Taylor 1999, xii). Widely theorised by social psychologists such as Frederic Bartlett and John T. MacCurdy in the 1940s, psychological warfare would be covertly practised by British and American propagandists during the Second World War.[3] Terrorism can thus be regarded as the continuation of the methods of psychological warfare, accompanied by violent action, from the Cold War period up to the present day. As political scientist Boaz Ganor argues,

> [m]odern terrorism is psychological warfare pure and simple. It aims at isolating the individual from the group, to break up a society into so many frightened individuals . . . Further, the terrorist aims to undermine the individual's belief in the collective values of society by amplifying the potential threat to the extent that security appears to outweigh all other political concerns . . . Terrorism uses the victim's own imagination against him or her. (2004, 40)

Therefore, terrorists must be able to access the mind of their victim – both civilians and the state – to predict their behaviour in advance of perpetrating acts of terrorism with a view to inflicting as much psychological damage as possible. Given that terrorism, like fiction, is predicated on the need to imagine the other (be it the victim or the reader), it is perhaps unsurprising that Muriel Spark and Doris Lessing, two writers who participated in twentieth-century political struggles, would subsequently engage with this phenomenon in their novels.

This chapter examines the psychology of post-war revolutionary terrorism in Muriel Spark's *The Only Problem* ([1984] 2018) and Doris Lessing's *The Good Terrorist* ([1985] 2007). It argues that accessing and manipulating the mind of the victim is at the root of the violence planned and executed by the terrorists Effie Gotham and Alice Mellings. Firstly, it considers the relationship between blackmail and terrorism in the novels, pointing to the potential for personal grievance to fuel violence against social and economic norms that are perceived to be unfair. Secondly, it explores the significance of terrorist language, which often misrepresents its objects and relies on media dissemination for political impact, and the symbolic targets of terrorist violence, which are based on readings of the victims' imagination. I draw on Joseph Conrad's *The Secret Agent* ([1907] 2000) as a model for the symbolic selection of terrorist targets in the novels under discussion. Finally, the chapter considers how gender and social class influence the construction of terrorist identities. I suggest that, notwithstanding their embracement of revolutionary terrorism, Effie and Alice remain subject to the patriarchy through their reliance on male material or intellectual support. In addition, they appropriate the general working class concerns they purport to defend and integrate them into their bourgeois ideology, thus displacing specific social and political injustices to the periphery. By analysing Spark and Lessing's depictions of terrorists as amateurish left-wing idealists, I argue that their novels enact a critique of the empty rhetoric of revolutionary groups amid 1980s conservatism and call for real engagement with the tangible social inequalities such groups tend to obliterate in their attempts to attract institutional and media attention.

Biographical Influences on the Literary Representation of Terrorism

From May to October 1944, Spark was employed by the Political Warfare Executive (PWE), a secret service created by the British government during the Second World War with the mission of spreading propaganda to enemy and enemy-occupied countries. Under the leadership of former *Daily Express* journalist Sefton Delmer, Spark was responsible for intelligence gathering rather than propaganda writing, but 'as a fly on the wall', she 'took in a whole world of method and intrigue in the dark field of Black Propaganda or Psychological Warfare, and the successful and purposeful deceit of the enemy' (Spark 2009, 147). As part of her PWE work, Spark operated a scrambler telephone – a green-painted telephone which made speech signals unintelligible in order to prevent enemy eavesdropping – to collect 'the details of the bombing, the number of planes that had gone out and those (not always all) that had returned' from the returning Allied bombers, which she would then pass on to Delmer (152). She was also tasked with answering a nightly call from the Foreign Office newsroom conveying 'general news not yet released for the next day's newspapers' (153). Such intelligence would be used to produce 'black propaganda' such as leaflets, broadcasts and rumours purporting to originate from Germany with the aim of damaging enemy morale and encouraging neutral countries to support the Allied cause. Unlike the 'white propaganda' originating from the BBC European Services, which prized accuracy and made no secret of its British origin, PWE 'black propaganda' featured information of disputable credibility originating from an undisclosed or falsely credited source (Jowett and O'Donnell 2012, 17–18). In fact, PWE propagandists cunningly mixed real facts with believable lies to create plausible stories capable of encouraging Germans 'to distrust their government and to disobey it' (Delmer 1962, 108).

Such emphasis on the psychological manipulation of enemy populations is not dissimilar to that of the terrorist groups that would emerge in the postwar period, even though PWE activities, unlike terrorist attacks, were carried out under the auspices of the British government. Following her employment at the PWE, Spark became a successful novelist and settled in Italy in 1967, first in Rome and later in the Tuscan countryside, where she lived until her death in 2006. Spark thus experienced the Italian 'Years of Lead' (1969–78), 'a decade marked by terrorist attacks and violent political protest, as well as by the shadow of the State's collusion with right-wing terrorism' (Sassi 2018, 1616). Red Brigade terrorism made Spark feel 'distinctly uncomfortable' and led to more prolonged absences from her Roman apartment (Stannard 2009, 424). Spark's representation of terrorist Effie in *The Only Problem* is arguably inspired by her lived experience of the Red Brigades during her time in Italy.

Whereas Spark is not deemed to be an overtly political writer, Lessing's literary career was significantly shaped by her overt engagement with revolutionary politics. Lessing's involvement in communist politics was initially driven by her critique of racial discrimination in the colony of Southern Rhodesia (now Zimbabwe), where she was raised and lived until her move to Britain in 1949. In her local Communist group comprising residents, European refugees and Royal Air Force (RAF) pilots, Lessing found like-minded individuals 'among whom thoughts about the Native Problem [she] had scarcely dared to say aloud turned out to be mere commonplaces' (Lessing 1995, 259). However, Lessing 'was never committed with all of [herself] to Communism' and often struggled to reconcile her personal and artistic integrity with the unconditional political commitment demanded by the Party (Lessing 1995, 284).[4] In particular, Lessing took issue with the Soviet Union's advocacy of socialist realism culminating in the Soviet Literary Controversy, which demonised modernist artists due to their celebration of the subjective interiority characteristic of bourgeois individualism. Nevertheless, Lessing would remain a member of the Communist Party of Great Britain (CPGB) from 1952 to 1956, finally quitting in response to the Hungarian Revolution of 1956. During her membership of the CPGB, Lessing's intellectual engagement with communism remained unenthusiastic: she 'did not go to meetings and was already a "dissident"' (Lessing 1995, 275). Lessing's growing scepticism towards organised communism would come to the fore in her later novel *The Good Terrorist* (1985).

This novel not only builds on Lessing's experience of belonging to a communist group in Southern Rhodesia, but was inspired by two further autobiographical events: Lessing's contact with neighbouring London 'revolutionaries', possibly members of the Angry Brigades, whose 'language was similar to that of the old communist and left-wing groups', and her knowledge of a young girl who became a revolutionary only to end up acting as the main carer of her group – a clear model for terrorist Alice (Lessing [1985] 2007, 11–13). Following publication of the novel, Lessing received several interesting letters which confirmed her understanding of the psychology of revolutionary groups, and in particular, their peculiar use of language as a means of enabling the perpetration of violence. For example, Lessing was contacted by someone

> who had been in on the early phases of the Red Brigades in Italy, and . . . said that . . . rackety amateur politicking was how many groups began, and then 'the language took them over' and they became ruthless and efficient killing groups (Lessing 1995, 276).

Such distrust of the language of revolutionary groups is at the core of Lessing's *The Good Terrorist*, as I will show later in this chapter.

Spark's *The Only Problem* follows scholar Harvey Gotham's attempts to write a monograph on the Book of Job in the solitude of the French countryside while being constantly disturbed by the lawless behaviour of his wife Effie, who has recently become a terrorist, and the police, who believe he is financing his wife's violent activities in the country. Most often analysed from a religious perspective as a result of scholarly emphasis on Spark's interest in the Book of Job and the problem of suffering, *The Only Problem*'s representation of the terrorist – in particular, the female terrorist – has remained largely unexplored.[5] Lessing's *The Good Terrorist* follows the activities of an amateurish group of revolutionaries based in a London squat, most likely modelled on members of the Angry Brigades, who benefit from the practical skills and motherly care of Alice. After its offers of help are disregarded by both the Committee for State Security (KGB) and the Irish Republican Army (IRA), the group moves from peaceful protest to violent action. This novel has often been read in the context of Lessing's avowed disenchantment with communist politics and her adoption of a more conservative stance; however, Lessing's satire of the revolutionary group is not simply a condemnatory critique but also a more positive indicator of the need for an intersectional approach attuned to gender and class difference. Both novels employ the figure of the terrorist to explore the precarious boundary between artistic autonomy and political commitment, as well as the suspicion of language arising from its appropriation by political ideologies.

Blackmail and the Ends of Terrorism

In an interview with Martin McQuillan, Spark remarked that 'terroristic actions and intentions . . . [go] along with a certain type of blackmail' which often originates in domestic environments (McQuillan 2002, 224). Spark's understanding of blackmail as the seed of terrorism suggests that she regards terrorism as a language governed by the imposition of an either/or logic which pits the terrorists' desired outcomes against the symbolic and/or physical violence resulting from failure to comply with such demands. The first of her novels to explicitly connect blackmail with terrorism is *Territorial Rights* ([1979] 2018), where Robert Leaver blackmails his ex-lover Curran by threatening to disclose his role in the murder of Victor Pancev, the man accused of poisoning the Bulgarian tsar Boris, before being recruited and 'sent to the Middle East to train in a terrorist camp' (Spark [1979] 2018, 189). Both *The Only Problem* and *The Good Terrorist*, however, locate blackmail in the immediate family circle. In *The Only Problem*, Effie is abandoned by her husband Harvey because she steals two chocolate bars from a supermarket, and becomes the leader of a left-wing terrorist organisation operating across Europe. Early in the novel, Effie's sister Ruth manages to get her husband Edward and herself invited to a holiday with Harvey and Effie by threatening to disclose to Harvey that Effie is sleeping with other men, thus being framed by Effie as 'a blackmailer' (Spark [1984] 2018, 35). However, Effie will ironically go on to blackmail her husband once she becomes a terrorist. For example, the movement of her violent activities into the Vosges region, where Harvey is writing his monograph on the Book of Job, arguably constitutes a retribution for his refusal to provide her with a large settlement: 'If Effie is involved, thought Harvey, plainly she is in this district to embarrass me' (63). Both Ruth and Effie use blackmail to control or punish others, thus exemplifying the terrorist logic Spark describes.

The Good Terrorist similarly shows that Alice's relationship with her parents is based on blackmail. When Alice receives a letter from the council saying that her father refuses to guarantee the electricity bill for her squat, 'rage took over [and] she exploded inwardly, teeth grinding, eyes bulging, fists held as if knives were in them' (Lessing [1985] 2007, 135). In a key rite of passage from good daughter to terrorist, a furious Alice 'reached her father's house [and] flung [a] stone as hard as she could at the glass of the bedroom window' (140). Through these examples of retribution, Spark and Lessing illustrate how everyday blackmail can easily become the testing ground for coercion on a bigger scale when feelings of anger at personal injustice and desire for revenge are displaced onto political objects. For Effie and Alice, personal grievance appears to be at the root of their desire to use violence to get revenge on a capitalist society whose social and economic rules, first encountered in the microcosm of the family, they consider unfair. Such representations also echo early portrayals of the female terrorist as 'dealing not with rational, but with emotional motivation' insofar as her violence 'stems not from dedication to the particular cause which she appears to espouse, but from blind obedience to another more personal cause' ('The Female Terrorist', 245).[6]

However, both Effie and Alice fail to understand what their ultimate political objectives are, exhibiting a disconnection between the means and the ends of their terrorist actions. For example, on stealing two bars of chocolate, Effie remarks: 'Why shouldn't we help ourselves? These multinationals and monopolies are capitalising on us and two-thirds of the world is suffering' (Spark [1984] 2018, 8). Effie's rebellious act is directed against the corporations which prioritise profit over human rights. In this context, her decision to steal chocolate may not be accidental given that its colonial production was based on the exploitation of African slaves; therefore, chocolate acts as a powerful symbol of the imperialist and capitalist forces she rejects.[7] Yet Effie's theft does not contribute to relieving the pain of others, and neither do her subsequent armed robbery, bombings of supermarkets or her eventual murder of a police officer. In fact, Harvey claims that Effie's misguided terrorism is wholly unproductive: he 'couldn't stand her sociological clap-trap. If she wanted to do some good in the world she had plenty of opportunity. There was nothing to stop her taking up charities and causes . . . But she has to rob supermarkets and banks. . .' (101). Whilst Effie is encouraged to take up causes that seek to minimise the social evils of capitalism, her attempts to completely dismantle this economic system are presented as delusional.

In *The Good Terrorist*, the revolutionaries are initially engaged in non-violent protest such as picketing, attending political demonstrations and painting slogans, which tends to foreground their self-centeredness at the expense of genuine social and political commitment. This is demonstrated by the fact that repeatedly getting arrested is applauded as the measure of success: '[Jasper] was always the first to be arrested, [Alice] thought proudly, he was so dedicated, so obviously . . . self-sacrificing' (Lessing [1985] 2007, 136). However, like Harvey in *The Only Problem*, Alice's mother can see through Alice's revolutionary pose, placing the excitement of mischief and the desire to attract attention at the root of her revolutionary activities:

> People go on demos because they get a kick out of it. Like picnics. . . . No one bothers to ask any longer if it achieves anything, going on marches or demos. They talk about how they feel. That's what they care about. It's for kicks. It's for *fun*. (359)

Such critique of the perceived egotism at the root of Alice's revolutionary group resonates with Lynne Segal's argument that the Angry Brigades served little political purpose and deployed illegality 'not so much [as] an act to fight and expose the class basis of bourgeois law, [but] as a necessary thrill' (qtd in Taylor 2015, 894). As a child of the 1960s civil rights and countercultural movements, Alice's belief that sacrifice consists of getting arrested narcissistically relegates the achievement of social and political justice to the background. In fact, such emphasis on 'how they feel' is ironically portrayed as an empty substitute for rational political discussion, again confirming the suggestion that the roots of terrorism might lie in personal grievance.

The Language and Symbolism of Terrorism

Like psychological warfare, terrorism is mainly 'a rhetorical product', based on 'the anticipated reactions to, and interpretations of, certain concrete acts of political violence' (Zulaika and Douglass 1996, 25). Terrorism can thus be described as a communicative act aiming to spread anxiety about the prospect of further violence among the target population. However, modern terrorists exhibit a 'disenchantment with words'; they 'are communicators who have lost faith not in their message but in their ability to affect the audience using non-violent language' (Rubenstein 1987, 10). By adopting stock phrases, terrorists render language bland and tedious, unable to communicate the significance of its cause. In a passage resembling Adolf Eichmann's mindless discourse during the representation of his trial in Spark's *The Mandelbaum Gate* ([1965] 2018), which is described as 'a dead mechanical tick' (215), Harvey draws on clock imagery to highlight the banality of terrorist language when listening to the news on the radio:

> The gang was going to liberate Europe from its errors. 'Errors of society, errors of the system.' Most of all, liberation from the diabolical institution of the *gendarmerie* and the brutality of the *Brigade Criminelle*. It was much the same as every other terrorist announcement Harvey had ever read. 'The multinationals and the forces of the reactionary imperialist powers. . .' It was like an alarm clock that ceases to wake the sleeper who, having heard it morning after morning, simply puts out a hand and switches it off without even opening his eyes. (Spark [1984] 2018, 84)

In her essay 'The Small Personal Voice', Lessing criticises precisely the failure of stock phrases to represent the world meaningfully. For example, she points to the demise of 'socialist art-jargon, the words and phrases of which have been debased by a parrot-use . . . to a point where many of us suffer from a nervous reluctance to use them at all' (Lessing 1975, 3). Her novel *The Good Terrorist* exemplifies this trend when Jasper, Alice's companion, addresses the other revolutionaries with 'the familiar phrases of the socialist lexicon, but as though he had only just that moment discovered them, so . . . people showed a tendency to laugh' (Lessing [1985] 2007, 235–6). In addition, as Margaret Scanlan notes, Lessing is aware that one's voice 'may not be a spontaneous authentic expression of a personality but a deception', an idea embodied in her representation of terrorists, who often 'depend on the media – BBC, *Coronation Street* – both to give them their speaking voices and to give voice to their actions' (2001, 79). Through her work for the PWE, Spark was also familiar with the use of voice for military deception. In fact, the PWE used prisoners of war to voice black propaganda broadcasts so as to maintain the illusion that they originated from within Germany. For example, Agnes Bernelle, a German actress and singer entrusted with broadcasting family news to the German Navy, is described by Delmer as 'incredibly good at it. The treacle in her voice would never let you suspect that this Circe had lost half her family in the gas chambers of Auschwitz' (Delmer 1962, 90).

Terrorism and the media in fact display a symbiotic relationship. Terrorism requires the amplifying effect of the media to exert psychological terror on the targeted population group, and the media, as its power to shock decreases, welcomes the 'excess of reality' contained in the terrorist image (Baudrillard 2002, 18). Both *The Only Problem* and *The Good Terrorist* are concerned with the instrumental role of the media in the creation of terrorist discourse. Although *The Only Problem* does not allow us access to Effie's consciousness, the novel suggests that her terrorist activities escalate following the encouragement of the press. Her early 'shoplifting in a supermarket in Trieste' was merely the subject of 'a small paragraph ... in the *Telegraph*, nothing in the other papers' while her later shooting of a policeman 'filled several pages of the newspapers' (Spark [1984] 2018, 49, 114). Similarly, the revolutionary group's first bombing in *The Good Terrorist*, which produces material damage but no casualties, is described as disappointing because it only filled '[a] paragraph in the local *Advertiser*!' (Lessing [1985] 2007, 337). Their subsequent bombing of the Kubla Khan Hotel, however, manages to secure radio coverage because '[f]ive people have been killed, and twenty-three injured, some seriously' (386). By indiscriminately attacking members of a population group, terrorists aim to make citizens feel unsafe and to disturb the fabric of everyday life with a view to coercing decision-makers into acceding to their demands. Banking on 'irrational anxiety', a fear that bears no relation to the actual statistical probability of being killed or injured in a terrorist attack, terrorists personalise violence so that 'the effect on the target population is made to extend beyond the immediate victims to include people who were not even in the area at the time of the attack' (Ganor 2004, 40–1).

Such 'irrational anxiety' is a temporal (future-oriented) feeling that 'involves intrusions of the (imagined) future into the present' (Frank 2015, 94). However, Sianne Ngai suggests that it is also a spatial feeling that subjects attempt to displace onto others as a form of unconscious self-defence, though Freudian psychoanalysis suggests that such an 'externalizing mechanism of "projection" may in fact constitute *part* of the phenomenon of anxiety, as opposed to a psychic operation subsequently performed *on* one's anxiety' (2005, 211). For example, when interrogating Harvey in *The Only Problem*, the police reconstruct the moment when the dead policeman's wife hears the news, pointing out that she 'is always worried when she hears of the death or wounding of a policeman', an assertion which precisely illustrates the psychological effect that the terrorists seek (Spark [1984] 2018, 118). The policeman's wife is presented as subject to the temporal dimension of 'irrational anxiety' – she 'is always worried' that her husband might be injured in a future terrorist attack – which might be spatially projected onto her immediate social circle, further perpetuating the terrorist logic of fear. While Effie shows no apparent moral qualms regarding casualties, Alice protests that 'if the bombs just go off, then we aren't going to know who's going to be around', a concern which the group quickly discards for the attainment of 'the greatest impact' (Lessing [1985] 2007, 371). In doing so, they acknowledge that the possibility of human fatalities, to be sensationally communicated to the public by the media, would increase their political leverage to influence the state.

As Zulaika and Douglass note, terrorists refuse to engage with the gradual progression of political negotiation, embracing instead 'the economy of an all-or-nothing decisive discontinuity through sudden, partial, arbitrary acts' (1996, 76). Such shifting of conflict into the symbolic and sacrificial sphere serves the purpose of challenging 'the system by a gift to which it cannot respond except by its own death and its own collapse' (Baudrillard 2002, 17). For this reason, terrorists often choose symbolic objects as the targets of their violence. In Joseph Conrad's *The Secret Agent*, Mr Vladimir – the First Secretary at the Russian Embassy – instigates a terrorist attack in the hope that it will turn public opinion in England against political refugees from the Continent. While explaining his scheme to the titular secret agent, Adolf Verloc, Vladimir takes pains to imagine the bourgeois mind in order to argue the case for the bombing of the Royal Observatory in Greenwich, the home of the prime meridian line:

> A bomb outrage to have any influence on public opinion now must go beyond the intention of vengeance or terrorism. It must be purely destructive. . . . Of course, there is art. A bomb at the National Gallery would make some noise. But it would not be serious enough. . . . But there is learning – science. . . . They believe that in some mysterious way science is at the source of their material prosperity. They do. And the absurd ferocity of such a demonstration will affect them more profoundly than the mangling of a whole street – or theatre – full of their own kind. (Conrad [1907] 2000, 66–7)

Mr Vladimir's peculiar choice of target is thus rationalised as an attack on science, which he perceives as the pillar of the capitalist forces that revolutionaries and anarchists seek to destroy. Although *The Secret Agent* describes a false flag operation instigated by state actors rather than an actual terrorist incident, the novel demonstrates understanding of the communicative dimension of terrorism, which relies on symbolism.

Both *The Only Problem* and *The Good Terrorist* inherit a similar concern with the symbolic significance of their terrorist targets. For Effie, supermarkets stand for an exploitative capitalist ideology that alienates the poor and police officers represent an authoritarian state that neglects dissenting views. Yet ironically, Effie's fight against the system requires wealth, the bourgeois weapon she claims to reject. In Harvey's words, '[m]oney; not enough money, but a lot. That's what Effie boils down to' (Spark [1984] 2018, 16). Alice's terrorist gang is also mindful of symbolism when selecting an object for their violence. In an episode mirroring that of *The Secret Agent*, they assess a series of bombing venues for maximum impact:

> It went on for hours. They discussed the merits of railway stations, restaurants, public monuments. The Albert Memorial was favourite for a few minutes, and then Faye said no, she adored it; she wouldn't harm a hair of its head. Hotels. No. 10. The Home Office. MI5's information computer. The War Office. (Lessing [1985] 2007, 343)

Their final decision to target the Kubla Khan Hotel suggests a twofold process of symbolism. On the one hand, its 'sedate luxury' stands for the acquisitive power of the middle and upper classes that the revolutionaries so much deride (378). On the other hand, the hotel's name echoes the Romantic imagination, described by Coleridge as 'the balance or reconciliation of opposite or discordant qualities' (2008, 319). In blowing up the hotel, the terrorists thus stage their rejection of the transient power of creativity, committing instead to a narrow-minded perspective which resists political negotiation and acknowledgement of the experiences of others. Like Effie, however, Alice shows a hypocritical attitude towards money. Despite her blatant hatred of the middle-class culture of saving, Alice finds herself thinking that 'she should put some money into the post office. For herself. Money no one should know about' (Lessing [1985] 2007, 206), which signals her internal commitment to bourgeois individualism rather than working-class collectivism.

Both Effie and Alice seem to confirm, rather than disprove, the counter-terrorist depiction of terrorists as 'kooks, crazies, demented, or at best misguided', based on viewing terrorism as an identity trait rather than a mode of behaviour (Zulaika and Douglass 1996, x). In an interview with Herbert Mitgang, Spark described Effie as 'that [Red Brigades] type. I think terrorism sometimes begins with a generosity of spirit, but some people have a built-in violence – almost as though there were a terrorist chromosome. Nobody can sympathize with the real terrorists' (Mitgang 1984). On discovering Effie's murder of a policeman, her brother-in-law Edward takes a similar view to his literary creator, noting that she is a fanatic who 'has always had this criminal streak in her' (Spark [1984] 2018, 146). Alice is similarly depicted as prone to rage attacks and her continuous forgetfulness mirrors Said's critique of the counter-terrorist representation of terrorism as a 'wholesale attempt to obliterate history, and indeed temporality itself', being 'ontologically and gratuitously interested in wreaking havoc for its own sake' (1988, 154). By insisting on placing the absolute narrative of revolutionary politics at the core of her life, Alice 'forgets' those items of information that disrupt her solipsistic existence. Feeling furious about her mother's decision to sell the family house, Alice fails to recall that she was the one communicating with the estate agents: 'For the thousandth time the situation was recurring, where Alice said, "I don't remember, no, you're wrong," thinking that her mother maliciously made things up; while Dorothy sighed and pursued interesting thoughts about the pathology of lying' (Lessing [1985] 2007, 350). In *The Only Problem*, Harvey leaves Effie because she is deceitful, egotistical and a petty criminal, yet her absence soon wipes out her worldly vices and similarly transforms her into a silent idol resembling Job's wife in Georges de la Tour's painting *Job Mocked by His Wife*, who communicates through 'the disinformation her terrorist act generates in the news' (Piette 2018, 1586). As a result, Harvey, much like the counter-terrorist discourse that Said condemns, dismisses the social and historical circumstances that inform Effie's terrorism and transforms her into a transcendent work of art.

The Female and Middle-Class Terrorist

The Good Terrorist is an early example of a novel that gives primary voice to the experience of a terrorist, even though Lessing's satirical stance still seems to resist, rather than enable, the possibility of readerly empathy. In contrast, *The Only Problem* links Effie with Job's wife through their mutual silence, giving us no insight into her thoughts or feelings. Referring to the biblical Book of Job, Ruth 'suppose[s] the wife suffered . . . But whoever wrote the book made nothing of her' (Spark [1984] 2018, 38). Significantly, both novels choose to focus on *female* terrorists, who are seen to 'interrupt stereotypical expectations of women as pure, innocent and non-violent' and are generally depicted as devoid of any agency of their own (Gentry and Sjoberg 2011, 4–5). From the beginning of the novel, Alice is depicted as the subject of physical and mental abuse by her companion Jasper despite contributing valuable skills to the revolutionary group: 'For her part she did not have to be told that she was wearing *her* look, described by him as silly. "Stop it," he ordered. His hand shot out, and her wrist was encircled by hard bone. It hurt' (Lessing [1985] 2007, 5). In fact, Alice behaves 'rather like a mother', running the household and caring for the emotional wellbeing of its inhabitants, but she is constantly belittled by other members of the group (205). For example, Alice's turning of the house into a revolutionary haven is mocked by Jasper, who considers it a symptom of Alice's bourgeois internalisation, and more generally, a threat to the group's mission: '"While you play house and gardens, pouring money away on rubbish, the Cause has to suffer, do without"' (160). Despite Alice's attempt to resist her feminine desires, for example, discarding a dress which 'was laying a claim on her, like an impostor demanding to be recognized', she remains a Victorian 'angel in the house' figure who is content to provide material and emotional comfort to the group and to defer to the male revolutionaries on ideological matters (165). For example, Lenin inspires in Alice 'a kind of bowing-down of her whole person, like a genuflexion, as to the Perfect Man', which resembles the female adoration of strong men evoked by totalitarian leaders (262). Such examples confirm Lessing's portrayal of 'women on the left [as] trapped in the patriarchy they despise' (Scanlan 2001, 87).

Despite their shared involvement in terrorism, Effie and Alice are in fact very different women. Effie, who 'was writing a thesis on child-labourers in the Western democracies', is depicted as 'not kind' and not 'a motherly type' (Spark [1984] 2018, 22, 47, 106), a cold and sinister intellectual character resembling Lessing's second husband Gottfried Lessing and Willi in Lessing's *The Golden Notebook* (1962), both of whom lead their revolutionary groups. Unlike Effie, Alice is a proud activist who condemns the intellectual approach to revolutionary action: 'She used to wonder how it was that a comrade with a good, clear and correct view of life could be prepared to endanger it by reading all that risky equivocal stuff', preferring to follow the ideas of others than to think for herself (Lessing [1985] 2007, 66). Lessing criticises Alice for her resistance to thinking independently; in contrast, Spark suggests that Effie's intellectual detachment might be precisely the attribute that enables her to come up through the ranks to become the leader of her terrorist group. Effie clearly belongs to the political sphere whereas Alice, despite her efforts to be an active participant in her revolutionary group, is relegated to the domestic sphere. Although both are heirs to the second wave of feminism, neither Effie nor Alice appears interested in upholding the gender equality principles that their female predecessors fought for. In fact, Alice follows the steps of her mother in '[c]ooking and nannying for other people' (353) and Effie fails to achieve financial independence because she cannot bring herself to sell her jewellery and eventually clings to her husband for material support.

Although Effie and Alice believe that they are acting on behalf of the working class when engaging in terrorist actions, they consistently fail to understand the needs of those they claim to represent. In fact, Alice patronises and demonises members of the working class as people who cannot help themselves – and therefore require the assistance of middle-class saviours like herself – to legitimise her superior claims to knowledge. For example, when observing a group of workers having breakfast in a café, Alice notes that:

> They had a pallid greasy look like bacon fat, or undercooked chips. In the pocket of each, or on the tables, being read, was the *Sun* or the *Mirror*.

> Only lumpens, thought Alice, relieved there was no obligation to admire them. . . . [I]t wasn't these men that would save Britain from itself! (Lessing [1985] 2007, 47)

Alice views the group of workers as a homogenous and passive mass, largely confirming her internalised and deep-seated stereotypes of the working class that turn their bodies into the staple 'fry up' breakfast they are seen to consume, and their minds into a thoughtless reflection of the conservative sensationalism of British tabloids. She similarly disdains her mother's new working-class friend, Mrs Wood, ironically on intellectual grounds, suggesting that 'she's never read anything in her life' (347). Alice is therefore portrayed as an heir to Bakunin insofar as she believes that a revolutionary elite is entitled to use terrorism as a lever to move the passive mass of working-class people to revolution, in contrast to the Marxist belief that the working classes constitute a thinking mass, capable of using their revolutionary will and self-government to act according to their own interests (Rubenstein 1987, 145–50).

While *The Only Problem* does not provide as much detail on Effie's attitudes towards the working class, we know that her thesis research is mostly based 'on Kingsley's *The Water Babies*', a Victorian children's fantasy novel that denounces child labour, thus seemingly focusing on fictional discourses at the expense of empirical research into the history of child-labourers. In addition, Effie's kleptomaniac gestures, described by Harvey as 'proletarian re-appropriation', become empty signifiers in the context of her wealth and privileged social position. In fact, the middle-class Effie and Alice unwittingly embrace the cultural logic of bourgeois morality that has been associated with the novel form since its 18th-century origins. If, as Nancy Armstrong argues, 'the novel's relationship to bourgeois morality [is] the history of the "impurities" that fiction either assimilated to bourgeois morality or else cast out of its imagined communities', then Effie and Alice may be seen to incorporate and subdue the general working-class struggle into their bourgeois ideology while displacing specific social and political injustices to the periphery (Armstrong 2006, 387). For example, on hearing that Comrade Andrew disapproves of the revolutionary group joining the pickets at Melstead, Alice protests that 'it is our struggle too. It is a struggle for all the progressive forces in the country. Melstead is a focal point for imperialist fascism, and it is not just the business of the Melstead trade unionists' (Lessing [1985] 2007, 138). Alice thus appropriates the fight against 'imperialist fascism' as a middle-class concern while erasing the importance of improving working-class labour conditions. In doing so, middle-class revolutionaries such as Alice enable criticism of abstract working-class dispossession while maintaining the everyday oppressions which contribute to the preservation of their social status.

Conclusion

Spark and Lessing appear conservative in their satire of the amateurish left-wing idealism upon which many post-war revolutionary terrorist movements were built, most likely because they failed to offer a viable alternative to capitalist evils. However, this does not mean that their novels advocate political paralysis. By considering the psychology of post-war revolutionary terrorism, Spark and Lessing illustrate how terrorists get into the minds of their victims in order to inspire anxiety, yet they are also attentive to their inability to bridge the gap between bourgeois representation of the working class and the actual needs of the working class itself. As a result, Spark and Lessing suggest, terrorists can easily fall into solipsism. In response, their novels advocate a less self-centred politics that prioritises an intersectional approach attuned to gender and class difference. Marx's famous evocation of terrorists as 'dangerous dreamers of the absolute' aptly applies to both Effie and Alice because, despite their interest in understanding the mind of the other, they tend to 'imagine the other from a perspective which discounts the other's perspective' (Mitchell 1996, 832).[8] Before becoming a terrorist, Effie's time was spent with her friends 'discussing their social conscience', but she did not attempt to grasp the views of those in need (Spark [1984] 2018, 34). Similarly, Alice patronises the working-class people who refuse her absolute perspective: 'Poor things, poor things, they simply don't understand!' (Lessing [1985] 2007, 393). In representing their terrorist characters as 'dangerous dreamers of the absolute', Spark and Lessing show that, despite being capable of accessing and manipulating the minds of their victims using the methods of psychological warfare, they are ultimately incapable of hearing and accepting any perspective different from their own.

Notes

1. The author wishes to thank Patricia Waugh, Michael C. Frank, Maria Flood, and the participants of 'The Figure of the Terrorist in Literature, Film and Media' conference for their helpful feedback on previous versions of this essay, as well as the Leverhulme Trust for the financial support to carry out this research.
2. Although the term 'terrorism' originally denoted state violence rather than the violent activities of sub-state actors, by the mid-twentieth century, sub-state terrorism had been adopted by ethnonationalist movements, whose desire for self-determination became 'the dominant motive behind the use of terrorism' (Law 2009, 179–80). Since this chapter focuses on literary representations of terrorism inspired by two sub-state terrorist groups – the Red Brigades and the Angry Brigades – in what follows I will equate 'terrorism' with 'sub-state terrorism' and 'terrorists' with 'sub-state actors' unless otherwise specified.
3. Frederic Bartlett wrote the seminal text *Political Propaganda* (Cambridge: Cambridge University Press, 1940) and John T. MacCurdy acted as psychological advisor to the

Political Warfare Executive, contributing to the creation of successful printed propaganda such as the malingering booklet (see Delmer 1962, 130–1).
4. Drawing on Lessing's letters to her RAF friends, Matthew Taunton has traced her sceptical attitude towards communism back to 1945. According to Taunton, Lessing 'wavered between a state of moral crisis about the fate of Communism in the Soviet Union, and a pragmatic acceptance of the Party line' (254).
5. A recent exception is Adam Piette's (2018) analysis of the relationship between fake news and terrorism in *The Only Problem*.
6. The early association of the female terrorist with a personal rather than political cause has largely been debunked and scholars now agree that women join terrorist groups for the same reasons as men – reasons which are often *both* political and personal (see Gentry and Sjoberg 2011).
7. Paul III's papal bull forbade the Spaniards to enslave the indigenous peoples of America, but the 'Middle Passage' of 'cargo' slaves did not come under any papal prohibition (see Coe and Coe 1996).
8. I was unable to find the source for this quotation, but it is widely attributed to Marx.

References

Armstrong, Nancy. 2006. "The Fiction of Bourgeois Morality and the Paradox of Individualism." In *The Novel, Vol. 2: Forms and Themes*, ed. Franco Moretti, 349–88. Princeton, NJ: Princeton University Press.

Baudrillard, Jean. 2002. *The Spirit of Terrorism and Other Essays*, trans. Chris Turner. London: Verso.

Coe, Sophie D., and Michael D. Coe. 1996. *The True History of Chocolate*. London: Thames and Hudson.

Coleridge, Samuel Taylor. 2008. *The Major Works*, ed. Heather J. Jackson. Oxford: Oxford University Press.

Conrad, Joseph. (1907) 2000. *The Secret Agent*. London: Penguin.

Delmer, Sefton. 1962. *Black Boomerang: An Autobiography; Volume Two*. London: Secker & Warburg.

"The Female Terrorist and Her Impact on Policing." 1976. *Top Security* 2, no. 4: 242–45.

Frank, Michael C. 2015. "Conjuring Up the Next Attack: The Future-Orientedness of Terror and the Counterterrorist Imagination." *Critical Studies on Terrorism* 8, no. 1: 90–109. https://doi.org/10.1080/17539153.2015.1005935

Ganor, Boaz. 2004. "Terrorism as a Strategy of Psychological Warfare." *Journal of Aggression, Maltreatment & Trauma* 9, nos 1–2: 33–43. https://doi.org/10.1300/J146v09n01_03

Gentry, Caron E., and Laura Sjoberg. 2011. "The Gendering of Women's Terrorism." In *Women, Gender, and Terrorism*, eds Laura Sjoberg and Caron E. Gentry, 57–80. Athens, GA: University of Georgia Press.

Hoffman, Bruce. 2006. *Inside Terrorism*. New York: Columbia University Press.

Jowett, Garth S., and Victoria O'Donnell. (1986) 2012. *Propaganda and Persuasion*. London: SAGE.

Law, Randall D. 2009. *Terrorism: A History*. Cambridge: Polity Press.
Lessing, Doris. (1957) 1975. "The Small Personal Voice." In *A Small Personal Voice: Essays, Reviews, Interviews*, ed. Paul Schlueter, 3–21. New York: Vintage Books.
Lessing, Doris. (1985) 2007. *The Good Terrorist*. London: Harper Perennial.
Lessing, Doris. 1995. *Under My Skin: Volume One of My Autobiography, to 1949*. London: Flamingo.
McQuillan, Martin. 2002. "'The Same Informed Air': An Interview with Muriel Spark." In *Theorizing Muriel Spark: Gender, Race, Deconstruction*, ed. Martin McQuillan. Basingstoke: Palgrave.
Mitchell, Robert W. 1996. "The Psychology of Human Deception." *Social Research* 63, no. 3: 819–61.
Mitgang, Herbert. 1984. "Echoes of the Red Brigade." *The New York Times*, July 15, 1984. https://archive.nytimes.com/www.nytimes.com/books/01/03/11/specials/spark-onlyproblem.html
Ngai, Sianne. 2005. *Ugly Feelings*. Cambridge, MA: Harvard University Press.
Piette, Adam. 2018. "Muriel Spark and Fake News." *Textual Practice* 32, no. 9: 1577–91. https://doi.org/10.1080/0950236X.2018.1533182
Rubenstein, Richard E. 1987. *Alchemists of Revolution: Terrorism in the Modern World*. New York: Basic Books.
Said, Edward W. 1988. "The Essential Terrorist." In *Blaming the Victims: Spurious Scholarship and the Palestinian Question*, eds Edward W. Said and Christopher Hitchens, 149–58. London: Verso.
Sassi, Carla. 2018. "Muriel Spark's Italian Palimpsests." *Textual Practice* 32, no. 9: 1615–32. https://doi.org/10.1080/0950236X.2018.1533184
Scanlan, Margaret. 2001. *Plotting Terror: Novelists and Terrorists in Contemporary Fiction*. Charlottesville, VA: University Press of Virginia.
Spark, Muriel. (1992) 2009. *Curriculum Vitae: A Volume of Autobiography*. Manchester: Carcanet.
Spark, Muriel. (1965) 2018. *The Mandelbaum Gate*. Edinburgh: Polygon.
Spark, Muriel. (1979) 2018. *Territorial Rights*. Edinburgh: Polygon.
Spark, Muriel. (1984) 2018. *The Only Problem*. Edinburgh: Polygon.
Stannard, Martin. 2009. *Muriel Spark: The Biography*. London: Weidenfeld & Nicolson.
Taunton, Matthew. 2021. "Communism by the Letter: Doris Lessing and the Politics of Writing." *ELH* 88, no. 1: 251–80.
Taylor, J. D. 2015. "The Party's Over? The Angry Brigade, the Counterculture, and the British New Left, 1967-1972." *The Historical Journal* 58, no. 3: 877–900.
Taylor, Philip M. 1999. *British Propaganda in the 20th Century: Selling Democracy*. Edinburgh: Edinburgh University Press.
Zulaika, Joseba, and William A. Douglass. 1996. *Terror and Taboo: The Follies, Fables and Faces of Terrorism*. London and New York: Routledge.

3. SYMPATHY FOR THE DEVIL? THE CHANGING FACE OF THE IRA IN AMERICAN SUPERHERO COMICS

Shane Walshe

INTRODUCTION

In 1986, an Irish Republican Army (IRA) plot to blow up the British Parliament was thwarted by the quick thinking of an American photojournalist. Four years later, a similar plan to kill members of the British royal family was foiled by the brave intervention of a US businessman. The heroic photojournalist was Peter Parker a.k.a. Spider-Man; the daring businessman was Oliver Queen a.k.a. Green Arrow. These events, which transpired between the covers of *Web of Spider-Man* #20 and *Green Arrow* #43, are just two examples of IRA violence spilling over onto the pages of Marvel and DC comics. Indeed, between the 1970s and 1990s, superheroes such as Shamrock, Jack O'Lantern, Metamorpho, Nightwing, and Speedy all found themselves inadvertently embroiled in what has euphemistically been called the 'Troubles', the ethno-nationalist conflict that raged in Northern Ireland during that period, sometimes extending to the rest of the island, neighbouring Britain and mainland Europe. The conflict originated in the differing constitutional aspirations of the two main communities in Northern Ireland, namely Catholic nationalists, who see themselves as Irish and aspire to a united Ireland, independent of Britain, and Protestant unionists, who regard themselves as British and desire to remain part of the UK. When civil rights marches protesting the inequalities between the nationalist minority and the unionist majority turned violent in the late 1960s, republican paramilitaries, such as the IRA, on the nationalist side, and loyalist paramilitaries, such as the Ulster Volunteer Force (UVF), on the unionist one, took up arms to protect their communities and fight for their interests. What ensued was a brutal conflict, with almost 3,500 people being killed by paramilitaries, local police and the British army, the last of which had originally been deployed in the area to restore order.

Despite the tragic human toll, the Northern Ireland conflict proved to be 'a thriller writer's dream' (Pelaschiar 1998, 19), spawning its own literary and film genre, the Troubles thriller. This genre was particularly popular in Hollywood in the 1990s, as evidenced in movies such as *Patriot Games* (Philip Noyce 1992), *Blown Away* (Stephen Hopkins 1994) and *The Devil's Own* (Alan J. Pakula 1997). In these films, renegade IRA terrorists[1] occupy roles previously held by Soviet spies, Libyan terrorists and South American drug cartels. However, unlike those groups, who have typically been portrayed negatively, Irish terrorists have generally enjoyed a privileged position in literature and film (Vanhala 2011, 222; Zywietz 2016, 94). Indeed, according to Richard Jackson, writers of contemporary fiction are much more likely to offer 'sympathetic portrayals' (2018, 384) of Irish terrorists than of other groups. The same applies in film, with Mark Connelly noting that filmmakers 'approach the IRA with a level of sensitivity and inherent sympathy they would never express in a movie about Serbian nationalists or Islamist militants' (2012, 243–4). This special treatment has been attributed both to the influence of the Irish diaspora in the US (Augé 2002; Connelly 2012) and to the fact that the conflict in Northern Ireland is typically framed as 'a classic colonial struggle between British occupying forces and the gallant freedom-fighters of the IRA' (McKittrick and McVea 2012, 146). The result is that Hollywood treats IRA violence as 'understandable' (Dodds 2008, 237), 'basically legitimate' (Blum and Heymann 2010, 174), and even as 'relatively "unterroristic"' (Zywietz 2016, 140). As Étienne Augé puts it, '[t]o Hollywood, the Irish struggle is fair; it is closer to resistance than terrorism' (2002, 152).

Although much has been written about the portrayal of Irish terrorists in film and literature (notably Magee 2001; Steel 2007; Pelaschiar 2009; Connelly 2012; and Zywietz 2016), little attention has been paid to their representation in comic books. This may be because 'comics that address terrorism usually focus on the victims rather than on the perpetrators' (Martin 2012, 472). This also applies to most US comics that deal with Irish terrorism, where the focus is primarily on those targeted by terrorists or caught in the crossfire (see *Primal Force* #0, *Marvel Comics Presents* #24, *Justice League Quarterly* #14). To redress that imbalance, and in keeping with the spirit of the present volume, this chapter analyses four storylines that foreground the figure of the IRA terrorist. Published between 1976 and 1991,[2] the series in question – *Iron Fist*, *Daredevil*, *Web of Spider-Man*, and *Green Arrow* – all involve encounters between superheroes and the Provisional IRA (PIRA).[3] As will become clear, although the earlier comic book depictions of the IRA are positive, reflecting cinematic tropes such as the 'reformed rebel' and the 'good' terrorist, they become increasingly unsympathetic over time, culminating in the trope of the 'fanatical hardliner'. These changing portrayals reflect an overall decline in American support for the IRA in the period under discussion, as evidenced, for example, in a marked shift in US political discourse, press coverage and donations to the Irish Northern Aid Committee (NORAID), an organisation which raised funds for the families of IRA prisoners (Clark 1977; Holland 1987; McKinley 1987; Wilson 1995). However, it would be reductive to suggest that this shift was linear in nature, as US support for the IRA ebbed and flowed depending on events on the ground. For example, in his research into popular support for the IRA, Jeffrey Sluka notes that the paramilitaries succeeded in winning the 'hearts and minds' of a significant portion of the civilian population both in Northern Ireland and abroad 'as a direct result of the repressive counterinsurgency tactics employed by the British army and police' (2010, 107). This notion is echoed by Jack Holland, who deduces from NORAID's tax returns that 'it was clear that the worse things were for Northern Ireland's Catholics, the better it was for NORAID's fund-raising efforts' (1987, 44).

If the police and British authorities were frequently guilty of turning public opinion against themselves, the IRA were equally adept at shooting themselves in the foot. Their shift of focus from economic and military targets to civilian ones resulted in growing condemnation of their violence and a gradual turn against militant republicanism.[4] Indeed, commenting on the murder of eleven civilians in the Remembrance Day bombing in Enniskillen in 1987, Tim Pat Coogan notes that 'even for supporters of the IRA, the terrorist line of acceptable targets can be crossed into unacceptability' (2000, 580) and, as will be shown below, this line was crossed increasingly frequently and is reflected in the more unsympathetic portrayals of the terrorists in the comic books as time passed.[5]

Sympathetic Portrayals of Terrorists

Before analysing the comics themselves, it is worth exploring the ways in which terrorists can be portrayed sympathetically. Research on this phenomenon in literature and film has tended to focus on three main areas: characterisation, motive and violence. In terms of characterisation, one can evoke sympathy for terrorists by, for example, portraying them as conflicted before they commit their acts of violence and as repentant afterward (Martin 2007, 3–4). Another way is by juxtaposing 'good' terrorists with 'bad' ones (Martin 2007, 3) or by making terrorists secondary characters rather than protagonists, thereby creating some narrative distance that 'permits a kind of safe and controlled form of sympathy and identification' (Jackson 2018, 379). In the same vein, findings from this chapter reveal that a close relationship between the hero and the terrorist serves to elevate the status of the latter – a form of honour by association.

When it comes to motive, audiences are more likely to feel sympathy if it is emphasised that the terrorists only resort to terrorism due to mistreatment, marginalisation or desperation (Martin 2007, 3–4). This is consistent with the observation that the IRA are often portrayed sympathetically by framing their violence in anti-colonial terms, as a case of 'David versus Goliath' (Zywietz 2016, 139). How sympathetic a perpetrator is perceived to be is also dependent on whether they themselves are allowed to explain their motives (Martin 2007, 3–4). When they are not given a voice, their motives are often attributed to them by others and 'described in terms of greed, revenge, rage, will to power, authoritarianism, fanaticism, bigotry, sadism, blood-lust, sexual dysfunction, and other reductive psychological explanations – rather than freedom, justice, idealism, nationalism, revolution, and the like' (Jackson 2018, 382).

Finally, with regard to violence, it is much easier to have sympathy for terrorists if the violence they commit is not actually shown, or is only shown indirectly (Martin 2007, 3–4). More importantly, as Jackson notes, the audience's sympathy has its limits and, thus, the intentional murder of the innocent would be a bridge too far (2018, 380). As will become evident in the analysis, the terrorists who are likely to be perceived most sympathetically are those who conform to most of the aforementioned categories. However, not all categories are equal and regardless of how understandable, for example, a terrorist's motives may be, if their violence is graphic, targets innocents or is carried out without remorse, it jeopardises how sympathetically they will be perceived.

The 'Reformed Rebel' in *Iron Fist* (1976–7) and *Power Man and Iron Fist* (1979)

During the first decade of the Troubles, there was a groundswell of sympathy in America for the IRA. This stemmed from the heavy-handed treatment that Catholics in Northern Ireland were receiving from the security forces, including illegal curfews, internment, police torture, and, most notably, the shooting dead of thirteen civilians by British paratroopers at a civil rights march on Bloody Sunday in 1972. Even though the IRA reciprocated with brutal violence of their own, including high-profile bomb attacks in Britain, as well as the murders of the British ambassador to Ireland and of Lord Mountbatten, a cousin of the British monarch, the group's underdog status and the highly publicised injustices that the nationalist community was experiencing in Northern Ireland were enough to retain American sympathy (Holland 1987, 35). Indeed, as would so often prove to be the case during the Troubles, '[t]he IRA's ability to maintain both its campaign and its support proved stronger than the public's capacity for sustained outrage' (Coogan 2000, 587).

In this light, it is perhaps not surprising that the first comic book encounter with an IRA terrorist is a positive one. It comes in *Iron Fist* #5 (1976), in which Danny Rand a.k.a. Iron Fist comes to the rescue of Alan Cavenaugh, who is being beaten by thugs in London. It transpires that the thugs are the IRA and that Cavenaugh is an IRA bomber who is haunted by his actions and is trying to leave violence behind. Although, as noted above, comics tend to focus on the victims of terrorism rather than on the perpetrators, this storyline explores the notion of the perpetrator as victim, someone who is traumatised by his deeds and trying to atone. This is a popular trope in portrayals of the IRA in film and has been variously labelled 'the troubled terrorist' (Einwächter and Kaczmarek 2014, 1), 'the reformed rebel' (Connelly 2012, 219), and the '"good" terrorist-hero' (O'Rawe 2004, 100). Given that such characters often engage in some form of 'rehabilitative penance' (Connelly 2012, 220), they are ultimately depicted as more tragic and positive than villainous and negative (Zywietz 2016, 141).

This also holds true for Cavenaugh. Right from the start, he is cast as a victim – an unarmed man in need of saving as blows from iron bars and chains rain down on him. Even when he reveals to Danny that he is an IRA bomber who has killed 12 innocent people, 'women an' children mostly', reader sympathy is still evoked for several reasons. Firstly, and most importantly, he is contrite and says that the killing was accidental as his bomb 'misfired'. Thus, he avoids the crime that, in Jackson's words, would put him 'beyond the pale' of reader sympathy, namely intentionally killing innocent people (2018, 380). Secondly, even though he served time in prison for his crime, the real punishment, he says, is the memories that haunt him. This notion is reinforced via a close-up of his closed eyes and pained expression as he remembers 'all those screams, all that pain.' Thirdly, his desire to atone is evident when he risks his life preventing an assassin from escaping from Iron Fist. Asked why he put his life on the line, he replies: 'I know a murderer when I see one – and I swore never to abide killers. If he'd gotten away, he would have killed again ... so I had to stop him.' By undertaking this rehabilitative penance, the former IRA man shows that he is indeed a reformed rebel.

Cavenaugh could have remained just another incidental character, but he befriends the hero and, thus, goes on to appear in subsequent issues, all of which are at pains to emphasise just how troubled he is. While this constant emphasis on his remorse may come across as heavy handed and repetitive here when all the comics are analysed side by side, it is less jarring when the volumes are read in isolation. After all, serial comics usually repeat information for uninitiated readers via editorial notes in captions, flashbacks and expositional dialogue. In Cavenaugh's case, these repetitions serve to show that guilt and regret are crucial to his characterisation, and they ultimately contribute to his sympathetic portrayal.

Iron Fist #11 (1977), for example, revisits some of the same territory as *Iron Fist* #5, emphasising that Cavenaugh is haunted by his terrorist past. However,

Figure 3.1 The 'Troubled Terrorist': Alan Cavenaugh's recurring nightmare (Source: *Iron Fist #11*, 1977).

what makes this issue interesting is the way that it conveys this notion. Unlike in the earlier comic, readers do not have to just take Cavenaugh's word that he is traumatised and repentant. Instead, they are taken inside his head and shown his recurring nightmare of the day he killed those innocent people (Figure 3.1). The nightmare is framed like a Dutch-tilt camera shot, a technique frequently used in cinema to suggest psychological discomfort. It shows Cavenaugh desperately running to warn shoppers about a bomb in a department store, and it zooms in on his devastated reaction when the bomb explodes before he can reach them. A caption explains that this is a recurring nightmare, a race he has run 'every night for the last few years ... run, and lost'. Thus, not only are readers shown that he tried in vain to prevent these deaths, but that he has had to live with that trauma ever since. Cavenaugh duly wakes up screaming, his face and shirtless body covered in sweat. At this point, another caption informs uninitiated readers who the traumatised man is: 'Depending on your point of view, he's a freedom fighter, a patriot, a solider, a terrorist, a bomber. The word Cavenaugh himself uses, though, is murderer.' These descriptors from the omniscient narrator show that Cavenaugh does not hide behind labels like 'freedom fighter' to comfort himself or justify his actions. Instead, he acknowledges that he murdered innocent people[6] and pays nightly for his crimes with his troubled dreams – a price 'far more terrible than a lifetime stretch in one o' her majesty's prisons'. If any doubts remain about how troubled he is, these are dispelled when the IRA men who are pursuing him hear him screaming from next door and comment 'there he goes again'. In *Iron Fist #13* (1977), the burden of Cavenaugh's guilt is shown to be so great that he even welcomes his impending death, saying, '[M]aybe now, my nightmare will end.' However, this is not the end of the Irishman (nor of the comic's reiterating just how troubled he is). Danny saves his life again and, as the pitiful Cavenaugh drifts off to sleep, the hero notes, 'He should rest easy for a time, until the nightmares come for him again', thereby evoking reader sympathy once more.

In keeping with the reformed rebel tradition, Cavenaugh earns the redemption he so desperately seeks in *Power Man and Iron Fist #60* (1979). Discovering that the Halwani Revolutionary Army, a fictional terrorist group, are planning to blow up an embassy, he rushes to the scene to dispose of the bomb. Unlike in his nightmares, he arrives in time and saves the day. This moment of heroism cements his status as a reformed rebel, and, having begun to make his peace with himself, he joins the Peace Corps, where he continues on his path to becoming a model citizen.

While reader sympathy for Cavenaugh is mainly achieved by demonstrating his remorse and atonement, it is also accomplished by having him befriend the hero. Because readers tend to align themselves with the protagonist (Smith 1994, 41), the fact that Danny is willing to see past Cavenaugh's crimes and give him a second chance means that readers are likely to do so too. To ensure that this is the case, Danny's friendship with the terrorist is repeatedly underscored. In *Iron Fist #7* (1976), for example, Cavenaugh is one of the few people that Danny thinks of when contemplating what he would be missing if he were to leave earth forever for the mystical city of K'un-Lun. The fact that Danny holds the self-confessed terrorist in the same regard as his closest friends, Colleen Wing and Misty Knight, is evidence of how positively the Irishman is viewed. However, the real strength of Danny and Cavenaugh's bond only becomes evident when it is tested after causing a rift between the hero and Misty. Misty, who lost her arm in a terrorist attack, cannot understand how Danny can be friends with 'a terrorist bomber – a murderer'. Nonetheless, Danny doubles down on his friendship with Cavenaugh, saying: 'Alan's not like that, Misty – he's a decent, tormented man, living in his own private hell! A man who's my friend – and if that isn't good enough for you – then maybe I'm not good enough either!' This ultimatum and the fact that the superheroes actually part ways over the matter reinforces just how loyal the protagonist is to the IRA man.

Although Misty and Danny eventually reconcile, the latter's friendship with Cavenaugh comes between them again when the Irishman reappears two years later in *Power Man and Iron Fist #59* (1979). Misty labels him a 'murderer', but Danny defends him, saying that he has never murdered anyone. This is a curious response given Cavenaugh's admission on their first encounter that he had killed a dozen innocent people, but it echoes what Connelly notes about former IRA men in Troubles thrillers, namely that their 'terrorist past is forgettable and forgivable' (2012, 183). When Misty reminds Danny (and uninitiated readers) of the innocents that Cavenaugh killed and then has a flashback to her own trauma in which she lost her arm, this should gain sympathy for her. However, Danny is not particularly sympathetic to her suffering and instead stands by his new friend, saying, 'Misty, Alan isn't the one responsible for what happened to you . . . He never wanted to hurt anyone. He's really suffered . . .' Here, again, the former IRA man's status as a victim is foregrounded, even placing his suffering above that of someone who was maimed in a terrorist bombing. Throughout the series, Misty is unable to dislodge Cavenaugh from Danny's affection and when she wrongly accuses the Irishman of having planted a bomb and has him arrested in *Power Man and Iron Fist #60* (1979), she only succeeds in securing further superhero support for him. Danny's partner, Luke Cage a.k.a. Power Man, who has never met the IRA man before, but who himself has been wrongly imprisoned, defends Cavenaugh, even trusting him enough to share Danny's secret Iron Fist identity with him. This divulging of the hero's secret identity – arguably the ultimate show of faith in the superhero genre – brings the former IRA man even further into Danny's inner circle, adding to his positive portrayal.

Throughout his story arc, then, Cavenaugh is shown in a sympathetic light. He did not mean to kill innocent people, is remorseful, and makes amends by preventing further loss of life. Moreover, the fact that Danny stands by him (as Luke will later do), even in the face of the challenges from Misty, raises his esteem in the eyes of readers. It should also be noted that although other members of the IRA are cast in the villainous role of Cavenaugh's pursuers, they still have redeeming qualities. They are never shown engaging in acts of terrorism and their main objective seems to be preventing someone with Cavenaugh's expertise from leaving their organisation. Indeed, rather than kill their former comrade when he deserts, they give him several chances to rejoin. Importantly, when they do use violence, they do not use it indiscriminately. In a shootout with Misty in *Iron Fist #13*, for example, they intentionally miss when returning fire, with one of them commenting, 'Nice an' easy, Pat – Remember we're after Iron Fist an' Cavenaugh. No one else!' In fact, their biggest flaw seems to be their slavish adherence to 'the cause'. In this regard, they fit the cinematic trope of 'the Republican fanatic' or 'hard man' (see below), 'who views compromise as surrender, denounces negotiation as treason, places abstractions above people, and ruthlessly uses violence to not only attack enemies but anyone within the organization who fails to follow his rigid standards' (Connelly 2012, 215). Thus, despite Cavenaugh once being their closest friend, they follow him to London and New York, arguing in *Iron Fist #11* that 'once you betray the cause, there's nowhere you can run to . . . an' no man or super-hero – who can protect you'. Interestingly, as in many cinematic treatments of IRA terrorism, their motives are never actually specified and 'it is up to the viewer to figure out what the supposed cause is' (Vanhala 2011, 222). This is not the case in subsequent portrayals.

The Renegade 'Psycho Republican' in *Daredevil* (1984–5)

Despite the mounting casualties of the IRA's terror campaign, the group still enjoyed considerable support in the US in the early 1980s, particularly following the slow and highly publicised deaths of ten IRA hunger strikers who were seeking recognition from the British government as political prisoners. Writing in retrospect on the significance of that moment, William B. Shannon, the former American Ambassador to Ireland noted that, '[t]he hunger strike was the greatest political propaganda coup for the IRA in the last decade' (Coogan 2000, 504). This notion is echoed by Connelly, who explains how it captured the hearts and minds of the American public: 'For the British, the face of the IRA was that of dead and maimed civilians killed in terrorist attacks. In America, it was the smiling innocent face of hunger-striker Bobby Sands depicted on posters, T-shirts, and buttons circulated in Irish bars and college campuses' (2012, 166). This positive perception of the IRA translated into another surge in donations to NORAID as well as increased illegal shipments of US weapons to the IRA, as evidenced in the high-profile seizure of the *Marita Ann* with seven tons of arms on board in 1984.

Such sympathy for the IRA also carries over into the group's next appearances in comic books, namely in *Daredevil #205* (1984), *#216* (1984) and *#217* (1985),[7] where they are depicted as 'good' terrorists in contrast to a 'bad' terrorist known as 'the Gael' – a crazed former IRA hit man who has gone rogue. If the 'troubled terrorist' trope, as in *Iron Fist*, allows authors and filmmakers to show at least one IRA member more sympathetically, then the renegade 'psycho republican' trope (McLoone 2000, 66), as here, enables them to portray the majority of the movement in a more positive light. This is a common strategy in Hollywood portrayals of the Troubles, in which the villains are often 'terrorists who are too extreme for the PIRA' (Vanhala 2011, 205). Indeed, the trope has been used so frequently in films that '[t]he tendency to blame violence on renegades or defectors has made the IRA repeatedly appear rational, restrained and reasonable' (Connelly 2012, 243). This is also the case in *Daredevil*, where the differences between the IRA and the Gael are evident in their respective uses of violence, their motives and their characterisation.

The IRA, for example, are never shown being violent. Although they initially appear to be the villains, bundling a young woman into a truck, it transpires that they are merely trying to hide her from the real villain, the aforementioned

Gael, who has already killed her father. While their story at first does not seem credible, Daredevil, whose heightened powers of perception function like a lie detector test, can tell from their heartbeats that they are telling the truth. Like the nightmare sequence in *Iron Fist* which takes readers inside the terrorist's mind and corroborates that he is haunted, this lie detector device takes readers inside the IRA men's hearts and confirms that they are indeed well-intentioned and that the real danger comes from the crazed renegade. This is substantiated in what follows, as the Gael proves to be a truly sadistic murderer, who takes perverse pleasure in slowly torturing and then strangling his victims, removing their gags, and relishing their screams as the 'life goes sputterin' out of [them]'. As he strangles a group of IRA men one by one in *Daredevil #216* (1985), having already paralysed them with a toxin, a close-up of his ecstatic face highlights the joy he takes in feeling the life extinguish from them. Pausing between killings, he taunts his helpless victims, saying ''Tis a fair thing . . . to rest an' to savor what's to come. For the anticipation can be the best part.'

In terms of his motives, the Gael also resembles IRA renegades in film, who are typically 'demented assassins' and 'do not represent the wider aims of the organisation' (Barton 2002, 103–4). This is reflected in his arbitrary choice of victims, ranging from innocent patrons in a bar to members of his own organisation, but not political targets. In *Daredevil #205*, he even admits that, although his first victim was a British soldier, he no longer kills out of political conviction: 'Over the years, I came to realize that the patriotism wasn't important to me. The killin' was.' In this respect, the Gael adheres to a long tradition, with Pelaschiar claiming that 'the list of brutal psychopaths who opt for a terrorist career as an outlet for their congenital violence in the Northern Irish political thriller is endless' (2009, 56). The Gael's bloodlust, however, is not shared by his former comrades, who are dedicated to a higher cause. They even voice this distinction in *Daredevil #216* (1985): 'Time was he was one of us . . . fightin' fer the cause. But he went off his nut, he did. Forgot his reasons fer killin' and did it fer the joy of it.' Although 'the cause' is not yet explained, it is implied that any killing that the IRA do is justified and that only someone who is 'off his nut' like the Gael would actually enjoy it. The effect of this type of contrast between the IRA proper and these renegade psycho republicans, according to Connelly, is that it grants 'a cloak of legitimacy to the IRA by blaming violence and extremism on lone malcontents' (2012, 215).

The ways that the Gael and the IRA are described in the comics further highlight their differences. Echoing the IRA's assessment of the Gael being 'off his nut', Daredevil, in *Daredevil #216* and *#217* respectively, calls him a 'complete homicidal maniac' and a 'madman'. These words carry even more weight coming from the hero and prove to be accurate, as, true to his psychotic nature, the Gael purposely burns himself in prison in order to be transferred to a hospital from which he can escape. There, a guard informs medical staff

Figure 3.2   Glorianna defends the 'good people' of the IRA (Source: *Daredevil* #217 1985).

(and new readers) that the Gael was 'a hit man for the Irish Republican Army* who went bad' (*Daredevil #217*). This description is particularly revealing, as the words 'who went bad' imply that the IRA ordinarily are good and that the Gael is an exception. Moreover, the editor's footnote, indicated by the asterisk, explains that the IRA are 'anti-government rebels', thereby framing them more positively than a label such as 'terrorists' would have done. The most positive description of the IRA, however, comes from Glorianna, the young woman who was being pursued at the beginning of the series and who in later issues is dating Daredevil's alter-ego, Matt Murdock. When it emerges in *Daredevil #217* (1985) that she has been arranging safe passage for IRA members into the US, the hero asks her: 'Why, Glorianna? Why were you helping those terrorists?' To which she replies: 'They're not terrorists, Mister Daredevil – or whatever your name is! They're the Irish Republican Army . . . good people fightin' to free their home from oppression . . . any way they can!' (Figure 3.2). Here, 'the cause' is articulated for the first time and the IRA are portrayed not as terrorists but as 'good people' who have become freedom fighters out of desperation. Not only are they described positively, but it is also stressed that they have nothing to do with the Gael: another editorial footnote explains that he is 'a renegade IRA agent', thereby distancing him from the legitimate organisation and its honourable cause. This strategy, as noted above, is common in cinematic portrayals, where renegade republicans are shown to be 'loose cannons working outside the moral codes and ideology of the IRA' (Barton 2004, 162).

As has become clear, *Daredevil* combines strategies to offer a sympathetic treatment of the IRA. This is also reflected in the hero's relationship with Glorianna. Concerned about whether his new love interest is on the right side of the law, Daredevil, in *Daredevil #217*, asks the superhero Black Widow, who is 'familiar with the international espionage terrorist scene', to investigate. She returns the verdict that 'Glorianna O'Breen is the soul of innocence' and 'has never committed a terrorist act in her life', thereby giving her blessing to the couple. Satisfied with that information, Daredevil continues dating Glorianna, seemingly happy to turn a blind eye to his girlfriend's aiding and abetting a recognised terrorist group.[8] Such tacit approval of IRA activity recurs throughout the series, with the IRA being shown to have many supporters in America who keep their eyes and ears open for them and offer them refuge. These include a jovial doorman, who informs them of Glorianna's whereabouts (*Daredevil #205*), and the owners of St. Brigid's Hostelry and Delahanty's Grill, which act as an IRA safe house and meeting point respectively (*Daredevil #216* and *Daredevil #217*).

Finally, it is noteworthy that the IRA are portrayed favourably not only by being contrasted with a psychotic renegade and by being given the superhero seal of approval, but also by being juxtaposed with evil international terrorists. Just as the IRA shared the page with the Halwani Revolutionary Army in *Power Man and Iron Fist #60*, they do so with Russian terrorists led by 'the Cossack' in *Daredevil #217*. Although no explicit comparisons are made, the presence of the Russians in a parallel storyline helps to cast the IRA in a positive light. Unlike the 'good people' of the IRA, who pose no danger to Americans, the Cossack is twice shown spreading panic by blinding New Yorkers with a neural transmitter and plotting to bring down an airliner over the city if he does not receive payment. Moreover, whereas the Russian threatens thousands of innocent people solely for financial gain, the IRA are framed as victims of oppression who have no choice but to try to liberate their country from invading British soldiers like the one the Gael killed ... before he went bad.

The 'Fanatical Hardliner' in *Web of Spider-Man* (1986) and *Green Arrow* (1990–1)

Following the signing of the Anglo-Irish Agreement in 1985, the US government began to take a more active role in the peace process in Northern Ireland, becoming the main contributor to the International Fund for Ireland, an organisation which supported economic development in the troubled region and encouraged dialogue between nationalists and unionists. This pursuit of a political solution to the Troubles was welcomed by Americans, and particularly Irish Americans, who were increasingly distancing themselves from militant republicanism (Wilson 1995, 249). They could not sympathise with the IRA's 1986 declaration that it was extending its list of legitimate targets to those who worked in any capacity for the security forces, thereby placing caterers, electricians, building contractors, civil servants and others in the line of fire. While civilians had been killed by the IRA in the past, this had never been a declared policy before. What is more, civilians had never previously been used as proxy bombs – a new IRA tactic in which alleged collaborators with the security forces were strapped into vehicles laden with explosives and forced to drive to checkpoints or military bases, while their families were held hostage. It was in the context of these changes in IRA tactics that the remaining series of comics were published.

The first negative portrayal of the IRA is in *Web of Spider-Man*, in which Peter Parker and fellow journalist Joy Mercado travel to England to cover PM Margaret Thatcher's speech on Irish terrorism. In theory, the depiction of the terrorists here should gain them sympathy, as they are given multiple opportunities to articulate their motives and to frame themselves as 'an oppressed people using terrorism against foreign occupation' (Connelly 2012, 176). They make their anti-colonial objective clear in their very first appearance, declaring, in *Web of Spider-Man #19* (1986), '[T]onight we strike a blow fer independence!' This nationalistic sentiment is then echoed throughout *Web of Spider-Man #20* in statements such as ''Tis fer Ireland we're united, lads, and 'tis a united Ireland we're fightin' for – ta the death!' and '[I]f the Brits won't get outta our country, we'll make *theirs* a livin' inferno!' However, as Jackson notes, just because a terrorist's cause is treated sympathetically, this does not mean that they themselves are (2018, 383) and this proves to be the case here, where several factors conspire against them. Firstly, unlike in *Iron Fist* and *Daredevil*, they do not have a personal relationship with the hero and, thus, lack the type of honour by association that is afforded to Cavenaugh and Glorianna. Secondly, unlike in the previous comics, they do not have the benefit of being cast sympathetically as either 'reformed rebels' or 'good' terrorists. Instead, they fit the mould of the aforementioned 'Republican fanatic' (Connelly 2012, 215) or 'fanatical hardliner' (Zywietz 2016, 151). Like their cinematic brethren, these hard men are 'wedded to the violent prosecution of "the cause"' (Hill 2006, 192), and it is this violence that distinguishes them most from sympathetic terrorists like Cavenaugh. Although, on the surface, there are certainly similarities between their bombing in *Web of Spider-Man #20* and Cavenaugh's in *Iron Fist #11*, there are also major differences. Like Cavenaugh's bomb, the IRA's device at Heathrow Airport detonates prematurely, killing innocent women and children rather than its intended target, Thatcher's advisor on counterterrorism. However, rather than be distraught or discouraged by this, as Cavenaugh was, the IRA proceed to shoot wildly around the airport with machine guns, killing and injuring even more civilians and yelling 'Up the rebels!' and 'Death ta the Brits an' Maggie Thatcher be dam–!'[9]

Thus, any sympathy that readers may initially have had for the IRA's cause is likely lost due to their unapologetic and indiscriminate violence. Moreover, unlike in *Iron Fist #11*, where readers could only imagine the horrors that Cavenaugh witnessed, here, the extent of the devastation is clearly shown. The comic opens with a splash page showing a huge explosion and people being thrown backwards by the blast. This is followed by images of bodies strewn across the terminal building, of the injured and dead being cradled in pieta-like fashion by loved ones, and, perhaps most poignantly, of a six-year-old girl being prised from her mother's arms and being given a blood-transfusion at the scene. This focus on the victims, and particularly on a young child,[10] ensures that even if one might approve of the IRA's motives, the comic makes it difficult to agree with their methods.

Furthermore, unlike Cavenaugh, these terrorists do not renounce violence after killing innocents. Instead, their resolve is hardened, and they plan to blow up the Houses of Parliament while Thatcher is delivering a speech. Again, they show no consideration for the collateral damage they might cause, making them just like IRA hardliners in cinema – 'ruthless fanatics, inhuman in their single-minded objective of uniting Ireland' (Schröder 1994, 485). One IRA man even voices this notion in *Web of Spider-Man #20*, defiantly shouting: 'Heathrow was just the start. Up the rebels! An' death ta anyone who'd keep Ireland divided!' His tone differs greatly to that used by Glorianna when articulating 'the cause' in *Daredevil #217*. Whereas her words, like her facial expression, convey desperation and even regret at having to resort to violence, his are tinged with hatred and anger and his face is twisted into an animalistic snarl that matches the literal description of him and his comrades as 'animals' elsewhere in the captions. This negative framing of the terrorists is also echoed by Spider-Man, who condemns their 'blowing up babies' and their 'fanaticism'. The extent of this fanaticism is highlighted later in that issue when the IRA leader, in a last-ditch effort to kill Thatcher, blows himself up. Fanatical to the end, he finds the strength to defiantly whisper the words 'Up the rebels!' as he is carried away half-dead on a stretcher. Although these words are intended as a final show of strength, they have been repeated so often in the storyline that, by the end, they come across as more of a deluded mantra than a call to arms.

Thus, although *Web of Spider-Man* is the first series to offer a more detailed explanation of the IRA's objectives, which should, in theory, work in the terrorists' favour, any sympathy gained is likely lost in their remorseless killing of innocent people and their depiction as mantra-spouting fanatics. Indeed, the real-world IRA were so upset by their portrayal in *Web of Spider-Man #20* that, soon after this comic was published, the Marvel building in New York had to be evacuated because of a bomb threat. This led to all references to the group being promptly dropped from subsequent comics in the series, leaving a very disjointed narrative, particularly as Peter and Joy depart for Belfast at the end of the issue to further investigate the IRA.

The least sympathetic portrayal of the IRA comes in *Green Arrow*, where, again, the fanatical hardliner trope comes to the fore. The fact that this portrayal is so negative comes as a surprise, as the storyline initially has all the makings of a positive depiction. Like *Iron Fist*, it features a friendship between the hero and the terrorist. Like *Daredevil*, it clearly articulates the IRA's cause and shows tacit support for it. However, like *Web of Spider-Man*, it also depicts the IRA's wanton disregard for innocent lives and, thus, ultimately condemns the violence.

The story begins with the protagonist, Oliver Queen, wandering onto a movie set in Canada and befriending the stunt coordinator, Terry Marsh. Unlike in *Iron Fist*, the hero does not know from the beginning that his new friend is a terrorist. Thus, when the revelation comes, it is even more shocking, particularly since, unlike Danny and Cavenaugh's friendship, which is mentioned repeatedly but rarely shown, Oliver and Marsh's friendship plays out on the page. In *Green Arrow* #41 (1990), they are shown choreographing stunts together, reminiscing about famous stuntmen and joking about the diminutive Hollywood star they are working with. They get drunk together, fight side by side in a pub brawl and stagger home afterwards arm in arm. Moreover, when Oliver, who in a recent storyline had been framed for terrorism, is accused of stealing a stockpile of weapons from the film set, Marsh provides him with an alibi. However, the twist is that Marsh has been using Oliver all along. He is the one who stole the weapons and who intentionally caused the brawl to secure an alibi for himself for the night of the theft. Furthermore, he duped Oliver into thinking he was drunk when he had hardly been drinking. This type of betrayal, while unexpected here, is common among cinema's IRA hardliners, who place loyalty to the cause above all else, even friendship. For such fanatics, 'the Cause is an absolute not to be violated by conciliation or weakened by personal considerations' (Connelly 2012, 220).

Although Oliver is upset, Marsh explains the reasons for his betrayal in *Green Arrow* #42 (1991), comparing the situation in Northern Ireland to that of colonial America:[11] 'Look at your own country and think what it must have been like under British rule. And think what it would be like now without the revolution . . . without men to stand up and fight for what you know is right. And then tell me I'm wrong.' By framing the argument in terms of the Revolutionary War, Marsh employs a similar strategy to the one used in Troubles thrillers. In *Patriot Games*, for example, the leader of Sinn Féin argues that 'when Americans talk of their own uprising against their British colonial rulers, they call the revolutionaries "patriots," not "terrorists"' (McBride 1992), while in *Hidden Agenda* (Ken Loach 1990), the point is made that 'George Washington was called a terrorist in his time' (Connelly 2012, 161). This colonial comparison is an effective strategy for eliciting sympathy for the cause, as one can imagine few American readers disapproving of the violence that attained freedom for their country. Indeed, the argument proves to be so persuasive for Oliver that he not only lets his friend walk away, but also lets him take the stolen weapons with him. Thus, despite initially feeling betrayed, the hero is ultimately shown to be sympathetic to the terrorist's cause.

It is only when Oliver is confronted with the nature of Marsh's violence that he changes his stance. This happens in *Green Arrow #43* (1991), when he is presented with police files cataloguing Marsh's IRA atrocities over the previous twenty years, including a car bomb attack in Piccadilly Circus that killed 11 people and injured 28, with photographs revealing the extent of the carnage. Reminiscent of the scenes from *Web of Spider-Man*, they show bodies being thrown by the blast. However, since this comic is intended for mature audiences, the images are even more graphic, showing blood splattering and, in one photo, brains exploding out of the side of a victim's head when Marsh shoots him from close range. As Oliver examines the evidence, his face remains expressionless, only changing when he learns of his friend's worst crime: sending a child through a British army checkpoint on a booby-trapped bicycle. Although many of Marsh's other victims were no doubt innocent, it is the intentional killing of the child – the embodiment of innocence – that puts the terrorist 'beyond the pale' and gives the hero the resolve to stop him.

When he arrives in Belfast to detain Marsh, Oliver sees what it is like to live under British rule. The British army are a constant presence, with heavily armed soldiers shown frisking a family and looming in the background as the hero walks through the city. The fact that the British are unwelcome is reflected by pictures of shamrocks graffitied over the Union Jack flags that are on display for a royal visit. The combination of these images suggests that the IRA's motive to liberate Ireland is valid, even if the way it is pursued is not. In this regard, the comic again echoes cinematic portrayals of the Troubles, which 'only question the means and never the goal of the IRA' (Connelly 2012, 216). Here, the IRA's methods are certainly criticised, particularly as Marsh intends to replicate his most heinous crime, this time by detonating a bomb while an unsuspecting child on an explosive-laden bicycle is presenting flowers to Lady Diana, Prince Charles and their young sons. When Oliver fails to dissuade Marsh from carrying out the attack, he takes his friend's life rather than allow further innocents to die. This killing of the IRA man by a hero – the only such killing in all the comics analysed – is the ultimate condemnation of the terrorist figure and transforms what began as a sympathetic portrayal into an unsympathetic one.

Conclusion

Much like Connelly's analysis of the Irish Republican Army on screen, this study of the group's portrayal in American superhero comics reveals the IRA terrorist to be a 'mutable icon who can be cast to serve as hero, victim, or villain' (2012, 244), with the depictions changing considerably over time. The earlier comics succeed in creating sympathy for the IRA either by portraying them as troubled terrorists seeking redemption or by contrasting them with psychotic renegade rebels who cast the legitimate organisation in a comparatively positive light. Likewise, early storylines feature other terrorist groups who are shown to be worse than the IRA, usually because they target Americans (see also Dodds 2008, 236). Finally, the fact that the IRA (or their associates) become close friends or lovers of the heroes elevates them in the reader's esteem. Unlike the earlier comics, the later ones are more likely to articulate the IRA cause, which should earn them the reader's sympathy. However, the fact that the terrorists show no remorse for killing innocents or even explicitly set out to do so, as in *Green Arrow*, means that any goodwill they may have had from the hero (and reader) is lost. This negative depiction is further exacerbated by the graphic portrayal of their violence.

This change in sympathy towards the IRA in US comics mirrors the situation in real life. While American support for the armed struggle was at its height in the 1970s and early 1980s, with NORAID succeeding in raising large sums of money for 'the cause' (see Hanley 2004), support for militant republicanism gradually declined as public outcry over the IRA's killing of civilians grew. High-profile attacks such as the Brighton Bombing (1984) and, particularly, the Remembrance Day attack in Enniskillen (1987) severely tarnished the image of the IRA, causing a major backlash against the movement. For many, however, it was the murder of Patsy Gillespie in a proxy bomb attack on a British army checkpoint (1990) that proved to be the last straw. Far from striking a blow for independence, this attack, which, like the one in *Green Arrow*, involved using a civilian as a human bomb, turned out to be 'the very incident that cause[d] the group to lose support once and for all' (Bloom and Horgan 2008, 582). After that, it was hard for even their most ardent supporters to refer in good conscience to these terrorists as 'good people' as Glorianna had done, and the label 'the souls of innocence' was best reserved for their victims.

Notes

1. During the period under discussion, the Irish Republican Army was regarded as a terrorist organisation under both national and international law. Accordingly, alleged members were convicted under the UK's Prevention of Terrorism Act and were also refused visas by the US State Department on the grounds of their being suspected terrorists. In light of this, and in keeping with the title of the volume, IRA volunteers will thus be referred to as terrorists in this chapter, except in cases where the comics themselves employ terms that challenge this description.
2. It is worth noting that the cover date on a comic is actually the 'pull date', i.e., the date on which it should be removed from shelves. The actual publication date is typically around three months previously. Thus, although *Daredevil* #217, for example, has a cover date of March 1985, it was already on sale in November 1984. One needs to bear this in mind when linking the content of comics to real-world events.

3. The decision to examine solely storylines with the IRA rather than balance the analysis with stories featuring loyalist paramilitaries was dictated by the absence of the latter in comics. This reflects a similar situation in cinema, in which '[t]here has been a paucity of film material which has dealt with the Unionists in Northern Ireland in any capacity at all' (McLoone 2000, 79).
4. In some quarters, however, such attacks actually led to an uptick in financial support for NORAID, due to what Michael McKinley calls 'the criminally perverse power of "blood in the streets" ("spectaculars") to loosen the purse strings of Irish-Americans sympathetic to the Provisional cause' (1987, 35). This was the case, for instance, following the murder of Lord Mountbatten in 1979 (McKinley 1987, 40).
5. This study does not mean to suggest that the comic book creators were themselves IRA supporters or that they condoned IRA violence. However, the portrayals of the terrorists in some of the comics are certainly sympathetic, which is in keeping with American attitudes at the time.
6. His intended target is never specified. Readers familiar with the Troubles may assume that it was the soldier outside the department store. However, since the IRA's cause is never explained, this remains open to interpretation.
7. Interestingly, the latter two were published following the murder of Sean Downes by Northern Irish police at an event to welcome NORAID publicity director Martin Galvin to Belfast. Photos of Downes doubling in pain as he was shot in the chest at close range with a baton round drew global attention once more to the police's use of lethal force on Catholics in Northern Ireland and was another propaganda victory for the IRA.
8. Although women were actively involved in violent activities in the Troubles (see Bloom, Gill and Horgan [2012] for an overview of their roles and backgrounds), none of the comics in this study feature female combatants. This reflects a broader trend observed by Danine Farquharson, namely that '[w]omen as active members in the IRA are few and far between in the fictional representations of Irish rebellion and republicanism' (2001, 140). This notion was reiterated a decade later by Fiona McCann, who noted that there was still 'a marked reluctance on the part of writers of fiction to engage with representations of female paramilitaries' (2012, 70).
9. In real life, the IRA had already attempted to kill Margaret Thatcher by blowing up the hotel she was staying at during the 1984 Conservative Party Conference in Brighton. Although she escaped unharmed, five people, including MP Sir Anthony Berry, died in the explosion.
10. The girl is later named, elevating her above the status of nameless victim. Her critical condition is described on the evening news and, at the end, it is revealed that little Annie has died. Her death is a further condemnation of IRA violence.
11. A similar colonial comparison is made by a drunk at the bar brawl who argues that 'Englan' should get outta Irelan' the way they got outta Canada'.

References

Augé, Étienne. 2002. "Hollywood Movies: Terrorism 101." *Cercles* 5: 147–63.

Barton, Ruth. 2002. *Jim Sheridan: Framing the Nation*. Dublin: The Liffey Press.

Barton, Ruth. 2004. *Irish National Cinema*. London: Routledge.
Bloom, Mia, Paul Gill, and John Horgan. 2012. "Tiocfaidh ár Mná: Women in the Provisional Irish Republican Army." *Behavioral Sciences of Terrorism and Political Aggression*, 4, no. 1: 60–76.
Bloom, Mia, and John Horgan. 2008. "Missing Their Mark: The IRA's Proxy Bomb Campaign." *Social Research* 75, no. 2: 579–614.
Blum, Gabriella, and Philip. B. Heymann. 2010. *Laws, Outlaws, and Terrorists: Lessons from the War on Terrorism*. Cambridge, MA: MIT Press.
Claremont, Chris. 1976. "*When Slays the Scimitar!*" Iron Fist #5. New York: Marvel Comics.
Claremont, Chris. 1976. "*Death Match!*" Iron Fist #6. New York: Marvel Comics.
Claremont, Chris. 1976. "*Iron Fist Must Die!*" Iron Fist #7. New York: Marvel Comics.
Claremont, Chris. 1976. "*The Dragon Dies at Dawn!*" Iron Fist #9. New York: Marvel Comics.
Claremont, Chris. 1977. "*A Fine Day's Dying!*" Iron Fist #11. New York: Marvel Comics.
Claremont, Chris. 1977. "*Target: Iron Fist!*" Iron Fist #13. New York: Marvel Comics.
Clark, Dennis. J. 1977. *Irish Blood: Northern Ireland and the American Conscience*. Port Washington, NY: Kennikat.
Connelly, Mark. 2012. *The IRA on Film and Television: A History*. Jefferson, NC: McFarland & Company.
Coogan, Tim Pat. 2000. *The IRA*. London: HarperCollins.
Dodds, Klaus. 2008. "Screening Terror: Hollywood, the United States and the Construction of Danger." *Critical Studies on Terrorism* 1, no. 2: 227–43.
Duffy, Jo. 1979. "*The Big Apple Bomber.*" Power Man and Iron Fist #59. New York: Marvel Comics.
Duffy, Jo. 1979. "*The Terrorist Manifesto.*" Power Man and Iron Fist #60. New York: Marvel Comics.
Einwächter, Sophie G., and Ludger Kaczmarek. 2014. "The Troubled Terrorist. Der IRA-Film als 'Kleines Genre'." *Montage AV* 23, no. 1: 161–75.
Farquharson, Danine. 2001. *Rebel Narratives. The Irish Gunman in Fiction and Film*. Unpublished Thesis. Memorial University of Newfoundland.
Grell, Mike. 1990. "*Hooray for Ollie-Wood.*" Green Arrow #41. New York: DC Comics.
Grell, Mike. 1991. "*Fall Guy.*" Green Arrow #42. New York: DC Comics.
Grell, Mike. 1991. "*Legends of Stupid Heroes.*" Green Arrow #43. New York: DC Comics.
Hanley, Brian. 2004. "The Politics of Noraid." *Irish Political Studies*, 19, no. 1: 1–17.
Hill, John. 1988. *Cinema and Northern Ireland*. London: Bloomsbury.
Holland, Jack. 1987. *The American Connection. U.S. Guns, Money, and Influence in Northern Ireland*. New York: Viking Penguin.
Jackson, Richard. 2018. "Sympathy for the Devil. Evil, Taboo, and the Terrorist Figure in Literature." In *Terrorism and Literature*, ed. Peter C. Herman, 377–94. Cambridge: Cambridge University Press.
"Little Wars." *Web of Spider-Man* #20. 1986. New York: Marvel Comics.
Lobdell, Scott. 1989. "*I Haven't Got Time for the Pain.*" Marvel Comics Presents #24. New York: Marvel Comics.
Magee, Patrick. 2001. *Gangsters or Guerrillas? Representations of Irish Republicans in "Troubles Fiction."* Belfast: Beyond the Pale.

Martin, Elaine. 2007. "The Global Phenomenon of 'Humanizing' Terrorism in Literature and Cinema." *CLCWeb: Comparative Literature and Culture 9, no. 1. Thematic Issue, Representing Humanity in an Age of Terror*, eds Sophia A. McClennen and Henry James Morello.

Martin, Elaine. 2012. "'I' for Iconoclasm: Graphic Novels and the (Re)presentation of Terrorism." *Critical Studies on Terrorism*, 5, no. 3: 469–81.

McBride, Joseph. 1992. "Patriot Games." *Variety*, June 3, 1992. https://variety.com/1992/film/reviews/patriot-games-2-1200430147/

McCann, Fiona. 2012. "The Good Terrorist(s)? Interrogating Gender and Violence in Ann Devlin's 'Naming the Names' and Anna Burns' No Bones." *Estudios Irlandeses*, 7: 69–78.

McKinley, Michael. 1987. "Lavish Generosity. The American Dimension of International Support for the Provisional Irish Republican Army 1968-1983." *Conflict Quarterly*, 2, no. 2: 20–42.

McKittrick, David, and David McVea. 2012. *Making Sense of the Troubles. A History of the Northern Ireland Conflict*. London: Penguin.

McLoone, Martin. 2000. *Irish Film. The Emergence of a Contemporary Cinema*. London: British Film Institute.

Michelinie, David. 1986. "*Humbug!*" *Web of Spider-Man #19*. New York: Marvel Comics.

O'Neil, Denny. 1984. "*The Gael!*" *Daredevil #205*. New York: Marvel Comics.

O'Neil, Denny. 1985. "*The Second Secret.*" *Daredevil #216*. New York: Marvel Comics.

O'Neil, Denny. 1985. "*The Sight Stealer.*" *Daredevil #217*. New York: Marvel Comics.

O'Rawe, Des. 2004. "The Northern Other: Southern Irish Cinema and the Troubles." In *Representing the Troubles. Texts and Images, 1970-2000*, eds Brian Cliff and Éibhear Walshe, 93–105. Dublin: Four Courts Press.

Pelaschiar, Laura. 1998. *Writing the North. The Contemporary Novel in Northern Ireland*. Trieste: Edizioni Parnaso.

Pelaschiar, Laura. 2009. "Terrorists and Freedom Fighters in Northern Irish Fiction." *The Irish Review*, 40/41: 52–73.

Schröder, Gottfried. 1994. "Nordirland im Film." In *Nordirland in Geschichte und Gegenwart/Northern Ireland – Past and Present*, ed. Jürgen Elvert, 469–86. Stuttgart: Steiner.

Seagle, Steven T. 1994. "*The Call.*" *Primal Force #0*. New York: DC Comics.

Seagle, Steven T. 1994. "*Flight.*" *Justice League Quarterly #14*. New York: DC Comics.

Sluka, Jeffrey A. 2010. "Losing Hearts and Minds in the 'War on Terrorism'." In *Iraq at a Distance. What Anthropologists Can Teach Us About the War*, ed. Antonius C. G. M. Robben, 106–32. Philadelphia: University of Pennsylvania Press.

Smith, Murray. 1994. "Altered States: Character and Emotional Response in the Cinema." *Cinema Journal* 33, no. 4: 34–56.

Steel, Jayne. 2007. *Demons, Hamlets and Femmes Fatales. Representations of Irish Republicanism in Popular Fiction*. Bern: Peter Lang.

Vanhala, Helena. 2011. *The Depiction of Terrorists in Blockbuster Hollywood Films, 1980–2001: An Analytical Study*. Jefferson, NC: McFarland & Company.

Wilson, Andrew J. 1995. *Irish America and the Ulster Conflict, 1968–1995*. Washington, DC: The Catholic University of America Press.

Zywietz, Bernd. 2016. *Terrorismus im Spielfilm*. Wiesbaden: Springer Fachmedien Wiesbaden.

4. TERRORISTS AND HOOLIGANS: RE-POLITICISING A DE-POLITICISED FIGURE IN CONTEMPORARY REPRESENTATIONS OF BRITISH FOOTBALL CULTURE

Cyprian Piskurek

INTRODUCTION

In a conference with journalists on 31 May 1985, Margaret Thatcher said that 'these violent people must be isolated from society' (qtd in Burgess 1985, 1). Thatcher was talking about football supporters whose behaviour a couple of days previously had contributed to the catastrophe at Heysel Stadium in Brussels leading to the death of 39 mostly Italian spectators. Before the European Cup Final between Liverpool F.C. and Juventus, Liverpool fans charged towards Juventus supporters in an adjacent block, causing a huge number of Italians to press against a wall which collapsed and buried many bodies. The behaviour of Liverpool fans was only one factor contributing to the disaster, however; the ruinous state of the ground and failure on behalf of the authorities to properly segregate rivalling fan groups were also to blame (Frosdick and Marsh 2005, 23). Yet, concern about violence in football stadiums was so common in 1985 that the catastrophe seemed to confirm what many observers, both at home and abroad, had come to expect from English fans. With more than 40 serious incidents in UK stadiums involving deaths and multiple injuries since 1888, the history of football in England and Scotland had always been closely linked to narratives of disaster (Elliott, Frosdick and Smith 1999, 13–14). The reason for most of these incidents was the derelict state of grounds or bad planning, but the figure of the football fan, which for large parts of the public equated with 'hooligan' and 'social pariah' (Dunn 2020, xvi), made it easy for press reports or politicians to latch onto preconceived notions of football crowds whenever disaster struck (Sandvoss 2005, 2; Piskurek 2018, 2–3).

In her statement to journalists, Thatcher made an interesting link between hooliganism and two other forms of violence in the UK, namely 'that on the picket lines and [that] in Northern Ireland' (Burgess 1985, 1). Crucially, moreover, the Prime Minister contrasted the perpetrators of all three types of violence with 'the good and decent citizens of our society' (qtd in Burgess 1985, 1). Terrorist violence, especially in the context of the Northern Ireland conflict, was an omnipresent threat in the Britain of 1985, and Thatcher herself narrowly escaped an attack on the Conservative Party Conference in Brighton in October 1984. The yearlong miners' strike with repeated battles between police and pickets had only ended in March 1985, and hooliganism was perceived as a continuous danger that allegedly kept respectable people from visiting football stadiums. Thatcher was not the first to suggest a link between these phenomena. Since the 1970s, media reports had taken the internationally recognisable label of 'terrorist' and selectively applied it to groups such as, for example, 'Scottish and Welsh nationalists, football hooligans and animal rights activists', even though 'none of these groups ... posed a serious threat to the British state' (M. Dunning 2021, 237).

The violence of picketing miners, terrorists, and hooligans was amplified in contemporary media reports. Together, these groups seemed to threaten the social order of Thatcherite Britain. As a 'disease of prosperous society' (Thatcher qtd in Burgess 1985, 1), they prompted the Conservative government to further advance the creation of a strong state. Similar measures and strategies were used to counter each of these threats: 'both covert policing and associated surveillance tactics' were deployed against terrorists in Northern Ireland, striking miners in 1984 and 1985, and football fans inside and outside the stadium (Armstrong and Hobbs 1995, 185). For football fans, the Thatcher government even tried to impose a highly controversial ID card scheme, which resembled the dragnet tactics of counterterrorism (A. King 2002, 85–6).

In what follows, I will explore the overlapping discourses surrounding hooliganism and terrorism in more detail. From the Thatcher era, this chapter then moves on to the turn of the millennium. I will discuss three fictional representations of terrorism at football grounds – Chris Cleave's novel *Incendiary* (2005), Scott Mann's film *Final Score* (2018), and 'To Be a Somebody' (1994), an episode from the crime series *Cracker* – to illustrate the dominant mythologies of terrorism and hooliganism in contemporary popular representations. As these examples illustrate, the mythologies of terrorism and hooliganism have developed in different directions since the 1990s: whereas neoliberal reforms in European football have transformed hooligans into an exotic remnant of a bygone age, terrorists continue to be de-politicised and tabooed.

De-politicisation, Discourse and Affect

One could take Thatcher's earlier-cited statement as anecdotal evidence of her rhetorical skill. Thatcher's 'antithesis-based oratory' (Crines, Heppell and Dorey 2016, 188) cleverly employed binary oppositions to exclude various groups from the societal majority. The linking of football hooligans and terrorists is of more specific interest, however, as it aims to de-politicise both groups. The intended effect of the Prime Minister's remark is to stigmatise hooligans and terrorists as antisocial pariahs who 'must be isolated from society' because they have rejected society. These young men (for both hooliganism and terrorism were explicitly gendered) contradicted the Conservative ideal of society, which posited the family as 'a critical site of control, especially in the potentially dangerous affluence and mobility of post-Fordist society' (A. King 2002, 79). There was a strong class bias against those who enacted violence against the state and its citizens. David Goldblatt notes that in Thatcher's Britain, 'now blooming on easy credit and rising house prices', football, still perceived as mostly a working-class sport, was considered as 'one of the few cultural zones in which the people and the disorder of rust-belt Britain clung on' (2006, 568). Mark Schmitt connects this with questions of ethnicity, describing the hooligan as 'a stigmatype of tainted whiteness' (2018, 225).

By likening hooligans to terrorists, Thatcher branded both groups as antagonists of the democratic consensus, disposable elements not to be negotiated with. Thatcher also bemoaned the fact that 'increased freedom of movement' for the young had led to an increase 'in the use of drugs and in violence and terrorism' (Burgess 1985, 28), which turned both hooliganism and terrorism into symptoms of 'the prosperous society' (1). At the same time, however, Thatcherite policies conceived of terrorism as 'something other than and outside of British civilisation' (M. Dunning 2021: 242). In public statements, which would ultimately find their way into the 1986 Public Order Act, Thatcher continuously called for vigilance, reminding the majority population of the threat posed by the few. In her oft-quoted Carlton Lecture of November 1984, the Prime Minister warned that various minority groups did not recognise the 'need to accept the verdict of the majority' and would 'coerce the system to meet their own objectives' (Thatcher 1989, 198–9). The use of vague umbrella terms like 'minorities' and 'special interest groups' allowed Thatcher to subsume striking miners, IRA terrorists, football hooligans and factions of the political left under one and the same category (see also Baudrillard 1993, 78). This reinforced her de-politicisation of these various groups.

I use 'de-politicisation' in a different sense than political science, where the term denotes strategic forms of delegating political decisions into indirect modes of government (Flinders and Buller 2006, 296). In the present context, 'de-politicisation' describes a process by which the actions of certain groups are discursively positioned outside the political sphere. Hooliganism and terrorism were attributed to villainy rather than a lack of political participation and representation. By de-politicising hooligans and terrorists, official discourse refused to acknowledge the agenda-driven nature of both types of actors. From such a perspective, the violence of hooligans and terrorists is not born from social inequality, which makes these groups try to 'obtain the leverage, influence, and power they otherwise lack to effect political change' (Hoffman 2017, 44); instead, hooligan and terrorist violence is seen as illegitimate and even pathological. In this way, the state ensures its 'monopoly on the legitimate use of violence' (Townshend 2011, 4). Thatcher's rhetoric thus helped to construct what Joseba Zulaika and William Douglass have, with reference to terrorists, called the 'quintessential proscribed or tabooed figure of our times' (1996, 6).

For the international discourse on terrorism, the exclusion of the voice and agenda of terrorists has always been essential (Palmerton 1988, 107), as 'terrorism is primarily a rhetorical product' (Zulaika and Douglass 1996, 25) and the rhetorical construction of the terrorist Other invariably serves an ideological end. As Richard Jackson points out, 'many of the key narratives and narrative strategies employed by writers of fiction function mostly to stereotype, dehumanize, and demonize the terrorist figure in ways reflective of dominant social and political rhetoric' (2018, 377). But by the 1980s, football hooliganism had equally been constructed as a major threat to society. The discourse on hooliganism was characterised by an amplification spiral evident in the media which dehumanised and demonised the figure of the hooligan (Cohen 2002, 226; Hall 1978, 25; Canepari 2020, 138). Observers in the stadium were often stunned at the extent to which a serious but not particularly common problem was blown out of proportion (Inglis 2001, 87). Yet, this amplification of the threat of hooliganism was an integral part of the official discourse on football, which was 'marked by a designation of soccer culture as equivalent to "disorder" or "violence"' (Redhead 1997, 11). At the height of public concern about football crowds, a *Sunday Times* editorial went so far as to ask whether this was not a 'slum sport played in slum stadiums increasingly watched by slum people' (1985, 16a).

A salient feature of both hooliganism and terrorism discourse is the objectification and silencing of the Other. Cass Pennant, one of the leading voices in the genre of the hooligan memoir, makes this explicit when he writes: 'Spurred on by the inaccuracies in accounts of the exploits of West Ham's InterCity Firm in various publications, I decided to use my unique position as a former member of the I.C.F. to set the record straight' (2002, 16). This is a way of working against what has been perceived as a misrepresentation, and it illustrates the importance of narrative power. In his discussion of terrorism novels, Tim Gauthier puts his finger on this problem: 'Is it possible to unconditionally inhabit the mind of the terrorist? Can common ground be established? . . . Or are texts about Islamic fundamentalists written in the West always going to be handicapped as outsider perspectives?' (2015, 41). Some recent works of fiction have attempted to subvert the dominant discourse by evoking empathy with terrorists and giving them a voice, but for the majority of Western texts, 'terrorists, when they are substantially portrayed at all, are portrayed in derogatory, dehumanizing, and immoral terms' (Jackson 2018, 378). This one-sided focus on the terrorists' alterity further de-politicises them.

Contemporaneous media representations depicted violence against state forces as a monolithic phenomenon, lumping together hooliganism, terrorism and even radical forms of trade unionism. As early as 1967, *The Sunday Mirror* talked about hooliganism as 'the animal terrorising of ordinary people' (qtd in Canepari 2011, 150); when a missile was thrown at the Manchester United team bus, *The Mirror* similarly spoke of 'Tear Gas Terror' (qtd in Melnick 1986, 4); and in 1988, a report on right-wing violence at Leeds United was titled 'Terror on Our Terraces' (qtd in Frosdick and Marsh 2005, 145). In his 1990 essay 'The Mirror of Terrorism', French sociologist and philosopher Jean Baudrillard compares the Heysel disaster to terrorism, stating that 'Today's violence, the violence of hypermodernity, is terror' (1993, 77). That same year, the Italian government sent counterterrorist forces to Cagliari to prevent hooligan riots by British fans at the 1990 World Cup. The word 'terrorism' is often used metaphorically, and one reason for its frequency may be its conceptual vagueness (Herman 2020, 3–5). Nevertheless, the examples cited above show that the association of hooliganism with terrorism was not uncommon between the late 1960s and 1990. This association exaggerated the threat of hooliganism, which was limited to specific contexts and in most cases targeted fewer people; at the same time, the characterisation of terrorists as hooligans delegitimised their politically motivated violence.

In order to have an impact, the public discourse on violence needs to cause an affect. The emotional response intended by both Thatcher's statements and tabloid headlines was that the audience should not only reject violent young males but also be afraid of falling victim to their violence. For that purpose, it was important to construct this violence as an attack on the social contract. After Thatcher herself escaped an attempt on her life at the 1984 Conservative Party Conference in Brighton, she stated: 'The bomb attack on the Grand Hotel early this morning was first and foremost an inhuman, undiscriminating attempt to massacre innocent, unsuspecting men and women staying in Brighton for our Conservative Conference' (1997, 213). By casting certain forms of physical violence as mindless and inhuman, other forms of violence – such as the structural violence of social exclusion, which became so central to the neoliberal project – were legitimised as necessary means of control in a strong state.

Recent studies in affect theory have highlighted the importance of negative affect – in Sianne Ngai's influential phrase, 'ugly feelings' (2007) – for the formation of community and social coherence, which rest on the exclusion of certain forms of violence. Thatcher's rhetoric instrumentalised affective reactions to both terrorist and hooligan violence to 'circulate, spur, and foment violent feelings to achieve [her] own agenda' (Dowland and Ioanes 2019, 2). Constructing a community of the righteous, based on the shared condemnation of physical violence, served to conceal the existence of structural and state violence. Thatcher's decade of success still baffles many intellectuals on the left because her politics seemed so logically incoherent (Hall 1988, 165). Yet, her thinking together of hooligans, terrorists and picketers, and constructing them as a uniform Other, exemplifies what Stuart Hall describes as the main purpose of organic ideology: 'articulat[ing] into configuration different subjects, different identities, different projects, different aspirations' (1988, 166). By appealing to the ugly feelings spurred by physical violence, Thatcher constructed 'a "unity" out of difference' (166). Whereas violent incidents related to football seemed to confirm Thatcherite ideology (A. King 2002, 84–5), other disasters in 1980s Britain (like the King's Cross fire or the capsizing of the Herald of Free Enterprise), often caused by structural neglect, were interpreted as freak accidents.

Constructing and Deconstructing Hooligans and Terrorists

When Thatcher made her remark about hooligans quoted at the beginning of this chapter, the Heysel catastrophe had seemingly confirmed essentialist notions about football crowds. Thatcher's statement is noteworthy because it conceives the hooligan as a monolithic figure, a well-known type just like 'the picketing miner' and 'the IRA terrorist'. Since the late 1960s, violent outbursts on the terraces of English stadiums had been framed as a growing problem, and by the mid-1980s a dominant discourse around hooligans had been established not only by media pundits, but also by academics: 'In a sport which had pioneered the concept of gentlemanly behaviour, the violence of the crowd was a denial of all that the game had been devised to project and embody' (Walvin 1986, 90). Tellingly, the first major investigation into the phenomenon of football violence was led by a team of psychologists. The Harrington Report of 1968 focused on individual pathology and characterised hooligans as immature and generally inclined towards violence. Depriving them of any agency beyond genetic disposition, the Report contributed substantially to the perception of the hooligan as a type (Frosdick and Marsh 2005, 87).

Although scholars like Ian Taylor (1971) or the so-called Leicester School (E. Dunning et al. 1988) soon began to take social factors into account, the public perception of hooligans continued to be shaped by the image of an incurably aggressive and antisocial bully. More helpful than approaches that describe hooliganism as a form of deviance are the theories of Stuart Hall and his Birmingham colleagues about the crucial role of media amplification. According to Hall, the discourse on hooliganism, like related discourses on juvenile muggers or other young working-class 'folk devils', must be understood as a *construction* rather than a *reflection* of a social phenomenon. By reporting about hooligans as a faceless group, a picture was disseminated that characterised the deviancy of violent fans as a disease:

> If the official culture or society at large comes to believe that a phenomenon is threatening, and growing, it can be led to panic about it. This often precipitates the call for tough measures of control. This increased control creates a situation of confrontation, where more people than were originally involved in the deviant behaviour are drawn into it – forced to 'put up a good show' or increase the wager, up the odds. Next week's 'confrontation' will then be bigger, more staged, so will the coverage, so will the public outcry, the pressure for yet more control . . . This is what is sometimes called an *amplification spiral* – and the press has a significant part to play in each twist of the cycle. (Hall 1978, 25)

Crucially, this style of reporting circumvents a deeper social diagnosis and structural explanations. In doing so, it denies the phenomenon any rational basis and overlooks the possibility that violence could be a symptom of circumstances which might call for inclusion rather than isolation.

Thus, a phenomenon which had been around for quite some time (Dunning et al. 1983, 19–31) was given a new label and a new degree of social relevance – a process that could also be observed in the changed perception of terrorism after 9/11 (Jackson 2005, 57–8). For at least two decades, most press reports about hooliganism followed what Hall calls the 'usual SAVAGES! ANIMALS! Story' (1978, 20). Fictional representations tended to reiterate that narrative. When football fans appeared on screen, they would hardly get a voice yet always spell danger, and even novels by writers that seemed to sympathise with the subculture, like Gavin Anderson's *Casual* (1996) or Eddy Brimson's *Hooligan* (1998), relied on easily recognisable stereotypes of mindless working-class thugs who were causing havoc for the fun of it. Once again, the parallel with 'terrorism discourse's penchant for ominous representations' (Zulaika and Douglass 1996, 8) is evident. Together, political rhetoric, media reports, and fictional representations established a narrative pattern that fit terrorists just as well as hooligans or picketing trade unionists. What united the discursive construction of these groups was the emphasis on the way they threatened the public order of the strong state. Since the new neoliberal order was meant to protect the freedoms of the conformist individual, the state could count on affective reactions, or 'ugly feelings', in the majority of the population to stabilise and legitimise its ideological position on how to deal with deviant groups. In the case of football, declining attendance figures in the 1980s, which reached a historic post-war low in 1984, suggest that many people shared these ugly feelings and avoided the terraces.

In the subsequent two decades, the meanings associated with both the figure of the terrorist and the figure of the hooligan moved in divergent directions. To a certain extent, this can be explained with different degrees of visibility. Whenever hooligan riots occurred in the 1970s and 1980s, they produced visual spectacles, the images of which would be readily reproduced and circulated in the media. In the course of the 1990s, however, hooligans were widely driven from British stadiums and thus moved out of focus of public attention. The 'spectacle of terrorism' (Baudrillard 2002), on the other hand, gained increased visibility and media presence with the 11 September 2001 attacks. In the words of Richard Jackson, 9/11 brought about a discursive formation, or public narrative, designed to stabilise an instable world: in this 'myth of exceptional grievance' (2005, 36), terrorism was narrated as a demonic threat. Meanwhile, the discourse around hooliganism was undergoing a significant change. Political and cultural transformations within football gradually excluded not only the hooligan, but a whole social stratum of football fans from English stadiums. Somewhat paradoxically, this led to a development where the figure of the hooligan was appropriated by many traditionalist fans as a residue of a bygone age. In contrast to the de-politicised figure of the quintessentially evil terrorist, the hooligan was now re-politicised as a romantic outlaw.

After the 1989 Hillsborough disaster, in which 96 fans were trampled and crushed to death on a terrace in Sheffield's Hillsborough ground, the UK government instituted a commission to come up with new regulations to clean up the game. The ensuing Taylor Report suggested, among other measures, the abolition of standing terraces in favour of seats as well as the wide-scale introduction of CCTV cameras, creating a climate around football grounds which drove hooligans away from first- and second-division grounds. Just one year later, the 1990 World Cup in Italy conveyed a colourful spectacle and a televised promise that football could look different. When private television companies promised lucrative deals for a cleaned-up new product, the top clubs in the country decided to break away from the lower divisions and founded the Premier League in 1992. This new product was mainly targeted at middle-class families rather than traditional working-class fans.

Published in the same year that the Premier League was founded, Nick Hornby's football memoir *Fever Pitch* showed how football could be appropriated by the intellectual classes, and a whole new genre, which was quickly christened New Football Writing, was born (Piskurek 2018, 95). Within this genre, a number of texts started to represent hooliganism in a more nuanced fashion. Rather than condemning hooligan practices, these texts created ambiguous narratives, negotiating a tension between fascination with and abhorrence of violence. Novels like John King's *The Football Factory* (1997) or Kevin Sampson's *Awaydays* (1998) and films like Lexi Alexander's *Green Street* (2005) or Nick Love's remake of *The Firm* (2009) represented football in the 1970s and 1980s from a hooligan point of view yet managed to move beyond the dominant perception of this subculture: Alexander's *Green Street* subtly suggests that her hooligan characters have middle-class jobs, thus refuting accepted forms of social essentialism; John King's characters are rooted in the working class, his novel contextualising football violence in the complex field of class struggle; and Kevin Sampson constructs hooligan subculture as a highly ambiguous field of identity formation. Together, such texts altered the perception of a social type who a few years earlier had been seen as a social pariah.

To understand this shift in perception, we need to consider that the Taylor reforms came at a price – quite literally, because clubs refinanced renovation and other costs via immense increases in ticket prices, of sometimes up to 900 per cent over twenty years (Conn 2011). The abolition of standing terraces limited interaction with others, and stadiums created 'docile bodies' in the Foucauldian sense. In previous decades, terraces had been characterised by the disorderly and unruly behaviour of a huge collective. By contrast, the panoptical world of the all-seater stadium, where CCTV, ground security and stadium layout literally kept each individual spectator in their place, replaced chaos with discipline, true to Michel Foucault's observation that 'the order does not need to be explained or formulated; it must trigger off the required behaviour and that is enough' (1977, 166). Thus, the watershed events of Hillsborough and the Taylor Report brought about less violent and more telegenic football crowds.

Moreover, clubs often changed their form of organisation and denied fan groups the right to democratic participation. These practices of social exclusion alienated many traditionalist fans. It is in this light that the ambiguous nostalgia of hooligan novels, memoirs and films gains significance. Texts of that kind position themselves against a commodified version of contemporary football and latch onto the figure of the hooligan in order to recall an age before the hyperregulation of Premier League stadiums. They reflect a reassessment of hooliganism at a time when the actual phenomenon no longer posed a tangible threat to English society. From a historical distance, it became acceptable, and possibly even appealing, to engage with this formerly stigmatised form of violence in narrative form. Somewhat paradoxically, in these texts, football violence of the 1970s and 1980s came to signify a form of resistance against the hypercommodified version of the sport after the Taylor reforms. Fans who would have rejected hooliganism at the time of its occurrence could now buy into notions of symbolic forms of violence against postmodern football.

The hooligan was a tabooed figure only for as long as he was perceived to be a real threat. As Brian Massumi explains, threats concern possible (future) events rather than actual (past) ones. He asks: 'How could the nonexistence of what has not happened be *more* real than what is now observably over and done with?' Massumi goes on to suggest that we 'live in times when what is yet to occur not only climbs to the top of the news but periodically takes blaring precedence over what has actually happened' (2010, 52). He refers to the rhetoric of Donald Rumsfeld and other officials in the Bush administration who understood the performative nature of threat as central to counterterrorist measures after 9/11. By this logic, an imagined threat is no less real than one rooted in actual events in the sense that it triggers the same future-oriented fear (Frank 2017, 8). This reads like an extension of Stuart Hall's media amplification spiral which works by anticipation rather than documentation. On that count, 'Fear is the anticipatory reality in the present of a threatening future' (Massumi 2010, 54). Once we subscribe to this affective reality, it does not matter if the next riot happens at all: 'A threat that does not materialize is not false' (Massumi 2010, 54).

The decisive turn in the discourse on hooliganism occurred when the reorganised football world managed to persuade people that the threat of violence in football was over. The anticipatory and performative nature of threat depends on the affective reaction of fear, but the sanitised panopticon of the Premier League stadium managed to literally exclude certain groups of fans – and thus also the fear of physical violence. The moment that a potential future threat is no longer thought likely to materialise is the moment in which a reassessment of the past is possible. Engaging with the hooligan mind in literary texts has become safe now that its referent in the real world has seemingly disappeared; today, the former threat of hooliganism can be remembered as something 'we' have overcome, but also as something that has been superseded by a new form of structural violence.

In the case of terrorism, a similar transformation seemed possible after the 1990s as well. The terrorist threat in 1980s Britain had emanated almost exclusively from the IRA and from Muammar Gaddafi's Libyan network. With the 1997 Good Friday Agreement, the threat of IRA terror seemed over. Despite the first World Trade Center bombing of 1993 and the 1998 attacks on US embassies in Africa, the 1990s were perceived by many as an era of security and optimism for the West. These hopes were crushed on 11 September 2001, and the subsequent War on Terror made it impossible for writers and directors to revaluate the figure of the terrorist the way New Football Writing had revaluated the figure of the hooligan. Whereas the figure of the hooligan now frequently serves as a foil to the subtler and less physical threat of social exclusion, the threat of terrorism is still alive, and it seems hard to imagine that the perception of this threat will change anytime soon. As Brian Massumi notes, 9/11 elicited fear of another attack, one that would be even worse than 9/11 itself. Massumi speaks of the 'nagging potential of the next after being even worse, and of a still worse next again after that' (2010, 53). This 'nagging potential' is one of the reasons why the terrorism taboo is still intact. According to Peter C. Herman, 'terrorism's unspeakability' serves to stabilise state formations under attack (2020, 7). For that reason, state-led discourses encourage a perception of terrorism as 'irrational, un-understandable, the result of a diseased mind, and so not amenable to reason' (9).

The revaluation of the figure of the hooligan in New Football Writing has not entailed a whitewashing of the practice of football violence as such, but it has challenged the dominant view of the hooligan as a radically anti-social and apolitical figure. In recent texts, the hooligan has acquired a voice. Whereas hooliganism has thus lost its 'unspeakability', Richard Jackson contends that fictional representations of terrorism still mostly 'reproduce (rather than challenge) the dominant cultural mythography of terrorism and maintain the taboo against engaging directly with the terrorist's subjectivity' (2018, 377). Peter C. Herman takes the more optimistic view that fiction 'can challenge the entrenched taboo against "rationalizing" terrorism' (2020, 13). In my next section, I will consider three texts in which fictional terrorists target football settings. By associating football violence with terrorism rather than hooliganism, these texts illustrate the changed perception of both phenomena since the 1990s and 9/11.

Fictional Terrorism at Football Grounds

Major sport events have always been sites of potential attacks – from the Gaelic Football massacre at Dublin's Croke Park in 1920, to the 1972 Olympic Games in Munich, the bombing of the 2013 Boston Marathon, and the misfired bombs outside the Stade de France in November 2015. In a less drastic episode, tabloid newspapers jumped at small hints which might have suggested a terrorist plot on Manchester United's Old Trafford ground in April 2004. These fears turned out to be unfounded (Frank 2017, 223–4), but the episode demonstrates how readily allegations about major sporting events, especially football stadiums, becoming terrorist targets fit the cultural imaginary of terrorism. It comes as no surprise, therefore, that terrorism has also found its way into football fiction.

Texts which evoke terrorist threats on football stadiums often use football's status in Western societies to reinforce the dehumanising representation of terrorists. Contemporary football has cleaned up its act and moved into the mainstream; violence on the terraces has been contained and the irrationalism and tribal tendencies of the crowd have been absorbed into the carnivalesque but harmless world of the stadium. Football has been habituated as a cultural asset, an ineluctable component of capitalist societies, and that elevates the symbolic value of the football stadium as a terrorist target onto another level. An attack on football can easily be narrated as an attack on global capitalism if, for example, the Premier League's glittering arenas are singled out by terrorist groups as the epitome of Western decadence. As spaces of leisure (for the spending of capital), stadiums are arguably invested with even more symbolic power than the World Trade Center as a space of work (for the generation of capital).

The affective response to violence in and around the football stadium has changed significantly over the last three decades. Whereas in the 1970s and 1980s hooligan violence was regarded as emanating from within the world of spectators, it is now seen as unrelated to genuine fandom. Although hooligan violence, if it occurred at all, was instigated by just a tiny minority of supporters, the discursive meanings of this kind of disorder saw it as symptomatic of a dangerous subculture that required the intervention of a strong state. The perceived absence of families from football grounds was used to emphasise the antisocial nature of football crowds, implicitly accusing the non-violent majority of complicity. Today, thirty years after the reforms and changes of the 1990s and the arrival of the commodified and consumer-friendly Premier League, any physical violence in the stands is interpreted as extrinsic to the game (Redhead 1997, 102). The instigators of these attacks are discursively isolated from the majority of the spectators, highlighting the abnormality of the attack. Football is now narrated as a central pillar of the West's cultural capital, concealing its function as a considerable asset of economic capital (Redhead 1997, 23). In this narrative, violence against the stadium crowd is not the product of, but an attack on the core values of society.

Scott Mann's 2018 action blockbuster *Final Score* is a case in point. Although the film reaches unforeseen lows in terms of implausibility of plot and one-dimensional characters, the way it represents violence in a football stadium is exemplary of the dominant mythologies of terrorism and hooliganism. West Ham United play their last ever home match at the Boleyn Ground, a European Cup semi-final against Russian side Dynamo. The lack of specification of the other club's name is significant (there is no evidence that this is meant to be Dynamo Moscow rather than some other Soviet team); in classic Orientalist mode, the only relevant thing is that this is some faceless entity standing in for the (post-)Soviet Other as a whole. Watching the match in the stadium among the Dynamo supporters is Dimitri Belav, a former leader of the military independence movement in the renegade Soviet republic of Sakovya, who after having faked his death is now living in London. Belav's brother Arkady leads a group of terrorists who take over the control room of the stadium and plan to detonate bombs if Dimitri, living in the UK under the protection of British government forces, is not handed over to the attackers. By 'resurrecting' his brother, Belav wants to rekindle the revolution in Sakovya.

The villains in this film are caricatures, prime examples of the tabooing of terrorists described by Zulaika and Douglass. There is not even the hint of a plausible motivation behind their actions, and the audience are left in no doubt as to the utter mindlessness of their violence. The nemesis of these demonised

Eastern Europeans is a US veteran, who does not even like football and only accompanies his dead best friend's daughter to the stadium, where he ultimately defeats the terrorists. The juxtaposition between those defying and those trying to save innocent lives is obvious, even if the film evokes the pre-9/11 hierarchies of the Cold War instead of summoning the spectre of Islamic terrorism.

In the lead-up to the actual match, scenes from outside the Boleyn Ground briefly show supporters of Dynamo with flares and smoke bombs, hinting at the dominant images associated with football hooliganism (11:04–11:20). There is no real danger emanating from these fans, just slight irritation, as the police are well able to contain the threat, but the sequence suggests that today, the hooligans are the Others. This is an explicit inversion of the conception of hooliganism as the 'English disease', which hooligan firms exported to the continent and paraded in various host towns during European cup campaigns (Spaaij 2006, 1). Instead, the sequence shows the barbarianism of foreign football fans outside an English football ground. Michela Canepari has analysed the language of tabloid press reports preceding the 2018 World Cup in Russia, and her results confirm this impression: many headlines from 2018 continued the sensationalist style of reporting about British hooligans established in the 1980s. The decisive difference is that this now happens elsewhere, 'backward' Russian football culture being contrasted with the reformed state of football in the British Isles (Canepari 2020, 143–7). In *Final Score*, the threat of hooliganism can be contained and kept under control, but this is hardly possible with the terrorist campaign that later unfolds inside the stadium. The logic behind this scenario is clear: in today's world, violence within the football ground cannot be related to hooliganism but must be of a terrorist nature.

This fictional scenario reflects a threat that is perceived to be real, and it is significant, therefore, that the perpetrators in the film are both dehumanised and de-politicised. The villains are the Sakovyans, and their potential target is the Western football crowd, including a 15-year-old girl, a senile and xenophobic old white lady, and a Pakistani ground steward. This is a panorama of contemporary British society rather than the stereotypical white male working-class football crowd of old. The British fans are eventually rescued by the traumatised American military hero. This is not a subtle reference to the presence of foreign investment in Premier League football, but a blatant reminder of global hierarchies in American-led counterterrorism after 9/11. The fact that the attack demolishes one of the oldest and most cherished London football grounds (foregoing the reading that the non-fictional West Ham itself decided to move and destroy the Boleyn Ground in 2016) emphasises the antisocial and sacrilegious nature of the foreign terrorist plot.

Final Score belongs to a genre which often opts for simple juxtapositions and seeks comfort in the stability of binaries. The fact that the film eschews any engagement with the terrorist mind conforms to the dominant mythography of the War on Terror, but its representation of the innocent football crowd can be read as a comment on the gradual extinction of football hooliganism as a threatening form of violence.

Chris Cleave's 2005 novel *Incendiary*, in which a working-class woman loses her husband and four-year-old son in a terrorist attack on Arsenal's new Emirates Stadium, offers a similarly de-politicised representation of terrorists. Written in the form of a letter to Osama bin Laden, the novel relates how the protagonist's life has unravelled since the suicide bombing. The novel's terrorist plot highlights the symbolic nature of the attack on a Premier League ground, a target epitomising what the attackers perceive as the decadence of Western society. Football, here, is the plaything of London's rich and famous. Right before the catastrophe happens, the narrator begins an affair with a journalist whose posh girlfriend teases him about his lack of cultural capital: 'She insists I must at least try to get up to speed with the game. I seem to be the last man in England who isn't. I'm failing to hold my own at dinner parties' (Cleave 2005, 41). Premier League football is stylised as a commodity or a social and financial asset of the rich. That Middle Eastern terrorists should target the Emirates Stadium, of all places, is ironic only at first glance; it shows how Western football has absorbed global money, and vice versa.

The social class of the protagonist's part-time lover also accentuates her own class background: living on a Bethnal Green housing estate, the woman is characterised by a myriad of stereotypical working-class markers, from the food she consumes and the tabloid papers she reads to the way she talks and tries to make sense of the world. The way that *Incendiary* employs her class position delegitimises the terrorist attack even further. In one of her letters, the narrator muses about bin Laden's possible motives and considers how the Arab world must feel underprivileged and exploited by the West. However, the constant reminders of her own social background indicate that the attack not only killed those who represent Western elites, but also people on the losing side of global capitalism in the West. Addressing the leader of al-Qaeda directly, the narrator asks: 'I saw the video you made Osama where you said the West was decadent. Maybe you meant the West End? We aren't all like that' (Cleave 2005, 5). In *Incendiary*, the victims of the stadium bombing represent those working-class fans who had to suffer the consequences of the processes of social exclusion described above. It is this group of people which New Football Writing has re-politicised to draw attention to the commodification of football. By contrast, Cleave's novel de-politicises Osama bin Laden and his faceless henchmen.

This juxtaposition is continued throughout the novel. The narrator's letters show a remarkable level of empathy and an urge to understand the terrorists' motives: 'Well Osama I sometimes think we deserve whatever you do to us. Maybe you are right maybe we are infidels' (Cleave 2005, 71). Her use of the pronoun 'we' is supposed to include all Britons. This position becomes sadly ironic when it transpires towards the end of the book that the authorities could have prevented the attack but decided to let it go ahead in order to protect an informer within the cell. The narrator and her social class are thus betrayed not only by the terrorists – whose motivation she seems genuinely interested in – but also by the UK government, which has sacrificed its own citizens.

While the book's ending, with London in a constant state of emergency and paranoia, can be interpreted as a warning against an 'overreaction to the current terrorist threat' (Frank 2017, 228), the text focuses primarily on the suffering of the victim and thus maintains the terrorism taboo. What is striking in this regard is the virtual absence of terrorists as agents in the novel. The suicide bombers are faceless and anonymous figures, not even important enough to feature in the narrative. Similarly, Osama bin Laden remains the silent addressee of the narrator's letter. For the narrator, the writing of the letter is a form of self-therapy, and her speculations about bin Laden's motives are an attempt to regain her voice: '[Y]ou'll have to bear with me because I'm not a big writer. I'm going to write to you about the emptiness that was left when you took my boy away' (Cleave 2005, 4).

The most complex of my three examples is a 1994 episode from the TV series *Cracker*, 'To Be a Somebody'. Here, Hillsborough survivor Albie Kinsella sets out on a killing spree ending in the failed attempt to bomb Manchester United's Old Trafford stadium. After his father, a co-survivor of the Hillsborough catastrophe, has died, Kinsella loses his last foothold and intends to take revenge on the authorities whom he blames for the mistreatment of Liverpool fans at Hillsborough. His original plan is to kill 96 policemen or journalists to match the number of supporters killed in the stadium.

There are some striking parallels between Kinsella and the nameless narrator of Chris Cleave's *Incendiary*. Hailing from a working-class background, both characters have a pent-up feeling of inferiority which is released once they are faced with the death of their closest relatives. Both characters are rejected by a society or nation they want to belong to, falling into the category of what Zygmunt Bauman terms 'disposable' or 'wasted lives' (2004, 6). The decisive difference between them – in line with gender stereotypes – is that the female narrator of *Incendiary* retreats into a state of depression whereas Albie Kinsella vents his frustration and anger by becoming a killer and terrorist. Tellingly, his first murder is triggered by a seemingly minor incident: a Pakistani shopkeeper refuses to sell Kinsella a newspaper even though he lacks just four pence. Before stabbing the man, Kinsella curses: 'Treat people like scum, they'll start acting like scum' (10:58–11:01). This rant against the discursive and performative power of stigmatisation allows Kinsella to justify the choice of his next victims: a sociologist attempting to explain his killings with theories about class, a *Sun* reporter who has misrepresented his deeds and the policemen whose colleagues' fatal decisions led to the Hillsborough catastrophe. In Kinsella's view, all of these people are either guilty of determinist assumptions about him or embody the political forces that deny him a place in society.

It is difficult, at first, to categorise Kinsella as a terrorist, as he starts with individual killings, but his methods change in the further course of the episode. He builds letter bombs before he starts to plan his attack on Old Trafford. Moreover, Kinsella has a political agenda, which is to fight against the social exclusion of traditional supporters in football and the structural violence exercised by the authorities (Piskurek 2018, 244–7). He accompanies his murders with messages, using his victims' blood to smear a number code for the date of the Hillsborough disaster on the walls of each crime scene. Kinsella is introduced as an alienated and mistreated football fan who sees violence as his only shot at gaining a position of agency, and we initially feel pity with him for the way that society seems to mistreat him. However, this premise is eventually undermined by his characterisation as a cruel murderer who randomly targets innocent victims to carry out his demented revenge plan. Although Kinsella is shown to be a cultured man who knows Rossini and Mozart, he ultimately remains in the position of the lone wolf terrorist.

Conclusion

In all the examples discussed here, the representation of terrorists relies on established formulas which at least to some extent acknowledge the personal or political motivation behind the terrorist act. At the same time, however, the terrorists' random targeting of civilians emphasises their lack of humanity and denies them moral legitimacy. It is significant that in each case, terrorism is linked to the world of football. Football is often superficially perceived as just a site of play, an unpolitical space for leisure activities; yet football is always political (Kuper 1994, 1–3). Thus, the intrusion of forms of violence into this space represents a disruption of social norms. Hooligans and terrorists who attack football grounds neglect the separation of social spheres and disregard social contracts; their actions encroach on a supposedly apolitical field as well as a quintessential global leisure activity. This is the reason why hooliganism could be singled out and constructed as a social problem in Britain during the 1970s.

The fact that, in the meantime, the hooligan has ceased to be perceived as a threat to society has made it possible to re-politicise him as a nostalgic figure of resistance. In recent football fiction, the void left by the hooligan as the villain of the story has repeatedly been filled by the figure of the terrorist. Unlike contemporary hooligans, stadium terrorists are perceived as a vital threat. Their attacks mostly target the large group of working-class football fans whose role has been so pivotal for New Football Writing and the genre's attempt to highlight processes of social exclusion. Even when a text like 'To Be a Somebody' hints at a form of empathy for the terrorist's motives, the terrorist still occupies the formulaic position formerly held by the hooligan. Nonetheless, as Margaret Thatcher's call for isolating both figures from society shows, these figures become deviant Others only by virtue of being discursively framed and constructed as such.

References

Alexander, Lexi, dir. 2005. *Green Street*. Universal Pictures. DVD.
Anderson, Gavin. 1996. *Casual*. Dunoon: Low Life.
Armstrong, Gary, and Dick Hobbs. 1995. "High Tackles and Professional Fouls: The Policing of Soccer Hooliganism." In *Undercover: Police Surveillance in Comparative Perspective*, eds Cyrille Fijnaut and Gary T. Marx, 175–93. The Hague, London, and Boston: Kluwer.
Baudrillard, Jean. 1993. "The Mirror of Terrorism." In *Transparency of Evil: Essays on Extreme Phenomena*. Trans. James Benedict, 85–91. London: Verso.
Baudrillard, Jean. 2002. *The Spirit of Terrorism*. Trans. Chris Turner. London: Verso.
Bauman, Zygmunt. 2004. *Wasted Lives: Modernity and Its Outcasts*. Cambridge: Polity Press.
Brimson, Eddy. 1998. *Hooligan*. Edinburgh: Mainstream.
Burgess, Charles. 1985. "Sports Writers Brief Thatcher on Heysel Riot." *The Guardian*, June 1, 1985, 1, 28.
Canepari, Michela. 2011. *An Introduction to Discourse Analysis and Translation Studies*. Milan: EDUCatt.
Canepari, Michela. 2020. "The Representation of National and International Football-Related Conflicts in the British Press: From Hooliganism to Terrorism." In *Investigating Conflict Discourses in the Periodical Press*, eds Giuliana Elena Garzone, Mara Logaldo and Francesca Santulli, 135–54. Bern: Peter Lang.
Cleave, Chris. 2005. *Incendiary*. London: Sceptre.
Cohen, Stanley. 2002. *Folk Devils and Moral Panics: The Creation of the Mods and Rockers*. 3rd edn. London and New York: Routledge.
Conn, David. 2011. "The Premier League Has Priced Out Fans, Young and Old." *The Guardian*, August 16, 2011. http://www.theguardian.com/sport/david-conn-inside-sport-blog/2011/aug/16/premier-league-football-ticket-prices
Crines, Andrew S., Timothy Heppell, and Peter Dorey. 2016. *The Political Rhetoric and Oratory of Margaret Thatcher*. London: Palgrave Macmillan.
Dowland, Douglas, and Anna Ioanes. 2019. "(Un)making the World: On Violent Feelings." *LIT: Literature Interpretation Theory* 30, no. 1: 1–4.
Dunn, Robert Andrew, ed. 2020. *Multidisciplinary Perspectives on Media Fandom*. Hershey, PA: IGI.
Dunning, Eric, Patrick Murphy and John Williams. 1988. *The Roots of Football Hooliganism*. London: Routledge & Kegan Paul.
Dunning, Eric, Patrick Murphy, John Williams and Joseph Maguire. 1983. "Football Hooligan Violence Before the First World War: Preliminary Sociological Reflections on Some Research Findings." In *Explorations in Football Culture*, ed. Alan Tomlinson, 13–49. Eastbourne: Leisure Studies Association.

Dunning, Michael. 2021. *Britain and Terrorism: A Sociological Investigation*. Cham: Palgrave Macmillan.
"Editorial." 1985. *The Sunday Times*, May 19, 1985, 16a.
Elliott, Dominic, Steve Frosdick and Dennis Smith. 1999. "The Failure of 'Legislation by Crisis'." In *Sport & Safety Management*, eds Steve Frosdick and Lynne Walley, 11–30. Oxford: Butterworth Heinemann.
Flinders, Matthew, and Jim Buller. 2006. "Depoliticisation: Principles, Tactics, and Tools." *British Politics* 1: 293–318.
Foucault, Michel. 1977. *Discipline and Punish: The Birth of the Prison*. London: Penguin.
Frank, Michael C. 2017. *The Cultural Imaginary of Terrorism in Public Discourse, Literature, and Film: Narrating Terror*. New York: Routledge.
Frosdick, Steve, and Peter Marsh. 2005. *Football Hooliganism*. Cullompton: Willan.
Fywell, Tim, dir. 1994. *Cracker*. Season 2, episodes 1–3, "To Be a Somebody." Granada Television. DVD.
Gauthier, Tim. 2015. *9/11 Fiction, Empathy, and Otherness*. Lanham: Lexington Books.
Goldblatt, David. 2006. *The Ball Is Round: A Global History of Football*. London: Penguin.
Hall, Stuart. 1978. "The Treatment of 'Football Hooliganism' in the Press." In *Football Hooliganism: The Wider Context*, eds Roger Ingham, Stuart Hall, John Clarke, Peter Marsh and Jim Donovan, 15–36. London: Inter-Action Imprint.
Hall, Stuart. 1988. "Gramsci and Us." In *The Hard Road to Renewal: Thatcherism and the Crisis of the Left*, 161–73. London: Verso.
Herman, Peter C. 2020. *Unspeakable: Literature and Terrorism from the Gunpowder Plot to 9/11*. Abingdon: Routledge.
Hoffman, Bruce. 2017. *Inside Terrorism*. 3rd edn. New York: Columbia University Press.
Hornby, Nick. 1992. *Fever Pitch*. London: Gollancz.
Inglis, Simon. 2001. "All Gone Quiet Over Here." In *Hooligan Wars: Causes and Effects of Football Violence*, ed, Mark Perryman, 87–94. Edinburgh: Mainstream.
Jackson, Richard. 2005. *Writing the War on Terrorism: Language, Politics and Counter-Terrorism*. Manchester: Manchester University Press.
Jackson, Richard. 2015. *Confessions of a Terrorist*. London: Zed Books.
Jackson, Richard. 2018. "Sympathy for the Devil: Evil, Taboo, and the Terrorist Figure in Literature." In *Terrorism and Literature*, ed. Peter C. Herman, 377–94. Cambridge: Cambridge University Press.
King, Anthony. 2002. *The End of the Terraces: The Transformation of English Football in the 1990s*. London: Leicester University Press.
King, John. 1997. *The Football Factory*. London: Vintage.
Kuper, Simon. 1994. *Football Against the Enemy*. London: Orion.
Love, Nick, dir. 2009. *The Firm*. Warner Bros. DVD.
Mann, Scott, dir. 2018. *Final Score*. Los Angeles: Saban Films. DVD.
Massumi, Brian. 2010. "The Future Birth of the Affective Fact: The Political Ontology of Threat." In *The Affect Theory Reader*, eds Melissa Gregg and Gregory J. Seigworth, 52–70. Durham: Duke University Press.
Melnick, Merrill J. 1986. "The Mythology of Football Hooliganism: A Closer Look at the British Experience." *International Review for the Sociology of Sport* 21, no. 1: 1–19.

Ngai, Sianne. 2007. *Ugly Feelings*. Reprint. Cambridge, MA: Harvard University Press.
Palmerton, Patricia. 1988. "The Rhetoric of Terrorism and the Media Response to the 'Crisis of Iran'." *Western Journal of Speech Communication* 52, no. 2: 105–21.
Pennant, Cass. 2002. *Congratulations: You Have Just Met the I.C.F.* London: John Blake.
Piskurek, Cyprian. 2018. *Fictional Representations of English Football and Fan Cultures: Slum Sport, Slum People?* London: Palgrave Macmillan.
Redhead, Steve. 1997. *Post-Fandom and the Millennial Blues*. London: Verso.
Sampson, Kevin. 1999. *Awaydays*. London: Vintage.
Sandvoss, Cornel. 2005. *Fans: The Mirror of Consumption*. Cambridge: Polity.
Schmitt, Mark. 2018. *British White Trash: Figurations of Tainted Whiteness in the Novels of Irvine Welsh, Niall Griffiths and John King*. Bielefeld: Transcript.
Spaaij, Ramón. 2006. *Understanding Football Hooliganism: A Comparison of Six Western European Football Clubs*. Amsterdam: Amsterdam University Press.
Taylor, Ian. 1971. "'Football Mad': A Speculative Sociology of Football Hooliganism." In *The Sociology of Sport: A Selection of Readings*, ed. Eric Dunning, 352–77. London: Cass.
Thatcher, Margaret. 1989. "The Carlton Lecture, London, 26 November 1984", In *The Revival of Britain. Speeches on Home and European Affairs 1975-1988*, compiled by Alistair B. Cooke, 193–201. London: Aurum Press.
Thatcher, Margaret. 1997. "Speech to the Conservative Party Conference, Brighton, 12 October 1984." In *The Collected Speeches of Margaret Thatcher*, ed. Robin Harris, 213–26. New York: Harper Collins.
Townshend, Charles. 2011. *Terrorism: A Very Short Introduction*, Oxford: Oxford University Press.
Walvin, James. 1986. *Football and the Decline of Britain*. Basingstoke: Macmillan.
Zulaika, Joseba, and William A. Douglass. 1996. *Terror and Taboo: The Follies, Fables, and Faces of Terrorism*. New York: Routledge.

5. SCREENING RAILWAY TERRORISTS: LIGHT MODERNITY, INVISIBLE THREATS AND THE AESTHETICS OF CONCEALMENT IN *THE 15:17 TO PARIS* AND *BODYGUARD*

Johannes Riquet

Introduction: Smooth, Light and Clean

At the beginning of Ang Lee's recent film *Gemini Man* (2019), Defense Intelligence Agency assassin Henry Brogan (Will Smith) shoots a terrorist on a moving high-speed train from about a mile away. The operation is presented as clinically precise and smooth: Brogan calmly lies in the grass as he watches the approaching train through the rangefinder of his rifle while communicating with his partner on the train. When the latter reports the speed of the train – '238 km/h and holding steady' – the second part of his statement could describe Brogan's position as much as it describes the train. In fact, the two forms of steadiness depend on each other: the high-speed train and state-of-the-art weapons technology are woven together into a hi-tech machine ensemble that announces the film's larger preoccupation with new technologies both on the diegetic level and through the extensive use of CGI. This link between (counter-)terrorism and the high-speed train is also signalled through editing; right after a shot of Brogan pulling the trigger, we see the train speeding towards a tunnel.

The film's concern with new technologies also manifests itself aesthetically. This is evident from the first shot, which shows the white and partly transparent steel-and-glass canopy of Liège-Guillemins, a new Belgian high-speed railway station that was opened in 2009 (Figure 5.1). Designed by the Spanish architect and engineer Santiago Calatrava, the futuristic structure 'soar[s] upwards, contriving to sculpture light (and the sense of the lightweight) out of steel and concrete' (Littlefield 2010, 109). The structure evokes the weightlessness that

Figure 5.1 Liquid modernity and high speed: the station of Liège-Guillemins at the beginning of *Gemini Man*.

Zygmunt Bauman (2000) sees as characteristic of contemporary 'light modernity' or 'liquid modernity'. The shift from the territorial grounding and bulky machinery of 'heavy' or 'solid' modernity to the flexible, invisible and extraterritorial power structures and software-capitalism of light modernity (Bauman 2000) has aesthetic implications, too. In *Gemini Man*, the 'soaring' structure of the railway station is connected to the smooth aesthetics of the high-speed train as the camera slowly tilts and pans to reveal the platforms, before we see a shiny white-and-blue train with large glass fronts picking up speed almost without producing any noise. In the entire scene, diegetic sound is reduced to a minimum, and the camera movements are calm and controlled.

The high-speed train scene with its light design and smooth cinematography is exemplary of the figurative relationship between the terrorist and the train in a set of recent films. As the present chapter will demonstrate, contemporary cinematic depictions of terrorist attacks on the railroad transform long-standing associations between the railroad and crime – especially political crime. Like earlier criminals in railway cinema, the figure of the terrorist in twenty-first-century films personifies the threat posed by technological modernity. However, this metaphorical relationship no longer revolves around the brute force and heavy machinery of 'solid' modernity, but around the smooth and light technologies and aesthetics of 'liquid' modernity. On the one hand, then, films like Clint Eastwood's *The 15:17 to Paris* (2018), my first case study, participate in the tabooing and silencing of the terrorist noted by Joseba Zulaika and William Douglass (1996). On the other hand, they also draw attention to the silent networks of communication, surveillance and intelligence surrounding contemporary terrorism. These networks resonate with the smooth technology of the high-speed train – or, as in my second example, the British TV series *Bodyguard* (2018), with the unobtrusive presence of the commuter train.

Murderer, Spy, Terrorist: Figurations of the Railroad

As cultural historians like Wolfgang Schivelbusch (1986) have emphasised, the railroad helped create an abstract spatio-temporal order of points, lines, networks and schedules. However, the ordered mobility of the railroad was accompanied by disruptive energies, too. Ralph Harrington argues that the railway journey in the nineteenth century was 'a shared cultural location through which the ill-defined but potent anxieties associated with the advent of mechanized mass transportation were focussed, collected and transmitted' (2000, 230). Ever since the nineteenth century, railway literature and cinema have used the train journey as a powerful narrative and poetic device to articulate the contradictions and tensions of technological modernity and thereby negotiate specific geopolitical concerns and anxieties (Riquet and Zdrenyk 2018).

The geopolitical constellations and technological anxieties negotiated in railway fiction have shifted over time. In the nineteenth century, a common metaphor for trains was that of the projectile (Schivelbusch 1986, 54). This association persists to the present day – the name 'bullet train' for the Japanese Shinkansen is a case in point. The figurative link has also persisted in the realm of literature and film, from William Barnes's 1859 poem 'The Railroad', where we read of a 'zweepèn[1] train' that 'Did shoot along the hill-bound plaïn' (2013, 5–6), to Bong Joon-ho's 2013 film *Snowpiercer*, in which the survivors of a global apocalypse circle the frozen earth in a train that is divided into social classes; the film contains a scene where the revolutionaries of the tail section put together a wheeled barrel-like structure that simultaneously looks like a giant cannon and doubles the train itself.

Since the mid-twentieth century, trains have also been associated with more explosive, even nuclear, kinds of weaponry and technology. In the fifties, an American physics professor, Lyle Borst, made plans for an atomic locomotive. According to a *Life* article from 1954, this 'designer's dream' of a locomotive 'could easily travel twice around the world without refueling once' ('The Atomic Locomotive' 1954, 78). In the second half of the fifties, following President Dwight D. Eisenhower's approval of the intercontinental ballistic missile (ICBM) programme, the United States Air Force developed a system for launching ICBMs from trains (Pomeroy 2010). The eighties saw a brief revival of the idea of a mobile missile launch system with the Peacekeeper Rail Garrison. On the other side of the Iron Curtain, similar projects existed; in

1956, the USSR Ministry of Transport announced plans for a nuclear-powered locomotive to be used in Siberia (Nilsen 2011).

In fiction, as well, explosive and nuclear energy has been linked to trains in manifold ways since the 1950s. In Ted Tetzlaff's 1953 film *Time Bomb*, for instance, we see a group of men pushing a series of large mines through a factory hall. The image anticipates the shape of the train that we see in the following shots, styled as a threatening force. In a Bollywood film from 1980, *The Burning Train*, an attacker plants a bomb on a new Indian high-speed train. Train and bomb are acoustically linked: the ticking of the bomb blends into the rhythmic sounds of the train, which becomes a figure for the darker sides of technology and modernity. The TV series *Supertrain* (1979) revolves around a stylish, nuclear-powered high-speed train travelling from New York City to Los Angeles, and much of the train's technological glamour derives from its power source. The locomotive of *Snowpiercer*, too, is nuclear-powered, and the shots of the slowly revolving circular engine hint at the possibility of destructive energy – indeed, at the end of the film the revolutionaries blast open an external train door with an explosive substance, which creates a giant explosion that triggers an avalanche so that the train derails. The possibility of explosive violence drives the narratives of the films I discuss in this chapter even while the metaphorical relationship between trains and terrorists in them revolves around yet another, newer kind of threat: the threat of silent, invisible technologies and networks.

These shifts in figurative associations are best understood if we take into account both the socio-historical context and the generic predecessors of twenty-first-century films about railway terrorists. The films discussed in this chapter transform and update long-standing associations between the railroad and crime that reach from nineteenth-century crime fiction to Cold War espionage narratives. Railway cinema's negotiation of geopolitical and technological anxieties has taken new forms in the wake of spectacular terrorist attacks on trains, notably the 2004 attacks on commuter trains in Madrid, the London underground attacks in 2005 and the attempted attack on the high-speed Thalys train between Brussels and Paris in 2015. These fictional discourses frequently went hand in hand with debates about public transport. In the nineteenth century, in the wake of the murder of bank clerk Thomas Briggs on a London commuter train in 1864, anxieties about the dangers of public transport were eagerly debated in the newspapers, and though violent crime on the railroad was actually very rare, murderers and other criminals all the more frequently appeared in popular fiction (Carter 2001, 167–201). In Emile Zola's *La bête humaine*, the figurative link between the murderer and the train is evident in the personification of the locomotive as a destructive force. The specific spatial arrangement of the train also allowed writers of crime fiction to develop a variant of the locked-room mystery (Cook 2011, 21–42), Agatha Christie's *Murder on the Orient Express* (1934) and *4.50 from Paddington* (1957) being among the most famous examples.

The next major development in railway crime fiction was the Cold War spy narrative, the James Bond franchise being a case in point. Attacks on the railroad are frequent especially in the early Bond films, in which the attacker is repeatedly linked to the train, as in the train scene in *The Spy Who Loved Me* (1977).[2] As agent Anya Amasova starts taking off her dress, the calm scene is interrupted by an outside shot of the fast and loud train. A few moments later, Jaws appears as suddenly as the train did before; both disrupt the peaceful scene inside the train. When Jaws appears, the horn pierces the silence and the sound of the train suddenly becomes louder. In this sequence, the train is linked to sexual violence and rape, and Jaws – with his metal teeth and superhuman strength – is himself part machine. His attack reflects the paranoid climate of the Cold War, the notion that violence may erupt anywhere and anytime.

These Cold War spy narratives form an important backdrop for recent narratives of terrorism on the railroad. As Joseba Zulaika and William Douglass write in *Terror and Taboo*, '[t]hriller writers . . . increasingly invoke terrorism as a substitute for espionage' (1996, 3). They argue that the disappearance of '[t]he evil other of the Cold War' created a vacuum that needed to be filled by new narratives and new threatening figures: 'Now we must visit terrorist haunts and contemplate desperate madmen from the beleaguered corners of the earth or the estranged sectors of society, their hands holding not just guns but nuclear devices and biological weapons as well' (Zulaika and Douglass 1996, 3). Twenty-seven years after the publication of *Terror and Taboo*, we should add digital weapons to the arsenal of terrorists that populate the pages and screens of contemporary literature and cinema, updating spy fiction's interest in all forms of remote communication for the twenty-first century.

As in the nineteenth century, these developments in twentieth- and twenty-first-century fiction have gone hand in hand with widespread public discussion. The public interest in railway terrorism is evidenced, for instance, by a series of studies by the Mineta Transportation Institute, sponsored by the US Department of Homeland Security (see, among others, Jenkins and Trella 2012; Jenkins and Butterworth 2018). While these studies state that railway terrorism in the US and in Western countries more generally actually constitutes a very small percentage of all attacks on trains (India and Pakistan are clearly in the lead), they focus primarily on jihadist attacks on the railroad in the US and the UK. One of the reasons for this seems to be the spectacular nature and symbolic force of attacks on the railroad. As the report notes: 'The terrorist bombings of commuter trains in Madrid in 2004 [and] the bombing of London Transport in 2005 . . . are some of the more *dramatic examples*' (Jenkins and Butterworth 2018, 44; emphasis added).

The awareness that such episodes are symbolic attacks on an icon of Western modernity is shared on both sides. Thus, a 2017 issue of the online jihadist magazine *Inspire* encourages mujahideen to plan attacks on railroads and includes detailed instructions on how to derail trains. And while one of the Mineta reports examines how different railway terrorists imitated earlier attacks (Jenkins and Trella 2012, 9–11), the article in *Inspire* includes a history of spectacular railway accidents in the US since 1904; mostly these accidents were not provoked by humans, which suggests an awareness of larger technological anxieties and their symbolic force. Indeed, the article explicitly discusses the benefit of such attacks beyond the possibility of a large number of casualties: 'In America, trains are considered to be among the most important means of transportation within the country ... All these means of transportation indicate that the world and the civilian life are very dependant [sic] on them' (Al-Asiri 2017). While the article may overstate the importance of trains in contemporary America, the writer clearly understands the dramatic potential of attacks on the railroad. What this example illustrates is that both sides in the so-called 'war on terror' become railway historians in their discourses about railway terrorism as they place recent (and potential future) attacks in a longer history of violence and accidents on the railroad.

Al-Asiri's discussion of railway accidents and their potential to create spectacular disruptions is rooted in an understanding of trains as 'the epitome of modernity' (Carter 2001). However, trains no longer represent technological progress in the same way that they did in the time of 'solid' modernity. Today, they can no longer unproblematically function as powerful figures of heavy machinery and the violence connected to it. The trains of what David Banister and Peter Hall termed the 'second railway age' almost thirty years ago (1993) are not predicated on the heavy machinery of high modernity, but on new technologies and a new aesthetics. As George Revill writes,

> the high-speed rail depends on the prospect of technologically mediated seamless interconnection. ... This is a pervasive concept in the realization of contemporary technology. It is present in the smoothness, simplicity, flow, efficiency and ergonomics of modern design. It is also evident in 'just-in-time' logistics which maximize availability on demand and the design and use of digital, mobile computers and communications systems ... (2012, 249)

This is a perfect description of the train in *Gemini Man*: smooth, light and clean, like the counter-terrorism operation performed by the protagonist. Along similar lines, the terrorists in recent railway cinema no longer pose a threat through their overpowering physical strength but represent a danger linked to invisibility and silence, a threat that Michael Barkun associates with contemporary discourses about terrorism: 'A strange world of invisible dangers was abruptly discovered by Americans in the fall of 2001' (2011, 17). Those invisible dangers include invisible weapons, the difficulty of spotting a terrorist in a crowd (for example at an airport or a railway station) and the silent communication in digital channels.

The threat of these invisible networks has led to a public concern with making the invisible visible in counter-terrorist tactics – and thus to a culture of screening, digital tracing and surveillance. In contemporary debates in media and politics, the emphasis on the possibilities of digital tracking tends to go hand in hand with anxieties about its potential inadequacies and failures, as well as about the possibilities that digital communications technologies in turn offer terrorists (Combs 2018, 185–211). As Brigitte L. Nacos writes, '[h]istorically, terrorists vied for publicity . . .; now they can exploit far-reaching, instant, and global media networks and information highways' (2016, ix). Indeed, a recent special issue on computer-assisted terrorism (Taylor, Horgan and Sageman 2015) attests that digital technologies have played an increasingly important role in terrorism and counter-terrorism, or at least in public perceptions thereof: 'informatics (the hardware of global telecommunications and the software of flexible interaction and communication) is changing the ways people on both sides of the so-called "war on terror" exercise, imagine and contest power and influence' (Williams 2015, 135).

The 15:17 to Paris, High Speed and the Aesthetics of Concealment

This association between terrorists and invisible digital networks takes on special significance in the context of the railroad because the digital transport of data frequently follows the existing infrastructure of railway lines, just like telegraph lines used to in the past. As Ingrid Burrington writes, 'telecommunications and transportation networks tend to end up piled on top of each other'; more specifically, she points out that it would be 'pretty much impossible to talk about American Internet infrastructure without talking about railroads' (2015, n.p.). With this association between the railroad and different forms of communication and data networks in mind, I would now like to turn to my two case studies, starting with Clint Eastwood's 2018 film *The 15:17 to Paris*. The film tells the story of the attempted attack on a Thalys train between Brussels and Paris in August 2015, which was prevented by the intervention of three Americans (Spencer Stone, Alek Skarlatos and Anthony Sadler), two of them soldiers with combat training, as well as a British and a French passenger. The film is based on the written account of the three Americans. In many ways, it performs the tabooing, depersonalisation and de-politicisation of the terrorist figure theorised by Zulaika and Douglass (1996). Thus, most of the film is devoted to the personal histories of the Americans, who acted their own parts while, as *The Guardian* wryly notes, '[t]he attacker, . . . being now incarcerated, was not available for filming' (Bradshaw 2018, n.p.). In the opening scene, when we see the attacker at the railway station, the cinematography renders him largely invisible (Kuhn 2019, 49). The scene is just over one minute long; while he is the first character to be introduced, we do not get a conventional character introduction, which would present the protagonist, their central traits and their desires to the viewer.

In fact, the film *refuses* to introduce the attacker as a character. While the Steadicam largely follows his movements, it fragments his body and persistently hides his face, cutting off his head or showing him from behind. In the first shot, we initially see the terrorist's back, with his head and most of his legs cut off; his back, in turn, is hidden by a black rucksack (whose content, we can infer, is much more significant than the person carrying it). When the camera eventually tilts up, the face remains mostly hidden, and what we do see is covered by large sunglasses. The shots that follow show us different body parts from various angles, focusing, for instance, on his chest and his feet. When the terrorist finally turns to face the camera upon entering the train, the sliding door immediately removes him from sight, covering the entire screen, before the film's title is displayed. The opening scene is thus presented as a prologue even though it introduces us to the main event and setting. In what follows, we meet the 'real' protagonists. We see the three Americans driving in a car while one of them gives us some facts about each in voice-over before the first of a series of long flashbacks takes us into their childhood and we learn about their individual struggles growing up as young Americans. They are presented both as rebels who have a complicated relationship to the state and its institutions but despite (or because of) that emerge as the ideal heroic American subjects (cf. Kuhn 2019, 49–51; Timss 2020, 52–3). Their introduction is thus diametrically opposed to that of the terrorist; while the latter is maximally hidden in terms of both screen time and information, the information about the protagonists and their background is excessive and distracts from what is supposedly the main event of the film – to the point of boredom.

The film's silencing of the terrorist is accompanied by a second form of invisibility, which is related to the narrative and aesthetic presentation of the high-speed train itself. On the narrative level, it is important to note that while the title foregrounds the train journey, the train scenes are actually very short: in terms of actual screen time, they jointly take up only seventeen minutes. Although the train journey is the most dramatic event of the *fabula* (or story), the prominence of train scenes and scenes that show the Americans elsewhere is inverted in the *syuzhet* (or plot)[3], at least in terms of duration. For more than an hour, the film shows the Americans as children and young men, accompanying them on their trip through Europe. The story of their experiences is punctuated three times by narrative fragments that return us to the events on the train. These scenes last between twenty seconds and one minute and are not in chronological order. In the first fragment, we get a glimpse of the beginning of the attack filmed from the floor. In the second, slightly longer one we see people wondering what the terrorist is doing in the bathroom until he steps out fully armed. In the third (again very brief) fragment, we see passengers further down the train running along the corridor in fear. The fragmentary and disjointed character of these scenes contrasts with the detailed and chronological account of the American protagonists' lives and their trip in Europe. Even in narrative terms, then, the elegant high-speed train seems to go almost unnoticed. Like the terrorist, it remains largely absent and invisible; like him, furthermore, it is only present in fragments when it does appear.

This narrative invisibility of the train goes hand in hand with an aesthetics of concealment that echoes the filmic presentation of the terrorist. In line with the conventions of railway cinema, *The 15:17 to Paris* includes both outside and inside shots of the train. However, the outside views are very different from the loud, violent shots of steam trains in earlier action and crime films. Instead, the Thalys train moves smoothly and silently through the landscape without conveying an open sense of threat. Thus, the second fragment begins with a panoramic shot of the train filmed from a green field. Because the camera is far away, the train's gliding movement looks deceptively slow. Aligned with the horizon as well as with the furrows in the field, the train seems to merge with the landscape organically. At the beginning of the third fragment, the camera approaches the barely audible train from the air (Figure 5.2). The camera's movement is as smooth as that of the train as it soars over and follows it so

Figure 5.2   An aesthetics of concealment: the terrorist and the train in *The 15:17 to Paris*.

that the two movements are aligned; in terms of the viewer's phenomenological experience, the train does not move forward at all. Furthermore, the train is initially partly hidden behind trees, and its silver colour as well as the sunlight reflected on the roof align it with the overexposed streak of sky at the top of the image. At the end of the fragment, after a scene of turmoil and chaos aboard the train filmed with a nervous hand-held camera, we again see the train from the outside, increasingly hidden by leaves until it completely disappears behind them. While we witness the outbreak of violence, this violence remains partly camouflaged, a process that is conveyed by the aesthetic presentation of the train.

The train shots of *The 15:17 to Paris* thereby exemplify the smooth and seamless aesthetics that Revill (2012) associates with the high-speed train. The threat linked to the train emerges precisely from the fact that it goes largely unnoticed. When it finally erupts, the violence appears all the more shocking; in the indoor scenes, the film repeatedly and abruptly switches from calm and quiet shots to agitated, disorienting and loud hand-held shots. This structure is repeated in the longest 'train segment', which is roughly divided into two parts, each about seven minutes long. The first part is very calm and slow-paced. Thus, we see the Americans on the train, where the most exciting activities are ordering drinks and uploading photos to social media. The camera, too, is mostly still or moves slowly. After the train leaves the station of Amsterdam, we see two panoramic shots that echo those already described in relation to the earlier fragments, with the camera soaring through the air to accompany the train's movement. In the second part, the deceptive calm of the first is suddenly shattered visually and acoustically.

It is when the film approaches its dramatic climax that both the terrorist and the train show their hitherto concealed faces. Thus, a shot of the terrorist's half-covered face in the mirror (Figure 5.2) is immediately followed by a shot of the train leaving Brussels, now louder and accompanied by an ominous clanging sound, before a cut takes us back inside and we see a frontal view of the terrorist's face. The scene of the Americans fighting the terrorist is interspersed with two further shots of the train. The low-angle shot of the train from the ground echoes earlier low-angle shots of the terrorist from the coach floor, making it appear equally threatening; the train is now very loud, and its dizzying speed becomes palpable because of the camera's proximity to the train. Conversely, once the threat is under control, we see one more high-angle outside shot, with the camera soaring over the train. Along with the terrorist, then, the train's violent energy is subdued by the end of the film.

The association between the terrorist and the high-speed train has important implications for thinking about the (geo)politics of the film, which is articulated through its relationship to the genre of the western. As Kenneth E. Hall notes, '[t]rains are central to the Western' (2014, 11). In the context of American frontier mythology, the railroad is a powerful symbol of manifest destiny (see, among others, Thomas 2011). In many classic westerns, the railroad represents the building of the nation; John Ford's *The Iron Horse* (1924) and Cecil B. DeMille's *Union Pacific* (1939) are well-known examples. However, many westerns also include attacks on the railroad by either Native Americans (again, *Union Pacific*) or outlaws (starting in 1903 with *The Great Train Robbery*). In these films, the attack on the railroad becomes an attack on the nation and its spatial order. Eastwood is well acquainted with the importance of the railroad in the western; he starred in various westerns that featured railroad scenes, including *For a Few Dollars More* (1965) and *Joe Kidd* (1972). Trains also appear in westerns directed by Eastwood himself; the most interesting of these, perhaps, is the Diesel train that the protagonists of *Bronco Billy* (1980) unsuccessfully attack by shooting at it on horseback and from a car; the prominent Union Pacific logo thereby creates a reference to the transcontinental railroad while the entire scene also ironically reflects on frontier mythology.

Indeed, Eastwood's relationship to the western is complex and ambivalent. After his farewell to the genre with *Unforgiven* (1992), he nonetheless revisited the western in other settings, sometimes adopting a more or less pronounced ironic distance. Thus, the story about a group of ageing astronauts saving America from nuclear threat in *Space Cowboys* (2000) both parodies American ideals of masculinity and pays homage to the cowboy figure; in *Gran Torino* (2008), a Korean War veteran battles Hmong gangs in the new frontier of suburbia while learning lessons about a new multicultural America; and in the biographical drama *American Sniper* (2014), a failed rodeo cowboy-turned-soldier fights against the new 'uncivilised other' in the Middle East, with the film only minimally challenging its patriotic message (see Kuhn 2019, 42–46). Against this background, *The 15:17 to Paris* emerges as yet another refiguration of the western. This time, the frontier is the corrupted space of Europe – indeed, the film was released at a time when Donald Trump was using the terrorist attacks in various European countries to justify his new immigration policies.[4] In this context, the train takes on further metaphorical significance. Thus, its linear progression and speed become linked to one of the Americans' feeling that 'life is . . . catapulting [him] towards . . . some greater purpose'; as the three debate whether they should skip the trip to Paris, they ultimately reject the idea and argue that fate seems to want them to undertake the journey as it did not stop them from doing so (see Timss 2020, 53). The sense of their being destined to be on the train is further supported by the film's narrative structure, which presents the train journey as the culmination and endpoint of their previous lives (see Kuhn 2019, 49). Finally, François Hollande's use of the train as a synecdoche ('to save those who were on that train, that is to say, humanity') at the end of the film supports the familiar narrative of America heroically civilising and saving the world. In *The 15:17 to Paris*, all ironic distance from this narrative seems to have disappeared (see Kuhn 2019, 51).

In Eastwood's refiguration of the western genre, the terrorist and the counter-terrorists operate in an entirely masculine world. The heroic masculinity of the Americans is thereby contrasted with the threatening masculinity of the terrorist, while the other passengers who helped prevent the attack – a French American academic with Armenian roots and a British businessman – are reduced to the roles of victim (the former) or peripheral presence (the latter). The heroes' masculinity is foregrounded throughout the film; they repeatedly flirt with attractive girls who seem to be invariably attracted to them; we see them dressed in American sports shirts; and the camera dwells on their muscular bodies. The terrorist's masculinity is presented in a very different way. When he steps out of the bathroom, he is not wearing a shirt; while the film displays his masculine body, this is a body stripped of all symbolic accoutrements, coded as a raw, threatening force. His bare body becomes a sign of unassigned otherness that complements his invisibility in other scenes and his silence throughout the film. While the American heroes embody a unified identity that is both national and religious (though not racial: the voice-over of Sadler, who is African American, emphasises the unity of black and white America in the first minutes of the film), the terrorist is given no national or cultural identity whatsoever – the only identity that is suggested is his Muslim religion, hinted at by his prominent beard. This absence of a specific identity extends beyond the boundaries of the film. The part of Ayoub El-Khazzani, a Moroccan who had moved from France to Belgium in 2015, was played by Ray Corasani, a little known Iranian American actor. While Stone, Skarlatos and Sadler have become public figures and are all over the internet, Corasani's role in the film has received almost no attention, and information about him is generally few and far between. His Iranian origins, furthermore, are not immediately apparent; the unconventional spelling of his surname – کوراسانی is usually transcribed as Khorasani – contributes to this, and the actor does not mention that he was born in Iran on his website. On the one hand, the fact that an Iranian actor plays the part of a Moroccan terrorist confirms the character's generic otherness. On the other hand, it unwittingly points to the long-standing conflict between the United States and Iran, newly erupted during Trump's presidency, as an unacknowledged subtext to the film's narrative. The invisible forces and threats associated with the train are thus also linked to the various social, cultural and political invisibilities that surround the terrorist.

Bodyguard: Silent Networks on the Terrorist Train

As we have seen, the figurative power of the high-speed train in *The 15:17 to Paris* extends in various directions: while it represents technological progress and the supposed 'civilising' mission of the United States, it also figures the invisible agents, networks and technologies of contemporary terrorism. This contradiction is partly resolved by the fact that the methods of terrorism and counter-terrorism frequently mirror each other and depend on the same technological possibilities (Nacos 2016). Indeed, the film hints at the networks of digital communications technologies in fittingly oblique ways. Thus, we repeatedly see a close shot of a glass door on the train with a large pink Wi-Fi sign. The repetition of this shot suggests an anxiety about invisible digital networks; railway hi-tech is here linked to hi-tech in communications technology. This link is made explicit in a shot of the toilet door next to which we see a poster, also pink, showing a cartoon-style drawing of a train, a butterfly and a globe emerging from a mobile phone screen, accompanied by the words 'Bleiben Sie in Verbindung/Stay in Touch'. The train and digital media are thus jointly associated with (global) connectedness. This shot is followed by the already discussed shot of the terrorist's face in the bathroom, figuratively linking him to both. The film thus gestures towards the digital networks that are hard to trace on either side of the frontline between terrorism and counter-terrorism. In this case, Wi-Fi actually motivates the Americans to switch to a first-class coach with a better internet connection; thus, it accidentally gets them into the right coach at the right time.

Similar concerns with digital communications technology appear in almost all other recent films about terrorists on trains. In Duncan Jones's *Source Code* (2011), the bomb is connected to and triggered by a smartphone, and the protagonist attempts to find out more about his supposed death with the help of mobile internet. Similarly, in Tony Scott's *The Taking of Pelham 123* (2009), a passenger manages to contact his girlfriend at home with a laptop. The first episode of the British TV series *Bodyguard* (directed by Thomas Vincent), too, obsessively shows us the Wi-Fi sign on the train's glass doors again and again (Figure 5.3). In the first scene of the episode, we see David Budd (Richard Madden), a police sergeant and war veteran suffering from PTSD, preventing a terrorist attack by a couple of suicide bombers on a train near London. Though the events take place on a commuter rather than a high-speed train, the train also has the smooth, calm and silent aesthetics of modern design. The camera is mostly still, and when it moves, it does so in slow and controlled pans inside the train that echo the quiet movement of the train in outside shots, an effect produced by the use of a telephoto lens. Many shots are taken from behind windows or through glass doors, creating a sense of reduced and mediated visibility; the few sounds that are audible are muted and soft, and the repeated use of telephoto lenses also inside the train creates out-of-focus backgrounds. Furthermore, the colour blue dominates the entire train sequence (and, to a lesser extent, the entire episode). Thus, the train itself is blue, as is the door of the toilet where the female suicide bomber is hiding; several blue light sources

Figure 5.3   Mediated views, digital communication and multiple screens in *Bodyguard*.

contribute to the almost dream-like aesthetics of the scene, including the lights on the coach ceilings and the flicker of blue light that enters the train from the police cars outside. Finally, the Wi-Fi sign is also blue; it therefore becomes a repeatedly foregrounded element of a larger aesthetic strategy.

The blue Wi-Fi sign plays a central role in this strategy because it links the many blue surfaces and lights of the train sequence to the blue light of digital screens. Indeed, literal and metaphorical screens recur throughout the sequence. Thus, the repeatedly shown control room to which the conductor withdraws is filled with (mostly blue) screens that feature various digital maps (Figure 5.3). On a figurative level, the windows – filmed from both inside and outside the train – evoke screens, an effect that is heightened by the blue colour of these framed 'images'. David and other characters are repeatedly shown gazing through these figurative screens. Thus, David's first glimpse of one of the terrorists is mediated through a train window. This mediated observation is connected to the presence of mobile phone and computer screens, which signify counter-terrorist efforts to track invisible terrorist networks throughout the series. As in *The 15:17 to Paris*, mobile phone technology also plays an important narrative role in the first episode of *Bodyguard* as David and the conductor maintain contact to first detect and then contain the terrorist threat. In one scene, the signal breaks down as the train moves through a tunnel, which has

David swearing and frantically trying to re-establish a connection – emphasised by an extreme close-up of the signal bars on his smartphone.

In several ways, then, the metaphorical links between the train and the figure of the terrorist are similar to those in *The 15:17 to Paris*: here, too, both are associated with silence, concealment and invisible networks. Thus, as the episode continues, the incident provokes national debates as politicians suspect that the bombers on the train might be linked to larger terrorist cells constituting a 'threat to national security', and the Joint Terrorism Analysis Centre raises the terrorist threat level to 'substantial'. Also, the male terrorist remains concealed for almost the entire train sequence. We see him through the window at the beginning of the episode (once from behind and once in the shadows), then briefly as he leaves the toilet unarmed, and again for a few seconds as he is apprehended by the police; we see him one more time in the background as he is taken off the train. His unobtrusive yet threatening presence resonates with the low-angle shot of the train gliding into the station in almost spectral fashion, accompanied by subtle ominous music.

In other ways, however, *Bodyguard* differs radically from *The 15:17 to Paris*, especially with regard to the representation of the female terrorist, Nadia. The camera repeatedly foregrounds her scared face in intimate close-ups and shot-reverse sequences that align her with the equally frightened David. As opposed to the anti-terrorist unit that boards the train, who treat her as a faceless threat and want to shoot her despite her cooperation, David creates a personal connection with her that culminates in a kind of hug and dance in which he shields her. David's backstory further supports this connection as he tells her about his own traumatic experience in Iraq and Afghanistan. The terrorist is thereby humanised as David locates the real culprits in politicians – both 'ours and theirs' – and he is linked to Nadia as a victim of political conflicts that disregard the lives of individuals who either serve those in power or are collateral damage (see Parry 2022). Indeed, as the episode progresses, the government's unwillingness to apologise for the mistakes made in the Middle East is foregrounded, and various characters portray the state and its apparatus of power – repeatedly present in the figures of political authority communicating via various channels – as the real threat. The parallel that is created between Nadia and an employee fired by the interventionist Home Secretary to whose protection David is assigned reinforces this: David is asked to calm down the angry former employee on the strength of his success in 'talk[ing] someone out of blowing up a train'. While the Home Secretary is glad that David has saved Nadia's life, her reasons are that they can now 'question her'. Madden's Scottish accent further emphasises David's complicated relationship to the London centre of the UK government.

The presence of two terrorists in the first episode of *Bodyguard* constitutes a gendered opposition. On one level, the invisibility of the male terrorist and the intimate portrayal of his wife rehearse a common pattern in political and cultural narratives about the Muslim world and the Middle East that portray men as uncivilised others while suggesting that women need to be protected and saved by the enlightened West. This gendered narrative, however, is complicated by the fact that the Western policeman 'saving' Nadia is himself subordinated to a threatening state power (personified by the female figure of the Home Secretary). While effacing the male terrorist, *Bodyguard* thus also critically interrogates the depersonalisation of individuals – terrorists and others – by the state apparatus. The cold blue world of the train is linked as much to the surveillance and communications apparatus of the state as to the terrorists and the networks they might belong to.

Conclusion

Films about crime on the railroad have long negotiated geopolitical and geo-technological concerns and anxieties. Contemporary filmic depictions of terrorists on trains are no exception. There are various continuities between the murderers and attackers of crime and spy films and the twenty-first-century figure of the railway terrorist. Thus, the 'the ill-defined but potent anxieties' about technological modernity that trains 'focussed, collected and transmitted' (Harrington 2000, 230) are still negotiated in the figurative relationship between attackers and trains. Like their predecessors, the films discussed in this chapter draw on the train's evocativeness as a figure of both order and violence to pose questions about the role of individuals in larger geopolitical conflicts. In these films, a concern with modern technology and its discontents is mapped onto a concern with the (in)stability of geopolitical regimes. Aesthetically, they draw on well-established iconographies of the cinematic railroad, notably when it comes to the interplay of inside and (metaphorically charged) outside shots as well as the alternation between calm and hypermobile shots.

At the same time, the films discussed here transform earlier figurations of crime on the railroad in ways that speak both to recent technological developments and to the changing contexts of global geopolitics – and, notably, to their intersection. In *The 15:17 to Paris*, the smooth, almost self-effacing technology and light aesthetics of the high-speed train figure what Barkun terms the 'strange world of invisible dangers' of the post-9/11 world (2011, 17), framed through the frontier mythology of the western. Though set on a commuter train, the first episode of *Bodyguard* creates similar links between the train and the figure of the terrorist through the sense of an unobtrusive presence that is threatening because it masks an underlying violence. Both *The 15:17 to Paris* and *Bodyguard* also connect the train to the invisible networks of digital communications technology, whose role in both terrorism and counter-terrorism they evoke. However, while the terrorist remains a depersonalised threat throughout Eastwood's film, in *Bodyguard* the female terrorist is individualised and aligned with David, and the cold blue world of the train is metaphorically connected not only to counter-terrorist tracking, but also to the surveillance technologies of the state more generally. In both, the figure of the terrorist is entangled with the technological and aesthetic regimes of 'light modernity' – where deceptively smooth surfaces hide violent forces that are always ready to erupt.

Notes

1. Sweeping.
2. The comments on *The Spy Who Loved Me* in this paragraph follow Riquet and Zdrenyk 2018, 14–16.
3. The distinction between *fabula* and *syuzhet* goes back to the Russian formalists: while *fabula* refers to the totality of events abstracted from the literary text – or, in this case, film – in chronological order, *syuzhet* refers to the (selective, jumbled, etc.) presentation of events in the work. In English-language film studies, these terms are commonly translated as *story* and *plot* (Bordwell 1985, 49–53).
4. The defence counsel in the 2020 trial (unsuccessfully) asked for Eastwood to be admitted as a witness because she thought the film had shaped public opinion of the attack.

References

Al-Asiri, Ibrahim. 2017. "Targeting Means of Transportation." *Inspire* 17.
"The Atomic Locomotive." 1954. *Life* 36, no. 25: 78–9.
Banister, David, and Peter Hall. 1993. "The Second Railway Age." *Built Environment* 19, no. 3/4: 156–62.
Barkun, Michael. 2011. *Chasing Phantoms: Reality, Imagination, and Homeland Security Since 9/11*. Chapel Hill: The University of North Carolina Press.
Barnes, William. (1859) 2013. "The Railroad." In *Train Songs*, eds Sean O'Brien and Don Paterson. Reprint, London: Faber and Faber.
Bauman, Zygmunt. 2000. *Liquid Modernity*. Cambridge: Polity.
Bordwell, David. 1985. *Narration in the Fiction Film*. Madison: The University of Wisconsin Press.
Bradshaw, Peter. 2018. "The 15:17 to Paris Review – Clint Eastwood Derails a Tale of Real-Life Terror." *The Guardian*, February 8, 2018. https://www.theguardian.com/film/2018/feb/08/the-1517-to-paris-review-clint-eastwood-france-train-attack
Burrington, Ingrid. 2015. "How Railroad History Shaped Internet History." *The Atlantic*, November 24, 2015. https://www.theatlantic.com/technology/archive/2015/11/how-railroad-history-shaped-internet-history/417414/
Carter, Ian. 2001. *Railways and Culture in Britain: The Epitome of Modernity*. Manchester: Manchester University Press.
Chopra, Ravi, dir. 1980. *The Burning Train*. India: NH Studioz. DVD.
Combs, Cynthia C. 2018. *Terrorism in the Twenty-First Century*. 8th edn. New York: Routledge.
Cook, Michael. 2011. *Narratives of Enclosure in Detective Fiction: The Locked Room Mystery*. Basingstoke: Palgrave.

Eastwood, Clint, dir. 1980. *Bronco Billy*. USA: Warner Bros. DVD.
Eastwood, Clint, dir. 2018. *The 15:17 to Paris*. USA: Warner Bros. DVD.
Hall, Kenneth E. 2014. "From the Iron Horse to Hell on Wheels: The Transcontinental Railroad in the Western." *Studies in the Western* 22: 11–22.
Harrington, Ralph. 2000. "The Railway Journey and the Neuroses of Modernity." In *Pathologies of Travel*, eds Richard Wrigley and George Revill, 229–59. Amsterdam: Rodopi.
Jenkins, Brian Michael, and Bruce R. Butterworth. 2018. *Train Wrecks and Track Attacks: An Analysis of Attempts by Terrorists and Other Extremists to Derail Trains or Disrupt Rail Transportation*. San José: Mineta Transportation Institute.
Jenkins, Brian Michael and Joseph Trella. 2012. *Carnage Interrupted: An Analysis of Fifteen Terrorist Plots against Public Surface Transportation, Research Report 11–20*. San José: Mineta Transportation Institute.
Joon-ho, Bong, dir. 2013. *Snowpiercer*. South Korea/Czech Republic: Moho Film. DVD.
Kuhn, Marius. 2019. "Holding out for a Hero – Clint Eastwoods *American Sniper*, *Sully* und *The 15:17 to Paris*." *Cinema* 64: 38–53.
Lee, Ang, dir. 2019. *Gemini Man*. USA: Skydance Media. DVD.
Littlefield, David. 2010. "Antwerp Central and Liège-Guillemins, Belgium." *Architectural Design* 80, no. 3: 106–9.
Nacos, Brigitte L. 2016. *Mass-Mediated Terrorism: Mainstream and Digital Media in Terrorism and Counterterrorism*. 3rd edn. Lanham: Rowman & Littlefield.
Nilsen, Thomas. 2011. "Russia Designs Nuclear Train." *Barents Observer*, February 24, 2011.
Parry, Kate. 2022. "Representing Public Service and Post-Militariness in *Bodyguard* (BBC, 2018)." *New Review of Film and Television Studies* 20, no. 2: 169–93.
Pomeroy, Steven A. 2010. "Highball! Missiles and Train." *Air Power History* 57, no. 3: 22–33.
Revill, George. 2012. *Railway*. London: Reaktion Books.
Riquet, Johannes, and Anna Zdrenyk. 2018. "Between Progress and Nostalgia: Technology, Geopolitics, and James Bond's Railway Journeys." *The International Journal of James Bond Studies* 1, no. 2: 1–24.
Schivelbusch, Wolfgang. 1986. *The Railway Journey: The Industrialization of Time and Space in the 19th Century*. Leamington Spa: Berg.
Taylor, Max, John Horgan and Marc Sageman. 2015. "An Introduction by the Editors." *Dynamics of Asymmetric Conflict* 8, no. 2: 95–6.
Tetzlaff, Ted, dir. 1953. *Time Bomb*. UK/USA: Metro-Goldwyn-Mayer. DVD.
Timss, Braden. 2020. "The Hero Industry: Spectacular Pacification in the Era of Media Interactivity." *Occam's Razor* 10: 48–61.
Thomas, William G. 2011. *The Iron Way: Railroads, the Civil War, and the Making of Modern America*. New Haven: Yale University Press.
Vincent, Thomas, and John Strickland, dir. 2018. *Bodyguard*. UK: World Productions.
Williams, Roy. 2015. "Fractured Narratives and Pop-up Diaspora: Re-theorizing the Capillaries of Power, Terror and Intimacy." *Dynamics of Asymmetric Conflict* 8, no. 2: 134–55.
Zulaika, Joseba, and William A. Douglass. 1996. *Terror and Taboo: The Follies, Fables, and Faces of Terrorism*. New York and London: Routledge.

6. 'NOTHING TERRORISTIC ABOUT HIM': THE FIGURE OF THE TERRORIST IN KARAN MAHAJAN'S *THE ASSOCIATION OF SMALL BOMBS*

Peter C. Herman

After 11 September 2001, a number of literary critics examined the figure of the terrorist in English literature, and they did not like what they found. Richard Gray fired the opening salvo with his 2008 article, 'Open Doors, Closed Minds: American Prose Writing at a Time of Crisis'. Surveying the rash of novels attempting to deal with that terrible day, Gray observed that 'a kind of imaginative paralysis' had 'set in', suggesting that, 'Perhaps it is too soon, perhaps it is impossible' to deal with these events (135). In his response to Gray, Michael Rothberg is even harsher, accusing 9/11 fiction of 'a failure of the imagination' (2008, 153). Gray and Rothberg's primary complaint is that 9/11 fictions 'retreat into domestic detail', as Gray (2008, 134) puts it. Rothberg agrees, and using Lynne Sharon Schwartz's *The Writing on the Wall* (2005) as his example, observes how 'the novel retreats back into the reified world of domesticity and "emotional entanglements"' (2008, 154). Consequently, both agree that most 9/11 fiction reduces the figure of the terrorist to a mere stick-figure, that most authors do not even gesture toward 'witnessing or explanatory piecing together of personal or cultural motive' (136). Robert Appelbaum and Alexis Paknadel (2008) broaden their focus to survey the representation of terrorism in novels from 1970–2001, and they conclude that Gray and Rothberg's criticisms of 9/11 fiction apply to a much wider range of literature. Most terrorist fiction, they argue, is all about the victim with little attention paid to the perpetrator: 'the main focus of most terrorist fiction in our period is the *target* of terrorism and the *injury* it inflicts' (Appelbaum and Paknadel 2008, 397). Richard Jackson (a co-founder of Critical Terrorism

Studies) similarly finds that most terrorist fiction depicts terrorists 'in largely derogatory, dehumanizing, and demonizing terms' (2015b, 402), and he calls for a new approach to terrorism in fiction, one that gives 'primary voice to the views of the terrorist' (397). Taking this approach would have two advantages, Jackson proposes:

> Allowing the terrorist to speak not only functions to discursively resist and undermine the terrorism discourse [i.e., that all terrorists are barbarians], but potentially also creates an agonistic moment in which the violent subaltern can speak on an equal footing directly to the counterterrorist – and by extension, to the reader. (397)[1]

While these criticisms refer primarily to novels written by American or British authors, the last fifteen years or so have seen the publication of novels by writers of South Asian descent that attempt to take a different approach to the tabooed figure of the terrorist by shifting the focus of their novels away from America or Britain to India, Pakistan or Afghanistan.[2]

THE ASSOCIATION OF SMALL BOMBS: THE VICTIMS

Like so many other instances of terrorist fiction, Karan Mahajan's novel *The Association of Small Bombs* (2016) is based on actual events: the bombings of two crowded outdoor Delhi markets, Lajpat Nagar (21 May 1996) and Sarojini Nagar (29 October 2005), by the Kashmiri separatist and Islamist group, *Lashkar-e-Taiba* ('Army of the Good').[3] The immediate context is the long-standing dispute between India and Pakistan over the northern province of Kashmir, presently unevenly split between the two countries, which have been in conflict since Partition (1947). The larger context is the long history of bloody, sectarian violence between Muslims and Hindus.

Initially, *Association* focuses on the victims, and so the book seems ready to confirm the criticisms of terrorist fiction levied by Gray and others. The novel starts, quite literally, with a 'Blast' (the first section's title), and 'Chapter 0' (an obvious reference to Manhattan's 'Ground Zero') describes in dispassionate detail the bombing at the Lajpat Nagar market on 21 May 1996 that killed, among other victims, Deepa and Vikas Khurana's two boys, Tushar and Nakul: 'The bombing ... was a flat, percussive event that began under the bonnet of a parked white Marutti 800' (3). The boys were accompanied by their Muslim friend, Mansoor Ahmed, who survives. The Khuranas, an educated, liberal, Hindu-Christian couple 'inordinately proud' of their 'few token Muslim friends' (Mahajan 2016, 72), 'had suffered the defining tragedy of their lives' (4), and Mahajan devotes a significant amount of the book to describing how they respond to their children's murder, the deterioration of their marriage, and

Vikas's descent into a fatal depression. The second section, entitled 'Victims: May 1966' (9–63), and the fourth, 'Mr. and Mrs. Khurana's Response to Terror: 1996-97' (65–113), are equally focused on 'the *target* of terrorism and the *injury* it inflicts', as Appelbaum and Paknadel (2008, 397) put it. The fifth, 'Mansoor Ahmed's Response to Terror: May 1996-March 2003' (Mahajan 2016, 115–180), once more centres the narrative on the victim. While Mansoor did not die in the blast, the damage to the nerves in his arms eventually makes using a keyboard so painful he must abandon his computer science education in the US. He does not see himself as miraculously saved: 'That's the meaning of having survived the bomb. I didn't survive at all. I just spent longer dying, rendered crippled and obsolete like that old 486 on which I acquired my first repetitive injuries' (160). The final section, 'The Association of Small Bombs' (235–76) brings together the lives of both terrorists and victims, showing how they unravel in the wake of a supposedly 'small' bomb. Deepa has an affair and wants to focus only on herself and her daughter: 'She wanted only to live in a nice house and to take care of Anusha and to take trips with her. She wanted no traffic with the larger world' (274). After Deepa reveals her transgression, Vikas runs away, and, 'alienated from everyone', works nonstop on a documentary about the bombing, subsisting 'only on bananas' and thus dying of a potassium overdose (274). Ayub, the terrorist who planted the Sarojini Nagar bomb, also dies alone on a beach 'from hunger and exhaustion' (269). Mansoor, while innocent, was arrested in connection with the Sarojini Nagar blast, and after a decade, is 'finally released for lack of evidence' (275). The book ends with the narrator telling us 'He never went out again' (276).

While these plot descriptions doubtless make the book resemble a soap opera, Mahajan does not focus exclusively on the personal in these sections. Instead, he sketches the background (usually but not exclusively political) that helps explain terrorism. Almost immediately after the first blast, the group known as the Jammu and Kashmir Islamic Force takes responsibility for the bombing. But rather than focusing on the immediate political reasons for their terror campaign, the Khurana's relatives resort to 'their normal scorn for Muslims' (25). 'They can't live in peace, these Muslims. Anywhere they show up, they're at war' (25), says one. Another repeats the same bias, calling Islam 'A violent religion of violent people' (25). A third expresses their disgust with Muslims in Kashmir, which this person calls a 'filthy people. The whole winter passes and they don't bathe. That's why Srinagar stinks so much' (25). They also repeat the myth about how Muslim terrorists 'believe they'll receive seventy-two virgins in heaven' (25).

American readers will likely recognise these sentiments as resonating with the Islamophobic tropes common after 9/11 and intensified by Donald Trump's vitriolic rhetoric.[4] But the more immediate reference for a South Asian audience would be the decades – centuries, really – of anti-Muslim bias and violence (see Engineer). Perhaps the best-known example today would be the sectarian violence that followed in the wake of Partition in 1947, when the land was split into two separate countries, one predominantly Muslim (Pakistan), the other predominantly Hindu (India). The partition, however, was far from peaceful. Although the numbers remain disputed, anywhere from 200,000 to 2 million people lost their lives (Talbot 2009, 405), and huge numbers migrated from one region to the other to live with their co-religionists. Anti-Muslim bias has remained a staple of Indian politics and mass culture, although it has recently worsened under Prime Minister Narendra Modi, who has, inter alia, overseen a surge in anti-Muslim violence of both a physical and cultural, such as renaming cities bearing Islamic names and rewriting history textbooks to promote Hindu nationalism (Ramachandran 2020, 15). In the words of a pundit for *The Hindu*, Modi and his party fundamentally believe that 'Muslims have made no contribution to India's cultural life' (Apoorvanand 2018). In 2019, Amit Shah, the head of the Hindu nationalist Bharatiya Janata Party (BJP) and Modi's right-hand man, called illegal Muslim immigrants 'termites', promising that his party would 'pick up infiltrators one by one and throw them into the Bay of Bengal', a statement which was widely interpreted as urging ethnic cleansing (Ghoshal 2019).

In Mahajan's novel, the protagonist's mother is well aware of the long history of Muslim oppression by Modi's BJP, and throughout the 90s she

> never stopped being alarmed. 'They're still angry about something that happened fifty years ago', she'd say, thinking of partition, and returning again and again to the images of party workers swarming the domes of the Babri Masjid [mosque], gashing the onionskins of cement with hammers. (Mahajan 2016, 122)[5]

The young Mansoor is bullied at school for his religious identity: 'he was taunted for being a Muslim, dubbed "mullah" and "Paki" and "mosquito"' (132), and his father, after nearly losing all his money in a real estate deal, thinks that his misfortune 'was punishment for staying on in an obviously hostile country. Many of his relatives had fled to Pakistan after the 1969 Gujarat riots [more on this event below]; only he, bullheaded, had stayed on' (152).

At first, surviving the bomb 'improve[s]' Mansoor's life (119) in that he is now chauffeured to and from school, and his classmates move from disbelief to 'bewilderment: What could this small Muslim boy have to do with the exploding market? How could he have survived?' (119). Five years pass and it seems that Mansoor has sufficiently recovered, except for the occasional ache in his wrists, so that he can study computer science at Santa Clara University in California, USA. But the past catches up with him, as does his alienation from the mainstream of American culture. First, 9/11 occurs, and even though

Mansoor obviously has nothing to do with terrorism, it does not matter. The fact that he is Muslim means that people look at him 'in a new way' (125). Even though Mansoor does not engage in political talk he is shunned because of his religion: 'When he said hello to acquaintances as they marched past in the dorms, they didn't wave back' (125). Mansoor realises that to the other students, 'I'm either a computer programmer or a terrorist' (126). Nobody is interested in *him*. Then, his injuries recur, making it impossible to use a keyboard, and so he returns to his parents' house in India. Curious about the ongoing trial of the accused Lajpat Nagar bombers, Mansoor attends a session where he meets a member of the NGO, Peace for All, and it is through this group that he meets Ayub Azmi, who will eventually plant the second bomb.

Mansoor's relations with Azmi demonstrate how the combination of social alienation and anti-Muslim bias allow Mansoor to sympathise with radical Islam without becoming a terrorist himself. While the primary purpose of Peace for All is to achieve justice, or at least, a trial, for the accused bombers, the underlying motivation for the group's creation is state-sanctioned extreme anti-Muslim violence:

> They had witnessed what Narendra Modi, the chief minister of Gujarat, had done in his state in March, how he and his administration had stood by, in localities like Naroda Patiya, Meghaninagar, and Bapunagar, as violent Hindu mobs, armed with swords, petrol bombs, tridents, and water postils to spray fuel, had set up Muslims, burning them alive, tearing infants from mothers and fetuses from wombs, raping women, killing a thousand. And they had realized that the Indian government wouldn't protect them, but in fact it had an incentive to demonize and exterminate them. (144)[6]

Modi's actions, however, are not just repulsive in themselves, they push Ayub and the rest of the group into sympathising with the radicalism of the Muslim Brotherhood and Sayyid Qutb, their theorist:

> The voice of reason, of knowledge, during these raucous meetings was Ayub ... With his quick-fire noun-laden sentences, he made knowledge *attractive*. 'The Brotherhood in Egypt is primarily a social organization. It only became politicized when they were persecuted, when their leaders were locked up in jail. I don't think Qutb was a great thinker as others do, but why martyr him?' (144–45; emphasis in the original).

Ayub, however, underestimates the Muslim Brotherhood's capacity for violence and terrorism. From the 1940s onward, the Brotherhood was responsible for a campaign of assassinations and bombings (Farahat 2017, 2–4).[7] To cite just one particularly prominent example, the Brotherhood killed Egyptian President Anwar Sadat in October 1981 because he signed a peace treaty with Israel.

As for Qutb, he was the Brotherhood's most influential theoretician, and he was jailed after the Brotherhood attempted to assassinate President Gamal Abdel Nasser (who took power via a military coup). In 1966, he was hanged. Qutb's primary message was to attack the West, indeed, all civilisation, for splitting 'the sacred and the secular' (Berman 2004, 87). Qutb also wrote a memoir, 'The America I Have Seen', of his time attending university in the United States, which he hated because of America's materialism and what he perceived as the unbridled sexuality of its women. America, Qutb writes, is defined by 'an enduring desire for wealth by any means, and for the possession of the largest possible share of pleasures and compensation for the effort expended to acquire wealth' (1951, 5). Qutb and the Brotherhood laid the foundation for al-Qaeda and the Taliban. This is, in other words, the philosophy of Islamist radicalism and Islamist terrorism (Berman, 52–102; Wright, 5–30; and Turner, 541–58).

However, in Mahajan's novel, 'the members of Peace for All were not radicals' (2016, 144). Their openness to the ideology of Islamism stems partly from ignorance ('People nodded their heads dreamily, not knowing much about Egypt or Qutb' [145]), but mainly from their sense of grievance at how Modi, his government, and, it seems, Hindu society generally, has excluded them. These are not wild-eyed radicals or religious fanatics: 'They were eminently reasonable people, students engrossed in careers' (144). They all want 'to be included in the mainstream' (144). And yet, each has a story of 'being personally pegged for a Muslim', of being told to 'go back to Pakistan', of someone saying, 'Oh, you don't *look* Muslim!' or of touching a friend's father's *Ramayan* (a Sanskrit epic) and then, of loudly being accused of polluting it (144). Mahajan's point is that exclusion and deep-seated bias lead otherwise reasonable people to sympathise with ideologies that support extreme violence and terrorism.

Mansoor moves even closer to al-Qaeda's ideology when, later in the novel, both Ayub (whose journey into terrorism I consider in the third section) and Mansoor agree that the West suffers from a lack of values. When Ayub says that he finally understands 'why al-Qaeda wanted to target New York. It's a place that prides itself on being the most awake, but it's asleep to reality' (171), he echoes Osama bin Laden's charge in 'Why We Are Fighting You': America is spiritually blind and its supposed 'pillars of "personal freedom"' have led the country into an abyss of political and sexual immorality (bin Laden 2007, 203). Mansoor asserts that the same problem with values afflicts India: 'Going deeper into learning about Islam, Mansoor could see how a crisis of values was afoot not only in the Western World but in India, which had become a lapdog of the West, eager to imbibe its worst ideas while ditching its best ones' (Mahajan 2016, 172). Like Qutb, bin Laden condemns the 'immorality and debauchery that has spread' in the West (2007, 202). In his many charges against America, he includes the exploitation of women as 'consumer products or advertising tools', and he adds: 'You are a nation that practices the trade of sex in all its forms, directly and indirectly' (bin Laden 2007, 204). In a similar fashion, Mansoor focuses on the West's obsession with debasing women, especially on TV, 'with its profusion of sex' (Mahajan 2016, 172). Ultimately, Mansoor believes India needs 'a revolution of values . . . a retreat from Western materialism', and that means returning to religion: 'People needed to be shown what religion could do for them in a practical way – how it could save them from depression, pain, meaninglessness, how it could connect them to a family beyond their small selfish nuclear units' (176).

Nonetheless, while Mansoor comes to agree with Qutb's and bin Laden's views on Islam, the West and morality, his involvement stops with greater piety and overt pride in his religion. Much to his mother's consternation, Mansoor starts wearing a *gol topi*, a skullcap, and she does not think this is a good idea: 'These days to call attention to yourself for being a Muslim', she starts to tell Mansoor, but he interrupts, telling his mother that anti-Muslim bias is why he wants to show off his religion to the world: 'But it's exactly because of this kind of shame that I'm wearing it! We have to get over all this shame and fear!' (Mahajan 2016, 209). But Ayub does not invite Mansoor to participate in his plot (Mahajan does not specify why), and Mansoor does not move from sympathising with radical Islam to jihad and terrorism.

Vikas and Deepa's daughter, Anusha, 'the daughter of the bomb' (124), born of her parents' desperate post-bombing sex, offers a different perspective on how and why someone could become a terrorist. Her father, we are told, 'hated his daughter' (239) because she reminds him of his lost sons. Even though she is adorable ('She was cute and round-eyed with flowing streamers of hair and an odd interest learning how things were made' [239]), Vikas 'didn't want to be near her' (239). Her mother treats her better, but both parents devote their time and energies to 'the Association of Terror Victims' (238), and while Vikas and Deepa find solace in this organisation because it allows them 'to eke a larger meaning' (248) out of their sons' murder, 'Anusha became neglected' (248). Whereas before she was a 'bright, soliloquizing, self-contained child' who loved dancing to Bollywood tunes, 'she now found she had no audience' (248). As an adult, Anusha looks at her abandonment as a reason for terrorism: 'Later, when she was older, she would tell her friends that she understood how such people, outwardly sensitive, could neglect their children to the point that they would go to a market and blow themselves up' (249).

Mahajan's portrait of Anusha follows the attempt in the 1980s to locate a cause for terrorism in family dysfunction. In 1983, a psychiatrist proposed that some become terrorists because of 'troubled family backgrounds' (Post 1984, 241), which of course perfectly describes Anusha's situation.[8] Neglected by both parents, doubtless aware of her father's antipathy toward her, Anusha traces the origins of terrorism to 'an act of retaliation for real or imagined hurts' (Post 1984, 243). For her, the motivation for terrorism is not political, but personal, and theoretical, as Anusha (so far as we know) does not blow herself up in a market.

Representing the Figure of the Terrorist: Shockie the Bomb-Maker

Both Mansoor and Anusha are characters the reader can easily sympathise with because neither commits any violence. They plant no bombs. They kill nobody. If anything, they are victims. But the same cannot be said for Shaukat 'Shockie' Guru, the man responsible for the Lajpat Nagar blast, and Ayub Azmi, who plants the Sarojini Nagar bomb. The challenge Mahajan faces with these characters is how to depict terrorists as anything other than monstrous. True, literature and popular entertainment are filled with examples of murderers, even mass murderers, who nonetheless retain some claim on our sympathies, even admiration. Shakespeare's Macbeth is a human killing machine who assassinates his king and orders MacDuff's wife and children slaughtered, yet audiences still admire him as a tragic figure. More contemporaneously, Walter White, the meth cook in the series *Breaking Bad*, kills approximately 274 people over the course of the show (according to fan sites), and his product destroys untold lives.[9] Yet the complexity of his character continues to draw us in. He is both responsible for any number of deaths, yet remains devoted to his family even as his family rejects him, and the audience is forced to admire Walter White's extraordinary skill (and luck) in neutralising his enemies and building his meth empire.

Both Richard Jackson (2015b), representing Critical Terrorism Studies, and Stephanie Bird (2020), representing the new field of Perpetrator Studies (which focuses primarily, but not exclusively, on the Holocaust), propose that literature can, and should, do better, especially since fiction 'can articulate multiple perspectives, imagine contradictions, and convey unresolved emotions and motivations' (Bird 2020, 302). And yet, the Western literary imagination generally recoils at treating terrorists sympathetically. For example, all the anarchists in Conrad's *The Secret Agent* are deformed in some way. Michaelis is 'round like a tub' (Conrad [1907] 2004, 31); the Professor is a 'dingy little man' with a 'greasy, unhealthy complexion' (46); and Verloc is 'Undemonstrative and burly in a fat-pig style' (10). The protagonist of Eoin McNamee's novel about the Irish Troubles, *Resurrection Man*, is a Protestant sectarian terrorist who may claim that he is responding to Catholic perfidy ('The Catholics in this town think they can just take over, the IRA, and all. Walk all over you, if you let them' [1994, 73]), but he is really a sadistic psychopath.

When Jackson calls for novels to give 'primary voice to the views of the terrorist' (2015b, 397), he means, as he writes in the preface to his novel,

Confessions of a Terrorist (2015a), to move away from depicting terrorism as 'deviant behaviour [resulting from a] combination of individual alienation and psychological vulnerability' (vii) and toward narrating the 'political origins' of terrorism, which 'follows a rational strategic logic' (viii). How closely does Mahajan follow Jackson's prescriptions?[10] While Ayub has one blast to his name, Shockie is 'the leading bomb maker of the Jammu and Kashmir Islamic Force' (33). Thus, he is responsible for killing 'dozens of Indians' (34) and for maiming many others. Therefore, he is a perfect candidate to fulfil Jackson's prescriptions for the figure of the terrorist, for exploring why, as Jackson puts it, 'an individual would choose to join a terrorist group' (2015a, vii). Yet the answer is oddly mixed, as Mahajan never indicates just how the reader is supposed to consider Shockie.

Mahajan is clearly aware of the tendency toward depicting terrorists as beyond reason. In an interview for the online magazine, *Guernica*, Mahajan underscores how terrorist violence is unspeakable, incomprehensible: 'The combination of those things [the graphic, political nature of the attacks as well as the randomness of the violence] makes it all the more horrible – what seems to be the senselessness of it' (Perlin 2016), and he folds these views into *The Association of Small Bombs*.

Towards the beginning, after Malik (the group's ideologue) is arrested, he faces a judge who repeats the usual depictions of terrorism: 'barbarous actions ... The killing of innocents' (Mahajan 2016, 63). And toward the end, Sharif, Mansoor's father, says about the Sarojini Nagar blast, 'You think's there's a reason? ... They [terrorists] hate everyone, especially themselves.' The goal, he says, is not a particular political result, but 'irrationality', because they themselves are 'irrational' (259).

Mahajan implicitly challenges this view by clearly and forthrightly giving the reason for Shockie's lethal violence; he creates bombs 'in revenge for the military oppression in Kashmir, expanding the JKIF's "theatre of violence," as the newspapers called it' (34). Specifically, the Lajpat Nagar blast that killed the Khurana boys is 'meant to be a signal to the central government about the elections they were organizing in Kashmir' (50). Afterward, one of the Khurana relatives, Mukesh, clearly gets the message: 'They wanted to disrupt the election in Kashmir', he tells Deepa (79). Therefore, there is no question about the reasons for Shockie's terrorism. As for irrationality, Shockie is aware of that charge and uses it to his advantage. When Ayub meets with Shockie to receive the bomb, he is stunned by the 'illogic' of having to wait at Mansoor's house for weeks. The group, he says to himself, '*prided* itself on irrationality' (223; emphasis in the original). However, Shockie explains, irrationality is a rational strategy for not getting caught: 'To be illogical. The more illogical you are, the better you are at this game. The shopkeepers even saw and noticed us – they told us to move on – but later, no one could remember our faces' (223).

However, the underlying motivation for Shockie's actions takes a backseat in Mahajan's narrative to the personal. In fact, other than the quotes cherry-picked above, we hear very little about the political situation in Kashmir, and nothing about why Shockie turned to political violence. Instead, we read more about Shockie's private life. Before leaving on his mission to blow up the market, he calls his mother, and worries when neither she nor the neighbour pick up (34). So here we have a terrorist who kills without compunction, yet loves his mother. It is not clear whether this detail is supposed to humanise Shockie or make him even more of a monster, since he seems to care deeply about his mother's welfare but is willing to commit mass murder. Additionally, Shockie is very concerned with his appearance. He pays close attention to the clothes he packs for the trip (35). When Ayub first meets Shockie, who acts as his handler, Ayub notes how 'he wore dusty black pants with astonishingly sharp pleats', and, as 'the son of a presswali, [he] took a dandy's pride, despite his thinning curly hair, in wearing ironed clothes' (203). Again, Mahajan provides no clues to the reader (or at least, no clues that this reader could find) as to how Shockie's vanity impacts our conception of him as terrorist.

Although Shockie is properly cautious about admitting Ayub to the group – 'he had learned from years of experience that no one could be trusted when it came to the work of revolution' (197) – he decides to trust Ayub not because Ayub shows any particular skill in bombmaking or because of his hatred of Modi, but because Ayub knows Malik, Shockie's friend who has been imprisoned for terrorism, and so 'an intimacy developed between them' (201). When he talks about Malik, Shockie starts to cry, and Ayub wonders how such a man can be a terrorist: 'You can't be a terrorist and be so emotional and unguarded' (206).

The question, then, for Ayub, and for Mahajan's readers, is how this man, who looks like 'a harmless middle-aged uncle' (198), or an 'electrician' (265), could be a terrorist when 'There was nothing terroristic about him' (264). The answer is not the vexed relationship between appearance and reality, as perhaps the reader might expect. Instead, Mahajan points the reader in a different direction by telling us that Shockie *compartmentalises* the violence. After he returns to his base in Nepal following the Lajpat Nagar bombing, he and Malik go swimming in a beautiful mountain lake, and Shockie wonders, 'How could it be that only four days ago I was in Delhi planting a bomb? . . . And now I'm here? The birds overhead were fervent in their high-pitched complaints. A surge of brightness passed over him. He hugged Malik and briefly fell asleep' (54). Returning to the town, Shockie 'crossed a puddle and was reminded of the deep lilac pool of mountain water from the morning. The bomb – all bombs – seemed far away' (55).

But while the bombs may seem far away after the fact, during a mission, he is another person altogether:

'It's normal', Rafiq told him [Ayub] later, 'He's always been an emotional person. Used to cry freely about his mother, his brother, Kashmir – he lost everything, you know. But don't underestimate how dangerous he is. When he's making bombs he's another person. He's possessed. His personality when he's making bombs has nothing to do with how he is normally. His speed changes too. He moves fast. It's almost as if by crying and being slow, he's saving up all his energies for the bomb.' (206)

But while Shockie may keep these two sides apart, it is not clear if the reader can do the same. Perhaps a terrorist can retain their humanity, and the reader's sympathy, only by repressing the violence after it's done, and by repressing one's emotions during the mission. But if you can manage this trick, just how fully human are you? And are we supposed to forgive Shockie, or appreciate that even terrorists have mothers whom they love? There are questions Mahajan raises, but leaves unanswered, possibly because they are unanswerable.

When the Political is Personal: Ayub and the Limits of Nonviolence

Mahajan takes yet another approach to the representation of the figure of the terrorist in the character of Ayub Azmi. At first, it seems that Mahajan wants to connect Ayub's journey to terrorism with Islamic radicalism (see Wattenbarger 2018, 687). After he and Mansoor become close and Mansoor tells Ayub about his health issues, Ayub says that he faced something similar but the pain went away after 'I gave myself to Allah' (Mahajan 2016, 157). As noted above, Ayub is fully briefed on the Muslim Brotherhood and Sayyid Qutb (145), and he repeats (with a soupçon of Frantz Fanon's theory of cleansing violence) the canard that America is at war against Islam: 'It's so touching, the sense of empowerment Islam gave to all these colonial people, to slaves. America's attempt to crush Islam is an attempt to destroy the self-esteem of the rising, conquered people' (183).[11] But Ayub does not turn to violence because of radical Islam.

When we are introduced to Ayub, he and his girlfriend, Tara, are part of the NGO 'Peace for All', whose purpose is to push for Muslim rights, including justice for those accused of perpetrating the Lajpat Nagar blast. They are fully aware that Modi's government not only has no interest in protecting them, 'in fact it had an incentive to demonize and exterminate them' (144). As noted, the group's members are 'not radicals' but 'eminently reasonable people, students engrossed in careers, people who wanted to be Indians but had discovered themselves instead to be Muslims and had started to embrace their identities' (144). They are not interested at all in violence, preferring instead demonstrations, sending letters to the editor of newspapers, and writing editorials. 'The voice of reason' in this group 'was Ayub' (144). So what happened?

Mansoor, Tara and Ayub write editorials about how the accused in the Lajpat Nagar blast have not been brought to trial, even though it has been years and mail had been sent 'to *The Times of India*, the *Hindustan Times*, and the *Pioneer*' they 'had not heard back; the editors at these papers, it seemed, were not interested in the unique slant of a victim asking for a terrorist's release' (180). So, they decide to organise a mass protest instead. At first, the protest seems like a massive success: 'hundreds of men and women chanting and holding up signs' (183). But the police are also there. Ayub tries to get himself arrested, but a policeman refuses, 'You're not worth an arrest' (184). Then, the protest ends in the worst possible way. Not, as one might expect, with police brutality, mass arrests, injuries, deaths and frontpage news headlines, but instead, 'something terrible happened on that spring day. The crowd dispersed' (184). Even worse, when Tara and Ayub open the next day's newspaper, 'there wasn't even a mention of the protest' (184). This is the fork in the road for Ayub, the moment he decides 'that nonviolence didn't work' (184). Therefore, the only recourse is violence and murder. Significantly, as we will see, at the same time Ayub has this epiphany, his girlfriend, Tara, '[breaks] things off with him' (185).

The problem is that nonviolence does not attract media attention: 'The media revelled in sex and violence – how could nonviolence, with its greying temples and wise posture, match up?' (185). Terrorism, on the other hand, is violence designed to attract as much media attention as possible (Juergensmeyer 2000, 139–44). As Don DeLillo puts it in *Mao II*, terrorism 'is the language of being noticed' (1991, 157). To be noticed, therefore, Ayub must resort to violence. Furthermore, for Ayub, nonviolence cuts against the fundamental truth of human existence: 'that the world was dictated by power' (199). If you want to rise up, then sweet reason will not help you: you must *force* your way to the top – or into popular consciousness. Previously, Ayub could make no sense of 9/11, 'a crime that had, for all its religious implications, always seemed opaque to him' (200). But 9/11 makes sense if you think of the world 'as a jungle' (200) where might makes right. Ayub turns to violence because he now understands that violence is the only way to get his message across: 'I had always thought you had to educate others about your pain, show them how to solve it. Now I realize you have to make them *feel* it' (200; emphasis in the original). The figure of the Sarojini Nagar bomber, it seems, is a political man driven to violence by the indifference of the Indian news media to his message.

But as he did with Shockie, Mahajan balances the political with the personal, and as such, recalls the arguments by Gray and Rothberg, among others, about how 9/11 novels fail because they focus so much on the effects of terrorism on the domestic sphere and ignore or render terrorists as inhuman monsters. But while Jackson, Appelbaum and Paknadel call for adding a full, sympathetic hearing of the terrorist's political motivations, Mahajan alters the figure of the terrorist as either an obsessed radical or a justly aggrieved freedom fighter by including motivations that are not in the least political. After Shockie gives him the bomb he will bring to the market, Ayub reconsiders his earlier understanding of 9/11 as exemplifying the role of force in society: 'Earlier he'd felt the attack was just revenge against American imperialism' (226), but now he thinks that the reasons are not political at all. Rather, 'the reasons for such aggression would have to be idiosyncratic, personal' (226). In fact, he reframes the planes crashing into the Twin Towers as a kind of rape:[12]

> Killing others and then yourself is the most visceral experience possible. Atta must have felt himself full of sexual hate for the people piled high in the towers, bodies in a vertical morgue. He saw the opening between the two towers as a vagina into which to shove the hard-nosed dick of the plane. Sitting at the controls, his curly hair tight on his skull, eyes rubbery, underslept, blackly circled, he must have seen someone appear at the window and look at him – a woman, maybe, a blond American woman. At that moment he got an erection. At that moment he slammed into her alarmed face. (227)

Ayub's sexualising terrorist violence explains why, after the bomb explodes earlier than expected and Ayub is caught in the blast, his last thought before he blacks out is not about politics. Instead, he turns to his love life: 'Tara will hear me now' (234).[13]

In effect, Mahajan inverts the 1960s phrase, 'the personal is the political'; in this novel, the political is the personal in that Ayub's terrorism results from his desire for Tara, not revenge for Muslim persecution. However, Mahajan provides no guidance as to how the reader is supposed to judge Ayub's motivations. Instead, he presents us with his imagining of the Ayub's interiority (which is exactly what Jackson, as well as Appelbaum and Paknadel say is missing in terrorism literature), and leaves it up to the reader to make of it what they will. On the one hand, by imagining the terrorist in this way, Mahajan restores what Jackson calls 'the humanity of the terrorist' (2015, 318). Ayub does what he does because of lost love. But once we understand that and perhaps empathise with Ayub's pain at losing Tara, we are still left with fact that he has murdered innocent people. The reader (this reader, at least) still must condemn him. Surely there are more productive ways of dealing with romantic disappointment and sexual frustration than setting off a bomb in a marketplace? But it may also be Mahajan's intention to illustrate how a terrorist act results from a panoply of overlapping and even contradictory motivations. And so, Mahajan refuses to reduce the figure of the terrorist to either a purely political (i.e., motivated by Hindu bias against Muslims) or a purely personal (i.e., romantic disappointment) figure. Instead, Ayub is a complex melange of both.

I want to conclude by looking at this novel's multivalent title: *The Association of Small Bombs*. The primary reference is to the organisation set up by the

Khuranas to help victims of 'small' bombs, that is, bombings that do not shake the world and whose victims are soon forgotten.[14] But both parts of the novel's title have additional resonances.

First, the book illustrates the ongoing 'associations' of a terrorist bombing, how the effects ripple outward with many overlapping, unintended consequences. Mansoor, a victim, decides to attend a court session for those accused of the bombing, there he meets a representative of the NGO (137), becomes involved with the group, and meets Ayub, who then commits the second bombing leading to Mansoor's imprisonment (269–70). The associations seem never-ending, and they include Anusha, not even conceived when the market bomb goes off, yet her life is inevitably shaped by this event, and not in a good way.

Lastly, 'small bombs'. Over the course of this novel there is an implied debate over which is worse or more effective, small bombs or larger ones? Shockie thinks that small bombs are useless and that his organisation's leadership does not realise 'that one big blast achieved much more, in terms of influencing policy, than hundreds of small ones' (52). Later in the book, another terrorist, Tauqueer, tells Ayub that large bombs are more humane because, well, misery loves company:

> It's better for the event to be big, to affect many. People say 9/11 was the worst terror attack of all time – was it? I think the small bombs that we hear about all the time, that go off in unknown markets, filling five or six are worse. They concentrate the pain on the lives of a few. Better to kill generously rather than stingily. (210)

But Vikas and Deepa provide a different perspective. Vikas tells a news channel that 'the small attacks are more deadly, because a few have to carry the burden of the majority'; worse still, the small attacks create even more enemies: 'Then, as these victims' grievances get forgotten, as the blasts themselves are forgotten, the victims of these small bombs turn against the government instead of the terrorists' (247). Furthermore, the damage caused by bombs is not restricted to the immediate casualties. Vikas and Deepa's marriage falls apart; Ayub dies of exhaustion; Mansoor's life is ruined; Vikas dies a shattered, broken man; and Anusha is psychically scarred by her parents' abandoning her. The damage just keeps going. In the end, Mahajan seems to be saying, there is no such thing as a 'small bomb'. They are all devastating.

Notes

1. While Jackson and the others are largely correct, I have explored how some authors and filmmakers give equal time to terrorists and terrorist motivations in *Unspeakable* (2020).

2. See, for example, Nadeem Aslam's *The Blind Man's Garden*, Joydeep Roy-Bhattacharya's *The Watch*, and Kamila Shamsie's *Home Fire*.
3. Since the early 2000s, Lashkar-e-Taiba have been designated a terrorist group by Britain, the United States and India. Pakistan, their sponsor, also banned the group.
4. See Johnson and Hauslohner for a timeline of Trump's anti-Muslim statements.
5. On December 6, 1992, the BJP organised a rally at the mosque which turned violent and led to the building's destruction, which in turn led to several months of communal violence between Hindus and Muslims. See Ramachandra 2007, 582–98.
6. Mahajan is not exaggerating in this passage. See Murphy 2009.
7. On the other hand, noting the tensions between the Brotherhood and Al Qaeda, some have regarded them as a 'firewall' against Islamist violence. See Vidino 2010, 200–2.
8. In recent years, however, this theory has been abandoned. See for example the summary of terrorist motivations by the American Psychological Association (DeAngelis 2009) and Borum 2004.
9. See, for example, this wiki: https://breakingbad.fandom.com/wiki/List_of_killings_by_main_characters
10. Sangeeta Ray observes that *The Association of Small Bombs* 'is deep and disturbing because it tries to express the interiority of characters who are most often dehumanized in an easily available script' (2021, 28).
11. For example, Osama bin Laden begins 'Why We Are Fighting You' thus: 'Because you attacked us, and continue to attack us' (197). In *The Wretched of the Earth*, Fanon proposes, 'violence . . . frees the native from his inferiority complex and from his despair and inaction; it makes him fearless and restores his self-respect' (1963, 94).
12. Shockie also finds terrorism sexually exciting. While waiting to get a key made for the car he will use for the Lajpat Narogini bombing, he goes to a 'local dhaba and admired the women at the tables with their gluttonous husbands. He wanted to ram his penis into their wives. He imagined pinning the dhaba owner's wife on a table and ripping off her kurta' (Mahajan 2016, 45).
13. Mahajan may be drawing on the persistent rumors that Atta and the other 9/11 hijackers visited strip clubs in Las Vegas. See Booth 2001.
14. The Lajpat Nagar bombing is a perfect example of a 'small bomb'. For example, the *New York Times* barely mentioned it. Instead of, say, a front-page article, the *Times* gave the bombing one sentence in 'World News Briefs'. Sandwiched between short articles on American and French aid pulling out of Central Africa, and the House preventing the CIA from using journalists as spies, we find this sentence: 'On Tuesday two Kashmiri groups said they had planted a car bomb that killed 13 people and wounded 38 in a crowded New Delhi market' (Reuters 1996). No more.

References

Appelbaum, Robert, and Alexis Paknadel. 2008. "Terrorism and the Novel, 1970–2001." *Poetics Today* 29, no. 3: 387–436.

Apoorvanand. 2018. "The Reason for Renaming Places." *The Hindu*. Last modified November 13, 2018. https://www.thehindu.com/opinion/op-ed/the-reason-for-renaming-places/article25478180.ece

Aslam, Nadeem. 2013. *The Blind Man's Garden*. London: Faber and Faber.
Berman, Paul. 2004. *Terror and Liberalism*. New York: Norton.
bin Laden, Osama. 2007. "'Why We Are Fighting You': Osama bin Laden's Letter to Americans." *The Al Qaeda Reader*. Trans. and ed. Raymond Ibrahim. New York: Doubleday.
Bird, Stephanie. 2020. "Perpetrators and Perpetration in Literature." In *The Routledge International Handbook of Perpetrator Studies*, eds Susanne C. Knittel and Zachary J. Goldberg, 301–10. London and New York: Routledge.
Booth, William. 2001. "Hijackers' Tracks in Las Vegas." *Washington Post*, October 14, 2001. https://www.washingtonpost.com/archive/politics/2001/10/14/hijackers-tracks-in-las-vegas/d8ac81a0-c4fd-4428-86d8-524996b92726/
Borum, Randy. 2004. *Psychology of Terrorism*. Tampa: University of South Florida.
Conrad, Joseph. (1907) 2004. *The Secret Agent*, ed. John Lyon. Reprint, New York: Oxford University Press.
DeAngelis, Tori. 2009. "Understanding Terrorism." *Monitor on Psychology* 40, no. 10: 60–4. https://www.apa.org/monitor/2009/11/terrorism
DeLillo, Don. 1991. *Mao II*. New York: Penguin.
Engineer, Ashgar Ali. 2002. "Gujarat Riots in the Light of the History of Communal Violence." *Economic and Political Weekly* 37, no. 50: 5047–54.
Fanon, Frantz. 1963. *The Wretched of the Earth*. Trans. Constance Farrington. New York: Grove.
Farahat, Cynthia. 2017. "The Muslim Brotherhood, Fountain of Islamist Violence." *Middle East Quarterly* 24, no. 2: 1–10. https://www.meforum.org/6562/the-muslim-brotherhood-fountain-of-islamist
Ghoshal, Devjyot. 2019. "Amit Shah Threatens to Throw Illegal Immigrants into Bay of Bengal." *Reuters*, April 12, 2019. https://www.reuters.com/article/india-election-speech/amit-shah-vows-to-throw-illegal-immigrants-into-bay-of-bengal-idUSKCN1RO1YD
Gray, Richard. 2008. "Open Doors, Closed Minds: American Prose Writing at a Time of Crisis." *American Literary History* 21, no. 1: 128–48.
Herman, Peter C. 2020. *Unspeakable: Literature and Terrorism from the Gunpowder Plot to 9/11*. New York and London: Routledge.
Jackson, Richard. 2015a. *Confessions of a Terrorist*. London: Zed Books.
Jackson, Richard. 2015b. "Terrorism, Taboo, and Discursive Resistance: The Agonistic Potential of the Terrorism Novel." *International Studies Review* 17: 396–413.
Johnson, Jenna, and Abigail Hauslohner. 2017. "'I Think Islam Hates Us': A Timeline of Trump's Comments About Islam and Muslims." *Washington Post*, May 20, 2017. https://www.washingtonpost.com/news/post-politics/wp/2017/05/20/i-think-islam-hates-us-a-timeline-of-trumps-comments-about-islam-and-muslims/
Juergensmeyer, Mark. 2000. *Terror in the Mind of God: The Global Rise of Religious Violence*. Berkeley: University of California Press.
Mahajan, Karan. 2016. *The Association of Small Bombs*. New York: Viking.
McNamee, Eoin. (1994) 2004. *Resurrection Man*. Reprint, London: Faber & Faber.
Murphy, Eamon. 2009. "'We Have No Orders to Save You': State Terrorism, Politics and Communal Violence in the Indian State of Gujarat, 2002." In *Contemporary*

State Terrorism: Theory and Practice, eds Richard Jackson, Eamon Murphy and Scott Poynting, 86–103. Oxford and New York: Routledge.

Perlin, Ross. 2016. "Karan Mahajan: On Small Bombings." *Guernica*. Last modified March 22, 2016. https://www.guernicamag.com/karan-mahajan-on-small-bombings/

Post, Jerrold M. 1984. "Notes on a Psychodynamic Theory of Terrorist Behavior." *Terrorism: An International Journal* 7, no. 3: 241–56.

Roy-Bhattacharya, Joydeep. 2012. *The Watch*. London: Hogarth.

Qutb, Sayyid. 1951. "The America I Have Seen: In the Scale of Human Values (1951)." Trans Tarek Masoud and Ammar Fakeeh. https://www.cia.gov/library/abbottabad-compound/3F/3F56ACA473044436B4C1740F65D5C3B6_Sayyid_Qutb_-_The_America_I_Have_Seen.pdf

Ramachandra, Guha. 2007. *India After Gandhi: The History of the World's Largest Democracy*. New York: HarperCollins.

Ramachandran, Sudha. 2020. "Hindutva Violence in India: Trends and Implications." *Counter Terrorist Trends and Analyses* 12, no. 4: 15–20.

Ray, Sangeeta. 2021. "Bombs and Bomb-Makers: Realism, *The Association of Small Bombs*, and the Post 9/11 Novel." *Studies in the Novel* 53, no. 1: 20–35.

Reuters. 1996. "World News Briefs; India Bus Bomb Kills 14 As Kashmir Vote Nears." *New York Times*, May 23, 7. https://timesmachine.nytimes.com/timesmachine/1996/05/23/issue.html

Rothberg, Michael. 2008. "A Failure of the Imagination: Diagnosing the Post-9/11 Novel: A Response to Richard Gray." *American Literary History* 21, no. 1: 152–8.

Shamsie, Kamila. 2017. *Home Fire*. New York: Riverhead.

Talbot, Ian. 2009. "Partition of India: The Human Dimension." *Cultural and Social History* 6, no. 4: 403–10.

Turner, John. 2010. "From Cottage Industry to International Organisation: The Evolution of Salafi-Jihadism and the Emergence of the Al Qaeda Ideology." *Terrorism and Political Violence* 22, no. 4: 541–58.

Vidino, Lorenzo. 2010. *The New Muslim Brotherhood in the West*. New York: Columbia University Press.

Wattenbarger, Melanie R. 2018. "When Person Becomes Problem." *Interventions* 20, no. 5: 681–96.

Wright, Lawrence. 2006. *The Looming Tower: Al-Qaeda and the Road to 9/11*. New York: Knopf.

PART TWO

GENDER, IDENTITY AND TERRORISM

7. MILITANCY, MATERNITY AND MASQUERADE IN SANTOSH SIVAN'S *THE TERRORIST*

Rajeswari Mohan

The Perplexities of the Female Suicide Bomber

In his discussion of suicide bombing, Talal Asad (2007) has argued that a suicide bomber's motives are always of primary interest but they can never really be known since he or she dies in the event. Discussions of suicide bombings therefore turn to the trials, confessions and testimonies of those who train for similar missions but do not complete them; they cobble together an explanation that is part fantasy, part history, part fiction and part ethnography. As such, Asad argues, 'the social scientist, novelist, and filmmaker endow the dead terrorist with the motives of the living' (2007, 45). It is in this sense that representations of 'suicide attacks are therefore, above all, histories. In recounting plausible histories, they also employ fiction' (41). While they might signal the occluded personal and collective histories of the terrorist, they are also driven by the dominant cultural values and tropes of the moment and place they represent. In doing so they convert the raw, partially understood continuum of violent acts and their consequences into socially meaningful, politically significant, morally compelling and, sometimes, aesthetically arresting narratives.

The narrative act of connecting events, causes and motives in a causal relationship has typically played a prominent role in rendering acts of violence meaningful in ways that direct us to moral condemnation, repugnance and retaliation. However, attention to the ways these narratives are plotted makes visible the evasions, dissimulation and occultation that are necessary and distinctive features of all ideological activity. We see a similar complex mix of source material and strategies in the plotting of Santosh Sivan's film *The Terrorist* (1998). As it depicts a young Sri Lankan woman preparing for a suicide bombing mission, the film enters a field of contradictory discourses that seek to explain terrorism in general or vindicate, in particular, the violent civil war waged by Tamil separatists between 1983 and 2009. While the film recognises the potential women's militancy holds for unsettling gender arrangements, it amplifies the anxiety provoked by the figure of the female suicide bomber by overlaying it with the possibility of motherhood. This anxiety finds a particular focus and expression in the protagonist's many acts of feminine masquerade whose implications the film simultaneously plays up and contains through its reliance on conventions of melodrama – especially in its moment of closure.

Sivan's film is based on the 1991 assassination of Rajiv Gandhi, the erstwhile Prime Minister of India and President of the Indian National Congress, by a female Sri Lankan suicide bomber who approached him on the pretext of garlanding and paying her respects to him. It depicts Malli, a female guerrilla, portrayed with taciturn intensity by Ayesha Dharker, in a militant Sri Lankan Tamil group, modelled closely on the LTTE (Liberation Tigers of Tamil Eelam) which emerged as the dominant separatist faction in the Sri Lankan Civil War. The film initially depicts Malli's life as a fierce soldier in army fatigues who is given an assignment to travel to South India and assassinate an unidentified 'VIP'. It then follows her movement through a dangerous terrain booby trapped with mines, patrolled by soldiers and controlled by army checkpoints. She crosses the narrow strip of ocean separating Sri Lanka from India, and awaits the day of her mission living – as a tenant pretending to be an agricultural researcher – in the home of an older man, Vasu. In her preparations for her mission, Malli is aided by two male handlers who provide her with appropriately feminine clothes and walk her through the process detonating her explosive belt. During this interregnum, disrupted periodically by flashbacks to her life in Sri Lanka, the film maps her mental journey from steely resolve to distress and confusion as she comes to believe she may be pregnant. The film depicts this change on two levels. When Malli leaves the women's brigade on her mission, she sheds her soldier's fatigues and puts on feminine clothes that help her get through a checkpoint, ease her way into Vasu's home and finally get close to her target. Here the film shows her astutely performing femininity to avoid detection. Against this public performance, the narrative inserts a private drama of Malli's changing relationship to her mission on account of her suspected pregnancy. Persistent in every element of the narrative plotting of the film is a contradictory fascination and anxiety over the body of the female militant, especially when it is associated with motherhood. Simultaneously, the film activates the melodramatic plot convention of an unexpected pregnancy and manipulates camera shots to create a cinematic identification that positions the audience to want her to fail in her mission.[1]

Speaking in an interview during the making of the film, Sivan describes his protagonist as 'mentally prepared to give up her life. It will be a difficult period for any human being. So, I want to creep into her mind and see what she thinks' (Sivan 1997). Quickly shifting from what she thinks to speculating about her motives, Sivan ponders whether anything would have made her change her mind, and lands on something that 'only a woman can offer the world', 'her creativity' (1997). Sivan's reference to woman's 'creativity' is simply and exclusively presented in the film as the potential and promise of motherhood. The ruse of pregnancy allows him to visually enact the overdetermined horror of the pregnant womb as a bomb in repeated shots of her belly being strapped with an explosive belt.[2] Further, by casting the central dilemma of the protagonist as a personal secret, the film undercuts the incipient understanding it opens up of the collectively shared motivations of Tamil insurgency in Sri Lanka in those moments when it gestures at not only the complex causes that have drawn women to the LTTE but also the contradictory effects of their actions on ideologies of gender and sexuality.

By presenting the change in Malli's identity from a dedicated soldier to one defined by the promise or expectation of motherhood, Sivan is able to highlight the tension between her inner and outward loyalties, between her obligation to the life she believes she carries within her body and her commitment to the future life of her people. Several commentators have pointed out the ways the film avoids setting up Manichean divisions between life and death, good and evil, discernment and zealotry. Nevertheless, Sivan locates the bomber's motivation solely in her psychology, with the expectation that if the cause of her actions is her mindset, therein lies the way to avert her violence. In this, he is part of a growing body of influential knowledge in the strategic analysis of terrorism that takes the psyche as its focal point of analysis to explain what is known in the intelligence community as 'violent substate activism' (Rai 2004, 544). These explanations, in which maternal failure is strikingly emphasised, understand 'terrorist violence' not as a political instrument but as personal, irrational, actions driven by compulsion, and precipitated by 'self-destructive urges, fantasies of cleanliness, disturbed emotions combined with problems with authority and the Self, and inconsistent mothering' (Brannan et al. 2001, 6). Amit Rai (2004, 547) has also shown that this approach 'masters the fear, anxiety and uncertainty of a form of violent political dissent by resorting to the banality of a taxonomy' that produces the terrorist as deviant, abnormal and indeed monstrous in ways that align it with orientalism. The focus on the suicide bomber's psychology is prominent in attempts to explain or represent terrorism by women, and overlooks the prevalent paradoxical belief among militant groups that the self-annihilation of the terrorist is a life-affirming act of sacrifice for the future of the community.

In an episode of the BBC's *Inside Story*, 'Suicide Killers', a spokesman of the Sri Lankan Army asserts that women militants in the civil war were likely drugged into carrying out suicide missions which could not in any way be undertaken by 'a normal human being' (1991). In another documentary, Neelan Thiruchelvam, a lawyer and politician who was a member of the Tamil United Liberation Front, makes a similar assessment when he says:

> When you don't attach any sanctity to your own life, you cross an important emotional threshold; this means you become almost the most perfect, the most complete fighting machine. It is a form of extreme nationalism which is capable of commanding the kind of passion, the kind of emotion that sometimes religious fervour is sometimes [sic] capable of calling upon people. (Black Bag 1996)[3]

As if to illustrate Rai's point, Thiruchelvam's acknowledgement of nationalism is quickly overshadowed by his emphasis on the bomber's 'emotion', 'passion', and 'fervour'. Consistently, these explanations downplay the political, historical and socio-economic motivations that propel not one or two but a steady and seemingly endless stream of men and women to annihilate themselves for their cause. Furthermore, speculations about the motivation of a female terrorist in terms of personal tragedy, rather than group, organisational and political goals, stand in contrast to similar investigations of men whose actions are more often explained in terms of ethnic or nationalist pride, religious duty, political agenda and a desire to protect loved ones.[4]

Women's Militancy and the Breakdown of Gender Arrangements

What this psychologising also overlooks is the way women's participation in militancy is often an expected outcome of their growing visibility as political actors. Feminists like Cynthia Enloe have pointed out that the direct and indirect 'militarization of women's lives' has been in part the result of women's increasing awareness of their rights, responsibilities and opportunities as citizens (1983, 16).[5] Sri Lankan feminists like Neloufer de Mel, on the other hand, argue that victimhood and the ensuing social and individual crisis offer opportunities for women to break with or reinvent tradition. 'This task is made easier because ... in the interregnum between the state as they know it and the anticipated state they struggle for, normalcy is suspended and prevailing rules do not apply' (de Mel 2001, 18).

The discourse of Tamil nationalism associated with the LTTE advances a similar account of women's militancy, even as it undercuts its effectivity. The name of its women's wing, *Suthanthirap Paravaigal* (Birds of Freedom), suggests an ambiguous link between women's militancy, national liberation and the empowerment of women: female militants might be harbingers of the free nation, and women's freedom would be one of promises realised only when the goal of a Tamil homeland is reached, but in all likelihood the militants themselves would be excluded from this future if they were to be successful in their missions. These women, the explanation goes, have joined the LTTE as the actions of the Sri Lankan military and the Indian Peace Keeping Force (IPKF) between 1987 and 1990 destroyed the homes of civilian Tamils and targeted women for sexual violence.[6] That is to say, women joined the LTTE as 'Black Tigresses' because the Indian and the Sri Lankan States, through the actions of their military, broke down the boundary between private and public spheres which determines customary gender roles in Sri Lanka, and targeted women for specifically gendered forms of violence. It is the State's attempt to hyperfeminise women as victims of rape, destitution and abandonment that ironically propels them into militancy. Put differently, the vulnerability of women caused by the breakdown of patriarchal order becomes the enabling condition of their radicalisation.[7]

This is the narrative put forth by scholarly writing in both the West and Tamil pulp fiction. Adele Ann Balasingham, who, after her husband's death in December 2006, was seen as the LTTE's ideologue, negotiator and spokesperson abroad, makes a similar point:

> The forces of social constraint which had obstructed [Tamil women's] deeper participation earlier, had left them exposed and defenceless in the face of violent racist hatred and State terror. Deepening genocidal oppression now propelled them out of their established social life into a new revolutionary world. Young women broke the shackles of social constraints, they ripped open the straight [sic] jacket of conservative images of women. The militant patriotism of Tamil women finally blossomed as they entered into a new life of revolutionary armed struggle. (Balasingham 1993)

This narrative of women's agency is prevalent not only among the LTTE and its sympathisers, but also, with a distinctively different spin, in Sri Lankan, Indian and international media accounts, as well as in studies by political scientists like Mia Bloom (2005, 142–65). My point here is not that charges of sexual violence are unfounded. Rape, as we have seen in Bosnia and Rwanda, is a well-documented practice of ethnic warfare, and while human rights organisations have found it difficult to document the scale of sexual violence in Sri Lanka, they allege that both the Sri Lankan Army and the Indian Peace Keeping Force were implicated in such acts against the Tamil population.[8]

While Balasingham presents the disruption of established social life by state violence as a serendipitous opportunity that allows women's patriotism to 'blossom' (1993), many other commentators understand it as trauma leading to fatalism, in language that casts the women militants as victims trapped between an essentialised sexuality and a backward culture (Pape 2006).[9] For instance, in an article in the international women's magazine *Marie Claire*, amidst articles on fashion and exercise, we read, 'Rape is something many female suicide bombers have in common. Considered spoiled goods and unmarriageable in their patriarchal cultures, they view becoming human bombs as a form of purification by fire' (Goodwin 2018). Purification by fire or *agni pariksha*, it should be noted, is a powerful trope underwriting female sexual purity in Hindu mythology. Goodwin's invocation of this trope, like the LTTE's frequent references to fierce Hindu goddesses or Sangam poetry (*Puranaanooru*, c. 200 BCE–100 CE) celebrating the bravery of a Tamil mother who is joyous upon seeing her young son slain on the battlefield, paradoxically relies on traditional codes of femininity to justify or explain militant women's radical departure from those traditions.

What is important to note is that the centrality of sexual violence in these attempts to narrativise women's militancy demands of us a contradictory response of moral condemnation and compassion. In doing so, such narratives block an understanding of the heterogeneous sociological and economic causes that have drawn women to the LTTE and the effects their actions have had on Tamil society. Such effects can be seen in the divergent accounts offered by the young Tamil women that Cathrine Brun interviewed, who say: 'women will be brave after seeing [the women cadres of the LTTE]. After seeing them we feel we can do everything!' They also say that they themselves are not like the LTTE women: 'They won't go back to their families; their society is somewhat different from our society. . . . We are not ready to lose our culture' (Brun 2008, 416). Their testimonies present militant women as both heroes and outcasts, as models of valour and cautionary examples.

Santosh Sivan's film enters the thick of these contending explanatory narratives of women's involvement in the Sri Lankan Civil War. The film opens in a rain-soaked jungle as a traitor is being interrogated and condemned to die at the hands of the person who witnessed his betrayal. A point-blank execution takes place, and when the executioner takes off a blood-spattered mask we realise that it is a woman, who turns out to be the film's protagonist Malli. For viewers of the DVD, this scene has already been presented proleptically in the introduction to the main menu where we are shown Malli washing her blood-stained mask in a river. As the camera closes in on her distressed face, it is transformed to a graphic image of a demonic face as the ambient sounds of the jungle morph into the characteristic screech of a horror film soundtrack (Sivan 2000). The same reversal of expectations occurs at the level of diegesis, in the film's layered repetition of acts of violence and compassion, and in its contradictory evocation of sympathy and horror. In the process, the film both underwrites and undoes the codes by which femininity is commonly presented in Indian films to emphasise male desire, maternal nurturance and responsibility to one's family.[10]

Feminine Masquerade and Sexual Dissonance

Sivan's film initially unsettles gender norms in its androgynous representation of the female militants, and simultaneously plays up Malli's treacherous masquerade of femininity in her covert mission. In the Sri Lankan sections of the film, Malli's masquerade is multidimensional and the film foregrounds both the admiration she generates and the sexual danger she poses in this role. Here, she is dressed in drab, loose-fitting clothes; she rarely smiles and looks directly at the camera with an intensity that withholds all promise of the pleasures of feminine spectacle that is typical fare in Indian cinema. Her character is cast as relentlessly unfeminine in other ways as well: in each of the three scenes where she kills a man, she is up close to her victim, and is presented as a coldblooded and excessively violent killer. In her initial interactions with Surya, aka Lotus, a young boy who serves as her scout in Sri Lanka, she is brusquely direct in her words and awkward when she tries to comfort him; she unabashedly tells her curious host in India that she can neither sing nor cook. She is thus presented as someone about whom there is nothing feminine. But when she has to cross a checkpoint, she dons a revealing costume that projects a docile, rustic feminine image, which exemplifies Amit Rai's analysis of the residual effects of Orientalism in representations of terrorists. Rai locates the figure of the contemporary Islamic terrorist within a genealogy of monstrosity in which the figure of the Oriental despot holds a prominent place (Rai 2004, 539, 548). Focusing on the dynamic of othering that structures this genealogy, Rai traces the discursive logic by which the murderous terrorist is seen as the result of the failure of 'a narrative space centered on the biopolitical apparatus of normalized domestic desire and kinship supposedly common in the West' (546). Even though Sivan focuses on the entirely different figure of the Sri Lankan terrorist, when the film highlights Malli's pointed rejection of the gender norms of the bourgeois heterosexual family it taps into the discursive structures Rai delineates. In the scene where she sheds her androgynously Western clothes and carefully puts on jewellery and clothing associated with the clichéd figure of a South Asian village belle, Malli cuts a striking figure of primitive, feminine docility in the middle of an emphatically modern scene of warfare. Malli's feminine masquerade occurs again when she arrives at the venue of her planned suicide mission. In these moments, the film orchestrates a volatile tension between what is presented as authentic interiority – of a committed anti-state militant in the first instance and a young woman experiencing the pull of maternal, nurturing love in the second – and a duplicitous masquerade of femininity. In the segments set in India, this tension is directed both at the representatives of the enemy state and the male handlers who share Malli's separatist loyalties.

Drawing upon Joan Riviere's foundational 1929 essay, "Womanliness as a Masquerade", Judith Butler addresses the implications of feminine masquerade in the context of patriarchal gender arrangements when she points out that it is often quite likely that 'the woman in masquerade wishes for masculinity in order to engage in public discourse with men and as a man as part of a male homoerotic exchange' (1990, 52). Mary Ann Doane's discussion of Riviere's ideas goes further to suggest that women often conceal this wish through a masquerade of hyperfemininity that transforms their transgressive desire, and the resulting fear of punishment, into seduction and flirtation (1982, 81). We have seen how women's participation in armed conflict provokes anxiety over their violation of gender roles and calls forth explanatory narratives that recast them insistently as women, albeit provoked to violence by their victimisation. Nevertheless, women's involvement in all-female combat units such as the Black Tigresses of the LTTE is bound to evoke fears of a femininity outside the heterosexual matrix, and a sexuality insubordinate to masculine desire.

The film introduces this issue early on, before Malli is selected for her mission. In a scene that pushes beyond what Adrienne Rich (1986) has called the lesbian continuum, a fellow soldier, Sumithra, express nothing short of romantic love for Malli, though it is cloaked in the language of inspiration that borders on spirit possession.[11] Her declaration, 'Malli, if only you were a man I would certainly have married you', is cut short by the sound of gunfire as if to severely reassert the heterosexual norm, and the scene shifts immediately to a pitched gun battle between soldiers and the guerrillas that ends with Malli searching out and shooting a soldier point blank. This and other scenes of homosociality that verge on homoeroticism show that the life of the female soldiers is not devoid of comfort or pleasure. In this, Sivan's film is joined by documentaries like the BBC's 'Suicide Warriors' (1996), in which we get multiple shots of the LTTE women doing their ablutions – washing their hands and feet, brushing their teeth, and combing each other's hair – as if to underscore the organisation's strict code of hygiene and chastity as well as to highlight the macabre irony of grooming bodies for death (*Inside Story* 1991).[12] In these instances, *The Terrorist* stays close to the conventions of South Asian films which, as Gayatri Gopinath (2005) has shown, repeatedly stage the dependence of national identity on the disciplining and controlling of women's sexuality within the rubric of heteronormativity.

Sivan's film likewise makes it clear through its starkly differentiated representation of Malli in the jungle and Malli at home that homoerotic bonds between the women soldiers are an abnormal effect of the suspension of traditional family structures during wartime when the rebels are forced to seek comfort in one another. The ensuing dissonant pleasure in the warzone is not allowed to last in the film's diegetic space, though, for Sumithra is soon killed in a gun battle and Malli is sent off on her mission. In a series of repeated flashbacks, we learn that sometime before Malli leaves on her mission, she spends a night of furtive passion in a ditch with a male comrade, whose capture and death shortly thereafter is the backstory to the film's opening scene of the point-blank execution by Malli. The film seals its displacement of homoerotic attachments by the heterosexual union when Malli comes to believe that she is pregnant.

The film begins its process of rehabilitating Malli into normative femininity when she leaves the world of destroyed families and deviant bonds of affection between women in Sri Lanka for Tamil Nadu, India, where she briefly experiences the calm routine of domestic order in a society that shares the language and culture of her native land. In the household of Vasu, a farmer, Malli's gradual integration into femininity is signalled by scenes where she shares meals with him, scenes that provide a striking contrast to the martyr's meal she has with the leader of the militants before her departure on her mission. She is shown to be gradually drawn into a domestic space secured by set daily routines, devotional music, food rituals and photographs alluding to a world beyond the confines of her life as a militant. The resulting tension between Malli's commitment to her mission and her involvement in Vasu's family is pushed to a crisis by her suspected pregnancy, and she is ostensibly set on a course of 'moral and emotional awakening' in a 'functional and lived culture' centred on conventions of authentic feminine deportment and maternal feeling (Pandit 2003, 96).

The threat that the masquerade of militant masculinity poses is signalled and controlled by Malli's recuperation into patriarchal family structures in the several instances where she shows pride and pleasure at being repeatedly identified by the male militants as the daughter of a revolutionary poet and the sister of one of the earliest martyrs to the cause. The masquerade of hyperfemininity in these instances is different from the obviously deceitful spectacle of femininity she mounts at the checkpoint in Sri Lanka and in Vasu's home. Rather, her hyperfemininity takes the form of her docile acquiescence to her duty as daughter and sister. The inner crisis precipitated by her later belief that she is pregnant becomes, for the viewer, another instance of compensatory hyperfemininity, this time activated by Sivan's narrative manoeuvre. Butler (1990) argues that attention to the masquerade of femininity can become a way of acknowledging the contradictions of women's gender performance as reinforcing and resisting gender norms. But the film redirects such an acknowledgement by overlaying Malli's taciturnity with the voluble efforts of the men around her to valorise her motives within the normative framework of the heteronormative, patriarchal family through their repeated invocations of her nationalist father and brother.

Melodrama and the Maternal Body

Even as the film markedly departs from the conventions of mainstream Indian film, it reverts back to the melodramatic narrative convention of a tragic or scandalous pregnancy resulting from a single, unexpected sexual encounter, and presents repeated shots of Malli's drenched body in visual echoes of the stock Bollywood convention of the 'wet sari sequence' (Figure 7.1). But since Sivan takes pains to ensure that there is nothing revealing, titillating, or conventionally sexy in the wet Malli scenes, it could be argued that he activates and blocks the promise of voyeuristic pleasure that operates in mainstream Indian film in ways that make us uncomfortably aware of the dangerous potential of feminine masquerade. One thing is clear: despite the sympathy Sivan shows for the cause of the Tamils by frequently conveying in the film their various justifications for the conflict, he is troubled by the way it can reconfigure sexual desire, especially given his professional investment as a cinematographer and director who has made his name and fortune by staging femininity for the male gaze.[13]

Drawing attention to the masquerade repeatedly, then, becomes the film's way of acknowledging and undercutting women's agency when they strategically perform femininity. We can recognise this in the two scenes where we see Malli explicitly playing at being a woman: in the first to get through a checkpoint and in the second to get close to the 'leader' who is her target. An important clarification is in order at this point: within the diegesis of the film, Malli's feminine masquerade is a simple and effective strategy in a world where political violence is seen as an overwhelmingly male arena of activity. However,

Figure 7.1 A close-up of Malli's face as she is bathing.

as Judith Butler explains, the woman who sustains masculine identification and dons femininity as a mask both refuses and 'hyperbolically incorporate[es]' the female Other in 'an odd form of preserving and protecting that love [for the female Other] within the circle of melancholic and negative narcissism that results from the psychic inculcation of compulsory heterosexuality' (1990, 53). The melancholia that attends Malli's masquerade is exacerbated by the proliferation of montage sequences from her life as a soldier in the jungle and flashbacks made up of long shots of Malli by the river near the militant camp in the jungle. These moments repeatedly interrupt scenes of domestic calm in the second half of the film and return us to her prior androgynous identity as well as to the scene of the sexual encounter that she believes has led to her pregnancy. The tension set up between Malli's private belief in her impending motherhood and public performances of hyperfemininity as a suicide bomber in training is further complicated by her growing attraction to the bourgeois family life offered by Vasu. As Malli grows closer to Padmavati, Vasu's wife who has fallen into a catatonic state ever since she heard news of her son's death, the film foregrounds Malli's internal identification as an agonised mother who is drawn to contemplating and refusing the loss of the object of her love, the baby she believes she carries within her. Malli's maternal identification creates a melancholia, musically underscored in the film, in which she mournfully internalises her position of militant motherhood as a prohibition.

Furthermore, in choosing maternity as the plot twist that would throw into disarray the ideological commitment of the suicide bomber, Sivan is tapping into the contradictory but powerful trope of motherhood in the discourse of Sri Lankan Tamil militancy. Adele Balasingham locates the women tigers of Tamil Eelam in the glorious tradition of 'selfless, sacrificing mothers' in early Tamil literature (1993). Motherhood is constructed within this tradition as symbolising sacrifice and self-effacement, and martyrdom is put forth as the fullest realisation of these ideals (Bloom 2007, 102). The masquerade of pregnancy has also been a tried and tested strategy for women suicide bombers. In April 2006, a suicide bomber posing as the wife of a soldier on her way to the maternity clinic managed to gain entry into a military hospital in Colombo (Bloom 2007, 95). The explosive vest worn by Rajiv Gandhi's assassin Dhanu also apparently led onlookers to believe that she was pregnant. In Sivan's film, Lotus, the young boy who guides Malli through the forest in Sri Lanka gradually activates maternal instincts in Malli even before she reaches Vasu's household. But as a child who participates in the armed rebellion, he is complexly coded. Children, in representations of terrorism, are the ultimate signifiers of the innocence of terrorism's victims, but Lotus is both perpetrator and victim, the cunning scout who can lead Malli through a minefield but who also childishly refers to the mines as apples. His account to Malli of the circumstances that drew him into the movement, told against a background score of the Carnatic raga of lullaby, juxtaposes a childhood destroyed by the state and a childhood reaffirmed momentarily in a chance encounter with a woman terrorist. In this, Sivan draws attention, with sympathy, to the militarisation of childhood that has been an important strategy through which the LTTE wins the hearts and minds of Sri Lankan Tamils.

Significantly, however, Sivan insists that the film presents Malli's dilemma as she *comes to believe* she may be pregnant. 'Please don't think that the story is about a pregnant girl. She is not actually pregnant', he reassures an interviewer with a caution that suggests that even a fictional representation of a pregnant suicide bomber is too horrific and scandalous for contemplation (Sivan 1997). The pregnancy then, is a ruse to make 'Malli think'. As Sivan tells us in his interview 'when she starts thinking, a change takes place inside her and she wants to run away, leaving everything' (Sivan 1997). In other words, when Malli is a soldier, she blindly follows orders or is swept away by militant rhetoric. When she comes to believe that she may be pregnant, her thinking self takes over, and her interiority gives her an autonomy unavailable to her previously masquerading self. However, Malli's 'thinking' is triggered and sustained by Vasu's repeated talks on motherhood and new life. We have known for some time now that when gender is constructed as an interior essence, 'that very interiority is an effect and function of . . . the public regulation of discourse through the surface politics of the body' (Butler 1990, 136). That is, Malli learns maternal feeling the same way she learns the proper way to fold a banana leaf after a meal: from Vasu. Despite the film's melodramatic portrayal of her perceived pregnancy, Malli's maternal thinking is also revealed to be no more original or authentic than her military thinking.

What the film offers, then, is a contradictory mix of historical fact, fiction, ethnographic detail and filmic convention that Talal Asad identifies in representations of suicide bombers. Equally, the film illustrates the barriers that block an understanding of a suicide bomber's interiority since, as I have pointed out, Sivan explicitly presents Malli's apparently pregnant body not in the spectacular realm of masquerade but as a secret, interior and private space of memory and longing. In the second part of the film, as flashbacks show her brief sexual encounter with a wounded militant, they are interspersed by heavily symbolic scenes where Malli hears the cry of an infant in her dreams, picks up a stranger's baby at a temple, and grieves over a nest blown to the ground by a thunderstorm. The disruptive diegetic and connotative codes of the first half give way to standard family melodrama in the sections set in India. Vasu, who has been telling Malli that his son is away on a photographic mission, confesses that his son has been dead for seven years. Malli, in turn, tells him that her baby's father is dead. Vasu joyfully reassures her that he will be the child's grandfather. At the same time, Malli's handlers (who are unaware of the suspected pregnancy) visit her regularly and train her for her mission, invoking her duty to their cause, to the martyrs who have shed their blood before her, and reminding her of her brother's sacrifice for the homeland. Through them, the deviant family structures of the separatists continue to disrupt Malli's full integration into the joys and comforts of the heterosexual and patriarchal family.

Sivan may well be aware of the intense pressure built up around these contrary understandings of familial ties, as the film's ending shows. The ending, which Sivan calls 'open', is prefigured in one of Malli's practice sessions when she hesitates to push the bomb's trigger button and the screen momentarily blacks out, as if to show her imagining her end. At the film's conclusion, Malli goes up to her target, garlands him, and as she bends down to touch his feet, she reaches for the trigger button. Just as her thumb flexes over the button, the screen goes blank, but a second later we are returned to Malli, her thumb still flexed over the button. This sequence is repeated three more times, and the third interval of blank screen lasts a little longer than before, and just as we think she has done it, we are returned to her hand, thumb still flexed over the button, a flower petal from the garland resting on her palm. The screen goes blank, and the credits start rolling. We may read this moment as showing Malli's inability to go through with the assassination.

Contrarily, the drifting petals take us back to an earlier moment in the film when Malli, a little girl, is standing by her dead brother's funeral bier, and as petals showered on him fall on her as well, she is exhorted to be brave and courageous like her brother. While the critical consensus about the ending is that Malli does not go through with her mission, what is more interesting to me is the movement, which would be teasing if it were not so macabre, shifting back and forth between annihilation and affirmation of life. Viewers are pulled between the fear that Malli would destroy the life of her target along with her own and that of her imagined unborn baby, and the hope that she would refuse the mission, thereby saving herself and her unborn baby but betraying the nationalist expectations of her comrades. What is powerfully staged is an oscillation between the mother who is a source of life and the mother who is the instrument of death. The stakes involved in this movement recall Freud's famous account of his grandson's fort/da game in his *Beyond the Pleasure Principle*. The game, Freud concludes,

> was connected with the child's remarkable cultural achievement – the foregoing of the satisfaction of an instinct – as the result of which he could let his mother go away without making a fuss. He made it right with himself, so to speak, by dramatising the [mother's] disappearance and return. (1922, 13)

We could say that the film's ending, too, plays out and makes right a generalised cultural anxiety about women's insurgency, which takes an overdetermined form in the discourses of maternity that circulate around the Sri Lankan Tamil insurgency. The narrative movement of the film, from its opening scene to its final shot, oscillates between absence and return in a way that establishes symbolic control over upheavals on the gender front that ask us to re-consider something that has been taken as a cornerstone of civilisation itself: the maternal body.[14]

In conclusion, as a useful point of contrast to the maternal body that Sivan presents, one may turn to the narratives of members of the Sri Lankan Mothers' Front that was formed in response to the 'reign of terror' in the late 1980s and early 1990s when thousands of young men disappeared. These activist mothers offer valuable counternarratives to official accounts of that period as they express rage for what was done to their sons and husbands, and also convey their tentative emergence as citizens, activists, leaders and organisers who are able to take on the state and rebuild their lives and their community. What they say over and over again is that being embroiled in violence, as victims or perpetrators, and working through their pain and guilt has altered their sense of who they are as citizens and what they can do for their community.[15] In their narratives one senses an important if muted discursive shift. In a world where violence is still seen to be a male prerogative, female violence has to justify its violation of the social order precisely in terms of that order's cultural values. Narratives like Sivan's seek to set aright the unbalancing of gender roles brought about by female militancy by trying to re-impose those self-same roles. Their anxious focus on violence's implication for gender arrangements forestalls whatever political intervention they may set out to achieve. The genius of the Mothers' Front in Sri Lanka, as elsewhere, is that in taking a stand against violence, women end up remapping the social imaginary and their position within it.[16]

Notes

1. David Deamer (2016) argues that this effect is produced on the viewer through the film's organising aesthetic of the closeup that conveys Malli's affective perceptions and its intensities.
2. These moments evoke the full resonance of Jasbir Puar's (2007, 216–20) elaboration of the 'body-weapon' which presents an intimate dissolution of the distinction between body and bomb, agent and instrument of destruction. Adriana Cavarero (2009) suggests that when this weapon is a female body, it is 'always, symbolically, a maternal body' that is 'the most repugnant core of the contemporary horrorist picture' (103, 99).
3. 'Suicide Warriors' was broadcast on 15 August 1996 on Channel 4 as part of the series *Black Bag*. It is important to note that Thiruchelvam played a role in trying to bring about a peaceful resolution to the conflict and was himself tragically assassinated by a suicide bomber.
4. See for instance, Cronin-Furman and Arulthas, 'How the Tigers Got Their Stripes: A Case Study of the LTTE's Rise to Power' (2021).

5. As the clearest example of this line of thinking, Enloe cites the legal brief filed by the National Organization of Women at the US Supreme Court in March 1981 in support of a challenge to a military registration law that applied exclusively to men. The brief claimed that the law 'perpetuated US women's second-class citizenship' (Enloe 1983, 237).
6. Cathrine Brun (2008) cites Adele and Anton Balasingham, who were influential spokespersons for the LTTE, as well as the young people she interviewed in northern Sri Lanka as holding this position.
7. For a discussion of this process in the Palestinian context, see Mohan (1998).
8. As Shahin Kachwala (2013) argues, nationalist discourses parallel the rape of the female body with the destruction of the community or nation and, in doing so, make visible the assertion of patriarchal power over women and the communities with which they are identified.
9. Pape (2006, 226–7) claims that Rajiv Gandhi's assassin Dhanu was a remarkably beautiful woman who was driven by desire to avenge the harm she suffered at the hands of the Indian soldiers (4 of her brothers were killed in the conflict, her home in Jaffna was looted, and she was gang-raped). According to Mia Bloom (2005, 160), she was avenging her mother's rape by the IPKF. See also *Kanavukku Veliyeyana ulaku: Tamililap Penkalin Cirukataikal* (2002). Many stories in this anthology identify rape as the primal trauma that propels women into militancy.
10. Ghaznavi, Grasso, and Taylor (2017) offer a comprehensive account of the enduring representation of women as objects of male desire in Indian films. For an account of the tradition in Indian film which presents women as nurturers who value their family responsibilities over all else, see Sharpe (2005).
11. Rich uses the term 'lesbian continuum' in her article, 'Compulsory Heterosexuality and Lesbian Existence', to address erotically charged homosocial bonds between women in a way that does not give a central and defining importance to sexual encounters. In an afterword to the essay, published six years after its initial publication, she clarifies that the term came 'from a desire to allow for the greatest possible variation of female-identified experience, while paying a different kind of respect to lesbian existence —the traces and knowledge of women who have made their primary and erotic and emotional choices for women' (1986, 73–4).
12. For an insightful discussion of the complicated play of necropower in the film, see Dillon (2009, 209–26).
13. Sivan has been an acclaimed cinematographer and director in Hindi, Tamil and Malayalam films since 1986. Among his many hits are *Dil Se* (1998), *Fiza* (2000) and *Asoka* (2001).
14. For an exploration of a similarly anxious preoccupation around women's bodies in the US after 11 September 2001, see Faludi (2007).
15. Malathi de Alwis (2009) offers a detailed and nuanced account of the 'contingent articulations of maternalized agonism' (84–5) of the Mothers' Front, and explores the challenges faced by Sri Lankan feminists and peace activists seeking to support the movement and prevent its co-optation.
16. For an account and analysis of women's actions and testimonies, see de Mel (2007).

References

Asad, Talal. 2007. *On Suicide Bombing*. New York: Columbia University Press.
Balasingham, Adele Ann. 1993. *Women Fighters of Liberation Tigers*. Jaffna, Sri Lanka: LTTE International.
Black Bag. 1996. "Suicide Warriors." Aired August 15, 1996, on Channel 4.
Bloom, Mia. 2005. *Dying to Kill: The Allure of Suicide Terrorism*. New York: Columbia University Press.
Bloom, Mia. 2007. "Female Suicide Bombers: A Global Trend." *Daedalus* 136, no. 1: 94–102.
Brannan, David W., Philip F. Esler and N. T. Anders Strindberg. 2001. "Talking to 'Terrorists': Towards an Independent Analytical Framework for the Study of Violent Substate Activism." *Studies in Conflict & Terrorism* 24, no. 1: 3–24.
Brun, Cathrine. 2008. "Birds of Freedom: Young People, the LTTE, and Representations of Gender, Nationalism and Governance in Northern Sri Lanka." *Critical Asian Studies* 40, no. 3: 399–422.
Butler, Judith. 1990. *Gender Trouble: Feminism and the Subversion of Identity*. New York: Routledge.
Cavarero, Adriana. 2009. *Horrorism: Naming Contemporary Violence*. Trans. William McCuaig. New York: Columbia University Press.
Cronin-Furman, Kate, and Mario Arulthas. 2021. "How the Tigers Got Their Stripes: A Case Study of the LTTE's Rise to Power." *Studies in Conflict and Terrorism*. https://doi.org/10.1080/1057610X.2021.2013753
de Alwis, Malathi. 2009. "Interrogating the 'Political': Feminist Peace Activism in Sri Lanka." *Feminist Review* 91, no. 1: 81–93.
de Mel, Neloufer. 2001. *Women and the Nation's Narrative: Gender and Nationalism in Twentieth Century Sri Lanka*. New York: Rowman & Littlefield.
de Mel, Neloufer. 2007. "The Promise of the Archive: Memory, Testimony and Feminist Domains." In *Militarizing Sri Lanka: Popular Culture, Memory and Narrative in the Armed Conflict*, 246–95. Los Angeles: Sage Publications.
Dillon, Mike. 2009. "'Patriotism and Valor Are in Your Blood': Necropolitical Subjectivities in *The Terrorist* (1999)." *Studies in South Asian Film and Media* 1, no. 2: 209–26.
Deamer, David. 2016. "*Theeviravaathi/The Terrorist*: Icon." In *Deleuze's Cinema Books: Three Introductions to the Taxonomy of Images*, 189–92. Edinburgh: Edinburgh University Press.
Doane, Mary Ann. 1982. "Film and the Masquerade: Theorizing the Female Spectator." *Screen* 23, nos 3–4: 74–88.
Enloe, Cynthia. 1983. *Does Khaki Become You?: The Militarization of Women's Lives*. Boston: South End Press.
Faludi, Susan. 2007. *The Terror Dream*. New York: Metropolitan Press.
Freud, Sigmund. 1922. *Beyond the Pleasure Principle*. Trans. C. J. M. Hubback. London: The International Psycho-Analytical Press.
Ghaznavi, Jannath, Katherine L. Grasso and Laramie D. Taylor. 2017. "Increasingly Violent but Still Sexy: A Decade of Central Female Characters in Top-Grossing Hollywood and Bollywood Film Promotional Material." *International Journal of Communication* 11: 23–47.

Goodwin, Jan. 2018. "When the Suicide Bomber Is a Woman." *Marie Claire*, January 16, 2018. https://www.marieclaire.com/politics/news/a717/female-suicide-bomber/

Gopinath, Gayatri. 2005. *Impossible Desires: Queer Diasporas and South Asian Public Cultures*. Durham: Duke University Press.

Inside Story. 1991. "Suicide Killers." Aired October 23, 1991, on BBC One.

Kachwala, Shahin. 2013. "The Body of the Nation?: Female Suicide Bombers and Derivative Agency in Mani Ratnam's *Dil Se* and Santosh Sivan's *The Terrorist*." *Journal of Postcolonial Cultures and Societies* 4, no. 1: 201–32.

Kanavukku Veliyeyana ulaku: Tamililap Penkalin Cirukataikal, 2002. Tamililam, Sri Lanka: Kaptan Vanati Veliyittakam.

Mohan, Rajeswari. 1998. "Feminism, Marginality, and Political Praxis: Leila Khaled's Subversive Bodily Acts." *Interventions* 1, no. 1: 52–80.

Pandit, Lalita. 2003. "Inside the Mind of a Suicide Bomber: Santosh Sivan's *The Terrorist*." In *Understanding Terrorism: Threats in an Uncertain World*, eds Akorlie A. Nyatepe-Coo and Dorothy Zeisler-Vralsted, 91–111. Upper Saddle River, NJ: Prentice Hall.

Pape, Robert Anthony. 2006. *Dying to Win: The Strategic Logic of Suicide Terrorism*. New York: Random House Trade Paperbacks.

Puar, Jasbir K. 2007. *Terrorist Assemblages: Homonationalism in Queer Times*. Durham: Duke University Press.

Rai, Amit S. 2004. "Of Monsters: Biopower, Terrorism ad Excess in Genealogies of Monstrosity." *Cultural Studies* 18, no. 4: 538–70.

Rich, Adrienne. 1986. "Compulsory Heterosexuality and Lesbian Existence." In *Blood, Bread and Poetry: Selected Prose 1979-1985*, 23–75. New York: W.W. Norton & Company.

Sharpe, Jenny. 2005. "Gender, Nation, and Globalization in *Monsoon Wedding* and *Dilwale Dulhania Le Jayenge*." *Meridians* 6, no. 1: 58–81.

Sivan, Santosh. Interview by Shobha Warrier. *Rediff*, December 5, 1997. "The Unmaking of a Terrorist." http://www.rediff.com/entertai/dec/05ter.htm

Sivan, Santosh, dir. 2000. *The Terrorist*, 1998. India: Wonderfilms. DVD.

8. THE FEMALE COUNTER-STRIKE: TERRORISING PATRIARCHY IN HINDI CINEMA

Harald Pittel

Introduction: Gender-Based Violence in a Terrorist Frame

Terrorism has become a recurring theme in Indian cinema. This development is very much in tune with the world-wide emergence, since the mid-1990s, of a 'new cinematic terrorism' responding to global forms of political violence (Shaw 2015, 185–6). But terrorism can also be understood as a characteristically Indian concern. More specifically, the emergence of cinematic terrorism reflects India's increased exposure to terrorist incidents since the 1980s, with the 1993 'Bombay bombings' and the surrounding events leaving an especially deep mark on the national imaginary (198). The surge of representations of terrorism in Indian film might also be symptomatic of a broader cultural tendency to showcase extreme brutality, cinematic terrorism being only one of its mediatised forms (Bannerji 2016, 3–7). The rise of spectacular depictions of violence in Indian visual media can be said to respond specifically to the society from which they emerge. It is unclear, though, if and to what extent such depictions contribute to serious discussions of the deeper causes underlying terrorism, or if they have a distorting effect on society by virtue of misrepresenting complex and often sensitive issues (3).

Among these issues is gender-based violence in India, a problem widely discussed in the country and abroad. These debates intensified in the wake of the death of Jyoti Singh in December 2012. A twenty-three-year-old medical student in New Delhi, Singh was beaten, tortured, and gang-raped on a private bus and died eleven days later. The repeated occurrence of such incidents calls for an investigation of the deeper social reasons for misogyny, structural discrimination, oppression, sexual harassment and violence against women and girls. While the problem is often downplayed as being over-represented by 'detailed and frequent reporting', critical commentators insist that the wider issue is evidently patriarchy, deeply anchored in traditional family-oriented social structures and typically safeguarded by corrupt institutions, all closely related to an aggressive neoliberal capitalism (Bannerji 2016, 3–7). More and more people are beginning to realise that respecting women's lives and securing their rights is hardly possible without undergoing a deeper process of societal transformation. However, such change is barely at hand, especially considering the cultural and political dominance of the governing far-right Hindu-nationalist Bharatiya Janata Party (BJP), which is known for undermining democratic institutions and processes as well as cementing traditional models of family and gender (Widmalm 2019). Official measures to improve the situation of Indian women typically reinforce ideas around purity and motherliness, evoking a conservative ideal of femininity as essentially to be protected. Yet paternalistic practices of 'caging' women 'reek not of care but of control' as they tend to exclude women from the public sphere – for their own good, as it were (Krishnan 2021). It is thus crucial to insist that any suggestions for taking action against gender-based violence, and the public discourses influencing such approaches, should not go uncontested; rather, they should be openly discussed and critically analysed, as many of these measures have a dark side.

Popular media like mainstream cinema might reinforce traditional mindsets, but they might also provide cues to reconfigure or even overcome them. Hence, studying products of popular culture is by no means of marginal significance. In general terms, mainstream cinema must be taken seriously as a major factor in establishing and maintaining ways of seeing, be they dominant, alternative or even oppositional. By the same token, popular films often capture the 'structure of feeling' of a specific historical situation, offering revealing insights into a group or nation's collective consciousness at the very moment that a crucial reconfiguration of the dominant outlook is in progress (Williams 1977, 121–7; Simpson 1995, 39).

Recent Hindi films like *Pink* (2016), *Soni* (2018) or *The Rapist* (2021) offer complex analyses of Indian patriarchy and draw on contemporary discussions of structurally conditioned violence. By contrast, the most popular depictions of gender-based violence in Hindi cinema tend to succumb to the fascination of the spectacle and in particular show a notable interest in the theme of terrorism. This chapter looks at three such blockbusters: *Neerja* (Madhvani 2016), *Tiger Zinda Hai* (Zafar 2017), and *Simmba* (Shetty 2018) illustrate common distortions in the discourse surrounding gender-based violence and patriarchy in India. More specifically, these high-grossing films share a peculiar representational strategy that constructs the patriarchal predicament in analogy to terrorism. This becomes most obvious in the way they cast terrorism as a metaphor for violence against women. At the same time, the films use terrorism-related tropes to dramatise female resistance to such violence, a scenario that I will describe as the 'female counter-strike'.

The analogy between terrorism and gender-based violence is not an invention of the films discussed in this chapter. Note for instance Rachel Pain's (2014) influential understanding of domestic violence as 'everyday terrorism'. Pain maintains that domestic violence should be grasped as a form of terrorism given that it relies on instilling fear to impose or disrupt an existing order (536). She adds that domestic violence is often more successful than political terrorism in generating fear for the purposes of power and control (540). Yet political terrorism is given much more attention than domestic violence, which is often tabooed and barred from articulation (542). Conceiving of domestic violence (mostly directed against women) as a form of terrorism might thus raise public awareness of this issue.

Such a representational strategy might seem particularly inviting in the Indian context. However, the three films under discussion here show that the comparison of terrorism and gender-based violence is fraught with ideological pitfalls. Not only does the analogy tend to exalt female suffering to mythical dimensions, it also shows little faith in democratic institutions by constructing female resistance as counter-terrorist self-entitlement. As I hope to demonstrate, representing female suffering and resistance as analogous to counterterrorism ultimately helps to reinforce rather than destabilise patriarchal structures.

Background: Terrorism in India and Cinematic Responses

Armed insurgencies have played a crucial role throughout Indian history, even though they were repressed or side-lined from dominant national narratives for a long time. The trajectory that led up to Indian independence in 1947 was by no means as 'non-violent' as official accounts attuned to M. K. Gandhi's leading ideal would have it, and armed struggles continued to play a major role in postcolonial India (Mehta 2018, 114–18). The shift of power from the British Empire to the newly founded states of India and Pakistan – the so-called Partition – not only entailed mass prosecutions and resettlements, but also failed to determine the status of the Kashmir region. Thus, it created a terrain in which the contestation of political power has been paired for decades with, on the one hand, civil-rights infringements under Indian hegemony, and, on the other hand, anti-Indian assaults, hijackings and assassinations partly supported by Pakistan (Mehta 2018, 120; Hingorani 2016, 63–93). However, Kashmir was not the only breeding ground for terrorism, and in many other areas in and around India, such as Punjab and Sri Lanka, secession movements and anti-Hindu insurgencies kept challenging the authority of the post-independence federal state. During the 1980s, this resulted in complicated tensions, culminating in the subsequent murders of two Indian Prime Ministers, Indira and Rajiv Gandhi, which effectively transformed terrorism into an issue of national relevance (Mehta 2018, 118–24).

Yet it was mainly the Kashmir conflict that was to shape the cultural meanings around terrorism after the Cold War in India. Islamic mujahideen fighters who had fought against the Soviet invasion of Afghanistan now turned against the USA, which had trained and supported them; this also led to the formation of al-Qaeda (Mehta 2018, 110–14). With Pakistani support many mujahideen fighters became involved in the Kashmir conflict, to which India responded by installing more and more army posts in the region (Mehta 2018, 110–11; Hiro 2012, 71–114, 135–53). The conflict was lifted to a global level after 9/11, with both Pakistan and India joining the US-led 'war on terror'; however, this development did not effectively settle the Kashmir conflict.

It is the dominant Indian perspective on that conflict which chiefly interests us here. While both states showed ambitions to become global economic and political actors, in India this development coincided with the rise of political 'Hindutva' (Hindu nationalism) with a strong anti-Muslim bias. This resulted in the strengthening of the extreme-right Bharatya Janata Party (BJP) as a dominant political and cultural force (Mehta 2018, 113–14), and they eventually became the ruling party in India between 1998 and 2004. They were re-elected in 2014 and remain in power at present. The surge of nationalism amplified the public discourse around terrorism, which increasingly focused on Kashmir, constructing the enduring crisis in that region as an existential threat to the Indian nation, often paired with strong anti-Muslim rhetoric. The two major terrorist incidents in this period – the 'Bombay bombings' of 1993, and the hijacking of an Indian aircraft in 1999 – were directly related to the Kashmir conflict and triggered massive military retaliations from the Indian state (Mehta 2018, 124–6).

It is against the historical background of India and Pakistan newly inventing themselves as actors on the global stage that a specifically Indian nationalist discourse around terrorism has proliferated. This discourse is marked by anxieties regarding the stability and vulnerability of the nation, the image of the latter shifting ambiguously between either the democratic state or a more mythical, Hindu-centred community. The propagandistic exploitation of such anxieties relies on medial repetitions of traumatic images of the nation under threat, and it is only fitting, therefore, that Indian cinema, and in particular Mumbai-based Hindi cinema, picked up terrorism as a major theme in the 1990s. First introduced by regional films like Mani Ratnam's *Roja* (1992) from Tamil Nadu, a state much exposed to violent insurgencies and secession movements throughout its history, cinematic representations of terrorism soon moved from the cultural and geographic margins to the national centre, where they became a staple Bollywood theme (Ahmed 2015, 189–90).

Generally speaking, Hindi cinema has a much greater impact on the Indian national imaginary than regional films in other languages. Accordingly, terrorist-themed films like *Border* (1997) or *The Hero: Love Story of a Spy* (2003) are blatantly jingoistic. They celebrate the strength of the Indian army and justify uncompromising brutality against people that they straightforwardly vilify as terrorists (Ahmed 2015, 189). At the same time, however, Bollywood has also adopted a contrary tendency which seeks to question binary oppositions such as 'us versus them', 'good versus evil', or 'Hindu versus Muslim', often tending to humanise terrorists to a considerable extent to make their actions appear psychologically plausible (Richter 2009). This emotionally empathetic outlook has given rise to the figure of the female terrorist, early instances of which can be found in Santosh Sivan's *The Terrorist* or Ratnam's *Dil Se* (both 1998).

The films discussed in what follows are somewhat different from the examples mentioned so far. As I will demonstrate, Hindi blockbusters like *Neerja*, *Tiger Zinda Hai* and *Simmba* tend to make more specific use of terrorism as a metaphorical lens for addressing the precarious situation of Indian women. Partly facilitated by Bollywood's enormous output of terrorism-related films since the 1990s, the respective media discourse in India employs the imagery and vocabulary of terrorism as a ubiquitous set of tropes, not only to vilify political dissidents, but also to dramatise all kinds of polarising issues, including human trafficking, the drug trade and violence against women (Ahmad 2014; Harindranath 2014; Simon 2002, 19–20; Taneja 2021; Wahab 2020). The labelling of such crimes as 'terrorism' may help to raise public attention; at the same time, however, it may also lead to the stifling of debates about the best way to deal with these issues: extreme counter-violence, often at the cost of legality, would typically offer itself as the indisputably 'right' response (Lakoff 2001). The examples of *Neerja*, *Tiger Zinda Hai*, and *Simmba* illustrate that Bollywood draws on terrorism not only to condemn violence against women, but also to aestheticise female *resistance* against such violence. The implications of this representational strategy are highly ambivalent and problematic: female resistance is couched as a struggle against those perceived as 'other' to the national collective, which leaves patriarchy at 'home' unmarked, thus effectively helping to keep it in place.

A Modernised Mother India: *Neerja*

Based on an actual terrorist aircraft hijacking, *Neerja* (directed by Ram Madhvani) is centred around the chief purser Neerja Bhanot (Sonam Kapoor), who was serving aboard Pan Am flight 73 from Mumbai to New York on 5 September 1986. During a stopover in Karachi, Pakistan, the plane was seized by Palestinian terrorists from the Abu Nidal Organization (a militant splinter group of Arafat's Fatah). The hijackers planned to abduct the plane and pick up Palestinian hostages from Cyprus and Israel. The operation resulted in a failure, and 21 passengers were killed during the incident. However, 359 were able to secretly escape from the aircraft. According to eyewitnesses, this was largely due to Bhanot's courageous interventions, which tragically caused her to be shot and killed by the hijackers. She was posthumously turned into a national icon, being bestowed India's highest peacetime award for bravery, the Ashoka Chakra.

Neerja fits in the Indian genre of biopic-as-hagiography, in which extraordinary human actions by ordinary people are exalted to near-mythical dimensions (Nayar 2017, 606–7). It is Neerja Bhanot's idealised actions that drive the movie forward. Her fearless interventions thoroughly undermine the hijackers' plans. First, she helps the pilots leave the plane. Then, when ordered to collect the passengers' passports, she protects American citizens from more severe cruelty by hiding their documents. At several points she directly confronts the hijackers; for instance, when she insists on serving water to the passengers against the terrorists' orders, claiming that when she caters to the passengers' needs, she is only doing her job, the same way the hijackers are doing theirs. Temporarily impressed by such boldness, the hijackers initially give in to Neerja's courage. At this point, a glimmer of understanding appears to show up in one of the otherwise brutal men, a dim echo of Indian cinema's earlier-mentioned tendency to humanise terrorists (Richter 2009). However, while the film is careful not to depict the Muslim hijackers as completely inhuman by showing them to be psychologically overstrained and unable to cope with the situation, their brutality prevails on the whole, and the movie's source of humanitarianism is clearly Neerja.

The implied analogy between terrorism and the situation of modern Indian women becomes overt when the terrorists' violence triggers traumatic memories in Neerja. As explained in several flashbacks, Neerja was in an arranged marriage with an Indian expatriate in Doha, Qatar, who humiliated and abused her, thus underwriting a widespread stereotype about non-residential Indians losing contact with Indian social values. To initiated viewers, this backstory sheds critical light on Qatar's instituted 'deep discrimination' impairing the rights of (not only) married women (Grant 2021). The correspondences between the hijacking and Neerja's fatal marriage are highlighted by means of a parallel montage, which shows her hiding from the terrorists in an aircraft toilet while suddenly remembering that she formerly had to hide in a similar way from her husband (Figure 8.1). The close relations between global terrorism and the 'everyday terrorism' of domestic violence, as suggested by Pain (2014), are evident here. Yet the film decidedly grounds its characterisation of the female protagonist in her ability to free herself from this troubled past. It strongly emphasises the fact that Neerja eventually managed to get a divorce, start a modelling career

Figure 8.1 Domestic violence equals terrorist violence: a parallel montage with flashback shows Neerja hiding from both male aggressors, terrorist and husband.

and become a flight attendant (this path of self-development is subtly conveyed to the viewer by an ad in the in-flight magazine featuring Neerja as a model). However, such hard-won freedom remains precarious, and the repressed memories of Neerja's abusive marriage keep coming back to her when the terrorists kick her, grab her, and push her around. By thus emphasising her traumatic past, the film exalts Neerja's heroism even more. In spite of her psychological struggles, she continues to stand against the hijackers and selflessly protects citizens of all nationalities, including an elderly woman and, especially, children. The transformation of Neerja into an icon becomes complete in the film posters. These crucial paratextual frames depict Neerja either with a gun pointed at her forehead or embracing children to shield them from violence.[1]

Neerja's courage culminates in a final humanitarian act that comes close to self-sacrifice. Having activated an emergency slide to help the passengers leave the plane, she lets everyone else go first and is tragically shot and killed by a terrorist. Yet this is not the last scene of the movie, which ends with Neerja's mother giving a glorifying speech in memory of her daughter. Neerja's mother appears repeatedly throughout the film, as she and her husband keep trying to obtain information about their daughter's situation during the hijacking. The film particularly emphasises the bond between mother and daughter. Neerja

Bhanot's real-life siblings have confirmed that their sister was indeed especially close to their mother, who always supported Neerja's freedom and bravery (A. Chatterjee 2016). In this way, the film establishes a significant link between Neerja and her mother, which would seem to be aimed at affirming a distinctly Indian ideal of womanhood. This ideal of womanhood is represented in the film in a variety of ways. As the head of a quasi-family of aircraft passengers, Neerja is fully committed to the well-being of the passengers, who belong to different generations as well as to different nations. Thus, Neerja represents the strong mother figure at the centre of a narrative of an inclusive and globally responsible nation. In times when family structures have long changed from more traditional forms to the model of the bourgeois nuclear family, the idea of an extended family represents a residual cultural element, which is precisely why it functions as a national narrative.

The idea of mother-as-nation has a long history in Indian cinema. Most influential in this regard was Mehboob Khan's 1957 film *Mother India*, which sought to ideologically deploy the mother persona in order to propagate a communitarian ideal designed to facilitate the transition from the traditional rural way of life to the modern Indian nation-state. According to a press statement originally released with Khan's film, the 'eternal theme of [the] Indian woman' is epitomised by a mother 'round whom revolves everything that is sacred and glorious in our culture, tradition and civilization' (G. Chatterjee 2020, 61). In other words, the mother embodies *sanatana dharma*, eternal order and duty as a collective ethic in terms of traditional Hindu law (Barlet 2010, 127–9; Michaels 2004, 15–20; Richter 2009, 496). As a representative of traditional values, the female protagonist, Radha, acts as the moral backbone of a small village community. As such, she personifies collective suffering in unstable times, as becomes obvious in her dealings with an unscrupulous and exploitative moneylender. Radha accepts the dharmic obligation to tradition without any compromises. When her son becomes a revolutionary and attempts to overthrow the oppressive social order, she does not hesitate to take a rifle and kill him. Caring for the larger community of the village and, by implication, nation, is more important to Radha than her own individual well-being and motherhood in the narrow sense of the word, even if the traditional foundations of the social order have become questionable.

Khan's influential figuration of the mother-as-nation has been reiterated countless times throughout the history of Indian cinema (Barlet 2010, 128). It implies a moral ideal of womanhood combining the extremes of suffering and endurance with a limited sense of self-empowerment (Richter 2009, 493–4). This conflation of disparate values is highly problematic for a number of reasons. The sense of greatness that the image of Mother India is charged with can be associated with a readiness to act courageously and in a self-entitled way on behalf of community values, while as a 'patriarchal ideal' it can also be associated with a nearly infinite female capacity for suffering, for willingly taking the burden of a whole nation (Richter 2009, 493).

A similar ambivalence is manifest in the protagonist of *Neerja*. She is introduced as a modern, independent woman who seems far removed from the image of Mother India. After all, Neerja has managed to free herself from the cultural bias against divorce and been able to overcome the traditional mindset that had made her accept an arranged marriage in the first place. Such an extent of self-determination is remarkable, especially considering that arranged marriages (though with stronger elements of love and consent) are still fairly common in India (Uberoi 2009, 24–6). Living the dream career of becoming both a model and a flight attendant, Neerja cultivates a Western lifestyle, which the film seems to advertise to a younger, particularly female, audience.

At the same time, however, there are strong indications that Neerja's femininity is still aligned to the Mother India myth. Not only is she about to marry again – being based on love, mutual respect and understanding, her new relationship is shown to be compatible with her sense of freedom and self-determination – but Neerja is also presented as a family woman. We first see her at a party with younger children, a subtle foreshadowing of her future life as a wife and mother. Later in the film, Neerja's willingness to resist and confront the hijackers while protecting the 'family' of passengers works as a glorification of motherly selflessness. The fact that the metaphorical family of people on board the plane is an international one reflects India's new role as a global actor. In *Neerja*, India's sense of international responsibility is coded in terms of characteristically Indian values. Most prominent among these is the Gandhian principle of non-violence (*ahimsa*), which is here embodied by a female character willing to suffer altruistically. Abstaining from any act of counter-aggression, Neerja's resistance is even more passive than Radha's in *Mother India*. All in all, then, Neerja's bravery and resilience resonate with, and even affirm, both liberal and conservative constructions of femininity. Ultimately, the film's implicit commentary on the situation of modern Indian women fails to overcome the ideological limits of its time, reflecting the obstacles to female emancipation in the contemporary cultural context.

A (Pseudo-)Feminist 'Song-and-Kill' Spree: *Tiger Zinda Hai*

While the Mother India narrative problematically constructs women as brave sufferers for the sake of the nation, it should not be forgotten that it also includes an element of female self-empowerment on behalf of dharmic 'higher justice'. Indeed, several terrorism-themed films draw on this aspect of the Mother India narrative to present female characters who actively 'fight back'. At first sight, such a representational strategy would seem to avoid the gender clichés reproduced in *Neerja*, according to which female resistance draws its strength from non-violent virtues such as will-power, equanimity and endurance. A recent, very graphic example of the 'women fight back' approach is the action thriller *Tiger Zinda Hai* ('Tiger is alive'), the second instalment of Yash Raj Films' burgeoning *Spy Universe* franchise. This film, too, links terrorism with patriarchy, but it features a scene in which the female characters are allowed to indulge in at least one act of counter-violence.

Like *Neerja*, *Tiger Zinda Hai* is based on a historical incident of national significance: the 2014 hostage-taking of a group of Indian nurses by terrorists of Islamic State (IS) in the Iraqi city of Tikrit. In the film, the fictive leader of the terrorist group (renamed ISC), Abu Usman, corresponds to the stereotype of the bearded Muslim terrorist modelled on Osama bin Laden. On the counter-terrorist side, the male action hero is Tiger (Salman Khan), a hyper-masculine secret agent. Working for the Indian secret service RAW (Research and Analysis Wing), Tiger is the best undercover specialist the country has to offer. His wife Zoya (Katrina Kaif) also works as a secret agent, but she is with Pakistan's ISI (Inter-Services Intelligence). Once again, the ideological narrative of the nation-as-family serves as the film's basic premise. This becomes apparent early on when an Indian husband and his apron-wearing Pakistani wife are having dinner with their child – a gendered allegory evoking a united nation, thus suggesting that post-colonial partition in South Asia might one day be overcome. The allegory is sustained throughout *Tiger Zinda Hai*, which reimagines the abducted nurses as a mixed Indian and Pakistani group. This gives rise to the first joint operation between both countries' secret services, led by the married superhero couple who successfully free the nurses before a scheduled US Army airstrike destroys the hospital and the terrorists.

The representation of the female protagonist is of particular interest here. In a crucial scene, Zoya leads an all-female killer commando team to obtain the hospital's construction plans from the Town Hall of Ikrit, which is heavily guarded by terrorists. A large number of terrorists are eliminated by Zoya's squad of specially trained Syrian women, who have entered the building posing as cleaners, all dressed in black abayas. The operation is also aimed at assaulting ISC's second-in-command, Al Amir Bagdawi, another bin Laden lookalike. In this scene, female insurgence is aestheticised, choreographed and set to music, thus turning the serial killing into a surprisingly conventional Bollywood song-and-dance sequence. Accompanied by the mystic-yet-pounding Sufi rock song 'Tera Noor', several of the fake cleaners are shown lifting their veils when presented to Bagdawi as sexual objects to choose from. When the terrorist leader selects Zoya and makes her undress in a luxurious bedroom, she takes a knife and cuts his throat (Figure 8.2). Likewise, the remaining women are shown bowing to terrorists and signalling willingness to have sex, only to eventually cut their throats and stab them in the back. In each case the men are taken completely off-guard and hence do not show much resistance. By placing

TERRORISING PATRIARCHY IN HINDI CINEMA

Figure 8.2 Low angle shot of Zoya undressing for Bagdawi, seconds before she cuts his throat.

women in the superior position of viewers and killers, the male gaze enacted in the Town Hall scene is arguably troubled by a rupture in the patriarchal order that reduces women to objects (Mulvey 1989). Once again, global terrorism is conflated with the 'everyday terrorism' of gender-based violence. Ikrit Town Hall resembles a stately mansion with lavish bedrooms and lavatories. While this setting links violence against women to domestic space, the building's interior decorations – which offer a wild mix of western luxury styles – point beyond India.

In its smoothness, the highly stylised sequence can be read as a form of musical relief. It is presented as a wish-fulfilment fantasy rather than a faithful representation of the female squad's operation. It would be wrong, nonetheless, to altogether downplay the scene's potential feminist appeal, which is reinforced by the lyrics of the accompanying song, 'Tera Noor' (Your Holy Light). Written in Urdu (by Irshad Kamil), the lyrics articulate a female singer's lament to God the creator about misogyny and male oppression. This is made explicit in the full version of the song, which has been uploaded to YouTube and other platforms, where a woman invokes the Lord to contend that His Adam, while 'born of me', is unable to see her beyond her body and constantly accuses her of weakness.[2] These opening lines are missing from the shortened version of the song that is played during the film's killing scene. The lyrics included there contain a more general lament to God about the lack of light, love and wisdom in a bleak, violent and materialist world. Significantly, however, the song still expresses the singer's (Jyoti Nooran) eagerness to 'explode'. It is up to the (female) audience to complete the scene's more specifically feminist message, and it seems that many viewers have indeed done so by leaving sympathetic comments below the video on YouTube. Emphasising that the film has given

153

them 'goosebumps', these comments register a strong affective response and often express the wish for a music video combining the scene from the film with an unabridged version of the song.

Even in its edited form, the prayer-like song seems to suggest that the women's brutal retaliation is, in a way, 'authorised' by direct contact with the divine. The fact that the song is sung in Urdu gives its notion of the divine an inclusive character. Having a long poetic and cosmopolitan tradition, Urdu is closely related to Hindi yet has undergone a long ideological history of cultural repression in India (Mufti 2014, 328–35). Still, it continues to be widely used in Bollywood songs, testifying to a 'desire' for the other language (334–5). Moreover, the lament about gross materialism and the absence of spiritual light in 'Tera Noor' is closely reminiscent of the mystical verse of Kabir, an eminent fifteenth-century Indian poet and philosopher who sought to reconcile Islamic and Hindu theological outlooks, also drawing on Christian elements (Underhill 1915, VI–XIX). From that perspective, the film's music and lyrics vaguely evoke an ethical and poetic common ground. They reference traditions that are often constructed as being incompatible with the dominant, culturally and religiously exclusivist Hindu-centred narratives of post-independence India. Following the conventions of Indian popular cinema, the song-and-dance scene offers an 'inside view' to illustrate characters' feelings; in doing so, it frames these emotions not only as female but also as a more generally felt transcultural experience. The 'feminist outburst' of the scene is thus safely couched in the film's larger reconciliatory politics, arguably shifting the focus away from female experience towards the broader and less specific endeavour of bridging cultural differences between India and Pakistan, or Hinduism and Islam.

Problematically, however, *Tiger Zinda Hai* displaces the issues of patriarchy and misogyny by locating them beyond the territory and institutions of the Indian nation-state. The film's basic premise – using a counter-terrorist operation in Iraq to dramatise female empowerment – projects male violence and patriarchy onto the political, cultural and religious other: a failed state associated with the image of the 'bad' Muslim. As a result, the film represents the oppression of women as an external threat rather than a problem existing within Indian society.

It is notable, moreover, that the 'female counter-strike' in *Tiger Zinda Hai* remains complicit with hegemonic masculinity, which tolerates such retaliatory violence only if it corresponds to the 'sexploitation' script. According to that script, women become violent only after having been exposed to (often sexualised) male violence first. In the words of Linda Williams, the 'female victim-hero' who eliminates male aggressors complicates the male viewer position by substituting scopophilic, sadistic desire with an illicit masochistic one (1999, 206–8). In *Tiger Zinda Hai*, however, Zoya closely follows the patterns of hypermasculinity: evoking the 'chicks with guns' cliché, the film's original poster sees

Zoya side-by-side with her husband in an armed gunfight against unidentified enemies.[3] Indeed, Zoya may be said to enact aggressive masculinity – 'in drag', as it were (Williams 1999, 207–8). The film is thus doubly designed to please a male heterosexual audience. Moreover, in an industry that is unwilling to critically engage with its own complicity in aesthetically sustaining patriarchal structures, the female killing scene seems tokenistic. In fact, it might even help to whitewash the transgressions of the male lead, Salman Khan, who has faced charges of sexual harassment, hit-and-run, expressing sympathy for terrorists and keeping unlicensed weapons (Pandey 2018; Sikdhar 2015). The extent to which Bollywood and other Indian film industries are entrenched within patriarchy is deserving of a separate paper (M. Pillai 2017).

Celebrating the Patriarchal 'Hidden State': *Simmba*

What *Tiger Zinda Hai* has in common with *Neerja*, then, is that it depicts terrorism and violence against women as foreign threats – as if they were 'external' problems. Things are different in my final example, *Simmba*, the third instalment of Rohit Shetty's highly popular *Cop Universe* franchise. This action comedy is set in India (more specifically, in the small tropical state of Goa) and, to a greater extent than *Neerja* and *Tiger Zinda Hai*, seems to be immediately concerned with contemporary Indian society.

Its anti-hero Sangram Bhalerao, aka Simmba, is a corrupt cop who, on being appointed the new inspector of a beautiful beach resort, makes a deal with a local gangster boss, Durva Ranade, and his brothers. Bhalerao comes to protect and even actively support the gang's Mafia-like criminal activities. Yet Simmba is not all bad; most notably, he makes several friends among virtuous women he respects. First of all, there is Shagun, who he falls in love with, and her mother, but there is also the young teacher Akruti, who reminds Simmba of his own teacher in the slums of Mumbai, where he led a rough life as an orphan child. The plot thickens as Akruti investigates a local drug problem, and it turns out that the illegal activities of Ranade's gang also include more heinous crimes such as drug trafficking and using children as drug dealers. When Akruti secretly enters a suspicious site owned by Ranade, using her mobile phone to document what turns out to be an illegal drug laboratory, she is discovered, raped and killed by Ranade's brothers. This marks a crucial turning-point for the movie. When given evidence that the gang is responsible for Akruti's death, Simmba breaks his ties with Ranade and vows revenge, beginning to change from bad cop to good cop.

This character transformation unfolds in several phases. Upon first hearing about the murder, Simmba quickly tracks down Ranade's brothers, confronts them, and makes them confess their deed to him. When they claim that there was no alternative to raping Akruti since she had said something that deeply hurt

Figure 8.3 Simmba's female police officers beat up Ranade's brothers under the watchful eyes of their male colleagues.

their manly honour, Simmba gives them a heavy beating. In addition, asserting that their egos will soon be injured even more, he hands the brothers over to his entourage of female police officers to extend the pounding (Figure 8.3). However, this is only the first instance of mob violence which pervades the film.

It should be noted at this point that there is a Bollywood convention of having an interval halfway through the movie. This cut allows for wild genre mixes distinguishing the movie's first part from its second part, contributing to an effect that is often compared to a Masala spice blend. In accordance with that convention, *Simmba* completely changes its tone after the break, shifting from action comedy to the more serious format of courtroom drama. Having brought Ranade's brothers to court for their atrocious crime, Simmba now has to deal with the massive power of the gangsters' boss. More specifically, Ranade manages to have Akruti's phone destroyed, which contained evidence of the rape, and he hires an excellent lawyer who plans to ask for a mistrial. This is when Simmba once again takes justice into his own hands: in a passionate courtroom speech, he directly addresses the female judge presiding over the trial. Highlighting the precarious situation of women in India, he draws attention to the much-debated 2012 Delhi gang rape and the dramatically rising number of rape incidents in India. He provocatively appeals to the judge's feelings, suggesting that such things might even happen to her own daughter. The judge temporarily loses her temper but eventually acts according to Simmba's wishes; she decides to adjourn the trial, thus giving Simmba an opportunity to come up with new evidence.

Simmba has different plans, however. When the two brothers are handed over to him to be locked up in a prison cell in his police station until the trial continues, he asks several people – mainly women – how they would treat rapists if they were in his place. The answers he receives are all the same: everybody agrees that rapists do not deserve to live, and that a police officer's job is 'to protect the good and to eliminate the bad' by killing rapists in 'direct encounters'. Following this advice, Simmba sets up a trap for the brothers, who are waiting in their cell for the trial to continue. A female crowd gathers in front of the cell, apparently to bring lunchboxes to the police officers. Simmba and his colleagues start insulting the rapists with sexually humiliating words. One of the brothers is unable to stand the provocation and brags about the rape, claiming that he would do the same to any of the women present. When the brothers ask to settle the matter in a hand-to-hand fight, the cell doors are opened and a scuffle begins. The officers put guns into the rapists' hands to pretend that the latter were planning an armed assault. Knowing that the CCTV cameras will document the staged scene in a slanted way, Simmba shoots and kills the brothers, making it appear as if extreme self-defence had been his only option. However, the manipulated CCTV footage thus produced is not accepted as evidence by the judge, and Simmba now faces charges for faking evidence while Ranade, the gangster boss, is about to evade justice through the help of his wily lawyer.

The situation is resolved by a *deus ex machina*, which not only saves Simmba but also justifies his actions. Singham, the glorified 'good cop' from the earlier two movies of the *Cop Universe* franchise, suddenly appears as the head of the special government investigation team that has been formed on the judge's demand to check the authenticity of Simmba's manipulated camera evidence. Even though Singham, unlike Simmba, is known for his firm anti-corruption stance, he wholeheartedly supports his colleague. Validating the CCTV material against his better knowledge, he saves Simmba from further prosecution. In the film's final scene, Singham explains his motivation:

> These monsters need to feel the fear, Bhalerao. Right now this fear exists only in the hearts of the parents whose daughters come home late at night. Even if she's returning from a party with her friends, or from her job, or moved to a different city to make a career. I only helped you because I wanted to instil this fear in those monsters who don't hesitate to commit horrible crimes like rape. Whenever they will have ill-intentions for a woman they must have this fear in their mind. That a few insane cops will come and shoot them dead. No arrest. No long court cases. Justice on the spot.[4]

Singham's position does not come as a surprise: he had already conducted extrajudicial killings in his two earlier films. It is certainly no coincidence that Singham's declared aim, to 'instil fear', evokes a crucial aspect of terrorism, a word derived from the Latin verb *terrere*, which means 'to bring someone to tremble through great fear' (Schmid 2011, 41). Singham's plan to prevent rape through fear follows a similar logic as counterterrorism, which aims to deter terrorists by means of state-endorsed violence. More specifically, the idea of 'monsters' within the population evokes the threat of 'sleeper' terrorists – a threat calling for increased security measures. The link between rapists and sleepers is reinforced by the sequel to *Simmba*, *Sooryavanshi* (Shetty, 2021), which reunites Singham and Simmba in a secret service mission aimed at eliminating Pakistani terrorists who have been living in India with false identities to repeat the 1993 'Bombay bombings' (a preview of *Sooryavanshi* is included at the end of *Simmba*, reinforcing the thematic connections between both films). However, whereas the terrorist cells in *Sooryavanshi* are part of a hierarchical organisation, the villains in *Simmba* operate as a network without clearly identifiable leaders. The figure of the rapist-as-terrorist remains faceless, lacking any stereotypically 'terrorist' features, which makes him all the more threatening – and thus justifies extreme measures on the part of the agents of law and order.

The film ends on this note of 'justice on the spot'. It implies that not all forms of unlawfulness are bad, as long as they reflect a higher sense of morality. This blatant encouragement of mob justice is striking, especially in the Indian context, where 'fake encounters' are often seen as a legitimate way to punish actual or alleged criminals, a measure endorsed even by high-ranking politicians (P. Pillai 2019). To fully understand the film's politics, it is necessary to once again focus on the representation of women as victims and avengers. The exaltation of female suffering along the lines of the Mother India narrative, as seen in *Neerja*, also features prominently in *Simmba*. This is most evident in the depiction of Akruti, a caring schoolteacher who embodies purity and motherly goodness. Like Neerja, Akruti risks her life for others. A complementary older mother figure is introduced near the end of *Simmba* (similar to the framing device in *Neerja*): unable to stand a chance against Durva Ranade's lawyer, Bhalerao convinces the top gangster's ageing mother to appear in court, and her mere presence makes Ranade confess his crimes.

Yet the film partially transcends the Mother India narrative. Much like *Tiger Zinda Hai*, it breaks with the construction of women as sufferers and instead empowers them to take justice into their own hands. In *Simmba*, this empowerment significantly exceeds the exceptional and displaced outburst of retaliatory violence seen in *Tiger Zinda Hai*. The key difference is that in *Simmba*, female counter-violence is encouraged as standard practice by a male police inspector, who is characterised as power-hungry and corrupt but also as acting according to a 'higher' sense of justice. Simmba serves as an extra-legal authority for handling social problems. When he intervenes, the rule of law is suspended. This enables various forms of vigilante justice, which in the Indian context have included violence against religious minorities, 'honour killings', and rape itself as a measure to 'discipline' women (Tully 2017; PTI 2021; Burke 2014). Even though he represents one of the institutions of the democratic state, Simmba acts against the law when he 'passes down' power to women. As mentioned above, this initially only concerns physical power – when Simmba has his female officers beat up Ranade's brothers. However, it later also involves a redistribution of power in a more political sense – when Simmba asks a number of women what they think is the right way to deal with rapists. This comes close to what Carl Schmitt (2008, 131–2) termed direct 'acclamation', whereby political decisions by leaders are immediately authorised, as it were, by the people (or rather, mob), without any clearly defined democratic process. The power of law is further subverted when Simmba orchestrates the extrajudicial killing of the rapists, systematically circumventing the legal process.

To better understand what makes this apparent vision of female empowerment so deeply problematic, it is useful to cross-culturally compare the film with Fritz Lang's *M* (1931), or more specifically, *M*'s central element of an undemocratic 'hidden state'. In Lang's classic of late Weimar-era cinema, the police are unable to track down 'M', an unidentified child abuser and serial killer terrifying Berlin. Primarily to protect their own illegal activities, an influential underworld association, including beggars and criminals, authorises itself to find M on their own. When they manage to identify M as a man named Beckert and arrest him, they arrange a secret trial in the city's sewers, including a prosecutor, defence lawyer and jury (all of whom are criminals), which results in a death sentence, and only a sudden police intervention saves Beckert from being executed on the spot. Reading *M* for its political dimension, there is a 'hidden state' manifesting itself in the underworld which only adopts the mere appearance of law and democratic institutions. Lang's intentions were critically motivated, and his film can be said to capture the structure of feeling of an impending change in Germany's society that would in fact see the erosion of its political system and civil rights, a drift which would eventually lead to fascism (Kaes 2021, 94).

One should always be careful when constructing historical analogies across times and cultures. However, without unduly generalising, there is a precarious tendency in today's India in which democracy is increasingly seen as disposable – a tendency that is closely related to the extreme-right government led by the BJP party and the strong cultural influence of Hindu nationalism endorsed by it. Against this background, it seems notable that *Simmba*, notwithstanding its half-satirical tone, is not a warning against corruption but takes the erosion of the democratic legal state for granted. More problematically, the film appears to actually advocate for the formation of an *M*-like 'hidden state' in which self-entitled groups with good connections to the undercurrents of society make the decisions that really count 'behind the scenes'. *Simmba* suggests that only in such an undemocratic hidden state will society open up for female participation. The seeming empowerment of women envisaged by *Simmba* is thus at the expense of democracy and civil rights.

It goes without saying that such pseudo-empowerment does not improve the overall situation of women but keeps the patriarchal system in place. Singham and Simmba's project of 'instilling fear' can be described as a form of terrorism, as their activities have the political aim of disrupting the democratic order in the name of patriarchy (Pain 536). Small wonder that all important decisions in the film are made or authorised by men. The actual subordination and powerlessness of women is thus cemented, as is illustrated by the most interesting, yet marginal, character in *Simmba*, namely the figure of the female judge. Representing a modern image of womanhood, as well as an uncompromising belief in law and order, the judge proves powerless against the machinations of Ranade's lawyer, Simmba's manipulations and Singham's final intervention. The fact that it is the appearance of Ranade's mother that brings the trial to a conclusion seems to indicate that the judge herself does not pass as a fully-fledged Mother India. When Simmba shoots and kills Ranade's brothers, it is Akruti's image which he sees in his mind's eye. The female victim thus comes to represent the guiding spirit of a 'higher' justice, which stands in contrast to the judge's less effective reliance on the conventional legal process. This denigration of the law, again, serves a patriarchal agenda, and it is only fitting, therefore, that the final still shows the undisputed heroes, Singham and Simmba, boldly walking into the end credits, as if to summarise the film's contention that there is a 'good' kind of male-authorised self-entitlement.

In conclusion, the three films discussed here expose the limitations of the widespread Bollywood strategy of drawing on terrorist discourse to represent both violence against women and female resistance to such violence. By using the overblown tropes of terrorism to dramatise misogynist oppression, the films seem to call for similarly overblown acts of saviourism and retaliation. Enduring myths such as the Mother India narrative mystify female experience, veiling the actual complexities faced by Indian women today. Moreover, as seen in *Simmba*, the films leave it to male characters and networks to initiate, authorise, and organise 'female counter-strikes' – counter-strikes that ultimately miss the relevant target, namely patriarchy and misogyny in Indian society.

Notes

1. See the Internet Movie Database (IMDb) entry on *Neerja* for these film posters: https://www.imdb.com/title/tt5286444
2. The translation referred to ('born to me') is from the *Return to Hades* blog entry 'Why Tera Noor is the feminist cheer you need' (L. 2017), which also includes a transcription of the original Urdu lyrics.
3. See: https://www.imdb.com/title/tt5956100
4. This is how the English subtitles included in the DVD, Blu-ray, and online streaming releases of *Simmba* translate Singham's speech.

References

Ahmad, Irfan. 2014. "Kafka in India: Terrorism, Media, Muslims." In *Being Muslim in South Asia: Diversity and Daily Life*, eds Robin Jeffrey and Ronjoy Sen, 289–329. Oxford: Oxford University Press.

Ahmed, Omar. 2015. *Studying Indian Cinema*. Leighton Buzzard: Auteur.

Bannerji, Himani. 2016. "Patriarchy in the Era of Neoliberalism: The Case of India." *Social Scientist* 44, no. 3/4: 3–27.

Barlet, Olivier. 2010. "Bollywood/Africa: A Divorce?" *Black Camera* 2, no. 1: 126–43.

Burke, Jason. 2014. "Thirteen Men in Court Over Public Gang-Rape in Indian Village." *The Guardian*, January 23, 2014. https://www.theguardian.com/world/2014/jan/23/court-gang-rape-indian-village-birbhum

Chatterjee, Avijit. 2016. "Death in the Clouds." *Telegraph India*, February 21, 2016. https://www.telegraphindia.com/7-days/death-in-the-clouds/cid/1314482

Chatterjee, Gayatri. (2002) 2020. *Mother India*. Reprint, London: BFI/Bloomsbury.

Grant, Harriet. 2021. "'We're Treated as Children,' Qatari Women Tell Rights Group." *The Guardian*, March 29, 2021. https://www.theguardian.com/global-development/2021/mar/29/were-treated-as-children-qatari-women-tell-rights-group

Harindranath, Ramaswami. 2014. "The Indian Public Sphere: Histories, Contradictions and Challenges." *Media International Australia* 152, no. 1: 168–75.

Hingorani, Aman M. 2016. *Unravelling the Kashmir Knot*. New Delhi: SAGE.

Hiro, Dilip. 2012. *Apocalyptic Realm: Jihadists in South Asia*. New Haven: Yale University Press.

Kaes, Anton. 2021. *M*. London: BFI/Bloomsbury.

Krishnan, Kavita. 2021. "Caging Women Is Violence – Not 'Safety' or 'Protection'." *The Wire*, January 17, 2021. https://thewire.in/women/freedom-women-violence-safety-protection

L., Sarina. 2017. "Why Tera Noor Is the Feminist Cheer You Need." *Return to Hades*, December 28, 2017. https://www.returntohades.com/2017/12/28/tera_noor_feminist_cheer/

Lakoff, George. 2001. "Metaphors of Terror." *In These Times*, September 17, 2001. https://press.uchicago.edu/sites/daysafter/911lakoff.html

Lang, Fritz, dir. 1931. *M*. Berlin: Nero-Film.

Madhvani, Ram, dir. 2016. *Neerja*. Mumbai: Fox Star Studios. YouTube Films India.

Mehta, Rini Bhattacharya. 2018. "The Nation-State's Other. Postcolonial Terrorism in the Indian Context." In *Terrorism and Literature*, ed. Peter C. Herman, 110–27. Cambridge: Cambridge University Press.

Michaels, Axel. 2004. *Hinduism. Past and Present*. Trans. Barbara Harshav. Princeton and Oxford: Princeton University Press.

Mufti, Aamir R. 2014. "Orientalism and the Institutions of World Literatures." In *World Literature in Theory*, ed. David Damrosch, 313–44. New York: Wiley Blackwell.

Mulvey, Laura. (1975) 1989. "Visual Pleasure and Narrative Cinema." In *Visual and Other Pleasures*. Houndmills and New York: Palgrave.

Nayar, Pramod K. 2017. "Biopics: The Year in India." *Biography* 40, no. 4: 604–10. JSTOR.

Pain, Rachel. 2014. "Everyday Terrorism: Connecting Domestic Violence and Global Terrorism." *Progress in Human Geography* 38, no. 4: 531–50.

Pandey, Geeta. 2018. "Salman Khan: The Superstar Who Lives Dangerously." *BBC News*, April 5, 2018. https://www.bbc.com/news/world-asia-india-21289358

Pillai, Meena T. 2017. "The Many Misogynies of Malayalam Cinema." *Economic and Political Weekly* 52, no. 33: 52–8.

Pillai, Priya. 2019. "Extrajudicial Killings: India's Long History of 'Fake Encounters.'" *The Interpreter*, January 29, 2019. https://www.lowyinstitute.org/the-interpreter/extrajudicial-killings-long-history-fake-encounters

PTI. 2021. "Honour Killing: Casteism Not Annihilated Even after 75 Years of Independence, Says SC." *The Hindu*, November 28, 2021. https://www.thehindu.com/news/national/honour-killing-casteism-not-annihilated-even-after-75-years-of-independence-says-sc/article37736850.ece

Richter, Claudia. 2009. "The Ethics of Coexistence: Bollywood's Different Take on Terrorism." *CrossCurrents* 59, no. 4: 484–99.

Schmid, Alex P., ed. 2011. "The Definition of Terrorism." In *The Routledge Handbook of Terrorism Research*. London and New York: Routledge, 39–98.

Schmitt, Carl. (1928) 2008. *Constitutional Theory*. Trans. Jeffrey Seitzer. Durham and London: Duke University Press.

Shaw, Tony. 2015. *Cinematic Terror. A Global History of Terrorism on Film*. New York and London: Bloomsbury.

Shetty, Rohit, dir. 2018. *Simmba*. Mumbai: Reliance Big Home Entertainment. Blu-Ray.

Shetty, Rohit, dir. 2021. *Sooryavanshi*. Dharma Productions and Reliance Entertainment. Netflix.

Sikdhar, Shubhomoy. 2015. "Salman Defends Yakub, Says Hang Tiger Memon." *The Hindu*, July 26, 2015. https://www.thehindu.com/news/national/salman-defends-yakub-says-hang-tiger-memon/article7466723.ece

Simon, Jonathan. 2002. "Governing Through Crime Metaphors." *Brooklyn Law Review* 67, no. 4. https://brooklynworks.brooklaw.edu/blr/vol67/iss4/6

Simpson, David. 1995. "Raymond Williams: Feeling for Structures, Voicing 'History.'" In *Cultural Materialism. On Raymond Williams*, ed. Christopher Prendergast, 29–50. Minneapolis: University of Minnesota Press.

Taneja, Kabir. 2021. "How India Is Weakening Its Case on Terrorism." *Hindustan Times*, February 18, 2021. https://www.hindustantimes.com/opinion/how-india-is-weakening-its-case-on-terrorism-101613569867532.html

Tully, Mark. 2017. "How the Babri Mosque Destruction Shaped India." *BBC News*, December 6, 2017. https://www.bbc.com/news/world-asia-india-42219773

Uberoi, Patricia. 2009. *Freedom and Destiny: Gender, Family, and Popular Culture in India*. New Delhi: Oxford University Press.

Underhill, Evelyn. 1915. "Introduction." In *One Hundred Poems of Kabir*, translated by Rabindranath Tagore, V–XLIV. London: Macmillan & Co.

Wahab, Ghazala. 2020. "How the Modi Government Has Used – and Dropped – the 'Terrorism' Bogey." *The Wire*, October 9, 2020. https://thewire.in/government/narendra-modi-terrorism-bogey

Widmalm, Sten. 2019. "Is India's Democracy Really in Decline?" *The Wire*, April 6, 2019. https://thewire.in/politics/is-indias-democracy-really-in-decline

Williams, Linda. (1989) 1999. *Hard Core: Power, Pleasure, and the "Frenzy of the Visible."* Berkeley and Los Angeles: University of California Press.

Williams, Raymond. 1977. *Marxism and Literature*. Oxford: Oxford University Press.

Zafar, Ali Abbas, dir. 2017. *Tiger Zinda Hai*. Mumbai: Yash Raj Films Home Entertainment. Blu-Ray.

9. CONTRASTING TERRORIST FIGURES: FAR-RIGHT EXTREMISTS AND JIHADISTS IN CONTEMPORARY FRENCH CINEMA

Sarah Davison

INTRODUCTION

On 13 November 2015, France's capital experienced the deadliest terrorist attack to occur on French soil since the Second World War. The multi-site attack took place at the Stade de France, the Bataclan theatre, and various cafés across the city, resulting in the deaths of 130 people. Of the 151 terrorism-related fatalities in Europe that year, 148 took place in France (Europol 2016, 10). The context surrounding the attacks on the offices of *Charlie Hebdo* earlier that same year famously ignited widespread public debate surrounding the limits of free speech and the extent of Islamophobia in France, a discussion which has since been explored in a wide range of scholarship and public discourse (Todd 2015; Plenel 2016; Wolfreys 2017). While the debate over Islamophobia in France continued, the increase in right-wing extremist terrorism was overshadowed. According to Europol, in 2014 France reported no right-wing terrorist attacks, compared to seven recorded in 2015, with a sharp increase in anti-Muslim violence in the immediate aftermath of the *Charlie Hebdo* attacks (2016, 41). Although these attacks were reported in French news media, they were often classified as *actes anti-musulmans* (anti-Muslim acts) by sources across the political spectrum (Beunaiche 2015; France 24 2015; Le service Metronews 2015; Les Echos 2015), downplaying their violent nature. With these events reported as terrorism by French authorities and recognised as such by Europol, but downplayed by French media simply as anti-Muslim 'acts' rather than 'attacks' or 'violence', a distinct tendency to euphemise far-right terrorism reveals itself.

These events have made terrorism a pertinent topic in France, and their portrayal on screen is now emerging as a burgeoning area of interest within French cinema. This chapter will argue that the tendency within French news media to euphemise far-right violence is carried over to contemporary mainstream French cinema. However, as this chapter aims to show, the favourable portrayal of white terrorists is not confined to those motivated by far-right extremism and extends also to white and white-presenting Jihadist extremists; in these portrayals of terrorism, racial bias can be seen despite the ideology of the terrorist figure. To demonstrate how white terrorists are depicted in less demonising ways, this chapter will consider two recent French-language representations of terrorist figures. The first, *Chez nous* (Lucas Belvaux, 2017), is a political drama and follows a small-town nurse who is recruited as a candidate for mayor by the fictional National Rally Party. She becomes romantically involved with a right-wing extremist, who commits terrorist acts without her knowledge. The second film this chapter will consider, *Made in France* (Nicolas Boukhrief, 2016), is a thriller-drama, and follows a French-Algerian journalist who infiltrates a Jihadist terrorist cell on the outskirts of Paris. Unlike *Chez nous*, *Made in France* follows an extremist cell consisting of Muslims from a wide variety of backgrounds, allowing a comparison and discussion of how terrorists are portrayed according to their ethnicity.

As this chapter deals specifically with the representation of the terrorist figure in contemporary French cinema, it is both necessary and illuminating to acknowledge the concept of race in the French Republican context. As a result of France's specific form of republicanism, which considers all individuals to be unquestionably equal under the constitution, markers of identity such as race, ethnicity and religion are considered to be legally irrelevant, or as Jean Beaman succinctly puts it, 'the only meaningful identity is a French one' (2019, 547). Consequently, data on race and racism in France is extremely hard to come by, and academics in France find it increasingly difficult to engage in research on race and ethnicity. Indeed, Emmanuel Macron's government has gone as far as to publicly question the need for academic study or university teaching of intersectionality, postcolonial studies, and other race-related fields, which the Minister of Higher Education, Frédérique Vidal, controversially termed 'islamo-gauchisme' ('islamo-leftism'; qtd in Assemblée nationale 2021).

Katya Salmi, a scholar in critical race theory, charts the history of French governmental and legislative resistance towards acknowledging or discussing race, racism, ethnicity and similar markers of identity. She highlights the problems lawyers have in arguing cases of racial discrimination in courts, the difficulty in acknowledging the lasting effects of French colonialism and the simultaneous ignorance towards racist discrimination and 'white privilege' (Salmi 2011). Beaman draws a similar conclusion, suggesting that 'just as French Republicanism denies the existence of race and racism ... it simultaneously denies the existence of whiteness and white supremacy' (2019, 553). In addition to the ignorance towards white privilege, Beaman convincingly argues that 'part of France's racial project is the continued production and reproduction of white as normal or default' (553), and that 'French identity is understood at macro and micro levels as white' (548). Thomas Deltombe and Mathieu Rigouste support this, suggesting that beyond the legal definition of French identity which disregards culture, religion or skin colour, another definition of French identity can be found in media discourse. This media-driven definition refers instead to the idea of a '"pure French stock"' – whom one naturally imagines corresponds to white, predominantly Christian populations who are instinctively faithful to the republican pact of separation of church and state' (2017, 117–18).

France's particular model of republicanism and its tabooing of race has allowed the privileged experience of whites to remain legally – and to a large extent, culturally – invisible. It has also precluded marginalised and racialised groups from forming 'non-mixte' ('non-mixed') dialogues – be they activist, work-related, civic or otherwise – where Black and Maghrebi individuals might discuss experiences of racism without the input of white individuals, as these are often labelled as purporting to 'anti-white racism' (Beaman 2019, 547). This ignorance towards white privilege and the consequent concept of 'anti-white racism' will be discussed in this chapter in relation to *Chez nous*. A further result of France's ignorance toward the specificity of individuals' experiences based on their race is, as Salmi argues, the 'disparate treatment of the histories of different marginalised minorities, whereby a certain concurrence occurs over whose history will be acknowledged' (2011, 186). While Salmi rightly highlights that 'experiences of Black people, as a racialized minority, have been overlooked for a very long time' (184), there remains a gap in the extent to which different minorities' historical suffering at the hands of the French nation has been recognised. This, she suggests, is evident in that 'steps have been made to recognise the deep cuts caused by slavery and racism towards Blacks', such as the 2001 law recognising slavery as a crime against humanity and President Jacques Chirac's 2006 decision to annually commemorate the abolition of slavery. By contrast, she suggests that 'there has been little progress in fully acknowledging the brutality of the Algerian war', but rather a series of laws have been introduced – such as the 2005 law citing the 'positive role' of colonialism – which actively demonstrate France's continued difficulty in appropriately dealing with its colonial past (186). Salmi does not suggest that the suffering of Black individuals in French society is less deserving of attention than that of second- and third-generation Maghrebi French people, but in underlining this disparity, she sheds light on the hierarchy operating in France based upon perceived race, influenced by factors such as appearance, religion, residence, clothing and speech. There is no singular academic agreement as to who falls at the bottom of this hierarchy; rather, scholars tend to focus on the various aspects which contribute to the racialisation of marginalised groups. While Salmi focuses on the disparate acknowledgement of France's involvement in the Algerian conflict and the transatlantic slave trade, Beaman argues that 'Muslim is a racialized category located at the bottom of France's racial and ethnic hierarchy' (2019, 555), focusing instead on religion.

This chapter will not attempt to challenge the views of either Beaman or Salmi, nor will it aim to introduce a new interpretation of which minorities are at the bottom of France's racial hierarchy. Rather, the first section will consider how the framing of the white terrorist in *Chez nous* perpetuates an ideology of whiteness as the default in France, encouraging audiences to sympathise with this figure. The second section will build upon this idea in relation to *Made in France*, arguing that the film attempts to challenge the white-centric modes of representation often found in Western media, yet, it nevertheless maintains a privileging of its white-presenting characters, relegating non-white characters to the margins.

What draws these films together, then, is the hierarchy of visibility ascribed to terrorist figures. As many scholars have noted, Western media habitually privileges the visibility of individuals it deems to be more valuable; generally Christian, Western, and usually white. In her highly regarded book, *Precarious Life*, Judith Butler discusses the hierarchy of public grief after 9/11: 'Certain lives will be highly protected ... Other lives will not find such fast and furious support and will not even qualify as "grievable"' (2006, 32). Referring specifically to the case of death and mourning, Butler suggests that the 'grievability' of an individual depends on whether they fall within the bounds of what is considered 'human' by Western society, and directly questions whether 'Arab peoples, predominantly practitioners of Islam, [have] fallen outside the "human" as it has been naturalised in its "Western" mold' (2006, 32). Maria Flood similarly highlights this 'differential distribution of compassion', referring to the victims of the attacks on the *Charlie Hebdo* offices and those of Boko Haram's massacres in Borno, Nigeria, which occurred simultaneously but with vastly different levels of attention (2016, 63). Flood also observes this inequality of compassion in relation to Xavier Beauvois' *Des hommes et des dieux* (2010), a film about the Algerian Civil War which privileges 'the deaths of a small group of French men over the elimination of approximately 100,000 Algerians' (67).

Indeed, this hierarchy of grief can be expanded to consider the visibility of the lives of Arab peoples, as well as their deaths. Carrie Tarr, for example, discusses the increasing visibility of Muslims in everyday life in metropolitan France and the ways in which Islam has 'come to be perceived in dominant discourses as a threat to the secularism of the state' (2014, 518). Tarr connects this perceived threat also to French postcolonialism, suggesting that France's Muslim population has been 'increasingly stigmatised to divert attention away from the failure of urban policies' which were meant to aid the influx of Arab and Berber migrants following the Algerian war (1962) and the thirty-year period of post-war reconstruction, but instead created multi-ethnic suburban ghettos characterised by poor social conditions (518). Tarr goes on to highlight how French cinema has tended to confine the practice of Islam to 'private, domestic spaces' (519), or 'less threatening settings outside metropolitan French territory' (520), seemingly suggesting that Islam is compatible only with France's secular society when it is not visible. The visible Muslim, and particularly the visible Arab or Berber Muslim, is therefore perceived in dominant discourses to be a threat to French society. This is compounded in relation to terrorism: as Jimia Boutouba suggests, there now exists the 'stereotype of the young disenfranchised Arab Muslim-turned-terrorist' (2019, 216).

As such, it is illuminating to consider how Arab and Berber Islamic terrorist figures are presented to audiences in comparison to their white, Christian counterparts. By applying these observations to recent French depictions of terrorist figures, we begin to see how racial biases are encoded into the narrative and form of these films. In *Chez nous*, narrative and framing choices maintain a proximity between the white far-right extremist, and encourage audiences to empathise and identify with the right-wing extremist terrorist while dehumanising and discounting his Arab and Berber victims. By contrast, *Made in France* attempts to dispel the stereotype of the 'Arab Muslim-turned-terrorist' (Boutouba 2019, 216), yet screens its Arab and Berber terrorist figures from audiences both through diminished space and time on the screen, and lack of contextualisation of their disenfranchisement. As such, the hierarchy of visibility can be identified in both films, ultimately creating a racially encoded dichotomy between 'good' and 'bad' terrorists.

The Figure of the Far-Right Extremist in *Chez nous*

Chez nous was produced on a relatively small budget of €5.3 million, financed by its producers Synecdoche, its distributers Le Pacte and Sofica, and a small contribution (roughly 3% of its total budget; Deruisseau 2017) from the French national public broadcaster France Télévisions. Directed by Belgium-born director Lucas Belvaux, *Chez nous* follows Pauline, a nurse in a small, northern French town who is recruited by the fictional National Rally Party to stand as mayor in local elections. During her recruitment, she rekindles a former romance with her high school sweetheart, Stéphane 'Stanko' Stankowiak, who unbeknownst to Pauline has become a member of a far-right extremist organisation which premeditates and commits terrorist acts against Muslims and refugees.

Critical reception of the film after its release in 2017 was largely mixed. While some critics suggested that the film takes shortcuts in its message (Kaganski 2017), many applauded the film for its satirical portrayal of Marine

Le Pen and the fanaticism of the far-right *Rassemblement National* party (formerly *Front National*), and Belvaux's ability to draw attention to the permeation of far-right politics among a wide variety of French citizens (De Bruyn and Gandillot 2017; Kaganski 2017; Tuillier 2017). Certainly, the film demonstrates strong satirical tones in its portrayal of far-right politics through a direct parody of the image of Marine Le Pen. The leader of the film's equivalent of the *Rassemblement National* party, Agnès Dorgelle (Catherine Jacob), is a staunch woman with a stark blonde bob haircut, mirroring almost exactly the image of Le Pen. Belvaux has not publicly admitted to this being a direct parody of Le Pen, but has been clear in his intentions of criticising the far-right. Indeed, in his statement of intention in the press kit for *Chez nous*, Belvaux proclaims that he does not intend for the film to only be addressed to those who are aware of the true nature of the far-right, but 'à tous et à chacun' ('to each and to everyone'; Belvaux 2017, 5). Far-right ideology is criticised throughout the film, with some scenes even challenging claims of 'anti-French racism'. At a garden party amongst Pauline's friends, debate breaks out as to who is and is not 'French'. Pauline's friend, Nada, takes issue with the anti-immigrant rhetoric that others are expressing, and leaves the party dismayed. Following her, Pauline attempts to calm her and bring her back to the party. Nada tells her that she does not want to return to eat with 'des beaufs', roughly equivalent to the pejorative Anglophone terms 'hick' or 'redneck'. Hearing this, Pauline suggests that Nada's words constitute anti-French racism. Nada counters by arguing that 'Il traite les Arabes de voleurs, personne réagit et je suis raciste?' ('He treats all Arabs as thieves, no one reacts and I'm the racist?'). Although critics have labelled this type of scripting as too heavily charged and didactic (Magnin 2017; Trouvé 2017), it would suggest that the message of the film is anti-racist and critical of racism rhetoric in France. While this may be true, closer reading of the film's narrative, framing and editing reveals that it nevertheless continues to privilege the white experience by encouraging audiences to empathise with white characters as victims, in particular the far-right extremist Stanko.

Although focusing on representations of right-wing terrorists in US cinema and despite the important differences in how race and ethnicity are approached in France and the USA, we might turn to John Marmysz to further elucidate the cinematic representation of white-presenting extremists as sympathetic. Marmysz suggests that in cinematic portrayals of these figures, such as the Anglophone *American History X* (1998) and *Romper Stomper* (1992) or the Francophone *Un Français* (2015), several key features emerge:

> The skinhead is portrayed as a misguided, though passionate and rather intelligent, rebel: a sort of tragic, alienated and wounded character who is in search of, yet constantly failing to find, a place in the world. Because

of these qualities, at the same time that we are encouraged to detest the way of life of the skinheads in these films, we are also encouraged to view them, and their struggles, with a sort of guarded sympathy and compassion. (2013, 626)

Stanko and his group closely mirror the 'images of young, white males sporting shaven heads with viciousness and racial intolerance' which most academics and media consumers associate with skinheads (626), as well as fitting the sympathetic and misguided image Marmysz highlights. Through narrative, framing and lighting, audiences are encouraged to relate to and feel sympathy for Stanko throughout the film.

As the audience acquaints themselves with Stanko, so too does Pauline as the pair reignite their former relationship. As their relationship develops, we see Stanko become involved with Pauline's children in various scenes, both inside of Pauline's home and externally during activities typically enjoyed by families, such as skiing and attending a football match. This development allows audiences to see Stanko within domestic and familial spaces, encouraging relation to and sympathy with his character. The audience's relation to Stanko is also encouraged consistently by the framing and *mise-en-scène* of the film. Often in close-up and medium close-up, Stanko's character remains visually close to the audience throughout the film. The majority of his appearances are shot in warm or bright natural lighting; he is almost never shot from the back, even in shot counter-shot sequences, in which he is shown in side profile when the camera focuses on his interlocutor. In fact, scenes of dialogue between Stanko and other characters often end with shots lingering on Stanko in medium close-up. This is particularly significant as the medium close-up typically allows audiences to relate to a character. Alison Landsberg, for example, highlights the close-up as a method used in cinema to 'create a preferred vantage point for us as viewers' (2009, 224). Landsberg suggests that even if the characters we see 'might have had radically different life experiences, convictions, and commitments' to us the viewer, close-ups and point-of-view shots are cinematic techniques that 'powerfully [foster] our sense of identification with a character' and can 'force us to confront, and enter into a relationship of responsibility and commitment toward, "others"' (2009, 225). In her discussion of the 'relationship of responsibility' associated with the close-up, Landsberg draws upon the theory of French philosopher Emmanuel Levinas. His philosophy centres around the concept of the self's simultaneous responsibility toward the other *and* acknowledgement of the alterity of the other. Ultimately, Levinasian ethics requires both an approach toward the other, and a degree of distance to allow for the inextricable alterity of the other.

Here, the lingering close-up shots of Stanko after conversations invite audiences to consider the character's thoughts, and subsequently confront the viewer with the Levinasian 'face' of Stanko, despite our knowledge that his extremism is something most audience members do not share. We recognise his alterity, yet are encouraged to forge the relationship of responsibility toward him.

Indeed, this relationship between Stanko and the audience comes to its peak during an interaction between him and Phillipe Berthier, a prominent local doctor who is involved with the National Rally Party, and has sponsored Pauline's campaign for mayor. After learning of Pauline's relationship with Stanko, whose criminal activity is known to Berthier, the doctor approaches Stanko and threatens to inform Pauline of Stanko's violent activity unless he leaves Pauline without further contact. During this interaction, all of the aforementioned techniques are present as they are filmed in bright natural light; Stanko is consistently in medium or full close-up and he never faces away from the camera, allowing audiences to maintain their identification with him and encouraging the 'relationship of responsibility' Landsberg refers to (2009, 225). The physical proximity and sympathetic portrayal are heightened, too, by emphasis of Stanko's features in a way that softens his appearance. Although he is shown as muscular with short hair and stubble, close-ups reveal his round features and large eyes, tempering the threat presented by his actions. As such, the proximity between the violent extremist and the audience of *Chez nous* is one which invites empathy and consideration from viewers. In this scene in particular, as Stanko is verbally threatened by Berthier with the dissolution of his relationship to Pauline, Stanko is positioned as the victim of the right-wing party. Combined with the physical proximity afforded by close-ups, favourable lighting and framing, this victimisation of the violent extremist not only deepens the potential for audiences to empathise with him, but restructures the film's conception of victimhood. Instead of the recipients of Stanko's physical xenophobic violence being considered as the film's victims, this position is assumed by Stanko himself.

By contrast, Stanko's victims in the film are given far less screen time and consideration. During a far-right attack on a group of residents in an impoverished area Pauline is canvassing, a man is shot and killed at random by Stanko's group. Pauline attempts to come to the man's aid as a former nurse, but is pushed away by the victim's friends due to her political position within the far-right political party. The wounded man does not occupy the screen for more than a few seconds. Rather, Pauline is the focus of the camera as she is ushered away from the scene. Moreover, in a targeted and premeditated attack by Stanko and his group, two refugees are taken hostage and pushed into a cage, and a large dog is tied up outside the cage as intimidation. The only moment during which the refugees' voices are heard is a short exclamation of panic in Arabic as the group descends upon them. Throughout the scene, the refugees are framed mainly in full and wide shots. In the few moments that they are

Figure 9.1 *Chez nous*: a refugee is placed in a cage by Stanko's group.

shown in medium close-up, the camera is placed behind the mesh of the cage, thereby physically separating the refugees from viewers (Figure 9.1). The shot is so dark that the refugees' faces are barely visible, and the dog receives as much time in the frame at eye level as the humans.

Here, the Arab victims of Stanko's violence are not only given a significantly diminished screen presence, but they are distinctly disadvantaged by the framing and lighting during the little time they do appear on screen. Although a close-up may typically encourage identification, here the mesh of the cage and the low lighting act as a barrier between viewers and the refugee. As such, the proximity afforded to the right-wing extremist terrorist figure contrasts starkly with the dehumanisation and lack of empathy encouraged for his victims, creating an imbalance of proximity and empathy within the film. While viewers are encouraged to forge a 'relationship of responsibility' towards the right-wing extremist, there is no such accommodation for his Arab victims, who are presented within the film as less 'visible'.

As a result, the hierarchy of visibility within the film becomes clear. The white, Christian Stanko is held visually and narratively closer to the audience, who are encouraged to consider his motivations and emotions, and see him as a victim of his own political party. By comparison, his victims are held at a much greater distance, remaining mostly out of the physical view of the audience, and therefore discounted as deserving of visibility and consideration. While the film may make an effort to denounce the Islamophobia and racism present in far-right French politics, it nevertheless privileges the experiences of white characters and continues to orientate the politics of viewing hierarchies toward the white, Christian 'Western' figure, and away from ethnic minorities who are subject to the physical and societal violence of the far-right in the real world.

Visual Hierarchies in *Made in France*

While *Chez nous* demonstrates that audiences are encouraged to feel empathy for far-right extremist terrorists, *Made in France* focuses instead on Islamic extremism, a topic which made the film difficult to distribute. Filming began at the end of summer 2014, and due to the limited budget, lasted only six weeks. Boukhrief had already encountered difficulty in securing funding for the production, which many producers considered to be too controversial at a time when Brussels, Kenya, northern Mali and many other territories had fallen victim to Islamic extremist violence (Bouchara 2016). Nevertheless, the film was eventually picked up by Pretty Pictures and Radar films, with backing from Canal+. Boukhrief continued to experience resistance, struggling to obtain filming permission from local councils; a hurdle he overcame by submitting a fake script in which the jihadists were reimagined as Russian mafia (Bouchara 2016). The release was set for 18 November 2015, just five days after the fateful attacks across Paris on 13 November. At the time of the attacks copies of the film's poster, an image of the Eiffel Tower composed in part of a Kalashnikov, were still pasted across Paris. The film's theatrical release was cancelled, and it was eventually released on the French television channel TF1's online streaming service on 29 January 2016. The DVD release begins with a 3-second flash of text on screen, which simply reads 'Ce film a été tourné avant les attentats de Janvier 2015' ('This film was made before the January 2015 attacks'; Boukhrief 2016). Despite the time elapsed between the November attacks and the film's eventual streaming release, no reference to the November attacks is made.

In its final iteration *Made in France* follows Sam, a Muslim journalist of mixed Algerian and French descent, who infiltrates an Islamic extremist terrorist cell in Paris and passes information to the French police about the cell's movements. The cell is made up of a Muslim of Malian descent (Sidi), a Muslim of Maghrebi descent (Driss), and two white Muslim converts (Youssef/Christophe and Hassan/Pelletier). The film tracks their plotting of a terrorist attack, which ultimately fails to materialise as all members of the cell perish by various means, with the exception of Sam. Although all of the main characters in *Made in France* are Muslim men, by birth or as a result of conversion, they are portrayed with varying degrees of proximity to audiences.

In an in-depth analysis of the film, Jimia Boutouba suggests that *Made in France* 'subverts the "colonial" legacy of Western films in which "the Western hero" inhabits the narrative foreground and embodies a universal subjectivity, while the racialised others, often reduced to deviant subjects or disposable bodies, remain in the background' (2019, 224). Indeed, the film's director Nicolas Boukhrief does create a film which subverts many of the stereotypes surrounding the terrorist figure, who is often presented as 'a depoliticised and dehumanised enemy' (Boutouba 2019, 219), reinforcing the conception of 'Western nations ... fighting one monolithic global threat that [has] suddenly raised its head' (Pargeter 2008, 98). In particular, Boutouba suggests that Boukhrief implicates French society in terrorist violence: 'the four terrorists he presents are all French. They all live in France' (2019, 220). Certainly, they are all French, and *should* be considered as such. However if, as we have already seen, within the popular imaginary 'whiteness [is] synonymous with Frenchness' (Beaman 2019, 552), then Arab and Berber characters, though French, might be said to separate 'Frenchness' into nationality versus (perceived) identity. While all of the characters are represented as French Muslims, they are afforded different levels of proximity to the audience, with white terrorists being allowed greater visibility than their Arab and Berber counterparts. Therefore, although Boukhrief opens up representations of terrorism to include apparently white-presenting extremists, he nonetheless reaffirms the favourable treatment of white terrorist characters in film, while the Arab and Berber terrorists Driss and Sidi are indeed 'reduced to deviant subjects and disposable bodies' (Boutouba 2019, 224).

Sam El Khansouri, the white-presenting journalist of mixed Algerian and French descent, is the film's protagonist. Like the film's director Boukhrief and the actor Malik Zidi who portrays him, Sam is born to a French mother and an Algerian father. Indeed, Zidi's own father was a Kabyle Algerian – a northern Algerian ethnic group whose skin is often very light, and who were recruited en masse as *harkis* (natives of the French colonies who served as auxiliaries) in the Algerian War (Hautreux 2006, 35). As Boutouba suggests, this character can be read as providing 'renewed understanding of what constitutes religious and national identity' (2019, 224), and as acknowledging how racialisation of Algerians in France is reductive, ignoring the ethnic diversity within the region. However, while this may be seen as a challenge to the idea of 'whiteness as synonymous with Frenchness' discussed above, Sam's role in the film can also be seen as problematically mirroring colonial attitudes towards Algerians. Discussing the construction of the 'Arab' in French media, Deltombe and Rigouste highlight that this image often relies on the republican assimilation model. Using the examples of Khaled Kelkal – the presumed co-author of the attack on the Parisian RER in 1995 – and the celebrated footballer Zinedine Zidane, they demonstrate the polarised characterisation of Muslims in France. Whereas Kelkal became the embodiment of social markers framed as threatening in the 1990s, such as the *banlieue* youth, immigrant, Muslim turned extremist, and delinquent turned terrorist (Deltombe and Rigouste 2017, 119), Zidane was framed as the exception to the 'Arab' rule: 'if an Arab tried hard enough or happened to be brilliant, there was no reason for them not to be loved by racists' (120). To describe the latter, Deltombe and Rigouste use the term *préfet* (prefect) to express the media-driven ideology that the 'Arab' can only be considered successful when in the entertainment industry, or when serving the Republic (119).

The term *préfet* in this sense refers to the 'promotion of "good Muslims" to positions of responsibility . . . in order to better keep the "native masses" in line' (121), much like the promotion of school students to the status of prefect with the expectation that they enforce discipline upon other students. Within this schema, Sam can be seen as the *préfet* figure of the film. He is a French-Algerian Muslim, who has supposedly successfully assimilated under the republican model: he lives in a spacious and clean Parisian apartment – always shown as brightly lit and containing brimming bookshelves – with his wife and child, he has a successful career as a journalist, and serves the Republic by allying himself with the police. This categorisation comes dangerously close to the role of 'harki', the name given to Algerian auxiliaries who fought on the side of the French during the Algerian War of Independence. As such, although the film does 'subvert the "colonial" legacy' (Boutouba 2019, 224) by challenging racialisation of the figures of the Muslim and the 'Arab' in Western media, Sam's role within the film remains ambiguous. Furthermore, the representation of the two other white members of the terrorist cell creates additional ambiguity regarding the film's subversion of racial biases in French media. Although the inclusion of terrorists with a variety of ethnicities and backgrounds may subvert the typical representation of terrorists within Western media, the portrayal of white and white-presenting terrorists in *Made in France* nevertheless perpetuates the privileged white perspective.

To demonstrate this, we can look to an instance in which audiences may be encouraged to relate to a character on screen – in the domestic space, as we saw in *Chez nous*. Abou Youssef, another white terrorist, known before his conversion as Christophe and continuously called Christophe by other cell members, is shown at two different family homes. One is his Catholic grandmother's house, where the cell is based. This home is littered with Catholic iconography of crucifixes, and when the cell leader orders that all Western influence be removed, Christophe protests particularly strongly to the removal of the crucifix above his grandmother's bed. The other family home Christophe is shown in is his Catholic parents' Parisian apartment, which is introduced by a slow panning shot of a statue of the Virgin Mary. Like Sam's house, the space is well-lit, brightly coloured, spacious and contains many markers of the middle-class Parisian bourgeoisie, such as brimming bookcases and antique artworks. Abou Hassan, also a white terrorist known before his conversion in prison as Pelletier, organises the cell and their criminal activity. He strictly observes Islam, has a Muslim wife, and is never referred to by his former Christian name by other characters. He has light skin, but no other information about his ethnicity is offered. Like Christophe, he enjoys a number of close-ups and intimate explorations of his character. Hassan's home is marginally more dimly lit than that of Christophe, although filters with warm tones of orange and yellow are used here. These warm, familiar presentations of white-presenting terrorists contrast significantly with those of the remaining terrorist figures, who are Arab and Berber in origin. Sidi, whose family emigrated from Mali, is shown briefly in his home helping his brother with homework. His home is nondescript, and our view is confined only to one grey room, in this fleeting medium shot. Similarly, Driss is shown once in his nondescript and dark home, aggressively boxing a punchbag – a shot during which he almost immediately goes outside to the balcony overlooking the darkness of the city at night, turning him into an aggressive figurative outsider even in his own home. Driss is continually portrayed as violent, removed from the domestic sphere, shot in extremely low lighting, and as such audiences are not encouraged to relate to his character at all. Here, we can certainly see how racial biases play into Bouhkrief's representations of terrorists, with their proximity to the audience depending on their ethnicity and relation to conceptual 'Frenchness'. Although they are all practising Muslims, we see that audiences are encouraged to empathise more with white terrorists than their Arab and Malian counterparts, who in turn are screened away from the audience.

Racial bias is also imbued into the narrative in the deaths of the terrorist characters. Christophe and Hassan, the two white-presenting terrorists, are the last characters to die, and although both converted Muslims, each is returned to their former Christian faith during their death. The death of Christophe by car bomb is shown in slow motion and medium close-up, giving the audience the time to see him perform the sign of the cross as he realises his fate, and encouraging viewers to consider his emotion, a proximity which, as we will see, is neither granted to Driss nor Sidi. Hassan is killed in a standoff with a RAID police unit. Although the moment of his death is in the form of a long shot, and does not focus on his face, it is preceded by a brief point of view shot from his line of vision, and he is shown with arms outstretched as a shower of bullets kills him (Figure 9.2).

Figure 9.2 *Made in France*: Hassan is killed by RAID police.

Undeniably couched in Christian iconography of Jesus Christ, the framing of Hassan's death combined with a point-of-view shot brings the audience into extreme proximity to him. The return of these white characters to their former Christian faith at the time of their death arguably suggests that their Muslim faith functioned merely as a mask. Boutouba makes the pertinent argument that this can be read as Boukhrief challenging the stereotypical representation of Jihadist terrorists as deeply rooted in religious doctrine, instead aiming to 'depict a more complex reality than the commonly accepted stereotypes' (Boutouba 2019, 229). However, we must also acknowledge that French audiences, as we have seen, are routinely exposed to visual hierarchies which privilege 'Western', Christian and predominantly white experiences. The return of Christophe and Hassan to their Christian faith therefore opens the characters up to being seen as more relatable to French audiences than other terrorists.

The contrast between the deaths of Christophe and Hassan compared to those of Driss and Sidi is striking, and furthers our understanding of racial bias in representations of the terrorist figure. One fruitful way of interpreting the deaths of Driss and Sidi is to turn to a concept established by E. Ann Kaplan, who discusses 'empty empathy'. By this, she refers to 'empathy elicited by images of suffering provided without any context or background knowledge' (2005, 93). Kaplan discusses this concept in relation to images of Rwanda and the Iraq War, but we can adapt and apply this concept to *Made in France* as a means of interpreting the differentiation in proximity in relation to the characters. Sidi, for example, is briefly shown as an emotional being. We see him question his affiliation with the terrorist group and admit to Sam that he joined because of the death of his cousin in Mali, but this is not further contextualised. At no other point in the film is there an allusion to the violence experienced abroad at the hands of French military. By Boukhrief's own admission in interviews, 'behind the young man who commits a suicide bombing, believing to have committed a heroic act, hides a human being rocked by social injustices and the glaring lack of possibilities for integration . . . France, since Mitterrand, has abandoned the poor . . . Radicalization is one of the consequences of this injustice' (Castiel 2016, 9; translation mine). Yet other than Sidi's extremely brief mention of Mali, *Made in France* does little to highlight the injustices and violence experienced by Malians at the hands of the French during Mali's colonisation. In fact, any exploration of Sidi's plight is cut short by his death at the midpoint of the film, as he becomes the first terrorist figure to die. Shot by an unseen policeman during a scene in which the group steals explosives from a warehouse, he dies on the roadside as Hassan refuses to take him to a hospital. Significantly, as Sidi nears death, the camera zooms in slowly on him, surrounded by the group, as he prays. However, at this point, in such an intensely intimate moment where the audience might be encouraged to relate to Sidi and consider his emotional turmoil, the camera pans up to focus on Sam's face. Here, the emotions of the white-presenting protagonist are privileged over those of the Black character's death. Not only is Sidi's experience as a Black character eclipsed by the experience of the white-presenting Sam, but exploration of the wider suffering experienced by his family in Mali under French occupation is also curtailed. His early death in the narrative with only brief mention of French colonial violence, I contend, solidifies his position as one of the stereotypical 'disposable bodies' (Boutouba 2019, 224) of racialised characters in Western media.

Indeed, Driss receives a similar treatment, but instead of the figuration of his character as a 'disposable body', he is portrayed throughout the film as the racialised 'deviant subject' (Boutouba 2019, 224). As seen above, the brief scene of Driss in his home offers audiences no context about his life, and unlike the other terrorist characters, viewers remain unaware of the reasons for his radicalisation. While audiences' empathy for Sidi may be empty, viewers are not encouraged to empathise with Driss at all during the course of the film. This is particularly prominent when he is murdered by Hassan. During a disagreement, the pair descend into a physical altercation which culminates as Hassan stabs Driss in the side, killing him. Although the camera captures Driss's face for a moment, cupped in Sam's hands, Driss drops to the floor and out of the frame, leaving the camera lingering on Sam's horrified reaction. This is reminiscent of the racially biased framing in *Chez nous*, as a young Arab man's emotion and humanity during his death is overlooked in favour of the reaction of Pauline.

Beyond solidifying them as 'disposable bodies', the deaths of Sidi and Driss play into a more widely observable tendency to have 'the colonial native . . . disappear in an instant through the auto-combustive agency of their own violence' (Gilroy 2007, 234). Paul Gilroy highlights one such example in Michael Haneke's *Caché* (2005), in which Majid, the son of two Algerians who were killed in the 1961 Paris massacre, commits suicide. Gilroy suggests that Majid's suicide becomes an 'exclusively aesthetic event, devoid of all meaning apart from what it communicates about Georges', who is the white, middle-class protagonist of the film (234). Certainly the same can be said for the deaths of Sidi and Driss, both of whom are killed as a result of their own violence: Sidi through his involvement in criminal activity, and Driss through his confrontation with Hassan. The focalisation of the framing during their deaths on Sam also renders their deaths meaningful only in relation to the effect it has on him, and allows the remaining third of the film to focus exclusively on the white terrorists. As such, not only are Sidi and Driss treated as disposable Arab and Berber bodies, but they are denied any character development beyond the stereotype of the self-destructive terrorist figure.

Both the deaths of Sidi and Driss in *Made in France* demonstrate once more that white terrorists are given priority in the visual hierarchy of the film, even at moments of intense humanity. Directing attention away from Sidi and Driss as they die, and instead privileging the emotion of the white-presenting Sam reinforces the audience's identification with the latter, solidifying the distance between the viewer and Arab or Berber terrorists.

Conclusion

This discussion of *Chez nous* and *Made in France* has demonstrated that regardless of the motivations of filmmakers to seek to communicate to audiences that right-wing extremist terrorism is a current threat in France, or that terrorism is also perpetrated by white individuals, the racial biases of French visual culture continue to permeate even the most recent and well-intentioned of representations.

While France has faced the widespread issue of Islamophobia for decades and continues to demonstrate this discrimination even at the legal level as a result of the nation's engrained values of secularism, anti-Muslim sentiment is not the singular driving force behind biased representations in these films. Instead, these representations are subject to more complex biases rooted in France's colonialism, which have left residual (although no less damaging) biases surrounding race, ethnicity and religion. While the trend of understanding and relating to right-wing extremist terrorists is now continued with the likes of *Chez nous*, it is not only right-wing extremist figures who benefit from a greater level of proximity to audiences, and who are priorities within the visual hierarchy of these films. As *Made in France* demonstrates, even when born and raised Muslim, the white terrorist is portrayed as somehow more relatable to audiences than the Black or Maghrebi terrorist. Moreover, while directors such as Boukhrief are beginning to acknowledge and challenge the stereotypes of representing terrorists, these representations remain couched in racial bias, privileging the visibility of white terrorists and their emotional experiences. Affording viewers proximity to white terrorists while denying non-white terrorists this familiarity risks categorising white terrorists as somehow more human, more worthy of visibility, imposing a racially-coded categorisation between 'good terrorists', or those we can empathise with, and 'bad terrorists', with whom we can and should not empathise. At a time when Islamophobia, resistance to postcolonial dialogue and anti-Arab sentiment is rife in France, the racial bias imbued in such screenings of the terrorist figure is extremely damaging.

References

Assemblée nationale. 2021. "XVe législature : Session ordinaire de 2020–2021 ; Séance du mardi 16 février 2021." https://www.assemblee-nationale.fr/dyn/15/comptes-rendus/seance/session-ordinaire-de-2020-2021/deuxieme-seance-du-mardi-16-fevrier-2021

Beaman, Jean. 2019. "'Are French People White?': Towards an Understanding of Whiteness in Republican France." *Identities: Global Studies in Culture and Power* 26, no. 5: 546–62.

Belvaux, Lucas, dir. 2017. *Chez nous*. France: Le Pacte. DVD.

Beunaiche, Nicolas. 2015. "Plus d'une cinquantaine d'actes antimusulmans recensés en France depuis l'attentat de 'Charlie Hebdo'." *20 Minutes*, January 12, 2015. https://www.20minutes.fr/societe/1515415-20150112-plus-cinquantaine-actes-antimusulmans-recenses-france-depuis-attentat-charlie-hebdo

Bouchara, Olivier. 2016. "Made in France, le film maudit." *Vanity Fair*, January 27, 2016. https://www.vanityfair.fr/culture/ecrans/articles/-made-in-france-le-film-maudit-par-olivier-bouchara/31201

Boukhrief, Nicolas, dir. 2016. *Made in France*. France: TF1 Video/Pretty Pictures. DVD.

Boutouba, Jimia. 2019. "Through the Lens of Terror: Re-Imaging Terrorist Violence in Boukhrief's Made in France." *Studies in French Cinema* 19, no. 3: 215–32. https://doi.org/10.1080/14715880.2018.1528536

Butler, Judith. 2004. *Precarious Life: The Powers of Mourning and Violence*. London: Verso.

Castiel, Élie. 2016. "Nicolas Boukhrief : Une Question de Prise de Conscience Morale." *Séquences : La Revue de Cinéma*, no. 302: 8–11.

De Bruyn, Olivier, and Thierry Gandillot. 2017. "'Chez nous', le film qui fait débat." *Les Echos*, February 2017. https://www.lesechos.fr/2017/02/chez-nous-le-film-qui-fait-debat-1114599

Deltombe, Thomas, and Mathieu Rigouste. 2017. "The Enemy Within: The Construction of the 'Arab' in the Media." In *The Colonial Legacy in France: Fracture, Rupture, and Apartheid*, 115–22. Bloomington, IN: Indiana University Press.

Deruisseau, Bruno. 2017. "'Chez Nous' le Film qui Fait Crier au Scandale Plusieurs Cadres du FN." *Les Inrockuptibles*, January 7, 2017. https://www.lesinrocks.com/cinema/chez-film-crier-scandale-plusieurs-cadres-fn-54487-07-01-2017/

Diastème, dir. 2015. *Un Français*. Mars Distribution.

Europol. 2016. *TE-SAT 2016: European Union Terrorism Situation and Trend Report 2016*. https://www.europol.europa.eu/activities-services/main-reports/european-union-terrorism-situation-and-trend-report-te-sat-2016

Flood, Maria. 2016. "Terrorism and Visibility in Algeria's 'Black Decade': *Des Hommes et des Dieux* (2010)." *French Cultural Studies* 27, no. 1: 62–72.

France 24. 2015. "'Charlie Hebdo': Plus de 50 Actes Antimusulmans Recensés en France." January 13, 2015. https://www.france24.com/fr/20150113-charlie-hebdo-multiplication-actes-antimusulmans-recenses-france-conseil-culte

Gilroy, Paul. 2007. "Shooting Crabs in a Barrel." *Screen* 48, no. 2: 233–5.

Haneke, Michael, dir. 2005. *Caché*. Les films du losange.

Hautreux, François-Xavier. 2006. "L'engagement des harkis (1954-1962). Essai de périodisation." *Vigntième Siècle. Revue d'histoire* 90, no. 2: 33–45.

Kaganski, Serge. 2017. "'Chez Nous' : Critiqué par le FN, le Film Est Assez Conforme à la Réalité." *Les Inrockuptibles*, February 17, 2017. https://www.lesinrocks.com/cinema/chez-nous-18543-17-02-2017/

Kaplan, E. Ann. 2005. "Vicarious Trauma and 'Empty' Empathy: Media Images of Rwanda and the Iraq War." In *Trauma Culture: The Politics of Terror and Loss in Media and Literature*, 87–100. Rutgers University Press.

Kaye, Tony, dir. 1998. *American History X*. New Line Cinema.

Landsberg, Alison. 2009. "Memory, Empathy, and the Politics of Identification." *International Journal of Politics, Culture, and Society* 22, no. 2: 221–9.

Le service Metronews. 2015. "Attentat contre Charlie Hebdo : les actes anti-musulmans se multiplient." *TF1 Info*, January 9, 2015. https://www.tf1info.fr/societe/attentat-contre-charlie-hebdo-les-actes-anti-musulmans-se-multiplient-1519699.html

Les Echos. 2015. "Charlie Hebdo : les Actes anti-musulmans ont plus que doublé par rapport à janvier 2014." *Les Echos*, January 19, 2015. https://www.lesechos.fr/2015/01/charlie-hebdo-les-actes-anti-musulmans-ont-plus-que-double-par-rapport-a-janvier-2014-198105

Magnin, Catherine. 2017. "'Chez nous' : Les idées d'extrême droite égratignées par un Belge." *20 Minutes,* March 7, 2017. https://www.20min.ch/fr/story/les-idees-d-extreme-droite-egratignees-par-un-belge-435829288410

Marmysz, John. 2013. "The Lure of the Mob: Contemporary Cinematic Depictions of Skinhead Authenticity." *Journal of Popular Culture* 46, no. 3: 626–46.

Pargeter, Alison. 2008. *The New Frontiers of Jihad: Radical Islam in Europe*. Philadelphia: University of Pennsylvania Press.

Plenel, Edwy. 2016. *For the Muslims: Islamophobia in France*. Trans. David Fernbach. London: Verso.

Salmi, Katya. 2011. "'Race Does Not Exist Here.' Applying Critical Race Theory to the French Republican Context." In *Atlantic Crossings: International Dialogues on Critical Race Theory*, eds Kevin Hylton et al., 177–96. Birmingham: C-SAP, University of Birmingham.

Tarr, Carrie. 2014. "Looking at Muslims: The Visibility of Islam in Contemporary French Cinema." *Patterns of Prejudice* 48, no. 5: 516–33.

Todd, Emmanuel. 2015. *Who Is Charlie? Xenophobia and the New Middle Class*. Trans. Andrew Brown. Cambridge, UK: Polity Press.

Trouvé, Pierre. 2017. "'Chez nous' : un film plombé par son message politique sur le Front national." *Le Monde*, February 23, 2017. https://www.lemonde.fr/cinema/video/2017/02/23/chez-nous-un-film-plombe-par-son-message-politique-sur-le-front-national_5084308_3476.html

Tuillier, Laura. 2017. "Chez Nous." *Cahiers du Cinéma*, no. 730: 46.

West, Joan M. 2017. "Chez Nous by Lucas Belvaux." *The French Review* 91, no. 1: 239–40.

Wolfreys, Jim. 2017. *Republic of Islamophobia: The Rise of Respectable Racism in France*. London: Hurst & Company.

Wright, Geoffrey, dir. 1992. *Romper Stomper*. Roadshow Film Distributors.

10. 'I WAS A BIG GIRL. I COULD PACK MY BAGS AND LEAVE': ISIS AND FEMALE EMANCIPATION IN TABISH KHAIR'S *JUST ANOTHER JIHADI JANE*

Zaynab Seedat

INTRODUCTION

When the Bethnal Green trio, Amira Abase, Kadiza Sultana and Shamima Begum travelled to Syria in February 2015, there was a palpable sense of shock and confusion among the British public as to why these schoolgirls from the West would travel to an area of extreme violence. Within a day, British news coverage labelled the girls 'jihadi brides' who were naive and had been groomed (Khan 2015). Days later, it emerged that a fourth girl from the same school, Sharmeena Begum (no relation to Shamima), had travelled to ISIS-controlled Syria a couple of months earlier, in December 2014. Aqsa Mahmood, nicknamed the 'bedroom radical', a radiography student turned high-profile ISIS recruiter, had been in contact with one of the trio on Twitter (Saul 2015; Buchanan 2015). Just a month after the trio's departure, a travel ban was imposed on five other girls – four of them from the same school as the Bethnal Green trio – after they showed interest in travelling to Syria (BBC News 2015). This exodus of East London girls to ISIS suggests a larger social context affecting Muslim girls which goes beyond personal factors. Issues including social alienation, identity crises, and political differences driven by religious considerations contribute to these women's radicalisation but are often downplayed in the media and political discourse.

Part of this deemphasis owes itself to the popular and misleading label 'jihadi bride', which infantilises girls by suggesting they join ISIS in search of romance. Newspaper articles such as a February 2015 piece by *Telegraph* columnist Allison Pearson perpetuate the label. In a parody of the coming-of-age story, Pearson dismisses the Bethnal Green trio's departure as a classic combination of teenage sexual frustration, strict parents and rebellion. What puzzles Pearson is that these girls seek out environments of known violence and repression rather than liberation. Her final witticism illustrates the image of the terrorist as the ultimate other: 'If you make your bed with barbarians, you can lie in it' (2015). Thus, Pearson reinforces binary 'us versus them' thinking.

Public concern surrounding ISIS members returning to their birth countries culminated in the infamous case of Shamima Begum. Her British citizenship was revoked in February 2019 by then-Home Secretary Sajid Javid, shortly after she had been discovered in a Syrian refugee camp by a *Times* journalist. Contributing to the public debate over Begum's expatriation, former *Good Morning Britain* presenter, the controversial and outspoken Piers Morgan, echoed Pearson: 'Don't let these terror brides come home – they made their ISIS husbands' beds, now let them rot in hell in them' (2019). The phrase 'terror brides' suggests that these women only have a marital and domestic role in relation to terror, one that is disproportionately concerned with bed-making. The dismissiveness of these labels, alongside Begum's banishment from the UK, indicates that terrorism is treated as an 'out of sight of, out of mind' problem, which leads to a continued lack of knowledge as to why women and girls from the West join ISIS.

Research demonstrates that women's motivations for joining ISIS are multi-causal and fall into push and pull factors (Saltman and Smith 2015; Hoyle et al. 2015). Some pull factors include religious duty; finding purpose; taking part in a humanitarian mission to relieve the suffering of Muslims, particularly the Syrian population; finding a spouse; belonging; and viewing the Caliphate as a utopic state for Muslims (Perešin and Cervone 2015; Perešin 2015; Saltman and Smith 2015; Hoyle et al. 2015; Shapiro and Maras 2019). Push factors span the persecution of the international Muslim community; anger or frustration at the perceived lack of international response and at the West's complicity; a lack of belonging in the West which contributes to an 'us versus them' dynamic; feelings of alienation and inequality caused by racism and the lack of religious freedom experienced by some Muslims in the West; and restrictive traditional and cultural values which Muslims, particularly females, experience in their diasporic communities (Perešin 2015; Saltman and Smith 2015; Hoyle et al. 2015; Shapiro and Maras 2019). These push and pull factors are multifaceted, encompassing both personal and political aspirations. Even factors which might be construed as being primarily of female concern – the hope of finding a spouse has popularised the 'jihadi bride' stereotype – apply across genders, meaning that women's reasons for joining are not wholly gender-specific.

Women's roles in ISIS are also diverse. They involve domestic duties; operational activities such as propaganda production and online recruitment;

tactical positions within militancy, like women-only brigades which keep women's morality in check; and state-building roles in teaching and healthcare (for a review of scholarship on the roles of women in ISIS, see Shapiro and Maras 2019, 94–5). This variety of roles proves the label 'jihadi bride' to be reductionist (Saltman and Smith 2015, 5–6). Even then, Katharina Kneip (2016, 89) finds that women's reasons for joining ISIS tend to be seen as less idealistic and political than men's because of their commonly assumed roles as wives and mothers rather than militants. Women's agency is overwritten by gendered frames which depict them as running to ISIS out of naivety and a misguided sense of romance. Media explanations of female radicalisation thus bypass individual or political motives and instead rely on stereotypical assumptions about the female gender.

As of 29 September 2014, the *Guardian* estimated that ten percent of those travelling to join ISIS from the UK, USA and Australia were women (Sherwood et al. 2014). This development represents a unique historical situation when compared with women's participation in past jihadist conflicts. The statistics accord with the general upwards trend of female terrorism identified by Karla Cunningham (2003, 172). While reasons for joining ISIS are not solely based on gender, the high number of females joining ISIS suggests a gendered consideration of the processes of recruitment and radicalisation which goes beyond the clichés of the 'jihadi bride' and 'women as wives and mothers'.

Whereas narrow gendered explanations obfuscate why women join ISIS, literary texts can help to rectify this lacuna. Published one year after the Bethnal Green trio made headlines, Tabish Khair's novel *Just Another Jihadi Jane* (2016) challenges the media narrative as to why British schoolgirls join ISIS. Khair's female-centric novel follows two second-generation South Asian Muslim high school girls from Yorkshire as they travel to join ISIS in Syria. Told from the first-person perspective of Jamilla, Khair's novel immediately signals a playfulness with gendered framing through its title, *Just Another Jihadi Jane*. The title alludes to Colleen LaRose, a white American woman convicted of several terrorism-related charges in 2011, who used the screen name 'JihadJane'. The name's connection to the idiom 'plain Jane' suggests a commonplace ordinariness (Conway and McInerney 2012, 11). Khair's adaptation of LaRose's alias not only implies a nod to an earlier case of female radicalisation, but illustrates that any girl, from any background – not just young, impressionable Muslim girls wanting to be 'jihadi brides' – can become susceptible to terrorist influences. The title also raises the question as to whether the girls are really only Jihadi Janes who have run away to ISIS in search of romance and adventure, or whether they are more than that.

Just Another Jihadi Jane is the only work of fiction so far dealing with women's recruitment to ISIS amid a growing corpus of podcasts, television shows, memoirs and scholarship, which Khair drew on while writing his novel.[1] As he explains in an interview, Khair read 'autobiographies of Muslims who joined and left fundamentalism as well as ideological tracts by Islamists', and he also used his 'own observations of Muslims being attracted to Wahhabism or being angry and frustrated at their inability to save other Muslims from persecution' (qtd in 'Addressing Xenophobia' 2016). Fictional representations can shed a fresh light on the phenomenon of female radicalisation. In his essay 'Why Literature is the Answer to Extremism', Khair argues that the complex readings which literature calls for contest extremism's desire for singular readings and easy answers (2019, xiii). The novel's very form escapes the demand for reductive explanations found in the media, but rather calls for complex reading which establishes empathetic connections between self and other.

By writing from the perspective of the terrorist, so often portrayed as other by the media and Western politics, Khair reveals an aspiration to provoke singular readings surrounding the naive, sexually frustrated, thrill-seeking 'jihadi bride'. In the novel, female emancipation proves an important factor in the duo's radicalisation. Although women's reasons for joining ISIS are often not confined to gender, as explored above, Khair includes and interrogates gendered explanations of why women join ISIS. My analysis follows suit, exploring the merits and limits of a gendered interpretation.

From her new home in Indonesia, Jamilla tells the story of herself and her best friend Ameena to an unnamed male novelist and essayist. The girls' motivations for joining ISIS are informed by the diverse push and pull factors mentioned earlier, which span across both personal (gendered) and political reasons. Although unlikely friends, Jamilla and Ameena's shared sense of isolation makes them vulnerable to ISIS recruiter Hejjiye. They travel to Syria to provide help at a women's only orphanage run by Hejjiye. Ameena marries ISIS commander Hassan and Jamilla finds work as a teacher, thus demonstrating the variety of roles available to women. Unbeknownst to one another, both girls become disillusioned. To help Jamilla escape, Ameena devises a complicated plot as part of a ceasefire operation involving her actual and Jamilla's supposed martyrdom. Jamilla, saved by the distraction Ameena's suicide attack and death provides, relocates to Bali where she approaches a male writer – after a talk of his arguing that former ISIS members should be barred from democratic states – to present her side of the story.

The Limits of Narration

Khair immediately signals a gendered focus through the title of his novel, enhanced by his writing from the first-person perspective of Jamilla. Her evasiveness concerning the details of the duo's story when addressing the male writer, such as the location of her hometown, conveys her awareness around storytelling. Jamilla is controlled in her narration and playful with fact and fiction, as she states, 'I am a woman who started off with the conviction that there should be nothing but truth. The One Truth, the Only Truth. I was suckled on that conviction' (Khair 2016, 1). Even the cover of the Periscope Book's 2016 edition showcases this elusiveness, depicting a page of text with passages concealed by black marker pen, leaving the words 'just another jihadi jane'. However, Clare Gallien (2019) interprets this kind of 'textual excision', often seen in government documents involving imprisoned terrorists, as a symbolic violence that is perpetrated by the state against terrorists. Redaction demonstrates that language is controlled by those in power (7–8). Rather than Jamilla's authority, the redaction of the cover page illustrates the mediation and violation of Jamilla's story by the male writer, who is perhaps symbolic of the general public.

The narrative style is reminiscent of Mohsin Hamid's *The Reluctant Fundamentalist* (2007), which similarly uses indirect speech to include the listener's interjections into the first-person narrative. Unlike Hamid's novel, however, *Just Another Jihadi Jane* presents a unique gender dynamic in the listener/speaker relationship as it is a secular, agnostic male who listens, and acts as a foil to, the Muslim female's oration (Chambers 2019, 178). This listener remains a shadowy figure at the borders of Jamilla's narration, a character that is never fully developed. The suggestion that he comes from a Muslim background – at one point Jamilla asks whether his parents had a set menu for *iftar*, the meal after breaking the fast (Khair 2016, 58) – seems to link his position against the repatriation of former ISIS members to conservative, right-wing sentiment in Muslim communities. It also foreshadows the stance of Home Secretary Sajid Javid on the revocation of Shamima Begum's citizenship. The inclusion of the male listener, a self-conscious nod by Khair to his positionality as an Indian man from a Muslim background, hints at a power dynamic inherent in Jamilla's narration: it is through the male writer and his bias that Jamilla speaks. So, the presence of this mediator distances Jamilla from the reader and hints at a narrative violence similarly seen in media stories about 'jihadi brides'.

Elena Igartuburu sees evidence of this violence in the fragmentation of Jamilla's narrative voice, which she describes as an 'agglutination' of different voices (2018, 457). Igartuburu does not develop this argument, however, which ends on an offhand and rather dramatic question: 'Are they even *girls* at all if their narrative is constantly disrupted by the voice of the author?' (457; emphasis in original). Contrary to Igartuburu, I would argue that the narrative intrusions into Jamilla's storytelling are related less to her girlhood than to the way stories are overwritten and retold. Jamilla's ardent statement, 'I am a woman' (Khair 2016, 1), answers Igartuburu's question concerning gender. Compounded as Jamilla's statement is by the maternal image conjured by the verb 'suckled' (1), Jamilla's opening proclamation concretises womanhood as central to her identity and to the novel.

Towards the end of Chapter 1, Khair chronicles a process of radicalisation closely tied to the struggles of second-generation Muslim women. Stuck between assimilating to British society and adhering to Islamic codes of living, Jamilla questions the male listener and implied reader:

> are you sure it was the mosque that radicalised Ameena? ... Or was it also Ameena's parents' divorce? ... Was it her lost love for Alex? Was it the way her friends snubbed her? Was it her mother's strong disapproval of the Islamic headscarf? (Khair 2016, 26)

Daniele Valentini (2019, 35) interprets this questioning as Jamilla's doubt around the exact cause of Ameena's radicalisation, a valid issue considering the unreliability of the narration. A different interpretation is suggested by Khair's explanation that narration represents an ontological limitation, 'an engagement with the fact that the language of the self can never fully express or "know" the other' (2019, xiii). In his novel, Khair explores the restrictions of storytelling and the politics of listening through Jamilla's questioning of the male writer. Rather than expressing personal doubt, the quoted passage challenges the listener/reader to consider whether the motivations for radicalisation can truly be uncovered. Curiously, Jamilla does not mention any political motivations here, even though over the course of the novel, politics are revealed to be another cause of the girls' flight to Syria.

Claire Chambers' work on sound (2019) and Igartuburu's on narration (2018) indicate that a specific gendered focus on *Just Another Jihadi Jane* is lacking in scholarship. My chapter seeks to rectify this by exploring how gender contributes to a sense of female radicalisation in the novel. More specifically, I consider women's participation in ISIS and the desire for emancipation through three female characters, Jamilla, Hejjiye and Ameena. Remaining mindful of Khair's contention that literature generates complex readings, I focus on the interplay of different factors in the process of radicalisation, considering the limitations of a gendered interpretation.

Jamilla: Mothers, Marriage and Muslim Community

Jamilla's narrative describes the difficulty of being both Muslim and female in the West. She dismisses the listener who cannot understand this predicament: 'you are a man' (Khair 2016, 77). As she explains, no Muslim man 'no matter how believing, how faithful, how orthodox, has to face a third of the difficulties that orthodox Muslim women encounter in the West' (77). Khair illustrates how Muslim women bear the brunt of Islamophobia as Jamilla is shouted at by an old woman on a bus – herself quirkily dressed in an antique gown and flowery bonnet – that she is letting down her sex and failing to assimilate (73).

Jamilla explains that this incident 'helped me make up my mind' (73) to join ISIS, as her anxieties around belonging in British society peaked. Thinking about her future in the UK as a practising Muslim, Jamilla laments, 'I did not belong here, I felt I never would' (67). Fully covered except for her eyes, Jamilla's orthodox Muslim women's dress presents a barrier in everyday life, which was 'under constant assault' (77). This metaphor of war applies to the ordinary interactions and commonplace choices influencing dress, food and social settings, which are restricted for Jamilla. Through these self-imposed constraints, Jamilla cannot fully partake in British society and is excluded; she tells the listener, 'some of us never had parks or parties to connect in. Some of us never will' (98). These restrictions build up a 'core of bitterness' within Jamilla, as she reflects that non-Muslims enjoy freedoms that can 'empower you as a person' (78). Jamilla believes that emancipation can be gained from living in the West as a Westerner, but this autonomy is not available to those on the periphery of being Western, like herself, who must compromise their religious beliefs to gain alleged freedoms.

Outsiders' views of her result in self-othering, as Jamilla feels she is like an 'alien from Mars', 'a monster or a curiosity' (78). It takes 'strength and character' (78) to be a Muslim woman in the West. These same qualities drive Jamilla's decision to join the Islamic State, 'a country where I thought I could be myself' (78). She sees ISIS as a utopia, allowing Muslims an escape from inhospitable home nations where religion must be compromised. Scholarship shows that laws governing hijab-wearing in some European countries are, indeed, a decisive factor in drawing Muslim women to ISIS, who hope to be freed from these Western restrictions (Kneip 2016, 95). Chambers (2019, 179) notes that Khair's novel reflects what Kirsten Holst Petersen and Anna Rutherford term 'double colonisation' (1986, 1), a phenomenon also known as the intersectionality of oppression (Crenshaw 1989, 140; 1991, 1244). Described by Jamilla as being 'lovingly browbeaten by her father', husband and 'incomprehensible new country', Jamilla's 'timid' mother epitomises the double oppression of patriarchy and colonialism that some Muslim women face (Khair 2016, 4). When Jamilla's father dies, mother and daughter are stopped from visiting his grave by male relatives who deem this to be anti-Islamic (20). Some women face the simultaneous oppression of living under a former colonial power and the tension of reconciling cultural and religious traditions, which are often patriarchal, with Western norms. Research shows that a further pull factor for women joining ISIS is the prospect of taking control of and making independent decisions about their lives that break from tradition (Kneip 2016, 92–3), thus overcoming their double colonisation.

Against this background, travelling to join ISIS can be interpreted as an emancipatory action. For Jamilla, the impetus to migrate comes from the epiphany: 'I was a big girl. I could pack my bags and leave' (Khair 2016, 79).

An encouraging phrase usually reserved for young girls to help modulate their behaviour, the term 'big girl' feels infantile, as if Jamilla were play-acting her independence. This emancipation cannot be judged by the standards of single-issue feminism, or *'freeing women from restraint or control'* (Kneip 2016, 92; emphasis in original). Rafia Zakaria takes care to indicate that ISIS is not so much concerned with women's liberation as 'presenting an alternative to Western hegemony' (2015, 122). Kneip proposes the term 'Islamicipation' to describe the emancipation from Western norms of culture, dress and socialisation (2016, 97). Living as part of an Islamic society is key to 'Islamicipation'. Jamilla recounts that among other reasons for ISIS' appeal there was the desire to live a simple life modelled on the Prophet Muhammad (Khair 2016, 79). Feminist aspirations like belonging to a sisterhood are used by ISIS to appeal to women, but 'Islamicipation', or living in a state that offers an alternative to the West, has just as much appeal, if not more, than feminism.

Coupled with a lack of belonging is a lack of empowerment that is acutely felt by Jamilla. With her plans for higher education fallen through, Jamilla faces pressure from her mother to marry. News of a potential suitor from Birmingham is framed in the language of warfare and terrorism, when 'Ammi dropped her bomb' (62). Jamilla expresses shock at this metaphorical violence even when marriage is a long-standing anticipation: 'All my life, I had been groomed to marry a man like him' (65). Instead of describing ISIS' recruitment tactics as grooming, Jamilla uses this word to convey her vulnerability and powerlessness in the face of an arranged marriage. Although '[m]arriage had been something like the rumour of a distant war; now, suddenly, the cannons were at my doorstep' (65). The imagery of cannons indicates that Jamilla is under siege by these long-range weapons aiming to breach her walls. Paradoxically, Jamilla replaces the symbolic battlefield of marriage with an actual one. Kneip notes that having free choice in marriage means the Caliphate offers freedom from restrictive family backgrounds where women are unable to make independent decisions about whom to marry (2016, 94). However, this new-found freedom is illusory. Paternal care is only temporarily removed. Marriage to a jihadi renews control by a male guardian, which, under ISIS territory, is even more prohibitive than parental decision-making (Kneip 2016, 98). As the novel unfolds, Jamilla finds the pressure to marry in Syria even more intense than back home.

It is also through this maternal pressure to marry that Jamilla first feels estranged from her family. She asks, 'Was this how I was going to end, another version of my Ammi?' (Khair 2016, 73). The distance between mother – an anxious, illiterate recluse – and daughter is made apparent as Jamilla thinks about her own vapid future as a wife. This conflict means Jamilla feels rejected: 'How easily they had all disinherited me! They had not done it consciously, sure, but then neither had this city' (68). The verb 'disinherit' has legal connotations;

Jamilla's marriage would mean forfeiting a claim to her father's flat while her new home in Indonesia shows that former ISIS members cannot return to Britain. 'Disinherit' also points to the more cerebral concepts of cultural heritage and belonging to a British society. Familial and societal dispossession compound Jamilla's psychological homelessness: 'they had allowed me to go, even encouraged me to drift out of their lives' (104). In Syria, Jamilla reflects that her being 'married off to a stranger' would have made her absence from the family home inevitable (103). Khair illustrates the complex interactions of push and pull factors and goes beyond scholarship by demonstrating that poor maternal relationships can also be a push factor. Although there was 'love between us', for Jamilla there was 'very little to express and even less to share' (103) with her mother. To escape the mundane, routine domesticity of her mother's life, ISIS provides Jamilla a seemingly emancipatory way out.

It is Jamilla's drifting away from her mother that makes Hejjiye, a female ISIS propagandist and recruiter, 'feel like a family member' (70). A beautiful woman who appears politically astute and religiously inclined, Hejjiye is someone whom Jamilla increasingly comes to trust, leaving her wishing for a 'mother – or an older sister – like her' (70). As Jamilla and Ameena's social circle diminishes after leaving school, a sense of belonging and acceptance is found through these online friends. In their midst, both girls feel like 'the norm, not the exception' (53). The protagonists' wish to belong to a group tallies with Marc Sageman's (2008, 66) examination of terror networks, according to which recruitment and radicalisation are driven by in-group love and out-group hate, rather than ideology. This is illustrated by Chris Morris' 2010 comedy film *Four Lions*, which suggests that a common pathway to terrorism is a 'bunch of guys' who collectively decide to join a terrorist organisation. In *Just Another Jihadi Jane*, Khair applies the same idea to a 'bunch of girls'. Lauren Shapiro and Marie-Helen Maras (2019, 98) found that for women who started alone and later joined a group, or women who started with a group and stayed with that group, their relationship with the group was a key factor in their radicalisation.

In Khair's novel, relationships and group dynamics make Jamilla feel part of an 'imagined community' (2016, 54). The passage echoes Benedict Anderson's notion that all communities larger than face-to-face groups are imagined, as individual members can never meet, let alone know, every other member (2018, 14). In *Just Another Jihadi Jane*, religion constitutes one such imagined community. At the orphanage, Jamilla realises that while the community created on the Internet erased the 'differences that existed with the brush of a hypothetical Islam' (Khair 2016, 54), she has little in common with the other girls besides this hypothetical Islam. Crucially, Anderson notes that for the construction of imagined communities such as nations, the lived realities of individual members are less significant than what they collectively imagine (2018,

14). Applying this idea to ISIS would suggest that the imagined sisterhood of Islamic belonging is more potent than the reality of differing socioeconomic and cultural backgrounds. Surprisingly, however, Jamilla's perspective shifts during her time in Syria. She later admits: 'The longer I stayed at the orphanage, the more I felt that I understood [my mother]' (205). As Jamilla's idealism of unconditional understanding with her fellow ISIS recruits falls away, she imaginatively reconciles with her mother instead.

Hejjiye: 'Jihadi Girl-Power'

In contrast to the meekness of Jamilla's mother, Hejjiye is a strong female role model at the ISIS orphanage which she runs, accessorised with a collection of Gucci handbags that makes her 'terrorist chic' (Igartuburu 2018, 451) or 'jihadi cool/chic' (Picart 2017, 7). Charlie Winter (2015b) describes this propaganda strategy as 'five-star jihad', where photos showcasing fast cars and weapons are used to romanticise the austere dystopic reality of ISIS to appeal to potential recruits. Added to her allure, Jamilla sees Hejjiye as maternal and compassionate. She admires her for preserving the safety and lives of women, children and orphans, 'creating an oasis . . . in the deserts of violence that surrounded them' (Khair 2016, 206). Through Hejjiye there is a sense of feminist emancipation, as Jamilla believes the purpose of the orphanage is women's education (102). Hejjiye thus epitomises the 'jihadi girl-power subculture' – to use Anita Perešin and Alberto Cervone's term (2015, 506) – found in social media propaganda. This new-found liberation translates into Jamilla's relief when going out in public, albeit with a male chaperone, and not being 'pierced by the occasional look of surprise or even disdain that my attire would elicit in England' (Khair 2016, 102). At this point, ISIS appears like a liberatory oasis for British Muslim women like Jamilla.

However, this oasis soon proves to be a mirage. In the course of the narrative, Jamilla becomes increasingly sceptical about Hejjiye, who is 'always in good humour – as if she were a model in a TV competition – and never with a shadow of doubt on her face' (94). This unlikely comparison of a burka-covered woman to a skin-bearing TV model highlights the performative nature of Hejjiye's role. Her unwavering enthusiasm, good cheer and confidence exhibit a singlemindedness that tips into ruthlessness, exemplified in her imprisonment of Kurdish fighters and her handling of Halide, a fellow resident at the orphanage, which I will detail later. Performance and reality blend so that '[t]he orphanage, or maybe Islamic State itself, was Hejjiye's catwalk' (134). This is an intensely feminine, even sexual image of an Islamic State held under the pointed heels of Hejjiye, especially when one considers the hypermasculine and patriarchal structure of the Caliphate, which demands modesty and subservience from its women (Winter 2015b). Fashion and modelling can be forms of empowerment in a secular Western world. The image of the 'catwalk' indicates that some women find a third way of existing in the Islamic State, beyond the roles of the 'jihadi bride' and the suicide bomber (which, as I shall explore, are the roles Jamilla finds herself caught between). Jamilla remarks that no matter if Hejjiye had been a racist politician in Europe or if she had worked in the banking or corporate sector, she would always have been in control: 'Whatever set of rules she found around her, she would use them to empower herself' (Khair 2016, 205). She adds that Hejjiye's 'route to power lay through the strictures of Islam' (205). The ISIS that Khair depicts here is driven by cultural politics and personal empowerment more than by religion.

Female emancipation is promoted by ISIS propaganda through practices such as veiling and gender segregation, which provide the opportunity for orthodox Muslim women to pursue careers in sectors like healthcare and education with more freedom than exists in the West (Khelghat-Doost 2017, 21). Jamilla finds herself living a more 'meaningful' (Khair 2016, 79) life after having become a teacher at the orphanage, a career denied to her by her family. These 'gender-segregated parallel institutions' (Khelghat-Doost 2017, 17) incorporate women more fully into the Islamic State and are speculated to be the principal reason behind women's prominence in ISIS (Saltman and Smith 2015, 14). However, Jamilla's narration reveals that veiling and gender segregation only afford so much protection in the Caliphate. Marriage to a man who can act as a chaperone is necessary for movement and participation in society, such as weekly trips to the market. Research shows that finding a husband is a significant theme in the online radicalisation and recruitment of women (Perešin and Cervone 2015, 500). Quite unusually, Jamilla is not urged to marry in her online rendezvous with Hejjiye, although Erin Marie Saltman and Melanie Smith find that women are openly dissuaded from travelling if they do not wish to marry (2015, 16). The omission of this detail in Khair's novel is significant: for Jamilla, marriage would have restricted her agency as well as any hopes of feminist emancipation she harbours.

ISIS does not provide a place for single women (Winter 2015a, 7). Halide, a fellow resident, suspects that while older women become teachers and younger women are intended as brides, some girls are trained to be suicide bombers (Khair 2016, 127). She is made to leave the orphanage because of these views, and although Jamilla remains ignorant, the reader deduces that Halide has been coerced into suicide bombing by Hejjiye. Jamilla is initially dismissive of Halide's speculations, assuming that women can freely choose between marrying or carrying out a suicide attack – another indication of her aspirational beliefs about ISIS. Later, she re-examines Halide's intuition and in a rare tone of dark humour wonders whether 'it was only the unattractive girls who got talked into becoming suicide bombers' (181). A hierarchy based on women's beauty is implied, which is ironic considering ISIS' precept of veiling this beauty. Pretty women secure powerful marriages, and Hejjiye enjoys fixing the marriages of the attractive women she surrounds herself with. By contrast, women considered to be ugly are forced to commit suicide bombings.

Ameena: Maternal Militancy or Emancipatory Attack?

Plain-looking Ameena, Jamilla's schoolfriend and eventual travel companion to Syria, contrasts with the beautiful and studious Jamilla's unwillingness to marry. Owing to romantic disappointment by high school heartthrob Alex, one of the pull factors identified by Perešin (2015, 24–5), Ameena quickly marries ISIS commander Hassan. Her abusive marriage leads her to plan a violent retaliation. In the Islamic State, women's militancy is considered a last resort as women are intended to have a domestic, home-bound role, caring for their husbands and children. Charlie Winter explains that women may be called to fight only under exceptional circumstances (2015a, 5). An Arabic document produced by the media wing of ISIS' all-female policing brigade, Al-Khanssaa, states that women are so important to the Caliphate that they must remain veiled and hidden away from society for their own protection (7). This 'jihadist perversion of feminism' (7) means that ISIS' hegemonic masculinity masquerades as a kind of benign feminism. It is important to note that the document never uses feminist terms such as 'empowerment', 'patriarchy' or 'objectification', but rather rejects feminism as a failed 'Western model' for society (19). ISIS' view of women is reminiscent of Elizabeth Hackett and Sally Haslanger's (2005) concept of gynocentric feminism which conceives of women as inherently non-violent because of their role as actual and potential mothers. As Umm Layth, the oldest woman in Hassan's household says, 'surely the role of a woman is to give birth, not to throw bombs' (Khair 2016, 202). The alliteration of 'birth' and 'bombs' emphasises the perceived contradiction of female-perpetrated violence: women should give life, not take it away.

Despite Umm Layth's viewpoint that women and militancy are incompatible, Jamilla reveals her suspicion that Ameena, with Hejjiye's help, must have calculated the details of a ceasefire plan during a Kurdish siege: 'It seemed to be beyond Hassan' (201). Here, women challenge the male hegemony on violence. With the ISIS orphanage under attack by Kurdish forces, Ameena brokers a ceasefire, using the orphanage's Kurdish prisoners to arrange her and Jamilla's martyrdom. Ameena volunteers herself and Jamilla, to the latter's horror, to escort the Kurdish prisoners to the other side, with this exchange designed to secure the safety of the women and children in the orphanage. Unknown to the Kurds, the duo will accompany the prisoners fitted with hidden suicide vests, enabling detonation by Hassan once they reach the Kurdish side (198). The irony for Jamilla – who has, among other reasons, joined ISIS to escape married life – is that finally she 'would have to choose between marriage or death' (196). Jamilla feels that she is being forced into martyrdom by Ameena. However, Ameena, attendant to the rules of veiling and modesty, realises that while her husband can fit her with a suicide vest, only she can fit Jamilla's suicide vest. Therefore, Hassan must teach Ameena how to administer a suicide vest. By using this opportunity to release the prisoners (211–12), Jamilla ingeniously exploits the modesty rules of ISIS' gendered social order. While Jamilla manages to free herself and the prisoners, Ameena stays behind, detonating her vest to kill herself, Hassan, as well as three of his henchmen. Thus, it is patriarchal control over women's militancy that leads to a female-perpetrated act of violence.

This is not the first time in the novel that Ameena subverts the gendered social order. In an earlier episode, Hassan discovers that Ameena has helped hide their young Yazidi slave boy Sabah from her husband's brutality. This results in Sabah's beheading and Ameena's public lashing. Ameena justifies her deed by referring to her maternal instinct, protesting to Umm Layth: 'Sabah reminded me of the son I do not have . . . I am a weak woman' (171). Jamilla suspects that Ameena's true reason for concealing Sabah was that she found his treatment by Hassan un-Islamic. Because Umm Layth would not have understood this, however, Ameena invoked the image of woman as mother to explain her actions and alleviate her punishment. The narrative distance caused by Jamilla's relation of Ameena's story makes it difficult to tell whether Ameena purposefully played on this trope to exonerate herself, or whether she really came to think of Sabah as her son.

If the latter is the case, then Ameena's suicide bombing does not entirely transgress ISIS' sanctioned role for women. The name she shrieks as a signal for Jamilla and the prisoners to take cover is Sabah. Thus, her act can be interpreted as that of a mother avenging the death of her son. The fact that Ameena is named after the mother of Prophet Muhammad strengthens her symbolic connection to motherhood. Katharina Von Knop (2007, 400) finds that many women join terrorist organisations to avenge male family members lost in counterterrorism operations, failed jihadi missions or successful suicide bombings. Such traumatic losses can lead to 'cognitive openings', a term coined by Quintan Wiktorowicz (2005) in his investigation of the UK-based radical Islamist group Al-Muhajiroun. By 'cognitive opening', Wiktorowicz describes the psychological alteration of an individual's previously held beliefs which makes that person receptive to new ways of thinking (5). This kind of transformation can be caused by a variety of factors, including economic factors (such as the loss of a job), social or cultural factors (racism), political factors (repression, discrimination) or personal ones (death, identity crisis) (20). Cognitive openings do not necessarily lead to radicalisation; they can also have the opposite effect, prompting individuals to question their previous commitment to an extremist organisation like ISIS (Hoyle et al. 2015, 27). In Ameena's case, her cognitive opening is highly gendered, but rather than renewing her support of ISIS, it turns her into a dissenter – to deadly effect.

While Ameena is not actually a mother but *performs* a symbolic motherhood, Clare Bielby and Jeffrey Stevenson Murer argue that dividing gender (being) from action (doing) is difficult as '"Doing" is always gendered' (2018, 4). Regardless of whether Ameena is a vengeful mother or whether this is just a front to violence, her attack must be understood through a gendered lens. One possible interpretation is that Ameena's actions adhere to what has been termed the 'maternal-sacrificial code': the denial of the self when raising children (Neuburger and Valentini 1996, 19). Ameena's suicide bombing, a violent act of self-effacement, is a radical version of 'giving all and taking nothing' (19). As Luisella de Cataldo Neuburger and Tiziana Valentini note in their book *Women and Terrorism*, maternal sacrifice feeds into a patriarchal order which frees men to take on other, more important roles (19). By killing Hassan and his henchmen, Ameena's attack overturns this patriarchal order. There is no question, therefore, that in *Just Another Jihadi Jane*, gendered violence *is* political violence, since Ameena's suicide bombing challenges a conception of women as mothers, child-bearers and nurturers.

However, viewing Ameena's bombing as maternal vengeance/sacrifice limits her actions to femininity and maternity. Caron E. Gentry and Laura Sjoberg explain that a mother narrative of violence denies a woman's agency while simultaneously contending that her actions are 'gender emancipatory' (2015, 82). Considering the patriarchal context within which Ameena's suicide attack takes place, her actions are at once emancipatory and fatalistic. Ameena's bombing can be viewed as a form of female empowerment, albeit one that results in her death. Her attack mirrors the gendered violence she experienced in her married life: by killing Hassan, she ensures an end to his violence, frees Jamilla and the female prisoners, and secures the release of the women at the orphanage. Thus, her bombing is a final, fatal way of exercising an agency usually reserved to men – although in her case, this agency is radically limited, suicide being her only means of escape.

Significantly, the freed prisoners interpret Ameena's actions according to notions of 'sacrifice, historical justice, national freedom' (Khair 2016, 216). This indicates that her suicide bombing can be viewed in a myriad of ways. For Jamilla, the reasons mentioned by the Kurdish prisoners are 'partly hollow' (216). Perhaps she is implying that something is lost in these references to warfare, steering the reader towards a gendered explanation instead. Jamilla lies to the prisoners about Ameena's cry of 'Sabah', claiming that he was Ameena's dead son (218). This creates an uncertainty around Ameena's attack, an ambiguity that stands against the rigidity of both Western media representations of 'jihadi brides' and the Islamic State's sanctioned gender roles. Avoiding a reductionist and depoliticising approach to female radicalisation and violent extremism, the mother narratives included in Khair's novel highlight the complex nature of women's participation in ISIS – an organisation intensely preoccupied with the correct way of being a woman.

Conclusion

Just Another Jihadi Jane offers a more comprehensive view of its two Jihadi Janes than the one generally followed in Western media. Starting out as the stereotypical 'jihadi bride', Ameena is transformed by violence into a person of careful action and intelligence, who challenges ISIS' conception of women while simultaneously conforming to the feminine norm through her maternal sacrifice. Likewise, Jamilla's unwillingness to marry subverts the label of the 'jihadi bride'. Ameena and Jamilla transcend the stereotype of naive romanticism that is associated with the original Jihad Jane (Conway and McInerney 2012). Khair depicts them as making a conscious decision to join the Caliphate on the basis of religious and political considerations, a decision that is informed by their respective backgrounds of racism, parental control and lost romantic love.

At the 2017 Jaipur Literary Festival, Khair briefly spoke about the representation of female ISIS recruits: 'I hear reports of girls being brainwashed. I have a problem with that perspective as it takes away their agency' (qtd in Sharma 2017). Female agency and emancipation are key concerns of Khair's novel, as is the need to understand willing female participation in the Caliphate's patriarchal control of women. In writing from the perspective of two Muslim girls, Khair's novel aims to uncover what he describes as 'the truth – the many truths – beyond facts' (qtd in Saha 2016). Khair's statement circles back to the beginning of this chapter. At the outset of the novel, Jamilla reflects on her previously held conviction about the 'One Truth' (Khair 2016, 1). The implication of Jamilla's reflection is that this singular religious conviction is waning. Thus arises the possibility of multiple truths and readings. By offering such a nuanced take on the topic, *Just Another Jihadi* counteracts the singlemindedness found in both extremism and media portrayals of extremism.

Note

1. See the BBC Sounds podcast *I'm Not A Monster*; TV shows include Channel 4's *The State* (2017) and Swedish series *Caliphate* (2020), available on Netflix; and memoirs span Farida Khalaf's *The Girl Who Escaped ISIS* (2016), Samer's *The Raqqa Diaries: Escape from Islamic State* (2017) and Nadia Murad's *The Last Girl: My Story of Captivity and My Fight Against the Islamic State* (2018).

References

"Addressing Xenophobia Through Writing." 2016. Red Elephant Foundation. http://www.redelephantfoundation.org/2016/09/addressing-xenophobia-through-writing.html

Anderson, Benedict. (1983) 2016. *Imagined Communities: Reflections on the Origin and Spread of Nationalism*. Reprint, London: Verso.

Baker, Josh, and Joe Kent. 2020-2022. *I'm Not A Monster*, produced by Joe Kent and Max Green, Podcast. https://www.bbc.co.uk/programmes/p08yblkf

Bielby, Clare, and Jeffrey Stevenson Murer. 2018. "Perpetrating Selves: An Introduction." *Perpetrating Selves: Doing Violence, Performing Identity*, eds Clare Bielby and Jeffrey Stevenson Murer, 1–13. Cham, Switzerland: Palgrave Macmillan.

Buchanan, Rose Troup. 2015. "Missing Syria Girls: Met Police Officers in Turkey to Search for Missing Schoolgirls." *The Independent*, February 23, 2015. http://www.independent.co.uk/news/uk/missing-syria-girls-met-police-officers-turkey-search-missing-schoolgirls-10063880.html

Chambers, Claire. 2019. "Sound and Fury: Tabish Khair's *Just Another Jihadi Jane* and Kamila Shamsie's *Home Fire*." In *Making Sense of Contemporary British Muslim Novels*, 169–211. London: Palgrave Macmillan UK.

Conway, Maura, and Lisa McInerney. 2012. "What's Love Got to Do with It? Framing 'JihadJane' in the US Press." *Media, War & Conflict* 5, no. 1: 6–21. https://doi.org/10.1177/1750635211434373

Crenshaw, Kimberlé. 1989. "Demarginalizing the Intersection of Race and Sex: A Black Feminist Critique of Antidiscrimination Doctrine, Feminist Theory and Antiracist Politics." *University of Chicago Legal Forum* 140: 139–67. http://chicagounbound.uchicago.edu/uclf/vol1989/iss1/8

Crenshaw, Kimberlé. 1991. "Mapping the Margins: Intersectionality, Identity Politics, and Violence Against Women of Color." *Stanford Law Review* 43, no. 6: 1241–99. https://www.jstor.org/stable/1229039

Cunningham, Karla. 2003. "Cross-Regional Trends in Female Terrorism." *Studies of Conflict and Terrorism* 26, no. 3: 171–95. DOI: 10.1080/10576100390211419

Gallien, Claire. 2019. "When Literature Becomes an 'Enhanced National Security Threat': Literary Interventions of the 'Terrorist' and 'Terrorist' Interventions of Literature." *The Journal of Commonwealth Literature*, 1–20. https://journals.sagepub.com/doi/10.1177/0021989419826366

Gentry, Caron E., and Laura Sjoberg. 2015. *Beyond Mothers, Monsters, Whores: Thinking About Women's Violence in Global Politics*. London: Bloomsbury Academic & Professional.

Hackett, Elizabeth, and Sally Haslanger, eds. 2005. *Theorizing Feminisms: A Reader*. Oxford: Oxford University Press.

Hamid, Mohsin. 2007. *The Reluctant Fundamentalist*. London: Hamish Hamilton.

Hoyle, Carolyn, Alexandra Bradford, and Ross Frenett. 2015. "Becoming Mulan? Female Western Migrants to ISIS." *Institute for Strategic Dialogue*, 1–48.

Igartuburu, Elena. 2018. "Productive Unease: Female Terrorists, Aesthetics, and Agency in Cultural Representation." In *El Desangramiento Latinoamericano: Un Panorama Político Contemporáneo Sobre La Reorganización Y La Reconfiguración Del Estado*

Neoliberal, eds Fernanda Pattaro Amaral, Fagner Firmo De Souza Santos, Astelio Silvera Sarmiento and Ana Cláudia Delfini Capistrano De Oliveira, 443–65. Colombia: Corporación Universitaria Americana.

Kapetanović, Goran, dir. 2020. *Caliphate*. Stockholm: SVT. Netflix. https://www.netflix.com/title/80240005

Khair, Tabish. 2016. *Just Another Jihadi Jane*. Reading: Periscope Books.

Khair, Tabish. 2019. "Foreword: Why Literature is the Answer to Extremism." In *Terrorism in Literature: Examining a Global Phenomenon*, ed. Bootheina Majoul, xi–1. Newcastle upon Tyne: Cambridge Scholars Publishing.

Khalaf, Farida. 2016. *The Girl Who Escaped ISIS*. Translated by Jamie Bulloch. London: Penguin Random House.

Khan, Sara. 2015. "'This Is a Form of Grooming': Jihadi Brides Heading to Syria." *Channel 4 News*. February 20, 2015. YouTube video, 4:01. https://youtu.be/O35nzXw5oPs

Khelghat-Doost, Hamoon. 2017. "Women of the Caliphate: The Mechanism for Women's Incorporation into the Islamic State (IS)." *Perspectives on Terrorism* 11, no. 1: 17–25. https://www.jstor.org/stable/26297734

Kneip, Katharina. 2016. "Female Jihad – Women in the ISIS." *Politikon: IAPSS Political Science Journal* 29: 88–106.

Kosminsky, Peter, dir. 2017. *The State*. London: Channel 4.

Morgan, Piers (@piersmorgan). 2019. "*NEW COLUMN* Don't let these terror brides come home – they made their ISIS husbands' beds, now let them rot in hell in them. https://dailym.ai/2V7vMw5." Twitter, February 18, 2019. https://twitter.com/piersmorgan/status/1097559337638064130

Morris, Chris, dir. 2010. *Four Lions*. London: Film4 Productions.

Murad, Nadia. 2018. *The Last Girl: My Story of Captivity and My Fight Against the Islamic State*. London: Virago.

Neuburger, Luisella de Cataldo, and Tiziana Valentini. 1996. *Women and Terrorism*. Trans. Leo Michael Hughes. New York, Macmillan.

Pearson, Allison. 2015. "Let's Stop Making Excuses for these 'Jihadi Brides'." *The Telegraph*, February 25, 2015. http://www.telegraph.co.uk/news/worldnews/islamic-state/11434343/Lets-stop-making-excuses-for-these-jihadi-brides.html

Perešin, Anita. 2015. "Fatal Attraction: Western Muslimas and ISIS." *Perspectives on Terrorism* 9, no. 3: 21–38. https://www.jstor.org/stable/26297379

Perešin, Anita, and Alberto Cervone. 2015. "The Western *Muhajirat* of ISIS." *Studies in Conflict & Terrorism* 38, no. 7: 495–509.

Petersen, Kirsten Holst, and Anna Rutherford. 1986. *A Double Colonization: Colonial and Post-colonial Women's Writing*. Sydney: Dangaroo.

Picart, Caroline Joan 'Kay' S. 2017. *American Self-Radicalizing Terrorists and the Allure of "Jihadi Cool/Chic"*. Newcastle upon Tyne: Cambridge Scholars Publishing.

Rajan, V. G. Julie. 2011. *Women Suicide Bombers: Narratives of Violence*. Abingdon: Taylor & Francis Group.

Sageman, Marc. 2008. *Leaderless Jihad: Terror Networks in the Twenty-First Century*. Pennsylvania: University of Pennsylvania Press.

Saha, Aditi. 2016. "Author Q&A Session #82: With Tabish Khair." *Book Stop Corner*, July 14, 2016. http://bookstopcorner.blogspot.com/2016/07/author-q-session-82-with-tabish-khair.html

Saltman, Erin Marie, and Melanie Smith. 2015. "'Till Martyrdom Do Us Part': Gender and the ISIS Phenomenon." *Institute for Strategic Dialogue* and *International Centre for the Study of Radicalisation*. https://www.isdglobal.org/wp-content/uploads/2016/02/Till_Martyrdom_Do_Us_Part_Gender_and_the_ISIS_Phenomenon.pdf

Samer. 2017. *The Raqqa Diaries: Escape from Islamic State*. Trans. Nader Ibrahim, co-edited by John Neal. London: Hutchinson.

Saul, Heather. 2015. "Aqsa Mahmood Warned Jihadi Brides They Must Prepare to Be Widows in Blog Post Weeks Before Missing School Girls Fled to Turkey." *The Independent*, February 24, 2015. https://www.independent.co.uk/news/world/middle-east/aqsa-mahmood-warned-jihadi-brides-they-must-prepare-be-widows-blog-post-weeks-missing-school-girls-fled-turkey-10067290.html

Shapiro, Lauren, and Marie-Helen Maras. 2019. "Women's Radicalization to Religious Terrorism: An Examination of ISIS Cases in the United States." *Studies in Conflict & Terrorism* 42, no. 1–2: 88–119.

Sharma, Supriya. 2017. "JLF 2017: 'Jihad Doesn't Mean You Chop People's Heads Off,' Says Tabish Khair." *Hindustan Times*, January 23, 2017. http://www.hindustantimes.com/books/jlf-2017-jihad-doesn-t-mean-you-chop-people-s-heads-off-says-tabish-khair/story-CkgGdPubuHqAT0IjT5aCWP.html

Sherwood, Harriet, Sandra Laville, Kim Willsher, Ben Knight, Maddy French, and Lauren Gambino. 2014. "Schoolgirl Jihadis: The Female Islamists Leaving Home to Join ISIS Fighters." *The Guardian*, September 29, 2014. http://www.theguardian.com/world/2014/sep/29/schoolgirl-jihadis-female-islamists-leaving-home-join-isis-iraq-syria

Third, Amanda. 2014. *Gender and The Political: Deconstructing the Female Terrorist*. New York: Palgrave Macmillan.

"Travel Ban Teenage Girls from Syria Trio's School." *BBC News*, March 27, 2015. http://www.bbc.co.uk/news/uk-32091822

Valentini, Daniele. 2019. "Tabish Khair's *Just Another Jihadi Jane*: Inside the Mind of a Foreign Fighter." In *Terrorism in Literature: Examining a Global Phenomenon*, ed. Bootheina Majoul, 20–44. Newcastle upon Tyne: Cambridge Scholars Publishing.

Von Knop, Katharina. 2007. "The Female Jihad: Al Qaeda's Women." *Studies in Conflict & Terrorism* 30, no. 5: 397–414.

Wiktorowicz, Quintan. 2005. *Radical Islam Rising: Muslim Extremism in the West*. Oxford: Rowman and Littlefield Publishers.

Winter, Charlie. 2015a. *Women of the Islamic State: A Manifesto on Women by the Al-Khanssaa Brigade*. London: Quilliam Foundation.

Winter, Charlie. 2015b. "Women of the Islamic State: Beyond the Rumour Mill." *Jihadology*, March 31, 2015. http://jihadology.net/2015/03/31/guest-post-women-of-the-islamic-state-beyond-the-rumor-mill/

Zakaria, Rafia. 2015. "Women and Islamic Militancy." *Dissent* 62, no. 1: 118–25.

PART THREE

INTIMATE ENEMIES: FEELING FOR THE TERRORIST?

11. CIRCUMVENTING THE CONDEMNATION IMPERATIVE: THE FIGURE OF THE FEMALE SUICIDE BOMBER IN AKIN AND EL AKKAD

Tim Gauthier

INTRODUCTION

The initial and visceral response to an act of suicide terrorism is often one of utter disbelief. How can it be that someone felt this horrific action was the most logical step to take? Surely there were other options than blowing oneself up and killing numerous others in the process. This incredulity causes one to attribute some kind of psychological disorder to the terrorist – no sane, or mentally healthy, person could commit such acts. In an earlier work, I noted a similar underlying impulse in much Western writing aimed at discounting the validity of the suicide terrorist's agenda (Gauthier 2015). This propensity reveals a reluctance to accept that terrorists may act while in full control of their faculties or that they have been driven by motivations whose foundations bear similarity to one's own (revenge, renown, meaningfulness, altruism). In fact, many critics and theorists posit suicide terrorists as rational agents performing what they believe are positive actions for the good of their community. In other words, gestures typically conceived of as acts of aggression should also be reframed as evidence of the individual's generosity, selflessness and sacrifice for the welfare of their community. Robert Pape, for instance, observes, 'the homicidal dimension of the act should not cause us to overlook an important cause leading to it – that many suicide terrorists are killing themselves to advance what they see as the common good' (180). In this iteration, suicide terrorists are no longer simply intent on the slaughter of innocent civilians, but young people who, misguided or not, sacrifice their lives in the hopes of bringing some measure of relief to their oppressed communities.[1]

But instead of recognising the altruistic motivations of the perpetrator, the observer feels the need to dissociate from, and condemn, the actions of the other. Few wish to risk being perceived as condoning, or worse supporting, murderous behaviour. In other words, not empathising with the terrorist becomes an act of (psychological) self-preservation. For these reasons, the 'condemnation imperative', as Ghassan Hage (2003) calls it, is present in much of the intellectual discourse pertaining to such actions. Hage contends that under these conditions,

> It is difficult to express any form of understanding whatsoever, even when one is indeed also condemning the practice . . . Only unqualified condemnation will do. And if one tries to understand, any accompanying condemnation is also deemed suspicious. (67)

The paradox is self-evident – any attempt at productive or revelatory discourse is immediately curtailed by the need to proclaim reprehension.[2] Noting these limitations, Richard Jackson suggests there is 'little doubt that literature has the *potential* to illuminate our understanding of terrorism through the empathetic entrance of the writer into the life world and subjectivity of the "terrorist" perpetrator' (2019, 377). The italicisation of the word 'potential', however, implies this is seldom the case. Much Western fiction, Jackson contends, effectively supports the dominant narrative in demonising and dehumanising the terrorist. Jackson further insists that a 'dominant mythography' about terrorism has been constructed, 'inform[ing] the way even ordinary people speak about (and understand) who terrorists are, what they want, and how to respond to them' (386).[3] In these circumstances, any consideration of motivations – to say nothing of personal, social or political drives – is severely handicapped.

Connecting with the perpetrator, then, requires that empathetic readers or viewers recognise this dismissive propensity. Having done so, they are better prepared to perceive the intractability of the others' circumstances; they can consider the possibility that no other form of recourse availed itself with the same power as did the choice of suicide bombing. Perhaps most importantly, they may recognise the extent to which the actions of others (including one's own) contributed to intolerable, and potentially unliveable conditions. Thus, empathy is not without its limitations. Entertaining the possibility of finding some common ground with the perpetrator, however, does not guarantee genuine conviction about that connection. A (sub)conscious sense that nothing essential ties one to the Nazi commandant, the serial killer or the suicide bomber is likely to persist. As Adam Morton suggests, considering oneself a 'morally sensitive person' necessarily constrains 'one's capacity to empathize with those who perform atrocious acts' (2011, 318). To complicate matters further, one may wonder whether one's ability to empathise with the atrocious actor is actually revealing of something (horrific?) lying within – a yet unconsidered potentiality to commit such deeds oneself. It is often said that one risks being contaminated by the other through empathy and that this explains a reluctance to engage.

Indeed, the language of contamination is frequently invoked in discussions of terrorism, as though the process of seeking to understand might lead one to sympathise with, or even condone, the terrorist's actions. Lisa Stampnitzky characterises this supposition as follows: 'Insofar as terrorists are understood to be inherently evil, it follows both that "evil" is the explanation for terrorism and that we ought not to seek to know terrorists, for such knowledge is potentially contaminating' (2013, 189). For her part, Eva Roekel suggests that the empathiser, 'is logically imbricated in the potential of becoming contaminated with what is immoral in the context of inquiry' (2021, 620).[4] But one may also refuse to empathise because one fears what the activity might tell one about oneself. As Morton observes, 'Overcoming [a barrier] may carry one along further than one wants' (322). And yet this is precisely the task for which empathy is best suited. An empathetic connection with the other should not put me at ease; on the contrary, it should disrupt and unsettle.

This chapter posits that such efforts on the part of a critical empathiser can be facilitated through engagement with a text that sets out to destabilise a tendency to discount the figure of the suicide terrorist. It thus examines two such fictional works – Fatih Akin's film, *In the Fade* (2017), and Omar El Akkad's novel, *American War* (2017) – that highlight the possibilities and limitations of an empathetic approach, as well as narratorial strategies for circumventing the condemnation imperative. Each text presents a female protagonist who is eventually driven to suicide bombing (though by very different circumstances). Both Akin and El Akkad resort to narratorial strategies that bypass the reader's biases and preconceived notions of suicide terrorism. Since these biases are not easily overcome, the authors resort to narrative strategies that induce readerly empathy for a character before the shadow of terrorism darkens the page/screen. Furthermore, the gender and ethnicity of these protagonists serve to subvert (stereotypical/biased) conceptions of the terrorist. As we shall see, the very use of a female suicide bomber destabilises the readers' conception of the terrorist. After all, if one extends any kind of understanding to these women, one is also obliged to reconsider one's stance towards others engaged in terroristic activities.

Of course, empathising with a fictional perpetrator (or any other character for that matter) is not an all-or-nothing proposition. A range of readers will no doubt exhibit a range of responses – some will necessarily connect more than others. Relatability is likely to occur to varying degrees and on a number of different levels. As McGlothlin observes,

> to assume that identification is either fully present or wholly absent disregards the dynamic character of narrative progression, the variability and

complexity of the relationship between readers and characters, and the idiosyncratic nature of an individual reader's engagement with representations of the inner experience of perpetrators. (2016, 266)

Readers will have their own motivations for connecting or not connecting with the fictionalised suicide bomber. Some, for instance, will empathise with the cause, but not the methods; others might be attracted to the terrorist's subversion or deviance; while still others may not be able to get past the killing of innocents, no matter how sympathetically the suicide bomber is portrayed. Nevertheless, I contend that there will be a commonality of responses. In other words, a majority of readers (though not all) will evince a qualitatively similar response to a character.

Critical Empathy

Empathy can be distinguished from sympathy or compassion in that it requires a conscious and willing effort on the part of the observer who must sublimate (if only momentarily) the self in order to better glimpse the other's perspective. In this regard, Karsten Stueber (2006) argues for a distinction between 'basic empathy' and what he terms 'reenactive empathy' (20–1).[5] Basic empathy allows us to recognise another's emotion, but not the reasons for his subsequent behaviour, and is thus insufficient. As I have noted elsewhere, Stueber insists that only reenactive empathy allows us to assess the actions of others, for 'only by using our cognitive and deliberative capacities in order to reenact or imitate in our own mind the thought processes of the other person – are we able to conceive of another person's more complex social behavior as the behavior of a rational agent who acts for a reason' (21). The key word here is 'deliberative', signalling an active and mindful effort to connect with the other.

This point is worth stressing, because a number of critics of the empathetic approach conceive of the reader as a passive receptacle, easily manipulated into identifying (that is, sympathising) with the perpetrator. Adherents of an empathetic approach, however, are not oblivious to its limitations. They are quick to point to the pitfalls awaiting any empathiser who strives to 'understand' the terrorist. As noted earlier, too great an identification with the protagonist, they contend, can adversely affect the reader's ability to properly judge the perpetrator's actions. Furthermore, this connection may detrimentally privilege the perpetrators' perspective over that of the victim. Critics such as Erin McGlothlin (2016, 266), however, posit that most readers possess a greater degree of autonomy than that for which they are given credit and are more than capable of calibrating their empathetic responses to the representation of the perpetrator. Identifying with the protagonist, after all, does not preclude assessing her actions with a critical eye. Robyn Bloch (2018, 128), for instance, asks, 'Is empathy always the same, no matter the person with whom we empathise? Or does empathy's nature change – or must it change – when we engage in it with perpetrators?' As Bloch observes, empathising does not equate with becoming the other. Eric Leake, for his part, argues that:

> [Empathy] does not require that we share the same feelings of another person's situation but instead that we use our emotional experiences to understand the feelings of another. This is a critical move in difficult empathy because it means that our feelings become a basis for understanding rather than a site of congruence. (2014, 177)

Critical empathisers retain the capacity to identify the ways in which they are like, and unlike, the other. Furthermore, empathy does not take place to the exclusion of all other faculties – one can be compassionate and rational at the same time.

These observations support the notion that engaging in empathy is an intentional and conscious act. Readers are unlikely to simply abandon their ethical compass (no matter how charming or conniving the perpetrator might be) so as to prove incapable of judging her actions – empathy and critical thought are not mutually exclusive. To this end, McGlothlin argues that 'activating empathetic responses on the part of readers may indeed achieve ethically desirable outcomes'. She prefers the term 'identification' over empathy, however, since the former 'better conveys the ethical dimension of the reader's relationship to a given character, as it implies a sense of active agency or conscious alignment on the part of the reader, even as unconscious mechanisms are also at play' (2016, 258). McGlothlin's terminology and taxonomy of identification accord with my preference for Stueber's notion of 'reenactive empathy', as they both place heavy emphasis on the agency of the empathiser.[6] What I hope is becoming clear is that I am advocating for an empathy that is conscious and intentional, rather than one that is emotional and instinctual.

Empathising with the perpetrator, however, poses its unique challenges: the provocation is greater if the person with whom one seeks to empathise has committed deeds one finds repugnant or immoral. Difficult empathy, as Eric Leake labels it, 'unsettles us and places easy empathy in question, showing us our vulnerabilities reflected in victims and our shared human capacity to victimize reflected in victimizers' (175). But to what extent is one truly willing to acknowledge a 'shared human capacity to victimize'? Those of us engaged in these discussions often talk about identifying that which we share with the perpetrators – a common ground – the question still remains: are we truly and genuinely committed to such identification? Might it not be the case that, left to our own devices, we can never quite make that leap, reassuring ourselves that we are worthier and more upstanding individuals? Seeking to prevent injury to one's ego, empathetic readers cannot help but imagine they would act differently. They would not molest that child, would not kill their spouse, would not blow up that mosque; they would find some reason to not commit the act, they tell themselves. One thus engages in the empathetic exercise, Adam Morton contends, even as one (privately) knows one is deceiving oneself:

> the fact is, that when we try to find anything like real empathy for people who commit real atrocities we come up against a barrier. We can describe the motives, and we can often imagine some of what it might be like to do the acts, but there are deep obstacles to the kind of sympathetic identification required for empathy. (2011, 321)

I would describe it somewhat differently – one does not fully empathise because one is fearful of what the activity might reveal about oneself. This dread of recognition explains the need to condemn, delegitimise and finally dehumanise the terrorist – to protect oneself against the possibility of sameness.

Returning to Stueber's concept of 'reenactive empathy' as a deliberate and intentional effort to connect with the other, we might ask just how intentional such a gesture can be without somehow acknowledging, and then attenuating, an instinctual response to distance oneself from the perpetrator and her actions. The importance of this directed recognition cannot be overstated. Because it is also incumbent upon the empathiser to acknowledge the power dynamics inherent in the empathetic gesture – who precisely is empathising and at whose expense? In other words, who gains? Since we know that empathy is not always altruistic – it can be misapplied for nefarious or instrumental reasons, for instance – empathisers should critically evaluate both their underlying motivations, as well as their justifications, for conducting the exercise. After all, the suicide bomber is irrevocably defined by her final action; she can never be thought of as anything other than a terrorist. This poses specific challenges for empathisers who must overcome a propensity to judge, to assess the protagonist solely in the light of that final action. The path to empathy lies not so much with connecting with the perpetrator's actions, then, but rather with his or her motivations. Fellow feeling is more easily elicited if readers are made to contemplate the possibility that they could be compelled to act in a similar fashion. In other words, it is not enough to put oneself in the terrorist's shoes, one must also identify the parts one shares with the terrorist. As Emile Bruneau (2016, 2) contends, 'the psychological processes that drive an individual to engage in terrorism are deeply human, common across cultures – and traits that likely reside in us all'. This is where fiction (both filmic and literary) may play a role, I argue, by discouraging a self-interested reading of the suicide terrorist through the presentation of scenarios that elide and bypass personal barriers, thereby exposing the viewer/reader to points of similarity that might have otherwise been discounted.

Recent perpetrator studies have focused their attention on the trauma of the perpetrators – either the trauma that contributed to, or compelled their actions, or that which resulted from having committed such deeds (see, for instance, McGlothlin 2020; Mohamed 2015). The perpetrator-protagonists examined here inhabit a different space. Since neither *In the Fade*'s Katja nor *American War*'s Sarat survive to experience their ultimate acts, they cannot be considered traumatised perpetrators as such, but rather women whose respective traumas lead to perpetration – or traumatised perpetrators-in-the-making. The respective texts thus allow the viewers/readers to trace each woman's respective emotional and psychological transformation from victim to perpetrator, but also to eventual non-victim (or no longer victim), as she exercises her form of deadly agency. In different ways, as we shall see, Fatih Akin and Omar El Akkad set out to map the affective trajectory of their respective protagonists, representing the societal conditions that contribute to their eventual self-annihilation.

(De)Othering the Suicide Terrorist: *In the Fade*

Fatih Akin's *In the Fade* (2017) deploys a traditional three-act structure and a not-so subtle mixture of cinematic genres. Its three parts – 'Family', 'Justice' and 'The Sea' – present a family tragedy, a courtroom drama and thriller respectively. In the first, we are introduced to Katja Sekerci who is married to Nuri, a once imprisoned and now reformed drug dealer. Together they operate a tax consulting agency specialising in aiding immigrants. Nuri is Turkish and the film suggests they are living in a multiculturally diverse district of Hamburg. Within moments the film offers an intimate portrait of pain and unbearable mourning; barely eight minutes in, Katja's husband and her six-year-old son are killed in a terrorist bombing. From this point on, viewers are provided little relief and made to feel the endless grief with which Katja now lives (conveyed, most dramatically, through Diane Kruger's raw and unwavering performance). Akin employs a number of closeups throughout the film, none more effective than that of Katja's face as she realises what has happened and is wrestled to the ground by police officers preventing her from approaching the crime scene (Figure 11.1). Her agony is writ large upon her face and, at moments such as this, many viewers will be compelled to empathise. Akin strives to temper these feelings, however, because in Katja, he has created a tattooed free spirit who often appears on the verge of imploding. Her obvious disdain for convention alienates her from both sides of the family who hold her responsible for Nuri's death. Her free-spiritedness causes her to act rashly, attenuating some of the viewer's empathy. Furthermore, the unrelenting quality of Katja's grief may also serve to keep the viewer at arm's length.[7] In this way, the film fosters a critical empathy that recognises flaws, but also encourages connection with a complex human being.

Figure 11.1 *In the Fade*: a closeup of an anguished Katja as she is wrestled to the ground.

Katja's grief, however, remains the predominant emotion of the film; Akin accentuates her sense of injustice and powerlessness. Since her husband was both a German of Kurdish descent and a former drug dealer, the police relentlessly question Katja about his possible fundamentalist or gang-related connections. Her sense of alienation grows, and the first part is punctuated by a nearly successful suicide attempt. She is 'saved' at the last moment by a phone call from her lawyer telling her that the terrorists responsible for the deaths of her husband and child – a neo-Nazi couple – have been caught. The courtroom experience, however, only twists the knife further. In this second part, Katja endures the recitation of a forensic report graphically describing the injuries her son suffered and the physical condition of his body after the explosion. Meanwhile, the defendants sit coldly and smugly in the box, while their unscrupulous lawyer twists the truth, eventually getting them released on a technicality (Figure 11.2). The viewer's empathy, which has been repeatedly engaged, is probably now at a high point. One reviewer reveals her own empathetic response, projecting it onto the viewer: 'When Katja suddenly charges at one of the attackers, amid the commotion of the trial, it's easy to imagine that you might have done the same' (Ebiri 2017).

In the final part of the film, Katja tracks the couple to a Greek island and exacts a particular form of vengeance. The film does follow, indeed wants the viewer to follow, the familiar patterns of a revenge film. We are intentionally shown Katja's construction of a nail bomb and its detonation device. The next day, she waits for the couple to leave their trailer and then plants the backpack containing the bomb. She sits and awaits their return, but eventually retrieves the bomb. Viewers may momentarily entertain the notion that she is having second thoughts – that she will not succumb to the cycle of violence that ensnared the couple (something some empathetic viewers might wish for).

Figure 11.2 The defendants sit coldly and unemotionally throughout the court proceedings.

Figure 11.3 Katja, bomb strapped to her back, the moment before she enters the trailer.

At the same time, Akin makes it clear that her grief and sense of injustice have not diminished. The film cuts to the next day, as we see the couple once again returning from their jog. They enter the trailer, and a long shot reveals Katja walking determinedly towards it, backpack and detonator in hand. For a few moments she stands at the trailer door – and viewers may imagine she is summoning up the resolve to place the bomb under the trailer. But, in a startling turn, she calmly re-straps the backpack to herself and walks into the trailer (Figure 11.3). Seconds later it explodes.

The trajectory of the film is such that two reviewers felt compelled to categorise it as 'a nihilistic Liam Neeson thriller' (D'Angelo 2017; see also Freer 2018), while another remarks that 'at its heart' it is not markedly different from movies such as *Death Wish* (Sobczynski 2017). These reviewers, however, conveniently ignore the manner in which Katja exacts her vengeance. The difference between *In the Fade* and these films, of course, is that the protagonist takes her own life as well as the lives of those who have done her family harm (this would never occur to Charles Bronson, nor are we likely to see it happen to Liam Neeson, no matter how many *Taken* sequels are made). Critics relegate the film to the tradition of 'revenge movies', even when the protagonist literally straps a bomb to herself. Utilising this perspective, critics have no need to resort to the condemnation imperative; Katja is simply a vengeful mother and wife – not a terrorist. This is problematic, however, because the reason they can see her as such emanates from a racialised and gendered notion of the terrorist. The possibility that a white woman might enact such self-annihilating violence runs counter to received knowledge – a narrow view of who the terrorist is and what he looks like (in the collective Western imagination the terrorist is male and almost always 'Muslim-looking' [Ahmad 2004, 1279]). Racialising the terrorist permits an othering which allows a distancing on the part of the viewer. Katja's whiteness, as well as her beauty, dismantle the stereotype, attenuate any attempt at such distancing, and question a restrictive conceptualisation of the figure of the suicide terrorist.

Framing these stories as 'revenge narratives' should further give us pause because such formulations raise the question as to what degree, and what form, of violence is considered palatable. In revenge narratives, viewers share in the protagonist's sorrow; they yearn to see things redressed. And, often, the social systems that are meant to serve the victim prove woefully inadequate. Feelings of injustice are thus exacerbated to the point where viewers may even endorse the violent measures enacted by the protagonist (or a 'very particular set of specific skills . . . Skills that make me a nightmare for people like you', as Liam Neeson warns his daughter's abductors in *Taken*). This is not to say that revenge is not a component of Katja's actions, but that such analyses ignore the ways in which the terroristic nature of her actions complicates the ways we think about both Katja and terrorism itself; her suicide bombing compels viewers to rethink everything that has come before. But, more importantly, it places them in a state of ethical ambivalence, forcing a re-assessment of the sympathy they may have felt for her plight. The unexpected gesture that ends the film creates a dilemma for viewers who may recognise that any understanding they experience for Katja's final action might also translate into an understanding of suicide-bombing more generally. Commenting on the final image in the film, Belgi Ebiri observes:

> All along, the movie has used Katja as a benign vessel of compassion, indulging her grief and replaying the trauma of her experience. . . . And now, just as it fades to black, *In the Fade* asks us – ever so briefly and troublingly – to imagine another world in which the terrorist is not a

beautiful white woman, but someone with whom we have been taught never to empathize. (2017)[8]

Ebiri emphasises that a reversal needs to be effected for the viewer to gain a renewed understanding of the terrorist. Through empathy with someone who looks like Diane Kruger may come some feeling for the bearded, darker-skinned individual who commits the same action. Akin thus flips the script, if you will, because up until then the viewer has thought of, and connected with, Katja as a victim. It is only in these final moments of the film that she must now be considered a perpetrator. In this way, Akin also causes the viewer to contemplate the boundaries separating victim from perpetrator, and the possibility that an individual can be both.

The film, however, might have done more here. Had the villains of the piece been a little less villainous or had there been some degree of ambiguity about their 'guilt', Akin might have explored questions of terror and responsibility more deeply. For though *In the Fade* is not a film strictly about terrorism, the fact that Katja straps on a bomb and blows herself up along with the neo-Nazi couple does compel the viewer to contemplate how and why one becomes a terrorist. But this happens perhaps in ways the director had not intended. Clearly, Katja's action is seen as more justified than that of the neo-Nazis. But, if so, why? The film goes a long way towards explaining Katja's ultimate act but, somewhat ironically, does not consider the gestures of the neo-Nazis, falling into the trap of making distinctions between good and bad terrorists. Even if Katja is 'innocent' – in contrast to the neo-Nazis – the film ignores the sources of resentment from which their actions may have sprung, dehumanising them and turning them into villains. By seeking to condemn neo-Nazi actions – the film is a direct response to a series of attacks on immigrants carried out between 2000 and 2007 by a neo-Nazi group calling themselves the National Socialist Underground (NSU) – *In the Fade* tends to take a one-sided approach to the subject.[9] Keeping these shortcomings in mind, the film nevertheless presents a possible strategy for problematising the urge to condemn, or to reconsider those who are condemned. It adopts an unconventional approach, eliciting empathy and a degree of understanding from viewers for a protagonist who commits an act they may ultimately find unforgivable.

Dislocative Fiction and the Unforgivable Terrorist: *American War*

As a work of dystopian fiction, Omar El Akkad's *American War* (2017) paints a frightening (and prescient?) portrait of a polarised United States tearing itself apart at the seams. The text concerns itself primarily with the Second Civil War (2074–95), and secondarily with the Reunification Plague (2095–2105). Climate change has transformed the North American continent, submerging much of Louisiana, Georgia and Florida under water. In response, the federal government seeks to ban the use of fossil fuels. Railing against this and other impositions, some Southern states attempt to secede. A southern suicide bomber assassinates the President and the country descends into civil war. El Akkad telescopes his perspective to focus on Sarat Chestnut and her ill-fated family, starting in 2075, when the country is enjoying a fragile peace. Despite evident deprivation, she and her siblings appear to live a life free of distress or pain. The family hopes to emigrate north, where there are better economic opportunities, but Sarat's father is killed in a suicide bombing and they end up being transported to a refugee camp near a contested border. Sarat is presented as a girl fascinated by the smallest living thing, and El Akkad depicts her as both innocent and trusting: 'She was a child still and the purpose of a lie eluded her. She couldn't yet fathom that someone would say something if they didn't believe it' (2017, 13).

In different ways, then, each of these text outlines how a loving and caring person can be broken and completely transformed through violence. Sarat's trajectory – from innocent to refugee to resistance fighter to political prisoner to suicide bomber – has a sense of inevitability about it. A groomer provides her with training and weapons, 'legitimate' motivation, and a terrorist is born. The tribulations undergone by Sarat and her family – the violent deaths of her parents, her brother's serious wounding, the torture and deprivation she herself is forced to endure – make it so that raising her hand against her oppressors is practically a *fait accompli*. El Akkad signals this objective:

> I didn't want a character who people would apologize for, sympathize with, or even like . . . The only thing I wanted was for people to understand how she gets to the place she ends up, because when we talk about extremists or people who end up doing horrible things, we tend only to talk about the finish line. (Crawford 2019)

The perpetrator's final act typically obliterates any conception of a self existing prior to that moment. El Akkad's assertion is that Sarat did not arrive at this endpoint on her own and, more importantly, that her final action does not define her. The attention paid to Sarat's evolution in *American War* raises a number of questions about existing limitations in conceptualising the terrorist. As Bielby and Murer ask: 'If perpetrating is a process and if the self is multiple and fluid, changing over time, what forms of self precede, follow and exist alongside the perpetrating self?' (2018, 3). The novel's extended consideration of Sarat's life pushes against the notion that perpetration defines that which is essential about her. As many have noted, one is not born a perpetrator; fuller understanding depends on knowledge of that which preceded the destructive act. Indeed, it is contingent upon recognising Sarat in all her complexity, as a victim-perpetrator.[10] El Akkad thus advocates for a critical empathy of the kind referred to earlier – one that allows for readers to connect with the feelings that pushed Sarat to act as she did, without necessarily sharing those feelings.

To empathise with the terrorist, however, one must conceive of a situation wherein one would be as dispossessed and desperate as she. To this end, El Akkad sets out to create a work he refers to as 'dislocative fiction': 'I take things that happen over there and I make them happen over here' (Doezema 2018). Upending readers from their usual surroundings – making the familiar unfamiliar – compels them to engage with their empathetic reluctance and prompts them to imagine how they might think or act in other circumstances. The novel thus presents a future in which citizens of the United States have become targets of the kinds of policies to which their nation subjects others: economic exploitation, drone attacks and refugee camps. As El Akkad tells an interviewer, 'It actually boiled down to pretending that the victims look and sound like you' (Arafat 2018). In other words, the novel speculates on what might happen if the horrors visited upon others by the United States were to come home to America. How might Americans respond if these anti-insurgent strategies were used against them to quell any kind of uprising?[11] At one point, for instance, Sarat comes to the dark realisation that:

> War broke [everyone] the same way, made them scared and angry and vengeful the same way. In times of peace and good fortune they were nothing alike, but stripped of these things they were kin. The universal slogan of war, she'd learned, was simple. If it had been you, you'd have done no different. (El Akkad 2017, 184)

In using the second person, El Akkad directly addresses his readers, compelling them to consider the proposed scenario. The sentence suggests that readers may flatter themselves into thinking that their higher principles would kick in, that they would act humanely when others have not. The truth of the matter, the novel suggests, is that they would not.[12] In reversing the tables, then, El Akkad aims to represent the suffering that could have been, and might be, theirs. *American War* actively subverts the notion that 'we' are never the terrorists and 'they' are always the terrorists.

As noted earlier, El Akkad works hard to enlist the reader's sympathy – anything bad that can happen to Sarat inevitably does. Having already lost her father, she is then orphaned when her mother is killed during the massacre at the refugee camp. Barely surviving herself, she discovers that her brother has been severely wounded and suffered irreparable brain damage. As a consequence, Sarat joins the rebel forces, taking part in guerrilla raids and assassinations. She is apprehended, imprisoned and relentlessly tortured until she is eventually released at war's end. These novelistic extravagances are tempered somewhat by the fact that these incidents are largely based on actual events. For instance, Sugarloaf, the island fortress where Sarat is incarcerated, bears a strong resemblance to Guantanamo Bay and the methods utilised to make her talk, including rendition and waterboarding, quickly bring to mind the inhumane treatment of prisoners at Abu Ghraib and elsewhere. The text problematises the urge to empathise, however, with Sarat's final gesture. Few readers are likely to concede that they would engage in an act that would take the lives of millions of innocent people. Sarat allows herself to be injected with a highly contagious biological agent, smuggles herself across the border, and unleashes a plague that will last ten years, killing 110 million people. In contrast to *In the Fade*, then, there is no ambiguity in terms of judging Sarat's guilt. The gargantuan nature of her crime leaves little room for equivocation. Furthermore, the narrator of the story, her nephew Benjamin, burns her diaries (from which the narrative is derived) claiming, 'It was the only way I had left to hurt her' (El Akkad 2017, 332). Even after her death, not surprisingly, pain and anger linger.

And yet, interestingly, the penultimate paragraph of the novel conveys a deeper understanding. Benjamin recalls swimming in a river with his aunt and seeing her surface: 'I saw a look on her face I'd never seen before. It was relief, as though she'd spent not a few seconds, but an entire lifetime suffocating, and was now finally free' (333). Sarat's nephew stands in for the reader in these final pages. He is unable to forgive her (despite sharing a strong and close bond with her – a crucial element of the final third of the novel), but he is able to connect with her feelings, to apprehend the ways in which she has been irrevocably damaged: 'I wonder, sometimes, if that's the way she must have felt the moment she put the poison inside her and readied to wheel herself into Reunification Square – an overwhelming relief, the opposite of drowning' (333). In these final lines, the reader witnesses a move towards empathy – 'if that's the way she must have felt' (333) – that seeks to understand, if not forgive.

'Between Normativity and Abjection': The Female Suicide Terrorist

The stories of Katja and Sarat thus differ significantly (and might be said to be thematically opposite) from those narratives that present a last-minute change of heart on the part of the would-be terrorist. Narratives such as Santosh Sivan's film *The Terrorist* (1998) or Slimane Benaïssa's novel *The Last Night of a Damned Soul* (2004) alleviate the readers' ethical dilemma. They care and sympathise with a protagonist and they are 'rewarded' when the potential terrorist fails to complete the intended mission. Their feelings have been corroborated; they were right all along to care for this person. In the case of Katja and Sarat, however, they have no such recourse – they must now come to terms with earlier feelings. Can they now simply disavow those moments of empathy? And if they are willing to extend some degree of understanding to Katja (and even

Sarat) are they not obliged to reconsider their nugatory stance towards others who have engaged in terroristic activities? Richard Jackson suggests that 'the boundaries of the terrorism taboo are maintained by a kind of schizophrenic desire to know but also *not* to know . . . how the "terrorist" thinks' (Jackson 2019, 388). With these texts, empathetic readers/viewers get to know the terrorists, and how terrorists are made, before the impulse not to know kicks in. We witness the progressive dehumanisation of these women and, in the process, have a better grasp of the humanity that has been lost through violence. Returning to El Akkad's notion of 'dislocative fiction', we can perceive how each text seeks to unsettle the reader, to disrupt the dominant mythography about terrorism to which Jackson has alluded. Both *In the Fade* and *American War* engage, in very different ways, in flipping the script: Akin through the use of a beautiful white woman as a suicide-bomber, El Akkad in making the United States itself the site of war, internment camps and drone attacks.

The other dislocative strategy deployed by these authors, of course, is in making their protagonists female. As Anne-Marie McManus (2013) observes, the gender of the perpetrator has very real effects upon reader or viewer, instigating diametrically opposed responses. Female terrorists are more likely to elicit empathy but, paradoxically, their actions will also arouse a greater degree of outrage from readers (than would those of their male counterparts). Women, after all, are meant to be life givers and caretakers, not life takers and murderers. This is further complicated by the fact that women are often conceived of as victims rather than perpetrators. Ironically, it is precisely because of these faulty gendered assumptions that the actions of the female perpetrator are so disturbing and unsettling. This disjunction inevitably elicits a greater degree of interrogation on the part of the reader. Anne Speckhard, for instance, observes that the use of female suicide bombers compels 'the horrified witnessing audience to probe more deeply for her motivations – something that garners far more attention to and often more sympathy for the terrorists' cause' (2008, 1001). This paradox also prevents the usual dismissal or condemnation of the terrorist, since readers are forced to wrestle with and reconcile what would seem to be contradictory characteristics: their femininity and their propensity for violence. McManus thus suggests that female suicide terrorists 'occupy a strange border between normativity and abjection' (2013, 81). The female presence in these texts insists upon a reconsideration of who and what a suicide terrorist is. Because even if one were to dismiss the female perpetrator as an anomaly, such a gesture problematises assumptions about the constitution of the terrorist.

Empathising with the perpetrator means to genuinely express curiosity for her humanity, to contemplate how she may have suffered, but not to relinquish the anger and pain we may feel as a result of her deeds. In other words, if we are truly to comprehend the terrorist, we must engage in a kind of Keatsian 'negative capability' where we keep these opposing elements in play, 'without any irritable reaching after fact or reason' (Keats 1958, I, 193–4). Texts that create ambivalence within their readers or viewers inevitably dispose them to reconsider the ways in which they (automatically and instinctively) conceptualise the suicide terrorist.[13]

Notes

1. See Ashis Nandy who notes that Western media seldom refer to suicide bombings as 'self-sacrifice' (2013, 119) or Johnston and Bose who suggest that 'the decision to engage in terrorism . . . is guided by love for, and a sense of obligation to, a community' (2020, 317). A recent text, *The Irrational Terrorist and Other Persistent Terrorism Myths* (Hudson et al., 2020), offers a variety of examples aimed at further dismantling and debunking this paradigm.
2. The impulse to not know the terrorist has been configured in ways different from Hage's 'condemnation imperative'. For instance, Joseba Zulaika identifies a faulty epistemology that begins 'with the placement of the entire phenomenon in a context of taboo and the willful ignorance of the political subjectivities of the terrorists' (2009, 2). Lisa Stampnitzky, for her part, speaks of a 'politics of anti-knowledge' (2013, 187) that governs much of the discourse of terrorism (particularly in the wake of the attacks of September 11, 2001). Finally, Quassim Cassam suggests that the discourse is further tainted by expressions of intellectual humility – often falsely invoked (2020, 430).
3. For his part, Michael C. Frank points to our tendency to fall back on 'comforting myths about the weakness, deviance, and abnormality of the terrorist "other"' (2019, 356).
4. Erin McGlothlin puts forth a similar argument: 'Narratives that attempt to humanize [perpetrators] . . . hazard the possibility that their readers will become too empathetic, that the critical space for ethical reflection . . . will shrink and that the reader will actually end up aligning with the perspective of the inhumane character' (2016, 255).
5. Paul Bloom labels these approaches 'emotional empathy' and 'cognitive empathy', respectively (2016, 17).
6. The title of McGlothlin's article makes the link between empathy and identification self-evident.
7. One critic at Cannes went so far as the call the film an example of 'rainy-day grief porn' (O'Connor 2017).
8. Interestingly, when a white woman is cast as the protagonist of a War on Terror narrative (see *Homeland*, *Eye in the Sky*, *Zero Dark Thirty*), it is in the role of the counter-terrorist, not the terrorist. I thank Maria Flood for this observation.
9. Akin tells an interviewer that the incidents took place 'in our neighborhood. So, it was close to me. I had to express my anger and my fear' (Ebiri 2018).
10. Javier Argomaniz and Orla Lynch (2018, 494–5) examine the role of victimisation in radicalisation and emphasise the need for a deeper consideration of these 'complex victims'.

11. Indeed, *American War* may resonate with some readers precisely because the polarisation it depicts is not too far removed from current conditions in the US. The insurgency of 6 January 2021 echoes El Akkad's text in discomfiting ways.
12. In his review, Thomas E. Ricks (2017) quotes an American soldier stationed in Iraq. The observation is most telling: 'Hell, if you came to Georgia and treated me and my family the way we're treating these Iraqis, damn right I'd be an insurgent'.
13. I would like to thank Michael C. Frank and Maria Flood: first for organising a wonderful conference, and second, for offering insightful and constructive comments to my work. Their efforts are much appreciated.

References

Ahmad, Muneer I. 2004. "A Rage Shared by Law: Post-September 11 Racial Violence as Crimes of Passion." *California Law Review* 92, no. 5: 1259–330.

Akin, Fatih, dir. 2017. *In the Fade*. Warner Brothers. DVD.

Arafat, Zaina. 2018. "American Dystopia: An Interview with Omar El Akkad." *Asian American Writers' Workshop*, February 28, 2018. https://aaww.org/american-dystopia-omar-el-akkad/

Argomaniz, Javier, and Orla Lynch. 2018. "Introduction to the Special Issue: The Complexity of Terrorism – Victims, Perpetrators and Radicalization." *Studies in Conflict and Terrorism* 41, no. 7: 491–506.

Bielby, Clare, and Jeffrey Stevenson Murer. 2018. "Perpetrating Selves: An Introduction." In *Perpetrating Selves: Doing Violence, Performing Identity*, eds Clare Bielby and Jeffrey Stevenson Murer, 1–13. London: Palgrave Macmillan.

Bloch, Robyn. 2018. "Innocent Superspy: Contradictory Narratives as Exculpation in a Woman Apartheid Perpetrator Story." In *Perpetrating Selves: Doing Violence, Performing Identity*, eds Clare Bielby and Jeffrey Stevenson Murer, 113–32. London: Palgrave Macmillan.

Bloom, Paul. 2016. *Against Empathy: The Case for Rational Compassion*. New York: HarperCollins.

Bruneau, Emile. 2016. "Understanding the Terrorist Mind." *Cerebrum*, November 1, 2016. https://www.ncbi.nlm.nih.gov/pmc/articles/PMC5198759/pdf/cer-13-16.pdf

Cassam, Quassim. 2020. "Humility and Terrorism Studies." In *Routledge Handbook of Philosophy of Humility*, eds Mark Alfano, Michael P. Lynch and Alessandra Tanesini, 427–38. New York: Routledge.

Crawford, Rachel. 2019. "Interview: *American War* Author Omar El Akkad." *City Newspaper*, March 19, 2019. https://www.rochestercitynewspaper.com/rochester/interview-american-war-author-omar-el-akkad/Content?oid=9837840

D'Angelo, Mike. 2017. "Even Diane Kruger Going After Nazis Can't Save the Blunt Courtroom Drama *In the Fade*." *AV Club*, December 19, 2017. https://www.avclub.com/even-diane-kruger-cant-save-the-blunt-courtroom-drama-i-1821430333

Doezema, Marie. 2018. "For Omar El Akkad, Journalism and Fiction Are 'Interlocking Muscles.'" *Columbia Journalism Review*, October 31, 2018. https://www.cjr.org/analysis/omar-el-akkad.php

Ebiri, Bilge. 2018. "'I Will Get Attacked for It, but F*ck That': Fatih Akin on *In the Fade*, Diane Kruger, and Neo Nazis." *Village Voice*, January 2, 2018. https://www.

villagevoice.com/2018/01/02/i-will-get-attacked-for-it-but-fck-that-fatih-akin-on-in-the-fade-diane-kruger-and-neo-nazis/

Ebiri, Bilge. 2017. "*In the Fade* Dares to Flip Expectations about Terrorism." *Village Voice*, December 22, 2017. https://www.villagevoice.com/2017/12/22/fatih-akins-in-the-fade-dares-to-flip-expectations-about-terrorism/

El Akkad, Omar. 2017. *American War*. New York: Alfred A. Knopf.

Frank, Michael C. 2019. "'Why do They Hate Us?': Terrorists in British and American Fiction of the Mid-2000s." In *Terrorism and Literature*, ed. Peter C. Herman, 340–60. Cambridge: Cambridge University Press.

Freer, Ian. 2018. "*In the Fade* Review." *Empire*, June 19, 2018. https://www.empireonline.com/movies/reviews/fade-review/

Gauthier, Tim. 2015. "'Toward These Uncanny Young Men': Entering the Mind of the Terrorist." In *9/11 Fiction, Empathy, and Otherness*, 127–65. Lanham, MD: Lexington Books.

Hage, Ghassan. 2003. "'Comes a Time We Are All Enthusiasm': Understanding Palestinian Suicide Bombers in Times of Exighophobia." *Public Culture* 15, no. 1: 65–89.

Hudson, Darren, Arie Perliger, Riley Post and Zachary Hohman. 2020. *The Irrational Terrorist and Other Persistent Terrorism Myths*. Boulder and London: Lynne Riener Publishers.

Jackson, Richard. 2019. "Sympathy for the Devil: Evil, Taboo, and the Terrorist Figure in Literature." In *Terrorism and Literature*, ed. Peter C. Herman, 377–94. Cambridge: Cambridge University Press.

Johnston, Nicolas, and Srinjoy Bose. 2020. "Violence, Power and Meaning: The Moral Logic of Terrorism." *Global Policy* 11, no. 3: 315–25.

Keats, John. 1958. *The Letters of John Keats*, ed. H. E. Rollins. 2 vols. Cambridge: Cambridge University Press.

Leake, Eric. 2014. "Humanizing the Inhumane: The Value of Difficult Empathy." In *Rethinking Empathy Through Literature*, eds Meghan M. Hammond and Sue J. Kim, 175–85. New York and London: Routledge.

McGlothlin, Erin. 2020. "Perpetrator Trauma." In *The Routledge Companion to Literature and Trauma*, eds Colin Davis and Hanna Meretoja, 100–10. New York: Routledge.

McGlothlin, Erin. 2016. "Empathetic Identification and the Mind of the Holocaust Perpetrator in Fiction: A Proposed Taxonomy of Response." *Narrative* 24, no. 3: 251–76.

McManus, Anne-Marie. 2013. "Sentimental Terror Narratives: Gendering Violence, Dividing Sympathy." *Journal of Middle East Women's Studies* 9, no. 2: 80–107.

Mohamed, Saira. 2015. "Of Monsters and Men: Perpetrator Trauma and Mass Atrocity." *Columbia Law Review* 115, no. 5: 1157–216.

Morton, Adam. 2011. "Empathy for the Devil." In *Empathy: Philosophical and Psychological Perspectives*, eds Amy Coplan and Peter Goldie, 318–30. Oxford: Oxford University Press.

Nandy, Ashis. 2013. *Regimes of Narcissism, Regimes of Despair*. Oxford: Oxford University Press.

Morel, Pierre, dir. 2008. *Taken*. 20th Century Fox. DVD.

O'Connor, Rory. 2017. "Cannes Review: *In the Fade* is a Compelling Socio-Political Revenge Thriller." *The Film Stage*, May 27, 2017. https://thefilmstage.com/in-the-fade-review-fatih-akin-diane-kruger-cannes/

Pape, Robert. 2005. *Dying to Win: The Strategic Logic of Suicide Terrorism*. New York: Random House.

Ricks, Thomas E. 2017. "Book Review: *American War* – a Grim Novel About a Second American Civil War." *Foreign Policy*, August 23, 2017. https://foreignpolicy.com/2017/08/23/book-review-american-war-a-grim-novel-about-a-second-american-civil-war-2/

Roekel, Eva. 2021. "On the Dangers of Empathy with the Military in Argentina." *Ethnos* 86, no. 4: 616–31.

Sobczynski, Peter. 2017. "In the Fade." Review of *In the Fade*, by Fatih Akin. *Roger Ebert*, December 27, 2017. https://www.rogerebert.com/reviews/in-the-fade-2017

Speckhard, Anne. 2008. "The Emergence of Female Suicide Terrorists." *Studies in Conflict & Terrorism* 31, no. 11: 995–1023.

Stampnitzky, Lisa. 2013. *Disciplining Terror: How Experts Invented "Terrorism."* Cambridge: Cambridge University Press.

Stueber, Karsten R. 2006. *Rediscovering Empathy: Agency, Folk Psychology, and the Human Sciences*. Cambridge, MA: MIT Press.

Zulaika, Joseba. 2009. *Terrorism: The Self-Fulfilling Prophecy*. Chicago and London: The University of Chicago Press.

12. DISCOMFORT AND DOCUMENTARY FILM: THE FIGURE OF THE WHITE EXTREMIST IN DEEYAH KHAN'S *WHITE RIGHT*

Maria Flood

White Right and Deeyah Khan's Filmmaking Practice

Deeyah Khan has directed two documentaries about political extremism. Whereas *White Right: Meeting the Enemy* (2017) follows neo-Nazi and so-called 'alt-right' groups in the US, *Jihad: A Story of the Others* (2015) portrays reformed radical Islamists in the UK. In these films, Khan reframes the parameters of the debate about radicalisation, moving beyond the question of ideology to consider what might be termed the affective conditions that she views as central to the pull of violent extremist and terrorist movements. She notes her frustration with the popular media discourse about extremism, and she also draws connections between far-right and Islamist extremists in terms of their motivations and personalities. In both cases, Khan argues that media narratives overplay the role of religion or ideology in radicalisation; instead, she suggests that the attraction of extremism is in part about 'human vulnerabilities (qtd in Urwin 2015), where 'the vast majority of the people [jihadis or far right extremists] are either lost and looking for a sense of belonging, or looking for a sense of purpose' (qtd in Saner 2017).

Khan foregrounds her own life story in each film, an autobiography that shows her deep familiarity with vulnerability and the quest for communitarian belonging. Khan was born in Norway in the late 1970s, a time when there were very few immigrants, and even fewer Muslims, in the country. Her mother is from Afghanistan and her father from Pakistan, and from an early age, she attended anti-racist marches with her father. Throughout her childhood and teenage years, Khan worked as a musician and singer, gaining renown in Norway. However, this drew the ire of extremists in the Muslim community, and at 17, Khan left for London to escape intimidation and death threats. Khan's experience of exile contributes to her ability to recognise feelings of isolation, longing and loneliness in the people she interviews.

A BBC interview about multiculturalism in the UK in 2016 sparked her notoriety among white supremacists (see Brand 2017). In the segment in question, Khan asserts that 'the fact of the matter is that the UK is never going to be white again'. She goes on to note that parents of Pakistani, Iraqi or other Muslim heritages must accept that the lives they had in their countries of origin cannot be recreated exactly in the UK. She concludes by stating that different communities are going to have to work together, asking 'what does it mean to build a society that includes all of us?' A vitriolic storm of hate mail and abuse followed, with threats that she would be raped, tortured, gassed and killed. Although Khan had been subject to racist abuse before – as a child in Norway she had been spat at, and her brother had been chased by racists – the scale of hostility in this case for a self-evident statement (Britain will not have a solely white population in the future) shocked and frightened her.

It is the conversion of this fear into intellectual curiosity and a search for empathic understanding that led to the making of *White Right*: 'I was done being scared . . . I realised I can hide and keep my head down or I can walk into this and see if I can understand any of it' (qtd in Malik 2018). The film features interviews with white supremacists in America in 2017, and Khan was present and filming at the Charlottesville Rally in August of that year when activist Heather Heyer was killed in a terrorist attack. These scenes make for harrowing viewing, as Khan is pictured with her camera amidst the increasingly frenetic crowds of far-right supporters. Yet much of the film is taken up with one-to-one interviews with adherents of various strands of far-right and white supremacist belief systems, from the mostly working-class members of the neo-Nazi National Socialist Movement (NSM, which claims to be the largest white nationalist organisation in the US) to the Ivy League-educated, self-styled leaders of the 'Alternative Right' (commonly called the alt-right). Khan is featured prominently in the film, visibly and/or audibly present throughout.

Her style could be categorised as 'performative' within Bill Nichols' schema of six documentary modes. This is a style that is emotionally driven and unequivocally subjective, laying emphasis on how the topic (in this case, white nationalism and its attendant racism and violence) affects the filmmaker personally (2010, 32). Unlike other documentarians of the white right in the US, such as Jon Ronson and Louis Theroux, Khan foregrounds rather than conceals her identity and ideological position, frequently highlighting to these men that she is a liberal, Muslim feminist. It is also a participatory documentary, given the involvement of the filmmaker with the subjects, where interviews are the primary mode of investigation and encounters that range from 'conversations to provocations' are depicted (Nichols 2010, 31). The interaction between the filmmaker and the subject is foregrounded, and indeed, Khan consistently adopts a direct, but non-aggressive, approach with the white extremists she meets, describing how their actions affect her personally and even showing them photographs of herself as a child.

Khan wants to focus on the 'human vulnerabilities' of her subjects, and indeed, the assumption that the subjects of a documentary are in some way vulnerable and deserving of protection has been a cornerstone of scholarly critiques of the form. In one of the earliest interventions into the debate on ethics, spectatorship and documentary, Calvin Pryluck stresses the potential hierarchy between person viewing a film (subject) and person viewed on film (object). Pryluck charts the various positions that documentary makers adopt towards their subjects, writing 'it turns out that the ethical problem is also an aesthetic one . . .; a simple human principle can be evoked here: those least able to protect themselves require the greatest protection' (1976, 28). This vulnerability can be socially inscribed, as in the 'injured identities' documentaries that Belinda Smaill identifies as a key contemporary form of the documentary (2007), or the vulnerability that can come about through the process of filmmaking itself. As Lisa Downing and Libby Saxton caution, the ethics of viewing is a complex process involving viewers and viewed: 'who is looking at whom, and how, and what kind of power relations are established or dismantled in this encounter?' (2010, 20). Nichols summarises the ethical challenge for documentary filmmakers in the following terms: 'How do we treat the people we film; what do we owe them as well as our audience?' (2010, 45).

The stakes for Khan in filming these subjects are radically altered by the fact that the subjects she works with have adopted polemical political identities and, in some cases, promoted or participated in terrorist violence. Not only does Khan meet and converse with the members and representatives of various far-right groups, including the NSM and Richard Spencer (a spokesperson for the alt-right); filming *White Right* also involved a degree of physical danger for Khan. Following the neo-Nazi rally in Charlottesville, Khan attended a subsequent gathering in the Virginia hills where some men began aggressively pointing their guns at the camera. Khan recalls thinking, 'I'm not going to make it out' (qtd in Saner 2017). Far from the vulnerable subject and the powerful filmmaker, the ethical stakes in *White Right* are in a sense reversed – it is the director who is potentially at risk, from the very people she is filming.

Thus, the human subjects in *White Right* are not, in Pryluck's words, people whose 'utter helplessness' demands 'utter protection' (1976, 28), but rather proponents of ethically abhorrent ideologies. Khan does not feature interviews with the victims of Islamist or white supremacist violence in these films; the focus remains entirely on the extremists. It is important to note here that this is not a question of humanisation or a lack thereof (see Jackson 2018). Khan at no point questions the humanity of her interviewees, and she films their amusing foibles and darker failings, their cruelties and kindnesses, their feelings and opinions, and accords them the dignity of being listened to unequivocally, even if she then interjects to disagree with them. The interviews Khan records often begin with a wide-angle two shot, which places Khan and her interviewee in the same visual frame; on this choice, she writes, 'I was interested in sitting down one-on-one with people like this and have the conversation where I am able to recognise their humanity and they are able to recognise mine' (qtd in Malik 2018). Indeed, *White Right* explicitly foregrounds confrontation, or at least communication: it is not about constructing a narrative or backstory of a subject's move into extremism (as she did in *Jihad*), but rather a film in which the story itself is structured around the interaction between Khan and those who consider her, and whom she considers, to be an enemy.

Khan states at the start of *White Right* that for many, right-wing radicals have come to 'embody hate in its purest form'; accordingly, the film importantly underscores the question of emotion. Indeed, it would be difficult to speak about white nationalism without evoking emotions like hate, anger, fear; many recent books on the topic directly reference these emotions (see Saslow 2018; Kimmel 2017; Russell Hochschild 2016; Anderson 2016). Additionally, these affective registers often overlap. As Sara Ahmed points out, far-right rhetoric often couches hate speech in the language of love. Thus, hatred of black, brown, Jewish, Muslim, female or homosexual bodies is framed discursively through the love that these groups feel for their own members, and for the nation itself: it is because 'we' love 'our' nation, 'our' white children, and 'our' white women, that we seek to defend and protect them from those who 'threaten' them (2014, 45). While Ahmed identifies the ways in which neo-Nazi propaganda draws on the language of love for the community to express hate for those outside of it, Khan suggests that love and the need for belonging are central to the motivations behind adherence to extremism: 'It doesn't start with hate. It starts out . . . with love and loyalty between the recruiter and the follower' (qtd in Urwin 2015). Khan draws on these emotional registers in her conversations with both current and former far-right radicals. However, because much useful work has already been done on how love, hate, anger and fear work in extremist ideologies, I want instead to consider how a different and thus far unexamined affective mode in relation to encounters with extremists plays out in *White Right*, namely the feeling of discomfort. I will show the ways in which social discomfort, i.e. not 'fitting', can lead individuals to join extremist groups, as evidenced by the interviews in *White Right*. I argue that what I call an ethics of discomfort operates throughout the film, deliberately evoked by Khan as a political, creative and emotional strategy.

White Right and the Ethics of Discomfort

When we use the word discomfort nowadays, we aim to describe a physical, emotional or mental state of unease, a form of distress. Discomfort is certainly more aligned with pain than pleasure in an Aristotelian understanding of emotion, or with the reality principle or death drive in Freudian terms. Contemporary definitions of discomfort highlight mental and physical disquiet as separate factors. The *Oxford English Dictionary* defines discomfort as 'the state, condition, or fact of being (mentally or physically) uncomfortable; uneasiness' (noun) and 'to make (mentally or physically) uncomfortable or uneasy' (verb). Yet what these definitions fail to capture is the ways in which physical, mental, social and emotional discomfort can go hand in hand. As anyone who has experienced even a persistent low-level chronic condition can attest, and as some doctors responding to the opioid crisis suggest, separating emotional and physical discomfort in pain patients is not always clear-cut (see McGreal 2018). Etymologically, the word discomfort is tied to emotional, mental and social distress rather than physical. Arising as the negative form of the Latin *confortare*, meaning 'to comfort, solace, or strengthen', around the fourteenth century the noun form came to signify 'misfortune, adversity' and 'grief, sorrow, discouragement', while the verb form in the same period signified 'to deprive of courage'. Thus, earlier definitions of the word are bound closely to the idea of confrontation and sadness (loss or misfortune at the hands of a foe or fate), and simultaneously connected to the term discomfit, meaning 'to defeat in battle, thwart, foil', or in more present-day usage, 'perplexity, confusion' (*OED*). It is also important to note that discomfort, medically speaking, is not pain – it can go from fairly mild to something that edges on, or rubs against pain, but is not acute suffering. Physical discomfort is useful as a diagnosis of potential future pain: when we get pins and needles, for example, the body is telling us that the position we are holding is no longer conducive to blood flow, and that we must move in order to free the circulation. Thus, discomfort has an important role to play in physiological health; as a form of unease, it signals the potential of future disease within the body – an idea we will return to in relation to Sara Ahmed's delineation of the social uses of discomfort.

The idea of discomfort I seek to elaborate in relation to Khan's ethics will draw on these earlier definitions of the term, but for now we must trace its present usage. The meaning of discomfort most widely used today as an absence of comfort or pleasure and to make uncomfortable arose in the mid-nineteenth century. Scholars like Walter Benjamin (1969) and Peter Sloterdjik (2013) have described the emergence of bourgeois capitalism and the shift from the early modern to the industrial era as a time of growing emphasis on material comforts. Moreover, these comforts were closely tied to ideas of the bourgeois household as a site of accumulating luxuries, both in terms of furnishings and machines that made the home a site of pleasure and leisure rather than work. We see the vestiges of this bourgeois desire for home and comfort in the (now waning) craze for *hygge* in the UK in 2015 and 2016: a Danish and Norwegian concept of home, most clearly defined as 'cosy and comfortable', the idea launched a wave of books and products designed to bring Scandinavian aesthetics and ease (and products) to the most uncomfortable British home.

Jacques Pezeu-Massabuau, who has written the first academic book-length treatise on the concept of discomfort, also connects it to ideas of space and belonging. He calls discomfort a 'topological disorder' (2012, 38) in terms of 'physical, psychological or cyber space' (118). He describes 'discomfort' as 'everything that causes friction or conflict with the material and human environment' (15). This analysis resonates with Ahmed's description of discomfort as a feeling of 'not fitting' into a space, where a space is a physical or psychological entity governed by what she calls the 'scripts' of normativity. She argues that comfort arises when a body can seamlessly 'sink into' a space that has already taken its shape – there is a pre-existing mould for such lives to exist, without disturbing or disfiguring the environment they seek to occupy. Speaking about the discomfort of queer bodies in heteronormative spaces, she writes that, 'discomfort is not simply a choice or decision – "I feel uncomfortable about this or that" – but an effect of bodies inhabiting spaces that do not take or "extend" their shape' (Ahmed 2014, 152). In fact, this connection between the human and the material in terms of space is central to some of the critiques of *hygge*: as Charlotte Higgins (2016) points out, *hygge* applies not only to the material space(s) of the individual home, but for many has come to be enlarged to the idea of the nation itself – there are those who 'fit' comfortably within its parameters, and those who do not, i.e. immigrants, asylum seekers and Muslims (see also Barry and Selsoe Sorensen 2018 on the Danish 'ghetto' policy).

There is some evidence to suggest that a feeling of discomfort, a lack of fit between an individual and the 'scripts' of a particular identity or nation, can lead to radicalisation. Like the immigrant bodies that do not 'sink into' or 'fit' the Danish nation (at least without some intervention), many of the individuals Khan interviews in her film *Jihad* speak of feelings of not 'fitting' into British society. In the case of white nationalists, the lack of 'fit' between the extremists and mainstream society may be more difficult to discern: after all, to use bell hooks' memorable formulation, we live in an 'imperialist white-supremacist capitalist patriarchy' (2004, 17). If anyone can be said to 'fit', surely it is these men? However, many critics have argued that changes to gender roles since the mid-twentieth century have meant that some men have struggled to find their place in contemporary society. For example, Susan Faludi analyses what she calls the post-war 'male paradigm of confrontation', which has been challenged by an era of growing Civil Rights, feminist, LGBT and environmental movements (1999, 598). She argues that 'as the male role has diminished ... many men have found themselves driven to more domineering and some even "monstrous displays" in their frantic quest for a meaningful showdown' (31–2). Thus, rather than contesting the script of normative white masculinity as economically and physically dominant, and reshaping it altogether, the loss of economic stability and the demographic shifts in American society have instead fuelled feelings of oppression, which far-right discourse exploits. Indeed, Khan has noted that 'a disproportionate' number of the men she interviews who adhere to far-right politics in the US are army veterans: the male paradigm of confrontation does not fit with civilian life and there is no space that accommodates their experiences of trauma. Khan describes these veterans as 'feel[ing] forgotten and abandoned by the country they've served' (qtd in Ruiz 2018).

A sense of stigmatisation, victimisation and fear of marginalisation is also made manifest in slogans like 'You will not replace us', shouted at the rally in Virginia, or in the words of the murderer responsible for the Christchurch massacre in 2019, 'white genocide' (Coaston 2019). Both these statements speak to the notion that white people will be ousted or 'replaced' by populations of colour, both in a literal sense (demographically) and figuratively (in the sense of co-opting white power in politics and society). This is the feeling of 'aggrieved entitlement' conceptualised by Michael Kimmel (2017): the sense of being disenfranchised by diversity, equality movements, and immigration, which strips white men of the economic benefits that baby boomer parents (in some cases) enjoyed in the post-war era. A quote from Willard Gaylin most clearly captures the sense of thwarted wanting that Kimmel describes: 'We can endure the fact that we do not have something unless we feel that something has been taken away from us. We will then experience a sense of violation' (qtd in Kimmel 2017, 25).

In *White Right*, we see the bodily and spatial nature of fit and discomfort, as well as the script of masculinity as confrontation, through the figure of Peter Tefft. Tefft's image was widely distributed in the media in the wake of Charlottesville, and for many he became an icon of hatred and violence. Yet in his interview with Khan, he appears vaguely bewildered by his infamy, and describes the reasons that he joined the movement as follows: he was depressed, and 'what bothered me most was myself'. Tefft speaks of an adolescent search for belonging, his self-hatred and depression, and 'body dysmorphia' – a mental health condition where the sufferer focuses obsessively on perceived flaws in their appearance – something that could be described as an extreme form of bodily discomfort. Tefft's evocation of dysmorphia recalls Ahmed's description of discomfort as 'an acute awareness of the surface of one's body, which appears *as* surface, when one cannot inhabit the social skin' (2014, 148). The 'others' that white supremacists falsely perceive as shaping the social skin that they believe they cannot inhabit are liberals, feminists, immigrants, Jews and people of colour. These groups are targeted with verbal abuse or physical violence. Tefft says that the neo-Nazi movement made him feel like a 'warrior' and gave him a sense of 'duty' to 'act heroically'. Indeed, there is a stark contrast to the awkward, reserved Tefft interviewed by Khan and the image of the wild-eyed radical that emerges at Charlottesville. This underlines the interconnectedness of bodily and topological comforts and discomforts, where 'discomfort is a feeling of disorientation: one's body feels out of place, awkward, unsettled' (Ahmed 2014, 148). Speaking to Khan alone, Tefft squirms and speaks quietly, almost gently. But placed amid the crowd of his co-ideologues, he 'sinks in', effortlessly inhabiting the 'social skin' that surrounds him.

In fact, the interviewees in *White Right* quite literally display their allegiances, their 'fit', on their skin. Their quest for comfort and 'fit' is written on the surface of the body, in the form of a profusion of tattoos; in the case of Ken Parker, a swastika is inked on one side of his chest, and the Ku Klux Klan symbol on the other. Moreover, the robes and printed T-shirts of the neo-Nazi garb of NSM members, as well as the collared pressed shirts and natty suit jackets of Spencer and his ilk are forms of dress that designate and forcefully delimit a community. As Ahmed continues, when 'one fits . . . the surfaces of bodies disappear from view. The disappearance of the surface is instructive: in feelings of comfort, bodies extend into spaces, and spaces extend into bodies' (2014, 148). This disappearance of the surface is the conformable sinking of the individual into the collective, where the hard lines between the self and the world are softened. Such visible manifestations of allegiance are part of the dynamic of the extremist's 'network'. Arie Kruglanski, Jocelyn J. Bélanger and Rohan Gunaratna argue that extremist movements feed the three N's: need, narrative and network. Need is a basic human motivation, 'the *need* to feel that one is significant and that one matters'; narrative is the ideological story that such groups tell to justify their use of violent words or actions; and network is 'the group or category of people whose acceptance and appreciation one seeks' and who validate the narrative (2019, 5). Uncomfortable feelings of weakness, isolation and worthlessness are redirected and channelled by the network into a comfortable sense of purpose and belonging, where anger and frustration are rewarded.

Khan references the discomfort or lack of 'fit' these men feel towards liberal American society, whose beliefs they regard as socially dominant – even as their belief system moves more and more towards the values of the Republican Party. However, discomfort is also deliberately generated by Khan – in herself, those she interviews, and occasionally, the audience. The scenes filmed at the Charlottesville rally render visible Khan's positionality: in the middle of the white extremists, holding her camera, while also being recorded by one of her colleagues (Figure 12.1). At one point, she gets hit in the face with pepper spray

Figure 12.1 Filming the 'Enemy': Khan amidst the crowd of NSM supporters at the Charlottesville Rally, 2017.

by anti-racist protestors. We see their anger and chants at the supremacists not from a detached position, but rather from the perspective of the white nationalists themselves, as Khan films within their ranks. If discomfort is about bodies inhabiting spaces that are not designed to fit them, watching Khan moving within a crowd of neo-Nazis shouting racist slogans as their ire, enthusiasm and energy swells, makes for deeply uncomfortable viewing. For, if being comfortable 'is to be so at ease with one's environment that it is hard to distinguish where one's body ends and the world begins' (Ahmed 2014, 148), Khan's body stands out as discernibly out of place in the crowd of white nationalists; her presence rather serves to underline the borders between her and those who surround her.

The feelings of discomfort Khan experiences in making this film never fully recede, although she does grow closer to some of the interviewees. As she notes, 'even when I started getting comfortable with some of the people, the people on the periphery could be very unpleasant' (qtd in Saner 2017). If comfort reduces the gap between a body and its environment and creates seamless spaces where the differences between bodies disappear, Khan continually inserts herself into situations where her body clearly does not fit. When she visits Detroit with Jeff Schoep, leader of the NSM, a number of eerily still long-shots capture Khan and Schoep (with his white supremacist T-shirt and tattoos) amid the crumbling ruins of Detroit's former industrial heartlands. Walking with trepidation over bricks, wires, cracked pavement, tall weeds and debris, these still long shots position Khan as a figure at odds with her physical environment. The environment itself is so unforgiving, it is hard to imagine any human body sinking with ease into its jagged concrete folds. But perhaps this is part of the point: Khan is here to talk to Schoep about how places like Detroit become fertile breeding grounds for white supremacy due to the hardships wrought by post-industrial joblessness and urban decay.

One of the most significant ways in which Khan generates discomfort in her interviewees is by bringing her own personhood to bear on their discussion. She routes the conversation away from ideology, and towards an encounter between individuals: as she notes in the voiceover, 'I wanted to get behind the hatred and extremist ideology to find out what they are like as human beings'. The opening sections of the film feature two interviews with Schoep. The first interview takes place in an anonymous hotel room and begins with the interviewee expounding upon his white supremacist beliefs, noting that they have gained members since the ascendancy of Trump whose 'talking points' are 'right out of our playbook'. Schoep is filmed in alternating side angle close ups in shallow focus with lead room to the right, and frontal medium shots in which his body fills the frame. By alternating these positions, Khan places the viewer alongside her, facing the interviewee, which also allows us to see his physical reactions and focus closely on his emotions.

Khan quickly turns Schoep away from this ideological and political path, which he speaks about with rehearsed and evident ease. Referring to his ideological beliefs, she asks him, simply, 'What if it's wrong?' Framed in a tight close up, we see Schoep's features twist, as he pursues his lips, frowns and tilts his head in an awkward and lingering silence. Khan then asks him about the fact that he read *Mein Kampf* at age thirteen; rather than questioning what influence it had on him, or how it informs his present-day credence, she asks him how he *felt*. Schoep is stumped by the question and cannot seem to access his feelings to find an answer. He hums and haws, takes a sip of water, taps his fingers on the sofa, before finally saying, 'my mind is wandering now . . . I'm getting burned out by these questions'. No such burnout was evident when he was speaking about his creed and traversing well-trodden rhetorical routes. As if to underline the relations of discomfort in the scene, it closes on an awkwardly composed shot: another close up of Schoep in which the lead room has shifted from right to left, the camera is very slightly canted, and a number of objects fragment the image – a bar running through the left foreground, the bend of a sofa, the corner of Schoep's white nationalist flag (Figure 12.2).

In the discussion that follows, Khan presses Schoep to confront the reality of where his actions habitually lead. Referencing the racist abuse she received online after her appearance on the BBC, she asks him about his invitation to the rally in Charlottesville: 'Would I be safe, just walking up there as a shit skin?' Schoep winces, looks away and smiles painfully. Khan probes: 'You don't like me saying that?', and Schoep merely grimaces, looks down and shakes his head. Placing herself in the frame with Schoep, we see her take out a photograph of herself as a child at an anti-racist march with her father. 'People that

Figure 12.2   Schoep's emotional and physical discomfort mirrored in the awkward shot composition.

represent what you represent made a 6-year-old child feel hated and unwanted and unwelcome and ugly', she tells him. 'The movement that you are a part of has this type of real-life effect on people like me. How does that make you feel?' 'Uncomfortable', he eventually answers. Discomfort is again made manifest by Schoep's physical gestures: he squirms, taps his boot and the sofa edge with his fingers, looks away and looks back at the camera, licks his lips, underlining the connection between emotive discomfort and the physical body.

Khan's discomfiting approach is also evident in her meeting with Ken Parker. Ken is a Navy veteran and a political science student at the University of Florida, and he is introduced as a striking and aggressive example of a member of the NSM. In the opening credits we see him on video saying, 'Jews and homosexuals, they should be exterminated, every single one of them'. Khan herself notes that 'Ken is exactly the kind of person I've always been afraid of'. She goes with Ken as he distributes flyers decked with swastikas in the local Jewish neighbourhood, and she tells him the leaflets will hurt people's feelings, statements Ken later says made him 'uncomfortable' and 'anxious'. At the time, however, he grumpily retorts that he 'can't control people's feelings', a statement which might be subtly referring to his own inability to control what appear to be growing feelings of fondness for Khan. It is perhaps at this point that we realise that Ken is more naïve than one might previously have suspected – he comes across as genuinely surprised and perturbed to discover that words have consequences.

This failure to connect his words and deeds to the real or potential suffering of others is further illustrated in a scene in which Khan interviews Ken in his home, reading some of the racist abuse and hateful Tweets she received following the BBC interview about multiculturalism. As he listens to her, Ken sits incongruously on a cosy couch, a cushion inscribed with 'I Love You' behind him. 'If I tell you these words hurt my heart . . .?' she asks, and Ken looks visibly distressed, saying 'I don't want to hurt your feelings . . . I consider you a friend'. He notes that Khan has been respectful, even if they have conflicting opinions ('It's nice to have friends, even if you disagree with them'). Khan also looks at a photobook with images from Ken's childhood, a technique which recalls her own use of childhood photographs in her interview with Schoep. In the end, Ken admits that Khan's questions have 'gotten under my skin'. He says that his opinion of Muslims has improved significantly and that he won't 'mess with the mosque anymore'. As is evidenced from the above account of their meeting, Khan generates discomfort in Ken by adopting a dual tactic of continued respect for him, his partner and their home, alongside constant probing questions and an evocation of emotion – her own, Ken's and the feelings of those he targets. Indeed, she shows how discomfort is generated through the lack of fit between a person's self-perception and what their actions say about them. Ken states, 'I don't consider myself a bad person', but Khan shows him that the effect of his ideology is to hurt others – not exactly the outcome for which a 'good person' would hope. If we consider ourselves to be good, it is uncomfortable to hurt someone's feelings – even if we believe we are objectively right – because it doesn't 'fit' with our sense of self.

AN ETHICS OF DISCOMFORT? THE POSSIBILITIES AND THE LIMITS

Returning to the idea of discomfort as 'misfortune, adversity' and its connection to the term 'discomfit' meaning 'to defeat' or 'perplex', we can say that Khan sits down with those who have caused her misfortune, who are her adversaries, engaging in a nonviolent encounter which generates feelings of discomfort and sometimes confusion on both sides. Indeed, it is the feeling of discomfort, the lack of fit between Khan and her interviewees, as well as the emotional (rather than ideological) discomfort she generates in them that produces an ethical encounter, that is in some cases, politically transformative. Effecting political change is often one of many documentary filmmaker's aims, and constitutes a profound potentiality of documentary film as a medium that is grounded in actuality. As Smaill notes, 'a documentary seeks recognition for actual subjects and communities of subjects in the same world the viewer inhabits', and the connection between the subject of the film and the world they share with the viewer is central to a documentary's 'political potentiality' (2007, 153).

What Nichols calls the 'unforeseen effects of a documentary' in the world (2010, 52) are quite astonishing in the case of *White Right*: Khan produces meaningful ideological change in some of her interviewees. Following his meeting with Khan, Ken Parker left the white supremacist movement and is now an active member in his local African American Church, All Saints Holiness Church, where he was baptised by Pastor William McKinnon III in July 2018 (Franco and Radford 2018). It is quite extraordinary to contrast images of Parker from before and after his renunciation of white supremacy. From a stern man in a shiny green KKK garb, or in black holding a rifle in front of an eagle and swastika flag, we see him dressed in a flowing white robe, wading into the sea hand in hand with McKinnon, head lowered. Parker describes his meeting with Khan as key to his eventual conversion, noting her kindness and the respect she showed him and his fiancé, in spite of their differences (Franco and Radford 2018). Parker is not the only individual de-radicalised by his encounter with Khan. Brian Culpepper, another member of the NSM, retired from 'active duty' after hearing the abuse that Khan received, saying 'it really did bother me, on a human level'. Finally, Jeff Schoep, former leader of the NSM and 'America's Poster Boy for Nazism', has left the organisation and is highly visible in American anti-extremist circuits, although there is some controversy surrounding the circumstances of his departure (Eligon 2020). Critics suggest this is a cynical move to avoid or mitigate the legal consequences he faces for his role in the violence that broke out during the Charlottesville rally (Mettler 2019). Nonetheless, Schoep also describes Khan as a 'friend' and underscores the importance of their conversations: 'being able to have that dialogue ... helped greatly in the deradicalization process' (Fuuse 2020).

Yet it is important to note that the drive to reform white supremacists, and the call to listen to them and engage with them, is itself 'uncomfortable' (Enzinna, 2018). As the case with Schoep, it can often be difficult to discern how much they have reformed ideologically on a deep level, and how much of their public personas of contrition may be due to a desire to avoid legal ramifications or seek attention. Nonetheless, Khan is not the only anti-racist activist who uses uncomfortable dialogue to change extremist's minds. Derek Black, godchild of KKK 'Grand Wizard' David Duke and son of Stormfront founder Don Black, left the movement after five years of patient and intimate interactions with fellow students at his liberal arts college in South Florida (see Saslow, 2018). In a speech to the New Zealand Parliament on 15 March 2019 in the wake of the murderous attack on a mosque in Christchurch, Prime Minister Jacinda Ardern echoed this call for more difficult dialogues, citing a young Muslim woman who said, 'we've now lost lives so I think it's time that we started having the uncomfortable conversations' (Ardern, 2019).

This process is inevitably fraught, yet it is undertaken by Khan with the hope of producing a discomfort, 'which is generative, rather than simply being constraining or negative' (Ahmed 2014, 155). Ahmed writes that the comfortable often escapes our notice – it is when ideas or people don't fit that they are brought to our attention: 'The "non-fitting" or discomfort opens up possibilities, on opening up which can be difficult and exciting' (154). Noticing discomfort, and the discomfort of others, points us towards the spaces in which we or others do not fit; it can bring us closer to those people and places and invite change. Ahmed writes that discomfort can show the 'failure of an ideal'; in the case of Khan and *White Right*, the interviewees' discomfort shows the failure of their white nationalist ideals, for she is a Muslim woman and they cannot help describing her as a friend. It might also highlight for the viewer the failure of some of Western society's liberal multicultural ideals – adherence to white supremacist ideas is rising – yet unexpectedly, so is the number of individuals trying to escape such movements (Enzinna 2018). Getting comfortable with discomfort means listening to opinions, beliefs and ideas that at best we disagree with, or at worst find abhorrent. Khan states that 'Judging and condemning jihadists and white supremacists "feels great"', 'but yields little' (Friedersdorf 2018). Her process, as I have demonstrated here, is instead to listen with both disagreement and respect, according her subjects dignity as human beings, while generating discomfort by challenging their views.

However, there is evidence in the film that this process of seeking out nonviolent, discussions with extremists is not always transformative. Discomfort has limits, and one of these is fundamentally physical: it can be dangerous for certain targeted groups to interact with extremists. Moreover, some bodies assume the weight of discomfort more than others. Although Khan notes that 'I don't believe it's the job of minorities to reform racists or to have to engage with their abusers' (Saner 2017), this is precisely what she undertakes and the reality remains that in many cases the hard graft of anti-racist campaigning and activism is undertaken by minority ethnic groups. As Ahmed argues, 'some bodies can "have" comfort, only as an effect of the work of others' (2014, 149). Khan's calm, empathic and reassuring presence guides the viewer through the film from beginning to end, and as viewers, we do not necessarily need to question our own complicity or relationship to racial inequality or economic injustice, nor do we have to engage in the difficult work of confronting prejudice head on in real life. Unlike Theroux, who often shields his own political opinions or ethnic origins from his subjects, Khan foregrounds her ethnicity and political left-wing views, so there is no uncomfortable ethical dissonance between audience members who 'know' and subjects who do not.

The fact that audience members are shielded from the discomfort Khan experiences highlights what Pezeu-Massabuau describes as the difference between controllable and uncontrollable discomfort. Pezeu-Massabuau outlines his morning routine: he goes for a fifteen-minute run in the early morning cold – an undertaking that generates significant physical discomfort. On returning home, he takes a hot shower, a physical pleasure that is all the more potent because of the discomfort that precedes it. This is an example of controlled discomfort, what Pezeu-Massabuau calls 'anti-comfort': this is the space where hope of relief exists, or where the subject knows that discomfort is finite, or can be terminated at will (2012, 58–62). However, as Sheena Culley writes in a review of the book, 'whether discomfort can really be harnessed to our advantage remains open to question . . . discomfort is only useful when we have agency over our well-being and can choose discomfort in the knowledge that comfort will follow' (2013). Khan shields her viewers from the uncontrollable discomfort of a live, face-to-face encounter with extremists, and we watch her discomfort and that of her interviewees from the safely controlled space of our homes and lives. We can switch off the film whenever we want, and we can make use of her ideas or simply forget them.

Moreover, as Pezeu-Massabuau points out, uncontrollable corporeal and psychological discomforts, such as those generated by poverty, illness, racial discrimination or bigotry can 'leave us passive and discouraged, neutralize our initiative and creativity and leave us defenceless against the seductions of the world and of soothing and protective ideologies' (2012, 33). He even notes that this is especially the case when these ideologies are 'aggressive and repetitive' (2012, 33), words that seem to describe the violent and virulent chanting of 'you will not replace us', from the white supremacist marchers at Charlottesville. When we feel the physical discomforts of social deprivation or the mental and emotional discomforts of being marginalised or excluded, 'soothing and protective ideologies', such as those offered by jihadism or white nationalism, can offer a space of fit, a kind of comfort. As Culley summarises, 'discomfort may potentially lead to revelation under some circumstances, but it is far from being revolutionary' (2013).

The limits of an ethics of discomfort are also related to scale, time and the type of interaction. As Conor Friedersdorf points out about the work of Khan and other non-violent anti-racist champions like Daryl Davis and Derek Black, 'even if their approach to anti-racism is effective, perhaps it cannot scale, as very few people possess the inclination, let alone the courage and patience, to engage extremists as they do' (2018). Thus, we can ask how Khan's model of listening to personal stories, asking awkward questions, and interacting with individuals in a respectful manner, can be scaled up to the level of an effective societal practice? Or to reframe the question: do the ideals of a collective multiculturalism only work on an interpersonal and local level, for those who live, work and interact with people from diverse cultural and social backgrounds? There is also the question of social media and its connection to rising tides of extremism of all kinds; as Khan notes, 'It's very easy to sit behind your laptop and send ruthless messages to somebody. It's very easy when you are in large groups and protesting and throwing up Nazi salutes' (Malik 2018). Social media might be said to combine the worst of all possible interaction types when it comes to the reproduction of extremist views: lacking the intimacy and accountability of a face-to-face interaction, it combines this with the group dynamics and anonymity of the crowd (see Littler and Lee 2020).

The question of ideology is also salient to this discussion. While Khan shows that individuals like Parker, Culpepper and Schoep can be successfully de-radicalised through a face-to-face encounter with their 'enemy', two far-right ideologues she encounters are not moved from their entrenched ideological positions. The film opens with an audio-visual image of physical discomfort in the person of Jared Taylor, a Yale-educated white supremacist, described by the Southern Poverty Law Center as 'a courtly presenter of ideas that most would describe as crudely white supremacist – a kind of modern-day version of the refined but racist colonialist of old' (SPLC n.d.). Taylor speaks directly to the camera, and says: 'My hair ok? It's not flying around in funny directions?' By opening the film on this moment, which Taylor surely imagined would be cut from the final version, Khan immediately decentres ideology and undermines Taylor's image as the polished, 'courtly' and articulate face of white supremacy. Setting the tone for the rest of the film, she then states outright: 'I'm a woman of colour. I am the daughter of immigrants. I am a Muslim. I am a feminist. I am a lefty liberal. And what I want to ask you is: am I your enemy?' Taylor pauses, before answering 'You're not subjectively my enemy' – a statement which demonstrates Taylor's awareness of the gap between confrontation on an interpersonal level ('subjectively') and on the level of ideological belief ('objectively'). This may be the central claim of the film: when we confront individuals as individuals, as subjects rather than objects, and face-to-face rather than through ideologically-driven, (digitally) mediated narratives, it is much more difficult to maintain hostility. This is not only about having a personal interaction, but also about the quality of the interaction, the 'respect' that all three men cite as central to their rapprochement with Khan, who herself notes that she has confronted and shouted at many racists groups in her life, and none of these exchanges resulted in positive change (see Rhor 2018).

Nonetheless, Taylor is not de-radicalised by his encounter with Khan, and neither is Richard Spencer, one of the poster boys and founders of the 'alt-right' movement and an ardent Trump supporter (Wood 2017). Khan introduces Spencer as one of the 'men from privileged and elite backgrounds' who form an ever-increasing strand of white supremacy in the US, and she interviews him in his lush and leather-furnished apartment in the wealthiest neighbourhood of Alexandra, Virginia. While she manages to discomfit Taylor enough to at least record him worrying over his appearance, Spencer presents a slick and apparently unperturbable façade of cool, detached ease. Spencer comes from a family of wealthy landowners (his mother inherited cotton farms in Louisiana), and he describes his desire to bring about 'a white ethnostate' ruled, unsurprisingly, by wealthy white people: 'people like me need to be in charge'. Like Taylor, Spencer seems to comfortably perform a script of wealthy Southern American whiteness, which is closer to the image of the colonial slaveholder than that of the angry, working class, black clad neo-Nazi. We witness Spencer admonishing his friend for not drinking his whiskey out of a whiskey glass,

Figure 12.3 Spencer and his friends surrounded by objects that evoke a well-worn iconography of wealth, power and masculinity.

and we see one of these friends (or followers) collapsed in a crumpled suit and tie on a leather armchair, presumably having imbibed too much of the aforementioned beverage, in front of row upon row of leather-bound books. Ornate gold-leaf patterned wallpaper adorns the background while Spencer is being interviewed, as does an image of Napoleon on a rearing horse (see Figure 12.3). This kind of painting, in which material wealth and domination over land and animals is explicitly connected to men and manliness, is the very image of what John Berger describes as art that 'serve[s] the ideological interests of the ruling class' by underscoring the connections between power, whiteness, masculinity, physical prowess, property and conquest (1973, 86).

Unlike the scenes with Parker and Culpepper, in filming Spencer, Khan does not place herself within the frame – we hear her voice off camera, but there is no two-shot which places her beside her interlocutor in the same visual field. It is unclear whether this relates to the limits of Khan's respect as a self-described 'lefty-liberal', with sympathy for those who struggle economically and socially, or whether Spencer simply cannot be made to feel uncomfortable. Certainly, in one scene, the latter seems to hold true: he meets a group of protestors outside his house, holding a vigil for Heather Heyer. They stare at him in silence holding candles, as one of them begins to sing the 1960s protest song made famous by Joan Baez: 'We Shall Overcome'. Spencer stands right in front of them, centimetres away from their faces, and says 'You guys just stare at me in a dead-eyed way', and laughs. This scene shows Spencer's confidence and callousness, but also perhaps hints at the insufficiency of 1960s left-wing activist strategies and a softer, empathically driven engagement in the face of the new threat of rising white radicalisation.

Conclusion: Future Directions and the Question of Empathy

The case of Richard Spencer highlights an issue that has been implicit in my discussion of Khan's work: the question of empathy. There may be limits to Khan's ability to feel empathy for some of the men she interviews, notable through the contrasting manner in which she films the scenes with Spencer and Taylor, versus Parker, Culpepper and Schoep. As the connotations of the Napoleon image make clear, Spencer and his ilk are not the consumers of an ideology that ultimately oppresses them (white supremacist capitalism), but rather its creators. Looked at from a class perspective, Parker, Culpepper and their kind can be said to labour under false consciousness: they feel oppressed and, in some cases, have suffered economically, but misidentify, or are led to misidentify, the agents of this oppression; by contrast, Spencer and his kind control and profit from this system.

It is perhaps not coincidental that Khan does not manage to discomfit these socially elite proponents of white nationalism, and they do not express empathy for her nor she for them. Rather than a joyful communion of human emotion, or a straight transfer or sharing of another's pain, empathy can also open space between self and other that is not always easeful. In fact, much research suggests that empathy itself may be a form of discomfort. Paulina Kukar describes a pedagogy of discomfort in a classroom context, where students and teachers resist the relatively facile impulse to feel sorry for characters in works of fiction, or even to imagine themselves in their place. Instead, she suggests that educators invite students to recognise the gaps in their experience and understanding of the suffering of another. More than this, Kukar proposes that students consider how they might be implicated in economic or social structures that cause or contribute to the suffering of others: 'recognizing [our] own implication in the suffering of another, [which] generates its own affective response, often discomfort' (Kukar 2016, 4).

Where does this leave us regarding the uses of discomfort in *White Right*? It is clear that more needs to be done on the connection between discomfort as a strategy for engaging with extremists, one that is underpinned by empathic listening and communication techniques. However, the chapter serves as a starting point for a consideration of how discomfort works in relation to encounters between those who are ideologically opposed, and perhaps also hints at the usefulness of discomfort as a critical paradigm when thinking about the ethics of directorial engagement with complex and polemical subjects in documentary filmmaking. Thus, while much work has considered the vulnerability of documentary characters, less research has been devoted to those individuals who are neither marginalised, victimised nor particularly precarious, and who may in fact be violent perpetrators. This chapter thus points to a way of thinking ethically about how filmmakers and perhaps even audiences engage with works that present communities and persons whose ideologies and actions may be abhorrent. Additionally, while love, hate, anger and fear have been frequently studied in relation to white nationalism, to my knowledge this is the first piece of work to consider how the feeling of discomfort relates to engagement with these groups.

As more and more individuals seek solace in the comfort of familiar conceptual tracks – a propensity propounded by the algorithmic incentives of social media – dwelling in the discomfort of ideological opposition, seeking neither to change nor defeat one's opponent, becomes a critically important endeavour. And though Khan does not set out explicitly to de-radicalise the men she meets, it is remarkable that her approach sometimes produces this outcome. The renunciations of Parker, Culpepper and Schoep are a testament to Khan's filmmaking techniques and the emotive relation she adopts towards her subjects. The film demonstrates the potential of this method to generate what could be called an ethics for extremists, one grounded in an acknowledgement of the generative power of discomfort as central to the encounter – something that many seek to avoid, instead engaging with problematic subjects in ways that are confrontational, friendly or neutral. This is a tactic for filming and engaging with adherents of radical and violent ideologies which never loses sight of either the subject's humanity or the profoundly hurtful and dangerous nature of their beliefs, yet holds both together – awkwardly, uncomfortably, but sometimes, effectively.

References

Ahmed, Sara. 2014. *The Cultural Politics of Emotion*. Edinburgh: Edinburgh University Press.

Anderson, Carol. 2016. *White Rage: The Unspoken Truth of Our Racial Divide*. New York: Bloomsbury Publishing USA.

Ardern, Jacinda. 2019. "Ministerial Statements – Mosque Terror Attacks – Christchurch." *New Zealand Parliament – Hansard Reports*, March 19, 2019. Document18https://www.parliament.nz/en/pb/hansard-debates/rhr/combined/HansDeb_20190319_20190319_08

Barry, Ellen, and Selsoe Sorensen, Martin. 2018. "In Denmark, Harsh New Laws for Immigrant 'Ghettos.'" *New York Times*, July 1, 2018. https://www.nytimes.com/2018/07/01/world/europe/denmark-immigrant-ghettos.html

Benjamin, Walter. 1969. "Paris: Capital of the Nineteenth Century." *Perspecta* 12: 165–72.

Berger, John. 1973. *Ways of Seeing*. London: Penguin.

Brand, Paul. 2017. "'The UK Is Never Going to Be White Again' – Muslim Deeyah Khan BBC Interview." September 19, 2017. YouTube video, 2:37. https://www.youtube.com/watch?v=FIivq4_VSZY

Coaston, Jane. 2019. "The New Zealand Shooter's Manifesto Shows How White Nationalist Rhetoric Spreads." *Vox*, March 18, 2019. https://www.vox.com/identities/2019/3/15/18267163/new-zealand-shooting-christchurch-white-nationalism-racism-language

Culley, Sheena. 2013. Review of *A Philosophy of Discomfort* by Jacques Pezeu-Massabuau. *Marx and Philosophy Review of Books*, June 3, 2013. https://marxandphilosophy.org.uk/reviews/7791_a-philosophy-of-discomfort-review-by-sheena-culley/

Downing, Lisa, and Libby Saxton. 2010. *Film and Ethics: Foreclosed Encounters*. London: Routledge.

Eligon, John. 2020. "He Says His Nazi Days Are Over. Do You Believe Him?" *New York Times*, April 4, 2020. https://www.nytimes.com/2020/04/04/us/jeff-schoep-white-nationalist-reformer.html

Enzinna, Wes. 2018. "Inside the Radical, Uncomfortable Movement to Reform White Supremacists." *Mother Jones*, July/August 2018. https://www.motherjones.com/politics/2018/07/reform-white-supremacists-shane-johnson-life-after-hate/

Faludi, Susan. 1999. *Stiffed: The Betrayal of American Men*. New York: Harper Collins.

Franco, Aaron, and Morgan Radford. 2018. "Ex-KKK Member Denounces Hate Groups One Year After Rallying in Charlottesville." *NBC News*, August 9, 2018. https://www.nbcnews.com/news/us-news/ex-kkk-member-denounces-hate-groups-one-year-after-rallying-n899326

Friedersdorf, Conor. 2018. "Perhaps the Most Effective Way to Fight Racism." *The Atlantic*, December 12, 2018. https://www.theatlantic.com/ideas/archive/2018/12/deeyah-khan-white-right/577834/

Fuuse. 2020. "Jeff Schoep, Former Leader of America's Largest Neo-Nazi Organisation." *Facebook*, June 7, 2020. https://www.facebook.com/Fuuse.deeyah/videos/jeff-schoep-former-leader-of-americas-largest-neo-Nazi-organisation/258002665276972/

Higgins, Charlotte. 2016. "The Hygge Conspiracy." *The Guardian*, November 22, 2016. https://www.theguardian.com/lifeandstyle/2016/nov/22/hygge-conspiracy-denmark-cosiness-trend

hooks, bell. 2004. *The Will to Change: Men, Masculinity and Love*. New York: Attia Books.

Jackson, Richard. 2018. "Sympathy for the Devil: Evil, Taboo, and the Terrorist Figure in Literature." In *Terrorism and Literature*, ed. Peter C. Herman, 377–94. Cambridge: Cambridge University Press.

Khan, Deeyah, dir. 2015. *Jihad: A Story of the Others*. Fuuse Films.

Khan, Deeyah, dir. 2017. *White Right: Meeting the Enemy*. Fuuse Films.

Kimmel, Michael. 2017. *Angry White Men: American Masculinity at the End of an Era*. New York: Bold Type Books.

Kruglanski, Arie W., Jocelyn J. Bélanger, and Rohan Gunaratna, eds. 2019. *The Three Pillars of Radicalization: Needs, Narratives, and Networks*. Oxford: Oxford University Press.

Kukar, Polina. 2016. "'The Very Unrecognizability of the Other': The Pedagogical Challenge of Empathy." *Philosophical Inquiry in Education* 24, no. 1: 1–14.

Littler, Mark, and Benjamin Lee. 2020. *Digital Extremisms: Readings in Violence, Radicalisation and Extremism in the Online Space*. London: Palgrave Macmillan.

Malik, Sarah. 2018. "A 'Sick, Broken' Masculinity Is Fuelling Extremism, Says Documentary Maker." September 13, 2018. https://www.sbs.com.au/topics/voices/culture/article/2018/09/06/sick-broken-masculinity-fuelling-extremism-says-documentary-maker

McGreal, Chris. 2018. "The Making of an Opioid Epidemic." *The Guardian*, November 8, 2018. https://www.theguardian.com/news/2018/nov/08/the-making-of-an-opioid-epidemic

Mettler, Katie. 2019. "The 'Race Whisperer'." *The Washington Post*, October 30, 2019. https://www.washingtonpost.com/graphics/2019/local/neo-Nazi-group-takeover/

Nichols, Bill. 2010. *Introduction to Documentary: Second Edition*. Bloomington and Indianapolis: Indiana University Press. First published 2001.

Pezeu-Massabuau, Jacques. 2012. *A Philosophy of Discomfort*. Trans. Vivian Sky Rehberg. London: Reaktion Books.

Pryluck, Calvin. 1976. "'Ultimately We Are All Outsiders': The Ethics of Documentary Filming." *Journal of the University Film Association* 28, no. 1: 21–9.

Rhor, Monica. 2018. "He Was a KKK Member, Then a Neo-Nazi: How One White Supremacist Renounced Hate." *USA Today*, November 1, 2018. https://eu.usatoday.com/story/news/2018/11/01/hate-group-white-extremist-radicalization/1847255002/

Ruiz, Christina. 2018. "Deeyah Khan." *The Gentlewoman* 18. https://thegentlewoman.co.uk/library/deeyah-khan

Russell Hochschild, Arlie. 2016. *Strangers in Their Own Land: Anger and Mourning on the American Right*. New York: The New Press.

Saner, Emine. 2017. "The Muslim Director Who Filmed Neo-Nazis: 'I Thought – I'm Not Going to Make It Out'." *The Guardian*, December 4, 2017. https://www.theguardian.com/lifeandstyle/2017/dec/04/the-muslim-director-who-filmed-neo-Nazis-i-thought-im-not-going-to-make-it-out

Saslow, Eli. 2018. *Rising Out of Hatred: The Awakening of a Former White Nationalist*. New York: Penguin Random House.

Sloterdjik, Peter. 2013. *In the World Interior of Capital: Towards a Philosophical Theory of Globalization*. Cambridge: Polity Press.

Smaill, Belinda. 2007. "Injured Identities: Pain, Politics and Documentary." *Studies in Documentary Film* 1, no. 7: 151–63.

SPLC. Undated. "Jared Taylor." SPLC: Southern Poverty Law Center. https://www.splcenter.org/fighting-hate/extremist-files/individual/jared-taylor

Urwin, Rosamund. 2015. "Deeyah Khan: What IS Do Is Like Grooming – They Prey on Guilt, Loneliness and Anger." *Evening Standard*, November 23, 2015. https://www.standard.co.uk/lifestyle/london-life/deeyah-khan-what-is-do-is-like-grooming-they-prey-on-guilt-loneliness-and-anger-a3121011.html

Wood, Graeme. 2017. "His Kampf." *The Atlantic*, June 2017. https://www.theatlantic.com/magazine/archive/2017/06/his-kampf/524505/

13. INTIMATE CONFLICTS: REBELS, HEROES AND DISFIGURED TERRORISTS IN BURMESE ANGLOPHONE LITERATURE

Pavan Kumar Malreddy

Disfiguring the Terrorist: Tropes, Figures and the Intimacy of Violence

In a post-war story about the intimacy of two amputated legs, an investigative team of inspectors descends upon a battle zone to collect evidence. '28 legs in all', cries out an inspector, '19 military personnel and 9 militants'.[1] 'No, our boss won't accept that', responds the officer, 'we can't have odd numbers, we need two legs per person'. Even if we assume that one of the military personnel was an amputee from a previous battle, we still have one militant leg to account for. So, the investigative team either needs to wait until one of the insurgents steps on a mine, or chase some of the local villagers from the militant-controlled areas in the direction of a mine field and hope that they will get an odd number of blasts to even the number of legs. But there will be a problem if one of the military personnel steps on a mine accidentally. That is exactly what happens in Mitali Perkins' novel *Bamboo People* (2010), in which a fifteen-year-old foot soldier of the Burmese junta, forcefully recruited, loses his leg in a landmine explosion. Left to die, with a missing leg, he is eventually rescued by another teenager from the enemy's camp, a Karenni insurgent, who takes pity on him and gifts him a prosthetic leg which was meant for the teenage amputees of his own camp.

The boy goes home to Rangoon, proudly displaying his 'Karenni leg' (Perkins 2010, 60) to his Burmese friends, in an overt gesture of political bonhomie that allegorically reinforces the notion that Burma the nation needs two legs to trundle along, one organic and one inorganic, one aesthetic and one prosthetic, the Burman and the Karenni, which stand side by side, as it were, but never even on ground or in life. The Burmese teenager can walk only at the expense of a Karenni amputee. The conflict that holds the two legs of the same body together and apart is therefore binding and intimate at the same time, as Moira Fradinger observes in the context of the Dominican Republic under the dictatorship of Rafael Trujillo: the violence between 'the most powerless and most powerful [is] part of a structure of enmity whose two polar opposites alternatively embody figures inimical to the fantasized unity of the nation' (2010, 188). It is the very intimate enmity which is conditioned by the paradoxical coexistence of harm and peace, division and unity that is characteristic of the Burmese texts featured in this chapter: Pascal Khoo Thwe's *From the Land of Green Ghosts* (2002) and Lucy Cruickshanks' *The Road to Rangoon* (2015).

Put simply, I refer to intimate conflict as a product of violence that is familiar, generational, inherited, inevitable and indispensable; it is a violence that turns brothers, sisters, neighbours and entire communities which share the same cultural space against each other in the name of new national identities and destinies. It is a violence in which the brush with the lover and the brush with the leader become the same thing; a violence in which the loss of an intimate partner and the loss of a national leader could trigger the same insurgent response; a violence which is unencumbered by the ideologies of redemptive justice, figural terrorism, mythic violence or any other sovereign arrogation of terror which is unleashed upon its populace in the name of the greater good; a violence which rallies around lovers, losers, limping insurgents, famished revolutionaries, unpaid mercenaries and rebels with more than one cause. The inimical 'conversion of kinsmen into enemies', as Shruti Kapila argues, can be traced to the decoupling of sovereignty from 'its mooring in the state' and its 'deposit[ion] in the political subject' by the postcolonial elites (2021, 7). This process, which holds the individual as the sovereign agent of violence rather than the state, enables the colonial fraternity to create an enemy within, in which the individual subjects, communities, and non-sovereign entities can be pitted against other such entities. Thus, by infiltrating violence to the societal and communal level, the state flexes its muscles and frees its hands of actual violence, and through 'logics of murder and affinity' promises 'the creation of fellowship' (8–9). And because intimate violence is so familiar to every stakeholder involved in the *longue durée* of conflict, and because it is carried out in *known* social sites and communal spaces, its ideological containers become so strained and porous that they render the essentialist as well as figurative categories such as terrorist and counterterrorist almost meaningless.

Nested between Thailand in the south, China to the north east and India to the west, perhaps no postcolonial nation is more susceptible to the intimacy of violence than Burma, not least because of a culture of dictatorship regimes which led to its isolation from the rest of the world for over half a century. Between 1824 and 1885, Burma was gradually annexed to the British Raj. From 1919 to 1937, the country was ruled as part of India with diarchic privileges, and was made into a separate colony in 1937. After the Japanese invasion in 1942, it became a Japanese colony until 1945, after which the British returned. Burma remained a British colony until its independence in 1948. The seeds of Burmese civic dissent can be traced to the intimate affects, such as trust and loyalty, vested in the colonial benefactors: while the Central Burmans, a Theravada Buddhist majority, fought on the side of the Japanese who had promised liberation from the British Empire, the ethnic groups of the frontier region – such as Karen, Kachin, Chin and Karenni – fought on the side of the British who had promised them political autonomy and sovereignty. As these promises remain unfulfilled today, both the conflict and the parties involved in the conflict remain equally, if not intimately, familiar to each other.

Given this conflictual heritage, Burma has been implicated in discourses of terrorism in myriad, often bizarre, and unpredictable ways. To begin with, the military junta that overthrew the democratically elected government led by Aung San Suu Kyi in 2021, has called the latter's shadow government a terrorist group for allegedly inciting violence against the military (DW 2021). It is the same military junta, known as the Tatmadaw, which has been labelled by many Western states a terrorist government since 1962. Yet, the insurgents fighting the junta, who had evidently been American allies, were classified as terrorists by the CIA and other agencies in the immediate aftermath of 9/11. The fact that Suu Kyi was awarded the Nobel Peace Prize also served to legitimise the perception of the junta as a terrorist or rogue government, a label which was used, ironically, to describe Suu Kyi's own political party – the National League of Democracy, which shared power with the Tatmadaw till the 2021 coup – on an earlier occasion, and for an entirely different reason: its passive compliance with the Rohingya massacre of 2016–17. This was followed by appeals from various statespersons and intellectuals, including former Nobel laureates such as Desmond Tutu to revoke her Nobel Peace Prize (Zhou and Safi 2017). Suu Kyi's is not alone in this: historically there has been an unavoidable collusion and complicity between Nobel Peace Prize winners and terrorists, as in the case of Menachem Begin, Nelson Mandela or Yasir Arafat, who were labelled as terrorists by their respective colonial governments but went on to win Nobel Peace Prizes (Scanlan 2001, 6). What such uncanny intimacy between the figures of terrorism and the icons of peace tells us is that if one is to aim for the Nobel Peace Prize, terrorism is actually a good place to start. Or quite inversely, if one does not have a good start with terrorism, aim for the Nobel Peace Prize, and one would eventually get there, or at least get to broker power or share governments with the terrorists – as in the case of Suu Kyi – and deservedly earn the title of terrorist.

This inverted paradox of the same person being the nation builder, terrorist or the pacifist of our times is also central to the disfigured subjects of intimate violence. Consider, for instance, how the fictional hero of Charmaine Craig's *Miss Burma* (2017), a Burmese-Jewish tradesman, reflects on the endless metamorphosis of Aung San who invited the Japanese to Burma to overthrow the British:

> Yet the past did encroach, particularly with news that trickled in – along with the occasional English-speaking Karen soldier – of the destruction of four hundred Karen villages ('not villagers, villages!') within the span of a few days by Aung San's army. ('Man, woman, child – no matter. They shot them and pushed them into heaps – eighteen hundred of them just in that one place.') News of Karen retaliation. Of race wars. Of a total British retreat to Assam. Of emptying prisons, and escalating murder rates, and thousands of released dacoits joining Aung San's ranks. (65)

In the same breadth the narrator recounts:

> The loyal are fully capable of deceit. That was something Benny told himself four months later, in May 1945, after the last of the Japanese had evacuated Rangoon and more than twelve thousand of their troops had been killed by Karen guerrillas supplied by British airdrop . . . Among the other intelligence and paramilitary groups working separately in Burma in support of the Allied cause were Kachin Rangers, Chin levies, Communist Party cadres, socialists, and even, in the final weeks of the campaign, Aung San's renamed Burma National Army . . . They had all fought the same enemy, yet what they had been fighting for apparently diverged widely. (81)

What is striking about Benny's fixation with Aung San is that his persona is split into polar opposites. Not long before Aung San was seated as the Prime Minister of Burma, he was regarded by both the colonial powers – the British and the Japanese – as an insurrectionist, a rebel, or an anti-colonial revolutionary of maverick proportions given his ability to switch sides to the British in March 1945 when the tide rose against his allies, the Japanese. For the British, yesteryear's rebel and anti-colonial insurgent became a peacemaker, or rather a piece-meal maker of a nation, who would eventually quell ethnic insurgencies by means of counterinsurgency: razing up of Karen villages, which – as Benny recounts – led to some eighteen hundred deaths of Karen minorities. In spite of this bloodthirsty and almost terroristic portrayal of Aung San, when Benny does encounter Aung San for the first time at a political rally, when it has become clear that Burma was going to gain independence, he makes this observation: 'There wasn't evil anywhere in the man's face that Benny could spot. There was anger, ancient anger, to be sure, and the focused ferocity of someone who would stop at nothing to free Burma's people' (92).

From being the leader of an insurgent national army, to an opportunist anti-colonialist, a murderer of eighteen hundred Karens, a man of 'focused ferocity', and to the 'father of the[ir] nation' (225), the label 'terrorism' uncannily eludes Aung San, but always lingers, especially in a nation where the familial, generational and national become inseparable. Consider, for instance, the views of Aung San's daughter as expressed in 1994, and then her fall from grace after the Rohingya massacre:

> The present armed forces of Burma were created and nurtured by my father. It is not simply a matter of words to say that my father built up armed forces. It is a fact ... Let me speak frankly. I feel strong attachment for the armed forces. Not only were they built up by my father, as a child I was cared for by his soldiers ... I would therefore not wish to see any splits and struggles between the army which my father built up and the people who love my father so much. May I also from this platform ask the personnel of the armed forces to reciprocate this kind of understanding and sympathy? For their part the people should try to forget what has already taken place, and I would like to appeal to them not to lose their affection for the army. (Suu Kyi 1995, 194–5)

Sympathy for the devil, and scorn for the terrorist. It is not that Suu Kyi's views have become aligned with the terrorist junta overnight, it is just that she now reloads and then relaunches the term 'terrorism' against another group of people: the Muslim minority in her own country (Safi 2017). The boundaries between the father, national father, family, military, foe and terrorists not only become porous here, but they do so precisely with the invocation of a collective threat by virtue of the same reductive principle that subsumes all social identities into the trans- and dis-figurations of a terrorist. This is particularly the case in a conflictual world where each life comes under a perceived threat, where every form of fellowship and intimate relationship could pose a potential 'terrorist' threat.

Such a strained, if not constrained, relationship to alterity in the context of threat, terrorism, social and civic unrest evokes two theoretical cues. The first one refers to Emmanuel Levinas' thesis on violence in the face of alterity, or our ethical bind to the familiarly unfamiliar Other. For Levinas, our very relationship to the Other is pure violence, because the face of the Other – not simply as a physical encounter of the visage but as an affective countenance – is vulnerable to the hazards of nonrepresentation. As he writes: 'The face is exposed, menaced, as if inviting us to an act of violence. At the same time, the face is what forbids us to kill' (Levinas 1985, 86). Yet, the face is also a source of invitation to violence and conflict as a trope of radical otherness: 'The Other is the only being that one can be tempted to kill. This temptation to murder and this impossibility of murder constitute the very vision of the face' (Levinas 1990, 8). Sure enough, in what Levinas (1998) terms the theodicy there is always a justification for the suffering of the Other in the name of the greater good or the preservation of the Self, which is being carried into the secular institutions of the day, that justify the killing, suffering and torture of the dangerous Other – in the present instance, the terrorist. Against this intimacy of face-to-face violence, Levinas does not call for the end of wars or pure violence as such, but for a primordial ethical imperative towards alterity, via a 'non-useless' or 'useful' suffering (Pugliese 2013, 5–11), by which the suffering in the Other can be made useful and meaningful by acknowledging the 'suffering in me for the unjustifiable suffering of the other' (Levinas 1998, 94).

Slavoj Žižek's interjection in, or rather rejection of, Levinas' face-to-face ethical pact serves as bridge to my second cue: rather than worship the face of the other as a pathway into transcendence, Žižek advocates for the smashing of the other's face because it is a sign of gentrified Otherness: 'Far from displaying "a quality of God's image carried with it", the face is the ultimate ethical lure . . . the neighbor is not displayed through a face; it is, as we have seen, in his or her fundamental dimension a *faceless monster*' (2013, 185; emphasis original). Ashis Nandy (1989) gives a face to this *faceless monster* of Žižek and calls him the intimate enemy, or Other within. For Nandy, the Other is not only encoded but is embodied within the Self, at least in the colonial context. In order to perform the hostile dominance, the coloniser and the colonised need to both invoke and negate the internalised Other within. This results in what Nandy (2010) calls the intimate animosity whereby 'what others can do to you, you also can do to your own kind': 'The colonial mantle is now worn by native regimes', Nandy affirms, 'who are willing to do what the colonial powers did' (ibid.). In an erstwhile colonial context, Elleke Boehmer and Stephen Morton (2015, 15), formulate Achille Mbembe's position on the violence employed by the postcolonial subject as follows: 'He who inflicts terror himself, having once been its victim, is the quintessential contested subject of the postcolony'. In other words, the violence that enters the colonised subject, is the violence that exits through him/her as cathartic terror: a form of release from a permanent state of being in pain.

Intimate violence is thus violence that is omnipresent, routine and endemic to the communal fabric, a violence that becomes an immediate response to myriad claims for agency. It is not only immediate but equally indispensable, as Kimberley Theidon puts it in the context of Peruvian villagers who suddenly find themselves in conflict with their fellow peasants and had to learn to kill their own brothers (2012, 208). Accordingly, Theidon argues, via Veena

Das and Arthur Kleinman, intimate violence concerns itself with 'how people engage in the tasks of daily living, reinhabiting worlds in full recognition that perpetrators, victims and witnesses come from the same social space' (384). In such a scenario, '[p]erhaps strategies that permit people to delay that full recognition – that permit people to mask the unbearable truth of intimate, lethal violence – are key to staying the hand of vengeance' (384).

If the victims of terrorism are those who are likely to use terrorism – both literally and metaphorically – against others, intimate violence is then both binding and divisive as Moira Fradinger argues in her work on Latin America:

> It is the friend whose difference is manufactured in times of crisis to be placed in liminal space, between the outside and inside, in order to differentiate the interior and exterior whose borders have been thrown into crisis. It is the friend become enemy who reminds us how a given political fraternity was built on foundational violence. (2010, 247)

The fact that Suu Kyi's shadow government is labelled as a terrorist group by a terrorist junta – the very junta instituted by her father and the one by which Suu Kyi was cared for as a child – is a glaring reminder of the interplay between intimacy and enmity bred by the foundational violence of power-harnessing in postcolonial Burma. The wheel now has turned full circle: in an ironic turn of events, the same Suu Kyi, showcased by the West as the champion of democracy and rights, denounced as a terrorist-ally when the Rohingya massacre was underway, begins to garner international solidarity as the last vestige of hope against the military junta that deposed her.

Such porousness of iconicity, including the tropological substitutions vested in the figure of the terrorists, military, militias, saviours of the nation and insurgents, is endemic to the notion of intimate violence. Here, the interchangeability of terrorist and nationalist or nation builder are made possible, according to Laura Sjoberg (2015, 393), precisely because of the epistemic intimacy of the violence involved: 'If the terrorist is the dissolution of order, the counterterrorist is its reconstitution'. Sjoberg further contends, via Cynthia Weber, that much like the power dynamics of the intimate relationships between the masculine and feminine, the '"terrorist"' is susceptible to the violation of the '"counter-terrorist" [which] is made possible by the epistemology of intimate (in)violability constituting the existence of "the terrorist" even without his/her materiality' (393). To put it differently, if masculinity is considered 'inviolable', any challenge to its constituent elements such as 'bravery, independence, protector status and honour' (394) leads to the construction of the other as a threat. Thus, the very existence of the category of 'terrorist', which serves as a fleeting and floating metaphor for those who are in a position to effectively impose it on others, is an exegesis of foundational violence through which nations are born, societies are made, and simultaneously, citizenship is gentrified and communities are destroyed. It is this very simultaneity of terrorism and counterterrorism – the dissolution and reconstruction of order – embedded in the *foundational violence*, such as the founding dominance of central Burmans over the minority tribes, that makes the enduring conflicts all the more intimate: 'the historical development and radical shifts in affinities within relationships that frequently involve a more powerful partner who, over the course of the relationship, exercises control' (Pain 2015, 67).

Rebels, Heroes and the Disfigured Terrorists in Burmese Literature

Pascal Khoo Thwe's *From The Land of Green Ghosts* (2002) features a series of allegorical cues on the intimacy of private and political violence. Thwe's memoir was written during his exile in Cambridge, after having been rescued by a Cambridge don named John Casey from the persecution of the junta for his role in student mobilisation.[2] Although Thwe inevitably joins an insurgency led by the Karennis during his flight from the junta, his decision to become an active political campaigner is shaped by the abduction and murder of his lover Moe, the daughter of a Burmese military officer who was killed in the conflict with the Shan insurgents. Since Moe is the only Burman in his life who shows unconditional affection and love in the land of 'Green Ghosts' (the name Thwe's Padaung tribe gave the Burmans), her murder marks a decisive moment in his subsequent encounters with violence. As Thwe writes: 'I believe that in the months to come, some part of her spirit and defiance entered into me, for this loss I have no words. Moe's body was never returned or recovered' (158–9).

Admittedly, this intimate loss manifests itself in Thwe's life as 'defiance', which in turn transforms into an act of rebellion against his father who, Thwe believes, had long been imprisoned by his own docility and submissiveness to the regime. From defiance to rebellion, Thwe channels his pent-up anger into an allegorical insurgency during one of his jungle hunts:

> I waited until the target could be seen distinctly. At the clearing in the bush a forked tongue appeared, an inch or two from the hutoo's nest. I pulled the rubber of the catapult. Off it went, and hit a dry twig and the snake's head. Such was the impact that the snake fell to the ground, sinking into a heap like a silk ribbon, but in slow motion ... The creature didn't die at once. Its center of life is not in the head, as it is with humans and animals – you can chop the head off and it will still wriggle and trash and not die. You must break the spine to render it lifeless. I held it in triumph ... Looking into the nest I found that it contained three baby birds, about two or three days old. Poor creatures, they almost ended up

in the snake's belly, I thought, without ever having the experience of flying freely. I took my trophy to the hut and rubbed it with ash. I cut off its head, skinned and gutted it, then buried in the inedible parts near the bush where it fell. I felt satisfied and had no wish for further hunting that day. (175–7)

Here, the hunt itself becomes not only a source of intimate psychological catharsis that brings Thwe much 'satisfaction', but its description alludes to a tropological substitution wherein Moe's loss stands in for the bird he could save, whose spirit, as it were *enters* into him (158-9) and invokes the insurgent impulse in him to shoot the head of the snake and save the bird. The synecdochic formulation 'the snake's life does not lie in its head' is indeed befitting of the intimacy of the singular body and the dismembering of its organic parts: if we read the junta's leader Ne Win as the head of the snake, the spine of the snake is his henchmen in the junta itself. Taken together, they make a toxic body of a regime splashing venom mixed with blood at the moment of their death, to say nothing of the satisfaction and triumph one gets from the crushing sound off each death blow to one's enemy. The perilous freedom of the birds in the nest that cannot fly shall remain. This organic allegory, or rather the allegory of dismembered organisms – the head, the body, the spine – resurfaces frequently throughout the text, most particularly in the form of a radio interlude between the Karenni militants and the Tatmadaw:

> 'So you don't love the old man anymore? I'm really shocked. By the way, how many men have you got? . . . And how many civilian porters?'
> 'They're all volunteers, all volunteers. It's a lie that we kidnap them.'
> 'Well, you said it. Pretty impressive that they volunteer to wear chains, volunteer to walk through the minefields, volunteer to be blown to bits. The Burmese like getting killed, then?'
> . . . 'Why are you trying to kill us?'
> 'Orders. And it's my duty.'
> 'I bet you enjoy your duty – you know, all the mowing down monks, women, unarmed students. You must feel pretty good after that, I suppose. After all, what could be more satisfying than murdering your own children'.
> . . . 'I'm not going to talk politics. I have a job. I have to feed my wife and family. Don't try to teach an old crocodile how to swim.'
> 'Talking of old crocodiles, how is your boss, your father? Still the benevolent ruler? Still ending the exploitation of man by man?' (241–2)

Again, the 'father' metaphor alludes to the junta 'head' New Win as the poisonous head of the snake and his henchmen as its spine (175–6) evokes the organic intimacy innate to one's body, but also the estrangement stemming from the presence of murderous venom in the same being. The radio banter, too, bears testimony to an indivisible belonging in a divided community, wherein duty and desperation are thrust upon each party to kill and to be killed in the name of preserving the self, the greater good of the community. Such indivisible presence of what can be called 'estranged familiarity' is akin to Patrick Rotman's reading of intimate enemies in the context of Algeria: 'having lived in close proximity as coloniser and colonised for almost 130 years, fighters on both sides had the sense of a foe at once completely other, yet strangely familiar' (qtd in Flood and Martin 2019, 173). Thwe captures another such intimate encounter with violence when he stumbles on the corpse of his enemy:

> When it was all over I walked up to the field of the battle. One of the Burmese soldiers was lying on his face. Curious, and with a feeling of presentiment, I turned him over. It was the same army officer who had told me in the restaurant in Mandalay that I was worth only one bullet. 'Surely', I thought, with a cruel and exultant sense that justice had been done, 'he was worth a lot of bullets.' Then I looked down at his puckered face, and all I could feel was pity at the waste of it. After all, he had been courageous, I could not sum up his worth by the number of bullets needed to kill him (2002, 250).

In this disconsolate encounter with the death of the enemy, it is as if only through certain familiarity, that is, an intimate understanding of violence, that an ethical alterity could be forged. A case in point, the bittersweet vengeance of seeing his enemy fall is immediately undercut by Pascal's acknowledgement of his enemy's courage, who like himself, knowingly walks into the enemy's jaws. Yet, in Thwe's exultant remark that 'justice had been done', there is an iota of vengeance that unravels its intimate bonds with violence. If vengeance is retributive of violence, then as Jacky Bouju and Mirijam de Bruijn (2014, 9–10) assert, 'in the course of this cyclical negative reciprocity, the permutations of the position of aggressor/victim ensure a replication of fears. In spite of this, revenge is always an opportunity as it remains the only recourse for defending one's interests or seizing lost power in an inescapable relationship'. However, Thwe converts his fleeting moment of vengeance into a moment of ethical alterity by virtue of his own intimacy with violence, one that enables him to acknowledge the suffering of the Žižekian faceless monster. Such suffering, however, does not necessarily amount to a useful suffering in a Levinasian sense, so long as Thwe's response is based on his encounter with the ill-fated visage of his enemy when he turns his body over, not its countenance that invokes his own suffering (for the Other). The chief culprit here is not the vengeance or the desire for retribution, but the inherent unpredictability and opacity, as well as the uncontrollability of redemptive violence, which, as Bouju and de Bruijn (2014, 10–11) observe, is so old that nobody knows anymore who the original aggressor or victim was and because the unexpected consequences and outcomes of violent deeds usually exceed the perpetrator's initial intentions. . . . Over the course of time, the initial conflict expands socially, involving unexpected new actors, witnesses or institutions, thus creating other sources of conflict and violence.

This is certainly the case with Thwe's own foray into the Karenni insurgency, the insurgent group that takes him under its wing, and its leader concedes that he is no longer sure who exactly his group is fighting, and that he prefers a federal solution to the multiple insurgencies because the separatists 'are tired of killing each other' (2002, 200).

An equally arresting tale, Lucy Cruickshanks (2015) *The Road to Rangoon* follows the lives of two orphaned siblings, Kyaw and Thuza, in the militarised zone in the small town of Mogok in the Shan State. While Kyaw becomes a member of the rebel army (Shan State Army), Thuza makes a subsistence living as a small-time ruby pilferer with the help of her brother from the rebel-controlled areas, and acts as a messenger between the Tatmadaw, the rebels and a Thai arms dealer. In the absence of any kin, except for an opium-addicted grandmother, Thuza comes under the paternal care of a Buddhist monk, Zwatika, a secret Tatmadaw agent, who tells Thuza that her parents were imprisoned in a jail near Rangoon, and manipulates her to accumulate as many rubies in order to bribe the prison officials and free her loved ones who, as we learn later, were killed by the Tatmadaw the moment they were abducted.

The subsequent story evolves through a series of intimate yet violent relationships between four sets of characters, each consisting of an entangled intimacy of friendships, loyalty and brotherhood: Thuza, Kyaw and Zwatika; the Tatmadaw officer Than Chit and his son Min; Michael, son of the British Ambassador, and Sein, the son of a university professor, both hailing from the upper echelons of Burmese society; and finally Thuza and Than Chit. Each of these dyadic, at times triadic relationships is bound by acts of violence, and in almost every instance by the loss of a loved one that sets them on a path towards vengeance, redemption and retribution. Since all the characters have lost something intimate through the conflict, their families are both split and bound by the war. This enables the acts and actants of violence from each end of the spectrum – rebels, civilians and the military – to morph and metamorphosise their roles at will: from the loyalists to the Union of Burma to infiltrators, smugglers, terrorists, and finally, to insurgents vis-a-vis the saviours of their nation. In each case, the manifestations of intimate relations, such as care, safety and justice, take a violent course, or rather take recourse to violence to such an extent that intimate acts and political acts can no longer be seen as separate. For the son of the British Ambassador, his own intimate feelings of shame and guilt for abandoning his friend Sein – a friend who becomes his sole companion by virtue of his class and habitus in a land of 'injured charm' (Cruickshanks 2016, 321) that he barely understands – during a bomb blast turn him into a rebel sympathiser. Yet, Michael's bid for affective redemption here is neither ideological nor lumpen, but one triggered by intimate feelings of pain, loss and guilt:

> This guilt was different from the constant, ignorable, low rumble of nervousness he had about Sein being his friend, and from the moment he had let the car drive away with his bleeding body in the boot, and even from the moment that he'd fled from the hospital. He realised now that he'd turned away often, in the way he admonished his father for doing – and Sein's father too, though he understood why. (154)

Upon learning that the bomb was actually planted by the Tatmadaw but was blamed on the rebels, Michael teams up with his teacher, a former member of the Shan State Army, and embarks on a risky venture to deliver a catchment of arms to the insurgents in the jungles of Burma. Despite the fact that he is visible, and risks being exposed, Michael grows intent on using privilege, and thereby risks one intimacy – that of his relationship to his father, an ambassador in service – to offset another, that is, the retribution for his friend's loss.

Like the dramatic metamorphosis of Michael Atwood's role, from a member of British diplomatic family to rebel aid, another significant exchange of roles occurs between the siblings Thuza and Kyaw, whereby the split in the intimacy of the family mirrors the split in their respective political ideologies and allegiances. In a clash of insurgent alternatives of their own peculiar brands, the siblings stand on opposite ends of the political spectrum:

> 'They taught you to fight, like I do. Why haven't you listened?' Thuza shook her head and stared at the ground. 'Our parents are nothing like you, Kyaw. They never touched a weapon.' . . . 'They wouldn't support you, Kyaw. You know that.'
>
> . . .
>
> 'I have hope Thuza, but I am a realist. You are the hopeless one. How many years have you saved? How much money do you have? Is it enough for a train to Rangoon? Is it enough to bribe a colonel or a general, to buy them a yacht and to break Mumma free?' He laughed and bared his beetle black teeth 'You are a joke'.
>
> 'Fuck off, Kyaw'.
>
> 'It's the daydreams in your head that keep you trapped. You're like those birds in your cage, like your little hidden bank notes. Every time you tuck another away, you're choosing to surrender. You're doing this, not me.

After all the Tatmadaw have done to our people – after all they've done to you, Thuza Win – I don't understand how you simply ignore them. Why don't you want to fight?'
'I'm fighting, brother. I am. Every day.' (227–9)

This everyday fight is indeed the most intimate aspect of violence, and if only for its familiarity, knowability, and its ability to naturalise itself, such violence risks being discounted as ordinary or unspectacular. Evidently, Kyaw discredits any 'fight' other than insurgent labour as a passive submission to the regime, in spite of Thuza's own 'fight' on an everyday basis: having lost her parents at an early age, she is forced by the circumstances of her life to be a ruby smuggler, bird catcher, pilferer and double agent. The extraordinariness of these occupations becomes transformed into a new 'ordinariness' of life. As Susanna Trnka argues in the context of Fiji,

> events that had previously been 'extraordinary' became a part of everyday life and discourse, but also in the ways in which the 'ordinary' events of daily living became implicated as sites of communication and understanding of political conflict. It was as if there could be no event that was not in some way narrated as a part of the political situation. (2008, 146)

In this sense, hidden from the 'extraordinary' and the 'spectacular', Thuza's 'everyday' insurgency, as Laura Sjoberg (2015, 386) would put it, is 'evidence that everyday/intimate violence is one of the greatest threats to people's security globally, and one of the greatest sources of terror to people – certainly as grave as, if not graver than, the acts that policymakers in global politics traditionally and easily label as "terrorism"'. By placing intimate violence at the heart of global terrorism debate, Sjoberg's appeals to policy makers to turn their attention to the intimate sites of violent production that are often misread as people's motives for terrorism. Much the same way, both terror and counter-terror reproduce violence 'in the intimate sphere, [which] manifest[s] as a violent act of control' (389), something that holds particularly true for the orphaned siblings who take divergent paths to insurgency – one fighting the odds of everyday violence, one fighting the everyday odds of violence – but are bound by an intimate cause, that is, to free their parents from the Insein prison. Thuza's aversion to *bona fide* insurgency remains somewhat short-lived, however, as she first turns to vengeance, indulging in the only intimate act of violence in her life: she kills her paternal figure Zwatika with her own hands upon learning that the monk was a military agent who had her parents killed, and evolves into a full-blown insurgent after the killing of Kyaw by the Tatmadaw.

But it is another intimate encounter of familial violence, almost as if mirroring the sibling's own forked path towards insurgency, between the Tatmadaw officer Than Chit and his wife Malar over the fate of their teenage son Min, that plays a decisive role in Thuza's journey towards insurgency. Ever since he was rescued from the streets by the Tatmadaw, Than Chit has channelled all his loyalty to the military institution. He even idolises Aung San, the founder of the Burmese National Army, and dreams of turning his son Min to a fine soldier of the Tatmadaw. But his wife Malar, who is a victim of intimate violence by way of her father who nearly died in the service of Tatmadaw, sees things differently:

> 'Why aren't you happy, Malar?' he said. 'Honestly. It's the only place a boy of his age should be. You know that. The people love and respect the Tatmadaw.'
> 'They fear them, Than Chit.'
> 'It's the same thing. They keep us together, sweetheart. What's not to love? Without strong men like Min and me to hold the insurgents at bay – all murderers and rapists wherever else they are – the whole country would collapse.' (180)

The tragic death of Min – who is sent to the battlefront by his superior unbeknownst to Than Chit – at the hands of the Shan insurgents is inimical to, if not proleptic of, the violent ending of the argument between the intimate partners: 'he slapped the wall beside her face and she yelped and flinched then scurried away' (181). Ironically though, it is not Kyaw's death, but Min's death that inspires Thuza to embark on an insurgent path of vengeance and redemptive justice in which a member of her enemy camp, Than Chit, becomes an unlikely ally. Even before the funeral of Min, the head of the Tatmadaw sends Than Chit on a mission to capture ruby pilferers, and when captured, Thuza makes an assault on the weaker constitution of a father who has just lost his son:

> 'You knew my brother was a rebel but you didn't make me say it. You knew he fought with the SSA. Their men killed your boy, but you didn't need to throw me with them ... You showed me mercy, Officer. You're a good man. You understood what I was feeling. My loss. You don't want others to suffer like you have done. That makes you more chivalrous than the Tatmadaw deserves. More gallant. Show me mercy again. ...
> The Tatmadaw has robbed us both. Your son was a soldier but he was a brilliant boy ... They sent you to work before your child was buried. Worse than that, they signed his murder warrant. They killed Min as eagerly as they killed my brother. ...
> Pass me the keys, sir. You won't be sorry. Pass me the keys and turn your eyes sideways, and I promise I'll punish them all for us both.' (356–8)

The fact that Than Chit sets Thuza free in order to avenge his son's death with her help, and sees the injustice he has done to Min by forcing his own ambitions upon his son, unravels what Ashis Nandy has called the intimate enemy, or the enemy within:

> Ultimately, modern oppression, as opposed to traditional oppression, is not an encounter between the self and the enemy, the rulers and the ruled, the gods and the demons. It is a battle between the de-humanized self and the objectified enemy, the technologized bureaucrat and his reified victim, pseudo-rulers and their fearsome other selves projected on to their 'subjects'. (1989, xvi)

In an unholy union of sorts, terrorist and counterterrorist join hands to kill *their* collective terrorist, the head of the Tatmadaw, who was indeed responsible for the killing of their loved ones. Through violence, the intimate loss at both ends of the spectrum – the military and the militant – forges a connivingly just political bonhomie among sworn enemies: the prisoner and the imprisoned – Than Chit and Thuza – join hands and pass on intelligence to the rebels to ambush the head of the Tatmadaw and blow him into pieces. In this intimate interplay of violence, no usurpers, no agent provocateurs and no agents of violence remain ideologically frozen or figuratively fixated: insurgents are repeatedly, and at times interchangeably, equated with terrorists (Cruickshanks 2016, 78), and a terrorist, such as Kyaw, in turn, is variably labelled as a 'notorious insurgent, a sniper, a bandit and a critical money-cow' (364); a ruby pilferer becomes an insurgent; a Buddhist monk secretly acts as a counterterrorism agent; an aspiring soldier models his career after the nation's father; and the father of the aspiring solider aids and abets the very terrorists who kill his son.

Conclusion

In view of these constantly morphing and metamorphosising agents of violence in the Burmese case, it is no overstatement to say that our preoccupation with deconstructing the figure of the terrorist, does much disservice to the presence and prevalence of diverse modes and modalities of violence in the postcolonial world. Against this background, rather than using the concept of terrorism or the figure of the terrorist as the departure point of our inquiry, there is a further need to take an inductive approach to registering the political modalities of violence for what they are: peasant wars, banditry, mass killings, mutinies, nationalist struggles, riots, insurgencies, acts of vengeance and unfulfilled emancipatory movements.

This chapter has argued that intimate violence as a concept helps understand not only the constant mitosis, if not the transfiguration the agents of violence undergo, but also sheds light on how violence becomes an inevitable yet indispensable tool to enliven all those very unfulfilled roles – a tribesman becoming an insurgent, a ruby pilferer becoming a rebel aid, or a military officer committing an act of treason – that risk being subsumed under the figural force of the terrorist. Like the disjointed legs of the violators and the violated, the terrorists or the victims of terrorism as evinced in the story of the Burmese teenage soldier cited in the opening of this chapter, it is the conjoining groin of the two legs that bespeaks of an intimacy of conflicts, enmity, solidarity and violence in the postcolonial world. The two separate(d) legs of the allegorical nation, as it were, are pivoted to the most intimate part of the same body, as captured in the mise-en-scène of Bapsi Sidhwa's novel *Cracking India* (1988) in which a man is tied to two jeeps and pulled apart, evoking an arresting imagery of violence that is congenital to the two communities and the(ir) respective nations – India and Pakistan – which are not only disjointed at, but are essentially conjoined by, the same severed groin.

Notes

1. The vignette presented here is loosely based on Minoli Salgado's (2019) short story 'Too Many Legs'.
2. A work of life fiction, which is in fact described as English literature of 'quality' (Thwe 2002, xvi) by the Oxford literary scholar Colin Burrow for its remarkable use of literary devices. Given its literary focus, this chapter makes a concerted attempt to steer away from the 'factual authority' of life fiction towards the execution of literary devices in Thwe's work.

References

Boehmer, Elleke, and Stephen Morton. 2015. "Introduction. Terror and the Postcolonial." In *Terror and the Postcolonial*, eds Elleke Boehmer and Stephen Morton, 1–24. 2nd edn. Oxford: Wiley Blackwell.
Bouju, Jacky, and Mirjam de Bruijn. 2014. *Ordinary Violence and Social Change in Africa*. Leiden: Brill.
Craig, Charmaine. 2017. *Miss Burma*. London: Grove/Atlantic.
Cruickshanks, Lucy. 2015. *The Road to Rangoon*. London: Quercus Publishing.
DW. 2021. "Myanmar Junta Designates Shadow Government as 'Terrorist' Group." May 8, 2021. https://p.dw.com/p/3t9Mn
Flood, Maria, and Florence Martin. 2019. "The Terrorist as *ennemi intime* in French and Francophone Cinema." *Studies in French Cinema* 19, no. 3: 171–8.
Fradinger, Moira. 2010. *Binding Violence*. Stanford: Stanford University Press.
Kapila, Shruti. 2021. *Violent Fraternity: Indian Political Thought in the Global Age*. Princeton, NJ: Princeton University Press.
Levinas, Emmanuel. 1985. *Ethics and Infinity*. Trans. R. Cohen. Pittsburgh: Duquesne University Press.

Levinas, Emmanuel. 1990. *Difficult Freedom*. Trans. Sean Hand. Baltimore: Johns Hopkins University Press.
Levinas, Emmanuel. 1998. *Entre Nous: Essays on Thinking-of-the-Other*. Trans M. B. Smith and B. Harshav. New York: Columbia University Press.
Nandy, Ashis. 2010. "Theorist: 'Real India: Ahis Nandy's 'Intimate Enemies'." Interview by Christopher Lydon. *Radio Open Source*, September 3, 2010. https://radioopensource.org/tag/theorist/
Nandy, Ashis. 1989. *Intimate Enemy: Loss and Recovery of Self Under Colonialism*. Oxford: Oxford University Press.
Pain, Rachel. 2015. "Intimate War." *Political Geography* 44: 64–73.
Perkins, Mitali. 2010. *Bamboo People: A Novel*. Watertown: Charlesbridge Publishing.
Pugliese, Joseph. 2013. *State Violence and the Execution of Law: Biopolitical Caesurae of Torture, Black Sites, Drones*. London: Routledge.
Salgado, Minoli. 2019. "Too Many Legs." In *Broken Jaw*, 48–49. Sutton: the87press.
Scanlan, Margaret. 2001. *Plotting Terror: Novelists and Terrorists in Contemporary Fiction*. Charlottesville and London: University Press of Virginia.
Safi, Michael. 2017. "Aung San Suu Kyi Says 'Terrorists' Are Misinforming World about Myanmar Violence." *The Guardian*, September 6, 2017. https://www.theguardian.com/world/2017/sep/06/aung-san-suu-kyi-blames-terrorists-for-misinformation-about-myanmar-violence?ncid=edlinkushpmg00000313
Sidhwa, Bapsi. 2010. *Cracking India: A Novel*. Minneapolis: Milkweed Editions.
Sjoberg, Laura. 2015. "The Terror of Everyday Counterterrorism." *Critical Studies on Terrorism* 8, no. 3: 383–400.
Suu Kyi, Aung San. 1995. *Freedom from Fear*. London: Penguin.
Theidon, Kimberly. 2012. *Intimate Enemies*. Philadelphia: University of Pennsylvania Press.
Trnka, Susanna. 2008. *State of Suffering: Political Violence and Community Survival in Fiji*. Ithaca: Cornell University Press.
Thwe. Pascal Khoo. 2002. *From the Land of Green Ghosts*. London: HarperCollins.
Zhou, Naaman, and Michael Safi. 2017. "Desmond Tutu Condemns Aung San Suu Kyi: 'Silence Is Too High a Price'." *The Guardian*, September 8, 2017. https://www.theguardian.com/world/2017/sep/08/desmond-tutu-condemns-aung-san-suu-kyi-price-of-your-silence-is-too-steep
Žižek, Slavoj. 2013. "Neighbors and Other Monsters: A Plea for Ethical Violence." In *The Neighbor: Three Inquiries in Political Theology*, edited by Slavoj Žižek, Eric L. Santner and Kenneth Reinhard, 134–90. University of Chicago Press.

AFTERWORD

Richard Jackson

It was a genuine honour to be invited to give a keynote lecture at 'The Figure of the Terrorist in Literature, Film and Media', the November 2019 conference in Zurich out of which this wonderful volume has arisen. It is an even greater privilege to be asked to write the afterword to this exceptionally interesting and insightful collection of papers, especially as I feel that I am the least qualified in the subject of all the contributors and there are many other more eminent scholars who could have been given the task instead. Unlike all the contributors to this superb collection, I have no legitimate expertise in literary studies or media studies. I trained in political science and international relations, and only came to the subject of terrorism in literature by happenstance.

In the following pages, I want to reflect briefly on some of the insights I have gained from this truly interesting, thoughtful and engaging collection of papers, in part through the prism of how and why I came to be interested in the figure of the terrorist, and how my concerns have changed since the terrorist attack on my home city of Christchurch, New Zealand, in March 2019. I commend this volume as a highly stimulating, rigorous and genuinely insightful addition to the growing literature on representations of terrorism in literature and visual media, and a major contribution to our understanding of the subject.

The Figure of the Terrorist

One day, somewhere around 2008, I was searching for a novel or film about terrorism which I could recommend to my students as a way of supplementing the academic books and articles I was making them read as part of a course. As a teacher, I had discovered that a good novel or movie could sometimes engage students and bring topics to life in ways that generally turgid, scientific academic writing could not. In this instance, however, when I thought about the many terrorism-related novels I had read, I realised that I could not think of a single example which I felt represented terrorism or terrorists in a realistic or credible way. That is, I could not recall any novel that told a story in which the terrorist protagonist had a believable psychology, motivation, history or characteristics, or any genuinely understandable reasons for what they did (Jackson 2015a; Jackson 2018). Certainly, no novel seemed to match my own research-based understanding of terrorism, my experience of talking to former terrorists and militants, or my reading of their biographical accounts. My students, I felt, would learn little about actual terrorism or the nature of real-world terrorists from the stereotypical and caricatured depictions that filled the pages of the thousands of terrorism novels which have been published in the Western context.

It was this experience, along with my growing interest in the so-called 'narrative turn' in international relations (Jackson 2015a), that eventually put me on a path to writing my own novel about terrorism (Jackson 2014). In *Confessions of a Terrorist* (2014), I tried to empathetically imagine why a real, historically situated person – as opposed to a caricatured, stereotypical, decontextualised Hollywood-style villain – would choose to commit acts of political violence and live the life of a hunted insurgent. I also wanted to create some fictional space for the figure of the terrorist to talk back against the stereotypical characterisations of his nature and motives – to challenge the essentialising reductionism of him to a dangerous caricature. Although the novel was a commercial failure, the experience of writing it, as well as my broader ongoing research on the discourse of the war on terror (Jackson 2005; Jackson 2007a), led me to focus some research time on the role of literature in the wider 'mythography of terrorism' (Zulaika and Douglass 1996) or 'terrorism discourse' that seemed to dominate Western societies at the time.

During this period, the primary problem or puzzle I sought answers to was, as the insightful and compelling introduction to this volume by Maria Flood and Michael C. Frank also discusses, why the figure of the terrorist, for the most part, continues to be represented in literature and visual media in essentialist, stereotypical, dehumanised and depoliticised ways. Or why, as Tim Gauthier's chapter explores, artists find it so difficult to ignore the imperative to morally condemn terrorists and accept their humanity. As the collection of papers in this volume goes on to explore, such a characterisation is somewhat complicated by the fact that more complex and nuanced artistic representations of the figure of the terrorist do exist, particularly in non-Western contexts, as well as in other, pre-9/11, eras. Shane Walshe's chapter demonstrates that comic book depictions of the IRA have changed over the years, from being constructed as understandable and basically legitimate, to increasingly unsympathetic portrayals of the 'fanatical hardliner'. Similarly, Rajeswari Mohan's chapter about the Sri Lankan film, *The Terrorist*, Harald Pittel's chapter on terrorism in Hindi cinema, and Zaynab Seedat's chapter on the novel, *Just Another Jihadi Jane*, all demonstrate that complicated, nuanced and sympathetic portrayals of the figure of the terrorist are perhaps more common than we think, but only when we shift our gaze from Western sources.

Nevertheless, it remains a puzzle as to why the figure of the terrorist, especially in the literature and visual media of Western societies, continues to most often be 'the paradigm of inhuman bestiality, the quintessential proscribed or tabooed figure of our times' (Zulaika and Douglass 1996, 6). This remains the case today, as the chapters by Beatriz Lopez, Cyprian Piskurek and Sarah Davison in this volume demonstrate, even while other deplorable figures – the violent criminal, the mafia don, the serial killer, the Nazi officer and even the paedophile – have received sympathetic, humanistic and realistic treatments in literary and visual media representations. As Peter C. Herman notes in his contribution to this volume, Walter White, the anti-hero of the television series *Breaking Bad*, becomes a ruthless meth dealer and kills approximately 274 people over the course of the show; and yet, he is depicted in ways which both plausibly explain his gradual transformation into violent criminality and maintain audience sympathy for his increasingly flawed humanity. If a drug-dealing murderer can be a sympathetic figure, why not a terrorist?

At the same time that I began to consider the puzzle of the literary terrorist, I was also continuing my research on the role of language and discourse in the generation of political violence (Jackson 2005; Jackson 2007b; Jackson and Dexter 2014). In this broader project, I could not help but note how art and literature can function as part of the discursive apparatus which dehumanises and demonises the enemy Other, legitimises political violence by the state, and constructs moral hierarchies of 'grievable lives' (Butler 2004). The puzzle of the dehumanised and demonised figure of the terrorist therefore, was much more than a simple issue of literary curiosity. In fact, such representations are a reflection, and co-constitutive of, the broader mythography or discourse of terrorism. In turn, the mythography of terrorism is a reflection, and co-constitutive of, the ongoing coloniality and racism of our institutions and wider societies, not least in the way that the figure of the terrorist is most often a person of colour, a Muslim or a person from a former colonial state (see Khan 2021). As Sarah Davison's chapter in this volume illustrates, even when cinematic depictions of terrorists attempt to be pluralising and sympathetic, white terrorists are more often coded as a kind of 'good terrorist' than non-white terrorists.

Perhaps more importantly, the dominant mythography of terrorism – and especially the essentialism, dehumanisation, and demonisation of the figure of the terrorist that is maintained – is directly implicated in a wide range of atrocities and human rights abuses: from the torture at Guantanamo, Abu Ghraib and Bagram, to drone killings, extraordinary rendition, shoot-to-kill policies, preventive detention, no fly lists, warrantless surveillance and a multitude of other infringements on human rights and dignity. From a more practical perspective, governments and researchers have begun investing a great deal in Preventing and Countering Violent Extremism (PCVE) programmes in recent years. However, their efforts are hampered somewhat by the culturally embedded dehumanised figure of the terrorist which obscures the real humans involved and blunts efforts to treat 'violent extremists' as human beings – not least because the public opposes such 'soft' responses to 'evil', threatening 'terrorists'. In other words, it is no exaggeration to suggest that the negative representation of the figure of the terrorist in literature and visual media, via its role in the mythography of terrorism, is harmful to a great many real human beings. Moreover, it is highly likely that this real harm is in turn a key factor in motivating individuals to engage in future acts of political violence.

One of the questions to consider at this point is, how did we arrive at this juncture? What explains the persistent recurrence of the dehumanised, demonised figure of the terrorist in Western literature and visual media? Why have artists, particularly in Western societies, shied away from challenging the dominant mythography? There is no single or definitive cause or explanation, but one part of it could be that 'terrorism' inhabits a special status in the broader hierarchy and types of violence which have been discursively established in Western society. As Lisa Stampnitzky (2013) has authoritatively demonstrated, from the 1970s onwards, 'terrorism' was (re)created by officials and scholars as an essential form of violence that was ontologically and morally different to other forms of political violence. It was discursively reconstructed as inherently irrational and morally wrong (after once being treated as one of many legitimate strategies of political violence), and ultimately, as completely unlike all the other forms of violence we tolerate and participate in, such as war, militarism, law enforcement, judicial violence, structural violence, cultural violence, domestic violence, racism, environmental violence and so on. Terrorism, in this respect, came to function as one of the key mechanisms maintaining the distinction between good violence and bad violence, legitimate violence and illegitimate violence; normal, acceptable, tolerable violence and abnormal, intolerable violence.

Other possible explanations lie in the effects of the 9/11 events themselves, and the way in which the spectacle of the attacks on the Twin Towers was co-opted and turned into a disciplinary tool against critics of the violence of US hegemony, those who would question the 'legitimate' use of violence by Western states in the global south, or those who would claim to be resisting Western imperialism. We might also point to factors such as the decline of revolutionary thought and practice in Western states, particularly following the end of the Cold War. In part, the broader historical loss of the figure of the revolutionary means that there is no real means of symbolically troubling the dehumanised figure of the terrorist. This is perhaps why the figure of Nelson Mandela does not trouble the figure of Osama bin Laden, despite both being labelled as 'terrorists' by the United States and others at certain points in their lives.

Additionally, we might consider the loss or subjugation of historical memory as another enabling factor in the construction of the dehumanised figure of the terrorist. That is, it is no longer possible to socially remember that a number of 'terrorists' previously won the Nobel Peace Prize, including Nelson Mandela, Yassir Arafat and Sean McBride – as Pavan Kumar Malreddy discusses in his essay in this volume. Nor is it that easy to remember official Western support for 'terrorists' like the mujahadin in Afghanistan, Unita in Angola, and the Contras in Nicaragua during the Cold War. Certainly, Israel's use of state terrorism in Egypt, Lebanon, the Occupied Territories and elsewhere, the use of terrorism in Nicaragua and Lebanon by US agents, and US-backed state terrorism in Latin America have been expunged from collective memory. We have forgotten our own terrorism, and our own terrorists, in order to maintain the fiction of the despicable figure of the terrorist Other.

A number of analysts would also point to the enduring material and discursive structures of coloniality which function to construct all anti-Western violence and all anti-US hegemony or anti-liberal order violence as inherently illegitimate and therefore a form of 'terrorism'. More broadly, as Sarah Davidson notes in her chapter, our societies are structured by race and racism; the figure of the terrorist is co-constitutive of this enduring social reality (see also Eriksson 2018). Lastly, we might also consider the character of the Western moral imagination which selectively views some forms of violence as inherently evil beyond comprehension. For example, at different times, some sections of Holocaust Studies have adopted this attitude, namely, viewing Hitler, the Nazis, and the genocide of the Jews as beyond comprehension and ultimately unknowable beyond the acknowledgement that it is an example of the human capacity for evil. It is more than just coincidental that the terrorism mythography frequently links terrorism and Nazism, thereby transforming terrorism into something which is both analytical and morally beyond the search for rational understanding.

None of these observations on their own can explain why Western literature and visual media has failed so miserably to provide credible human representations of the figure of the terrorist. However, considered collectively, they furnish a level of understanding of the broader, and very powerful, discursive structures and forces which have made it so difficult for artists to break the taboo on representing an understandable human terrorist, or to go beyond the 'condemnation imperative', as Tim Gauthier puts it. In addition, this state of affairs is a reminder that art cannot be considered outside of its historical and material conditions of production; literature and visual media are as much products of history as they are products of imagination. This provides an admittedly blunt explanation for why Western-centric literature and film support the dominant mythography of their own imperialistic societies, while the literature and visual media of non-Western societies take a more sympathetic view towards those who would violently challenge the status quo. At the same time, this observation suggests that there is a decolonial opportunity present in the current moment: if artists in the Western world cannot muster the imaginative moral courage to challenge and resist the dominant discourse and humanise terrorists, see the world through their eyes, consider their grievances, contextualise and historicise their political struggles, then perhaps it is up to non-Western artists to deconstruct the dominant mythography. As a number of the contributions to this volume attest, this is exactly what non-Western artists seem to have been doing, even if Western audiences and artists remain unaware of them.

The Figure of the Terrorist 2.0

The figure of the terrorist in Western literature and visual media arguably had its most compelling origins in the anarchist violence of the late nineteenth century (see Herman 2020). As this volume demonstrates, variations in its form and depiction occurred over the next century, such as the differential and more human treatment given to Irish terrorists, as Shane Walshe's chapter illustrates. Other variations occurred in the literature and visual media of non-Western societies, again as we have seen in several chapters in this volume. Nevertheless, the present incarnation of the figure of the terrorist was given its strongest impetus following the 9/11 terrorist attacks and the launch of the US-led Global War on Terrorism. This figure of the terrorist has dominated artistic representations for the past twenty years, particularly in Western societies. It is a heavily racialised figure – Muslim, predominantly but not exclusively male, and essentialised as religious, fanatical, blood-thirsty, hate-filled and threatening. The figure of the terrorist is, as already noted, the tabooed evil Other.

However, the growing number of white terrorist attacks in recent years, such as the Pittsburgh synagogue shooting in October 2018, the Christchurch mosque shootings in March 2019, the El Paso shooting in August 2019, and the Buffalo supermarket shooting in May 2022, among others, have thrown this established figure of the terrorist into existential crisis and highlighted some of its inherent contradictions. For example, the white terrorist fundamentally challenges the racialised aspect of the taken-for-granted figure of the terrorist. No longer is the terrorist automatically assumed to be a foreign, Muslim man. The terrorist is in fact, a white citizen. He is no longer the alien Other; he is Us. In this respect, the increased presence and visibility of the white terrorist destabilises the primary discursive function of the figure of the terrorist, namely, to be the outside Other to the identity of the Western Self.

In some ways, the real-world white terrorist has given material form to the criticisms of the figure of the terrorist made by critical scholars, including myself and many of the contributors in this volume. I, and many others, have long argued that the notion that the terrorist other is always Muslim, religious, fanatical, non-political and alien is simply wrong, misleading, harmful and dangerous; the existence of the white terrorist, and the growing threat he poses, fully supports our contention. At the same time, I and others, particularly those who adopt a critical sensibility, have argued that there are good reasons to humanise the figure of the terrorist and express empathy with them, as a way of resisting and deconstructing the terrorism mythography. And yet, the increasing visibility and presence of the white terrorist makes this an uncomfortable position to maintain.

The Christchurch terrorist attacks in March 2019 were a genuine shock to me, and to most New Zealanders, particularly the white settler population. It was a shock that went beyond the understandable shock of close proximity to violence and empathy for the victims. Not only was this the city where I had gone to university, got married and worked, but I had friends and family living there. Additionally, New Zealanders, especially Pākehā New Zealanders, believed that we were a basically fair society, we had not been greatly involved in the war on terror, and there seemed to be no obvious reasons for such a violent attack. Geographically isolated, New Zealand is far from the global centres of conflict and had until then remained relatively unaffected by the war on terror.

However, in the period of intense and emotional reflection which followed the attacks, one of my growing realisations was that I had not included white supremacist terrorism as one of the types of terrorism for which I expressed sympathy in my article from a few years earlier, entitled 'Confessions of a Terrorist Sympathiser' (Jackson 2015b). In this article, I had argued that 'sympathy for the terrorist is what is most needed right now if we are to break the current international cycle of violence and find more ethical and peaceful ways of responding to the challenge of contemporary political violence'. I went on to list and explain how I understood how a young woman from Gaza, or a young Sunni man in Baghdad, or a Muslim woman in France, or a Northern Irish Catholic man, or even a young American woman who witnessed the 9/11 attacks, could come to the decision that they would take up arms and fight back against the injustices and violence done to them. The aim of the article was to resist the dehumanisation and demonisation of terrorism discourse so that space could be created for the consideration of more effective, nonviolent and socially just responses to political violence. Such space had, I believed, been closed down by the language of the war on terror, and it had led directly to invasions, war, Abu Ghraib, torture, drone killings and more.

However, as I contemplated the horrific events which had occurred in my city, I realised that I had never expressed any sympathy for someone like the Christchurch attacker. My opposition to the demonisation and dehumanisation of terrorists had always excluded white supremacist terrorists, and, to an extent, state terrorists. It seemed that the racist, conservative violence of the white supremacist terrorist was so anathema to my 'critical' anti-establishment, liberationist sensibilities and values that it was too painful and difficult to contemplate empathising with, and giving voice to, such individuals. In effect, white supremacists were the only terrorists I did not mind calling terrorist. Following the attacks, in New Zealand this willingness to dehumanise and demonise the figure of the (white) terrorist played out in the way that his name was erased from public discourse, his manifesto was legally suppressed, and politicians framed the response within the narrative 'he is not us', and 'this is not who we are' (Toros 2022). It was as if we might become infected with his racism and violence if we were to know his name or attempt to understand his reasons. It seemed that at long last, the figure of the terrorist was now a white (Christian) man instead of a non-white Muslim man, and he was being treated in the terrorism taboo-prescribed, condemnatory manner.

Of course, this situation is highly problematic and contradictory. The figure of the terrorist and the terrorism mythography does not stop being misleading and harmful when it is applied to white terrorists. It is wrong-headed to treat a new category of terrorists with the same ineffectual, harmful and self-defeating policies as those that came before, and the same dangers persist in dehumanising, depoliticising and demonising certain categories of people. If the War on Terror 2.0 repeats the same mistakes as the initial War on Terror, it is also likely to end up with the same harms, mistakes and ineffectiveness. The logical answer is that we should resist and deconstruct the terrorism mythography with the same vigour today as we have in the past, notwithstanding the new identity of the terrorist. The figure of the terrorist overall needs to change, because it is wrong and it hurts people for no good reason.

However, now that the terrorist is a white nationalist racist, we are faced with some tricky challenges. For example, we might ask: is an empathetic artistic depiction of the white supremacist terrorist even possible, and if so, what are some of the main challenges of such depictions? Are there limits to the empathy which can be shown for the white supremacist terrorist? Does such empathy risk justifying or normalising white supremacy? Moreover, is an empathetic, humanised depiction of the white terrorist necessary or needed? What should or would such a depiction do, and are there any dangers in attempting it?

In the first instance, as noted in this volume, there is a well-established taboo and mythography of terrorism in which any kind of empathetic exploration and encounter with the terrorist is likely to result in extreme negative reaction and social sanction. Such a discursive context makes any attempt at empathetic engagement with the terrorist – whether Muslim, Irish, female or white supremacist – an act of counter-cultural rebellion and a kind of blasphemy. Related to this, a challenge is posed by the present global de-colonial moment in which a great many societies are waking up to the ongoing legacy of colonialism, racism and the oppression of non-white people. In such a context, the attempt to empathise with the white supremacist terrorist is in real danger of being seen as endorsing, normalising or justifying the racist ideology or sentiment of the terrorist. While empathetic engagement with the previously defined (insurgent) figure of the terrorist has a normative foundation in that it can often be viewed as an act of solidarity with the oppressed subaltern, empathetic engagement with the white supremacist terrorist has no such normative basis and is thus an ethically fraught prospect (see Toros 2022).

Another challenge here is that, as Mia Eriksson suggests, 'the discourses available for comprehending terrorism in the West today are shaped by, and continue to re-shape, a world structured by whiteness as the norm' (2018, 270). In fact, as already mentioned and as many studies have shown, the terrorism discourse is an identity producing discourse in which the evil non-white terrorist Other defines through negation the good white Self. In this context, confronting or even contemplating the *white* terrorist is a potentially identity-rupturing and highly destabilising process in which we come face to face with the terrorist Other only to realise that this Other is the Self. This challenge to the dominant sense of identity cannot be tolerated, and so, following a terrorist attack, the white terrorist has to be expelled from the Self.

As I have already noted, in New Zealand following the Christchurch terrorist attacks, political and cultural elites quickly proclaimed 'He is not us', even though more than a hundred years of colonial violence against non-white Others would suggest that such violence is in fact, very much who we are. It was a desperate discursive effort at disassociation and expulsion of the attacker from the dominant identity. Similarly, in Norway and in the US, among others, the white terrorist is most frequently labelled as mentally ill, deviant, abnormal or a lone wolf (Eriksson 2018). They are not representative of a community or an identity. At the least, there is a strong sense of incomprehension that such a person (a white person) could engage in an act of barbaric terrorism – which is by definition confined to the barbaric Other. Within such a powerful and sensitive national identity structure, empathetic engagement with the white terrorist who is clearly part of the Self is a potentially dangerous and fraught exercise.

From another perspective, there is no denying that the aims and grievances of white supremacists are in large part rooted in a conservatist fantasy, a nostalgia for the return of a violent and unjust order, a desire to restore the perceived loss of privilege, 'white fear' or 'white fragility', and no small amount of conspiracy thinking. This is in direct contrast to a great deal of the terrorism of the past few decades which has often been rooted in nationalist struggles or revolutionary ideologies. The challenge is: can or should we really give voice to the politics of the white terrorist when they appear to be rooted in racism, hatred, toxic masculinity, superiority, paranoia and privilege? Is it in any way similar to giving voice to the subaltern, oppressed terrorist?

This danger of giving voice to the violent fantasies of the white supremacist terrorist would seem to be borne out if we consider the well-known impact of *The Turner Diaries*, the most famous novel about white supremacists by William Luther Pierce. As we know from numerous real-world white supremacist terrorists, *The Turner Diaries* has acted as a powerful form of propaganda and has directly inspired the actions of terrorists like Timothy McVeigh, Anders Breivik and other more recent white terrorists. Might sympathetic portrayals of white terrorists similarly serve to inspire, rather than deter future acts of violence? More broadly, we have seen the effects of normalising white nationalist politics in numerous countries; it emboldens extremists and can lead directly to increased levels of violence and harm towards non-white people, women and vulnerable minorities.

In other words, the issue is that empathetic engagement and humanisation of the figure of the terrorist is not sufficient simply on its own; it must be part of a deeper human-to-human dialogic engagement that does not justify and inspire further violence but rather creates the possibility for transformation. It must be empathy rather than sympathy (Toros 2022), while recognising that quite often the perpetrators of violence can also simultaneously be victims of violence. Whether and how such an engagement is possible in artistic representations is not a question easily answered.

Lastly, and without going into areas that I am not fully equipped to navigate, as Tim Gauthier and others in this volume remind us, the employment of empathy in literary and visual media depictions is not without risk, as empathy can be instrumentalised, manipulated for non-altruistic purposes, or a hallow gesture that merely salves the conscience of the empathiser. It can be invoked under false pretences or be a substitute for meaningful political change, thereby reinforcing the unjust status quo. In situations where there is a power imbalance between the empathiser and the empathised, empathy can be seen as another form of colonisation or domination. Empathy for the terrorist, or any violent Other, can also be harmful for the artist or researcher. As Toros, expresses it, 'empathy requires an openness that leaves us vulnerable to violent and insidious ideas that hurt the soul as well as the mind' (2022, 231). Perhaps such hurt to the soul is also one of the reasons why artists have struggled to find an empathetic connection with their terrorist subjects. In the end, the challenge is to practise a kind of empathetic engagement that avoids these pitfalls and instead minimally, and through a deliberate activation of imagination, overcomes the denial of subjecthood, constructs a shared humanity that works against continuing victimisation, gives voice to the structurally voiceless, and creates space for transforming away from all forms of violence.

Conclusion

I do not purport to have any answers to the challenges posed by the figure of the terrorist, either the racist, dehumanised terrorist figure of the dominant Western mythography, or the white terrorist figure who challenges that depiction and who is beginning to haunt our collective imagination today. I am grateful to the editors of this volume, however, for organising a genuinely interesting and productive conference, and then producing this wonderful collection of papers which makes a real attempt to grapple with many of these complicated issues, examines critical questions from different vantage points, and explores possible solutions from within relevant critical theoretical frameworks. It is clear to me that critical concepts like 'difficult empathy', as explored in Tim Gauthier's chapter, and the 'ethics of discomfort', as explored in Maria Flood's chapter, are important steps towards finding possible solutions to these challenges.

In the final analysis, I believe that critically examining the figure of the terrorist in literature and visual media, as this volume has set out to do, remains a vitally important task. There is still a great deal we do not know about how the figure of the terrorist is constructed, and to what effect in society. We also continue to be largely unaware of the literature and visual media of the non-Western world. Moreover, there continue to be very good reasons for resisting and deconstructing this figure, in part through engaging with the more nuanced and complex non-Western depictions, not least because of the way it functions to maintain the broader mythography of terrorism and war on terror policies. In fact, it is implicated in the maintenance of many forms of violence in society, all of which cause immeasurable harm to individuals and communities. I believe that this volume provides an incisive analysis and makes a huge contribution to this broader emancipatory project. Every single chapter in this book is informative, eloquent and hugely interesting. I feel privileged to have been at the conference where this project began, and deeply grateful to have been asked to read the final manuscript and write this afterword. It is a tremendous achievement which I highly recommend.

References

Butler, Judith. 2004. *Precarious Life: The Powers of Mourning and Violence*. London and New York: Verso.
Eriksson, Mia. 2018. "Breivik and I: Affective Encounters with 'Failed' Masculinity in Stories About Right-Wing Terrorism." *NORMA: International Journal for Masculinity Studies* 13, nos. 3–4: 265–78.

Herman, Peter. 2020. *Unspeakable: Literature and Terrorism from the Gunpowder Plot to 9/11*. New York: Routledge.
Jackson, Richard. 2005. *Writing the War on Terrorism: Language, Politics and Counterterrorism*. Manchester: Manchester University Press.
Jackson, Richard. 2007a. "Constructing Enemies: 'Islamic Terrorism' in Political and Academic Discourse." *Government & Opposition* 42, no. 3: 394–426.
Jackson, Richard. 2007b. "Language, Policy and the Construction of a Torture Culture in the War on Terrorism." *Review of International Studies* 33: 353–71.
Jackson, Richard. 2014. *Confessions of a Terrorist*. London: Zed Press.
Jackson, Richard. 2015a. "Terrorism, Taboo and Discursive Resistance: The Agonistic Potential of the Terrorism Novel." *International Studies Review* 17, no. 3: 396–413.
Jackson, Richard. 2015b. "Confessions of a Terrorist Sympathiser." *richardjacksonterrorismblog*, November 27, 2015. https://richardjacksonterrorismblog.wordpress.com/2015/11/27/confessions-of-a-terrorist-sympathiser/
Jackson, Richard. 2018. "Sympathy for the Devil: Evil, Taboo, and the Terrorist Figure in Literature." In *Terrorism and Literature*, ed. Peter Herman, 377–94. Cambridge: Cambridge University Press.
Jackson, Richard, and Helen Dexter. 2014. "The Social Construction of Organised Political Violence: An Analytical Framework." *Civil Wars* 16, no. 1: 1–23.
Khan, Rabea. 2021. "Race, Coloniality and the Post 9/11 Counter-Discourse: Critical Terrorism Studies and the Reproduction of the Islam-Terrorism Discourse." *Critical Studies on Terrorism* 14, no. 4: 498–501.
Stampnitzky, Lisa. 2013. *Disciplining Terror: How Experts Invented "Terrorism"*. Cambridge: Cambridge University Press.
Toros, Harmonie. 2022. "Better Researchers, Better People? The Dangers of Empathetic Research on the Extreme Right." *Critical Studies on Terrorism* 15, no. 1: 225–31.
Zulaika, Joseba, and William Douglass. 1996. *Terror and Taboo: The Follies, Fables, and Faces of Terrorism*. London: Routledge.

INDEX

#MeToo movement, 22

4.50 from Paddington (1957), 90
9/11 (September 11, 2001, terrorist attacks)
   aftermath and retaliation, 6, 19, 76, 168, 266, 268
   in literature, 105–6, 116–17
   rhetoric following, 1, 3–4, 74, 107
   understanding of reasons for, 5, 9
   see also Islamophobia; War on Terror
11'09"01 (2002), 19
15:17 to Paris, The (2018), 17, 88–9, 93–6, 98–9, 100–3
   in the tradition of the western, 96–8

Abu Ghraib, 216, 266
Abu Nidal Organization, 147–8
accidental terrorists, 15
affect theory, 71–4
Ahmed, Saifuddin, 19
Ahmed, Sara, 226–30, 235–6

Akin, Fatih, 209, 213; *see also In the Fade* (2017)
Al-Asiri, Ibrahim, 91–2
Algerian terrorists, 8, 18
Algerian War of Independence 1954–62, 167–9, 175–6, 254
'alien' terrorists, 4
al-Qaeda, 110, 146
Alternative Right (alt-right), 224–5, 238–9
altruism, 203–4
America, 213–5, 267
   anti-Americanism, 14, 110–11, 146
   support for the IRA, 49–50, 55, 58–9, 61, 63
   see also 9/11; *White Right: Meeting the Enemy* (2017)
American History X (1998), 170
American Revolutionary War, 61
American Sniper (2014), 7–8, 97
American War (2017), 22, 205, 209, 213–17
anarchism, 29, 268

INDEX

Anderson, Benedict, 191
Anderson, Gavin, 73
Anglo-Irish Agreement 1985, 58
Angry Brigades, 29, 32–3
anti-Americanism, 14, 110–11, 146
anti-colonialism, 50, 59, 61–2; see also colonialism
anti-racist activism, 236–7, 239
anti-Western bias and violence, 110–11
anxiety, 37–8
    associated with technology, 90–3, 102
    see also fear
Appelbaum, Robert, 13–14, 105, 107, 116
'Arab' in French media, 175–6
Arafat, Yasser, 247, 267
Ardern, Jacinda, 235
Armstrong, Nancy, 42
arranged marriage, 20, 148, 151, 190–1, 193–4
artistic autonomy and political commitment, 32–3
Asad, Talal, 125, 136
Ashcroft, John, 4
Aslam, Nadeem, 14
assimilation, 188–9
Association of Small Bombs, The (2016), 17–18
    characterisation and motivation of the terrorists, 112–17
    family dysfunction as the cause of terrorism, 111–12
    meaning of the title, 117–18
    political and religious context and motivations, 107–11
    the victims, 106–7
Attack, The (2005), 14–15
Aung San, 248–9, 258
Aung San Suu Kyi, 247, 249, 251
Awaydays (1998), 75

Baker, Howard, 3–4
Bakunin, Mikhail, 42
Balasingham, Adele, 129, 135
Bamboo People (2010), 245–6
Banister, David, 92
Barkun, Michael, 92, 102
Barnes, William, 89
Bartlett, Frederic, 30
Baudrillard, Jean, 71
Bauman, Zygmunt, 81, 88
Beaman, Jean, 166–8
Begin, Menachem, 247
Begum, Shamima, 183–5, 187
Bélanger, Jocelyn J., 230
Belvaux, Lucas, 169–70
Benaïssa, Slimane, 216
Benjamin, Walter, 227
Berger, John, 239
Bethnal Green trio, 183–5, 187
Bharatiya Janata Party (BJP), 108, 144, 146, 159
Bielby, Clare, 196, 214
Bin Laden, Osama, 3–4, 10, 80–1, 110–11, 152, 267
biological weapons, 216
Bird, Stephanie, 112
Black, Derek, 235, 237
blackmail, 33–4
Blind Man's Garden, The (2013), 14
Bloch, Robyn, 206–7
Bloody Sunday 1972, 50
Bloom, Mia, 129
Bloom, Paul, 23
Blown Away (1994), 48
Bodyguard (2018), 17, 89, 99–103
Boehmer, Elleke, 250
Boggs, Carl, 21
Boko Haram, 168
Bollywood film, 90, 134, 154, 156, 160; see also Indian cinema
Bombay bombings 1993, 143, 146, 158
Bond, James (fictional character), 91

INDEX

Border (1997), 147
Borst, Lyle, 89
Bouju, Jacky, 254
Boukhrief, Nicolas, 174–5, 178, 180
bourgeois morality, 42
Boutouba, Jimia, 169, 174–5, 178
Breaking Bad (2008–13), 112, 265
Breivik, Anders, 272
Brighton Bombing 1984, 63, 68, 71
Brimson, Eddy, 73
Britain, 183–6, 188–9, 191, 224
British Empire, 247–8; see also colonialism
Bronstein, Phoebe, 12–13
Brun, Cathrine, 130
Bruneau, Emile, 208
Buffalo supermarket shooting 2022, 268
burkas, 192
Burke, Edmund, 2–3
Burma, 22–3, 245–9, 251–2, 259–60; see also From the Land of Green Ghosts (2002); Road to Rangoon, The (2015)
Burning Train, The (1980), 90
Burrington, Ingrid, 93
Bush, George W., 4
Butler, Judith, 4, 6–7, 9, 23, 132–3, 135, 168; see also 'ungrievable life'

Cache (2005), 179
Canepari, Michela, 79
capitalism, 20, 35, 38–9, 77–8, 227–8, 240
Casual (1996), 73
Catholicism, 176
Cervone, Alberto, 192
Chambers, Claire, 188–9
characterisation of terrorists, 49, 112–17; see also comic books
Charlie Hebdo attack 2015, 165, 168
Charlottesville Rally 2017, 224–5, 229–31, 235, 237, 239

Chez nous (2017), 20, 166–73, 179–80
childhood, militarisation of, 135–6
Chirac, Jacques, 167
Christchurch massacre 2019, 229, 235, 263, 268–71
Christianity, 176–8
Christie, Agatha, 90
cinema studies, previous works on representation of the terrorist, 10–14
civilian targets, 49
class see social class
Cleave, Chris, 17, 80
close-ups, 171–3, 176, 209, 232
cognitive openings, 195–6
Cold War, 91, 267
Coleridge, Samuel Taylor, 39
collective memory, 267
colonialism, 35
  in Burma, 247–8, 250
  French, 166–7, 175–6, 178–80
  legacy of, 271
  and patriarchy, 189
  see also Northern Ireland conflict
comedy, 11
comic books, 17, 47–9, 62–3; see also DC Comics; Marvel Comics
  fanatical hardliner figure, 58–62
  'good' terrorists and 'bad' terrorists, 55–8
  reformed rebel trope, 50–5
common good, 203–4
communications technology, 99–100, 102
Communism, 32–3
community, belonging and altruism, 191–2, 203–4, 223, 226, 230
'condemnation imperative', 5, 9, 22, 203–6, 212, 264, 267
Confessions of a Terrorist (2015), 113, 264
conflicted terrorists, 49, 137

277

INDEX

Connelly, Mark, 48, 55–6, 62
Conrad, Joseph, 14, 31, 38, 112
consumerism, 227–8
contamination, fear of, 205
Coogan, Tim Pat, 49
Corasani, Ray, 98
counterterrorist tactics, 68, 74–5, 93, 100, 103, 157–8, 266
counterterrorist terminology and rhetoric 1–5, 16, 67–70, 72, 74, 107; *see also* terrorist and counterterrorist, fluidity of labels
Cracker (1993–5), 17, 68, 81–2
Cracking India (1988), 260
Craig, Charmaine, 248
Cruickshanks, Lucy, 22–3, 246, 255–9
Culley, Sheena, 237
Cunningham, Karla, 185

Daredevil (1984–5), 55–60
Das, Veena, 250–1
Davison, Sarah, 20, 265, 267
DC Comics, 17, 47
de Bruijn, Mirijam, 254
de Mel, Neloufer, 128
Death Wish (2017), 211
dehistoricisation of terrorism, 16
dehumanisation of the terrorist, 3–6, 9–12, 18, 79, 93–4, 98, 169, 213, 264–7, 270; *see also* humanisation of the terrorist
DeLillo, Don, 14, 116
Delmer, Sefton, 31
Deltombe, Thomas, 19, 167, 175
depoliticisation of terrorism, 13–14, 16–18, 69–70, 79–80, 128, 178, 264; *see also* motivations of the terrorist
de-radicalisation, 235, 237–8, 241
Derrida, Jacques, 8
Des hommes et des dieux (2010), 8, 168
Devil's Own, The (1997), 48

Diderot, Denis, 3
digital networks and weapons, 91, 93, 99–100, 102; *see also* technology and terrorism
Dil Se (1998), 147
discomfort, notion of, 227–9, 234, 236–7, 240–1; *see also White Right: Meeting the Enemy* (2017)
dislocative fiction, 215, 217
disposable bodies, 179
Doane, Mary Ann, 132
documentary filmmaking, 224–5, 234–5, 240–1; *see also White Right: Meeting the Enemy* (2017)
domestic violence, 145, 148–9, 153, 194
Dominican Republic, 246
'double colonisation', 189
Douglass, William, 1, 38, 70, 88, 91, 93
Downing, Lisa, 225
Drif, Zohra, 18
dysmorphia, 229

Eastwood, Clint, 7, 17, 97
Ebiri, Belgi, 212–13
Eichmann, Adolf, 36
Eisenhower, Dwight D., 89
El Akkad, Omar, 22, 205, 209, 214–15, 217
El Paso shooting 2019, 268
emancipation for women, 189–90, 192–4, 197
empathy
  basic and reenactive, 206–8
  critical, 206–9, 215
  difficult, 22, 23, 207, 273
  and discomfort, 240–1
  empty, 178
  passive and active, 22, 23
  of the terrorist, 3–4
  with the terrorist, 2, 4–6, 9, 15, 20–3, 40, 71, 80–1, 212–13, 216–17, 272

with victims of terrorism, 13–14
with white terrorists, 270–2
see also 'condemnation imperative';
humanisation of the terrorist;
sympathy for the terrorist
Enloe, Cynthia, 128
Eriksson, Mia, 271
estranged familiarity, 254
ethics of discomfort, 234–9, 241, 273
ethics of viewing, 225
ethnicity, 69, 166–9; *see also* racial bias; racism
Evans, Brad, 21

Faludi, Susan, 228
family dysfunction as the cause of terrorism, 111–12
Fanon, Frantz, 115
fear
as a domestic weapon, 145
as a political weapon, 30, 36, 37–8, 43, 157–8, 160
of future violence, 75–7
female counter-strike, 145, 147, 151–60
female emancipation, 189–90, 192–4, 194, 197
female terrorists, 16–17, 18, 20, 196
caregiving and maternal feeling, 18, 33, 40–1, 133
gender norms and subversions, 130–3, 217
ISIS recruits, 183–6, 188–90, 192–7
militancy, 128–30, 131, 138, 194–5
motivation of, 18, 19, 34–5, 126–8, 195–6, 214
operating within the patriarchy, 31, 40–1
sexual violence against, 129–30
suicide terrorists, 19, 101–2, 135, 193–6, 205, 211–12, 216–18
see also American War (2017); *Good Terrorist, The* (1985); *In the Fade* (2017); *Just Another Jihadi Jane* (2016); *Only Problem, The* (1984); *Terrorist, The* (1998)
femininity, 126, 133, 144, 151, 158, 192
masquerade of, 126, 131–5
feminism, 41, 128, 153–4, 190, 194; *see also* emancipation for women
Fever Pitch (1992), 74
Fiji, 257
film as a means of understanding the terrorist, 205–6, 208–9
film posters, 149, 154–5
film studies, previous works on representation of the terrorist, 10–14
Final Score (2018), 17, 68, 78–80
Firm, The (2009), 75
Flood, Maria, 12, 22, 168, 264, 273
football disasters, 67, 71, 74–5, 81–2; *see also* hooliganism
Football Factory, The (1997), 75
football matches as terrorist targets, 77–82; *see also* hooliganism
forgiveness, 22
Foucault, Michel, 1, 75
Four Lions (2010), 191
Fradinger, Moira, 246, 251
framing, 6, 8, 171–3, 179, 232, 239
Français, Un (2015), 170
France, 20, 165–9, 170, 174–5
French colonialism, 166–7, 175–6, 178–80
Frank, Michael C., 264
French cinema, 166, 169, 174; *see also Chez nous* (2017); *Made in France* (2016)
French Revolution, 2–3
Freud, Sigmund, 37, 137, 227

INDEX

Friedersdorf, Conor, 237
From the Land of Green Ghosts (2002), 22–3, 246, 252–5

Gaddafi, Muammar, 76
Gallien, Clare, 187
Gandhi, Indira, 146
Gandhi, M. K., 145, 151
Gandhi, Rajiv, 19, 126, 135, 146
Ganor, Boaz, 30
Gauthier, Tim, 20, 22, 70–1, 264, 267, 272–3
Gaylin, Willard, 229
Gemini Man (2019), 87–8, 92
gender and terrorism, 18–20, 40–1, 101–2
   norms and subversions, 130–3, 135, 144, 194–7, 217, 228–9
   see also female terrorists; femininity; masculinity
gender-based violence, 129–30, 143–5, 147–9, 153–8, 160, 194, 196
Gentry, Caron E., 18, 196
Germany, 159
Gilroy, Paul, 179
Giroux, Henry A., 21
Goldblatt, David, 69
Golden Notebook, The (1962), 41
Good Friday Agreement 1997, 76
Good Terrorist, The (1985), 16–17, 30–1
   blackmail, personal grievance and narcissism, 34–5
   gender, 40–1
   Lessing's biographical influences, 32–3
   rhetoric and media attention, 36–8
   social class, 41–3
   symbolic targets, 38–9
   terrorist identity, 39–40
'good' terrorists and 'bad' terrorists, 55–8, 169, 180, 213, 265

Gopinath, Gayatri, 132
Gray, Richard, 105–6, 116
Green Arrow (1990–91), 60–3
Green Street (2005), 75
Guantanamo Bay, 216, 266
Gujarat riots 1969, 108
Gunaratna, Rohan, 230

Hackett, Elizabeth, 194
Hage, Ghassan, 5, 9, 204; *see also* 'condemnation imperative'
Hajjat, Abdellali, 19
Hall, Kenneth E., 96
Hall, Peter, 92
Hall, Stuart, 72–3, 76
Hamid, Mohsin, 19, 187
Harrington, Ralph, 89
Harrington Report 1968, 72
Haslanger, Sally, 194
hate speech, 226
Herman, Peter C., 14, 17–18, 76, 265
Hero: Love Story of a Spy, The (2003), 147
hero with personal connection to terrorist, 49, 51, 53, 58–9, 61–3
heteronormativity, 131–2, 133, 135, 228
Heysel Stadium disaster 1985, 67, 71–2
Hidden Agenda (1990), 61
hidden state, 159–60
Higgins, Charlotte, 228
hijab, 188–9
hijacking of aircraft, 147–8; *see also* 9/11
Hillsborough disaster 1989, 74–5, 81–2
Hindi cinema *see* Indian cinema
Hindu nationalism, 146, 159
Hinduism, 154
Hindu animosity with Muslims, 106–10, 145–6; *see also* India

Holland, Jack, 49
Hollande, François, 97
Hollywood cinema, 10–11, 21, 48, 55;
    see also *individual films*
Holocaust Studies, 267
Home Fire (2017), 14–15
homoeroticism, 132
homosexuality, 132, 228
Hooligan (1998), 73
hooliganism, 17
    changing nature of football, 74–8
    de- and re-politicisation of, 69–70, 74–5, 77, 82
    equated with terrorism, 68, 71, 82–3
    fictional representations of, 73–5, 77
    fictional terrorism at football matches, 77–82
    in the media, 70–1, 73, 79
    perspective of the 'hooligans', 70–1, 77
    rhetoric and media coverage, 67–9, 71–2, 79
    social construction of, 72–3
Hornby, Nick, 74
Horses of God (2012), 11
hostages, 152
humanisation of the terrorist, 11–13, 17–18, 101–3, 117, 147–8, 217, 226, 265, 269; *see also* dehumanisation; empathy
hunger strikes, 55
Hurt Locker, The (2008), 8

identification with perpetrators, 207; *see also* empathy
identity *see* terrorist identity
Igartuburu, Elena, 187, 188
imagined communities, 191–2
immigration policies, 97
imperialism *see* colonialism
In the Fade (2017), 22, 205, 209–13, 216–17

Incendiary (2005), 17, 68, 80–1
India, 19, 106, 108, 110–11, 126, 145–6, 154, 159, 260
    gender-based violence in, 143–5
    see also Association of Small Bombs, The (2016)
Indian cinema, 19, 90, 134, 143–8, 154–6, 160, 265
    Mother India trope, 149–51, 158, 160; *see also Neerja* (2016); *Simmba* (2018); *Tiger Zinda Hai* (2017)
Indian Peace Keeping Force (IPKF), 129
Inside Story (1991), 128, 132
Inspire (jihadist magazine), 91–2
intervals in films, 156
intimate enemies, 21–2, 246, 250–2, 254, 259–60; *see also* violence: intimate
invisible threat of terrorism, 89, 92–3
    technologies and networks, 98–101
IRA, 17, 47–9, 76, 112
    American support for, 49–50, 55, 58–9, 61, 63
    changing degrees of sympathy for, 48–50, 58–9, 62–3, 265, 268
    equated with football hooliganism, 68–9
    fanatical hardliner trope, 58–62
    'good' terrorists and 'bad' terrorists, 55–8
    reformed rebel trope, 50–5
Iran, 98
Iraq, 7–8, 152; *see also* War on Terror
Ireland *see* IRA; Northern Ireland conflict
Irish Northern Aid Committee (NORAID), 49, 55, 63
Iron Fist (1976–7), 50–6, 59, 61
irrational anxiety, 37–8
irrationality, 113, 266

INDEX

ISIS, 15, 152, 194–7
   female recruits, 183–6, 188–90, 192–4, 197; see also *Just Another Jihadi Jane* (2016)
Islam, 154
Islamic radicalism, 14–15, 19–20, 91–2, 109–10, 115, 131, 166, 169, 174–80, 223; see also ISIS
'Islamicipation', 190
Islamophobia, 19–20, 107–11, 165–6, 168–9, 176, 180, 223–4
   women's experiences of, 188–9
Israel, 5, 267
Italy, 32

Jackson, Richard, 74
Confessions of a Terrorist (2015), 113, 264
dehumanisation and tabooing of terrorists, 4, 9–10, 14, 70, 77, 217
   literature and empathy, 112–13, 204
   sympathy for the terrorist, 5, 15, 48, 50, 59, 105–6, 116, 117
James, William, 14
Japan, 247–8
Javid, Sajid, 184, 187
Jihad: A Story of the Others (2015), 223, 228
'jihadi brides', 183–6, 193–7; see also *Just Another Jihadi Jane* (2016)
jihadists see Islamic radicalism
Just Another Jihadi Jane (2016), 20, 197, 265
   assimilation, alienation, emancipation, 188–90, 192–4
   community and belonging, 191–2
   context, 185–6
   marriage and maternal relationships, 190–2, 194–7
   narration and gendered focus, 186–8, 196

Kabir, 154
Kapila, Shruti, 246
Kaplan, E. Ann, 178
Kashmir, 106–7, 114, 145–6; see also *Association of Small Bombs, The* (2016)
Keats, John, 217–18
Keen, Suzanne, 5–6
Kelkal, Khaled, 175
Khadra, Yasmina, 14
Khair, Tabish, 20, 185–8, 197; see also *Just Another Jihadi Jane* (2016)
Khan, Deeyah, 22, 223–6, 230–4, 236–8, 241; see also *White Right: Meeting the Enemy* (2017)
Khan, Salman, 155
Kimmel, Michael, 229
King, John, 75
Kleinman, Arthur, 251
Kneip, Katharina, 185, 190
Kruger, Diane, 209, 213
Kruglanski, Arie, 230
Kukar, Paulina, 240

La bête humaine, 90
LaCapra, Dominick, 23
Lajpat Nagar bombing 1996, 106, 109, 113
Landsberg, Alison, 171–2
Lang, Fritz, 159
Last Night of a Damned Soul, The (2004), 216
L'attentat (2005), 14–15
Le Pen, Marine, 169–70
Leake, Eric, 9, 13, 207
left-wing activism, 29, 35, 69, 71
left-wing terrorists, 16–17, 29–31, 43; see also *Good Terrorist, The* (1985); *Only Problem, The* (1984)
legal process, 156, 159–60; see also mob justice
Leicester School, 72

Lessing, Doris, 16–17, 30–3, 36, 41, 43; *see also Good Terrorist, The* (1985)
Levinas, Emmanuel, 171–2, 249–50, 254
Liberation Tigers of Tamil Eelam (LTTE), 126–30, 132, 135–6
Libyan terrorists, 76
'liquid modernity', 17, 88, 103
literary studies, previous works on representation of the terrorist, 13–15, 105–6
literature as a means of understanding the terrorist, 204–6, 208–9, 215
London bombings of 2005 (aka 7 July attacks or 7/7), 90–1
Lopez, Beatriz, 16–17, 265

M (1931), 159
Macbeth, 112
McBride, Sean, 267
MacCurdy, John T., 30
McGlothlin, Erin, 205–7
McManus, Anne-Marie, 217
McNamee, Eoin, 112
McQuillan, Martin, 33
McVeigh, Timothy, 272
Macron, Emmanuel, 166
Made in France (2016), 20, 166, 168–9, 174–80
Madrid train bombings of 2004, 90–1
Maghrebi people in France, 167
Mahajan, Karan, 17–18, 106, 113, 115, 117; *see also Association of Small Bombs, The* (2016)
male gaze, 134, 153, 155
Mali, 178–9
Malreddy, Pavan Kumar, 22–3, 267
Mandela, Nelson, 247, 267
Mandelbaum Gate, The (1965), 36
Mao II (1991), 116
Maras, Marie-Helen, 191
Marmysz, John, 170–1

marriage, 20, 148, 151, 190–1, 193–5, 197
Martin, Florence, 12
martyrdom, 12–13, 135, 194–5; *see also* suicide terrorists
Marvel Comics, 17, 47, 60
Marxism, 42–3
masculinity, 98, 154–5, 239, 251
  crisis of, 228–9
  violent young men, 69, 71, 81
Massumi, Brian, 75–6
maternal body, 138
maternal feeling, 126–7, 133, 135–7, 194–7; *see also* Mother India trope
maternal relationships, 190–2
Matthes, Jörg, 19
Mbembe, Achille, 250
media coverage of terrorism, 19, 68, 223
  amplification, 36–7, 73, 76
  in France, 165–6
  hierarchy of grief, 168
  representation of 'jihadi brides', 183–5, 196–7
  violent vs non-violent action, 116
melodrama, 134
middle classes *see* social class
militarisation of women, 128–31, 138, 194–5
Mineta Transportation Institute, 91–2
Miss Burma (2017), 248
Mitgang, Herbert, 39
Mitterrand, François, 178
mob justice, 156–60
modernity, 17, 88–9, 92, 103; *see also* technology and terrorism
Modi, Narendra, 108–10, 115
Mohammed, Marwan, 19
Mohan, Rajeswari, 18–19, 265
Morag, Raya, 21
Morgan, Piers, 184
Morton, Adam, 204–5, 208

Morton, Stephen, 250
Mother India (1957), 150
Mother India trope, 149–51, 158, 160
motherhood, 126–7, 135, 194–7
motivations of the terrorist
    attempts to understand, 5, 9, 21, 80–1
    and audience sympathy, 50, 112–15
    community, belonging and altruism, 191–2, 203–4, 223, 226, 230
    and empathy, 208, 214
    female terrorists, 18–19, 34–5, 126–8, 195–6, 214
    grief, 252
    IRA comic book portrayals, 55, 57–61
    'jihadi brides', 184–5, 188, 193–4
    the personal and the political, 17–18, 115–17
    personal grievance and narcissism, 34–5, 111–12
    psychological explanations, 13, 127–8, 203, 271
    suicide terrorists, 125, 127–8, 208
    see also depoliticisation of terrorism; tabooing of terrorists
Moulessehoul, Mohammed *see* Khadra, Yasmina
Mountbatten, Lord, 50
multiculturalism, 236–7
Murder on the Orient Express (1934), 90
Muslim Brotherhood, 109, 115
Muslims
    animosity with Hindus, 106, 145–6
    anti-Muslim bias and violence, 19–20, 107–11, 165–6, 168–9, 176, 180, 223–4
    women, 183–6, 188–9, 193–7
    see also Islamic radicalism
mythography of terrorism, 264–71, 273

Nacos, Brigitte L., 93
Nandy, Ashis, 250, 259
narration, 186–8, 205
Nasser, Gamal Abdel, 110
National Socialist Movement (NSM), 224–5, 231, 235; *see also* Charlottesville Rally 2017; white supremacists
Nazism, 267
Neerja (2016), 19, 144, 147–51, 155, 160
Neeson, Liam, 211–12
neoliberalism, 71, 73, 144
neo-Nazism *see* right-wing extremists
Neuburger, Luisella de Cataldo, 196
New Football Writing, 74–5, 76–7, 80, 82
New Zealand, 229, 235, 263, 268–71
Ngai, Sianne, 37, 71–2
Nichols, Bill, 224–5, 234
Nigeria, 168
Nobel Peace Prize, 247, 267
non-violence, 35, 115–16, 138, 151
non-Western representations of terrorists in literature and film, 11–12, 15–16, 264–5, 268, 273
Northern Ireland conflict, 47–50, 58–9, 63, 76, 112; *see also* IRA
Norway, 223–4, 271
novels and bourgeois morality, 42
nuclear energy and weaponry, 89–90

Of Gods and Men (2010), 8, 168
Only Problem, The (1984), 16–17, 30–1, 33
    blackmail, personal grievance and narcissism, 34–5
    gender, 40–1
    rhetoric and media attention, 32–3, 36–8
    social class, 41–3
    Spark's biographical influences, 31–2

symbolic targets, 38–9
terrorist identity, 39–40
Orientalism, 78, 131
otherness, 70–2, 83, 98, 249–50; *see also* counterterrorist terminology and rhetoric; dehumanisation

Pain, Rachel, 145, 148
Pakistan, 106, 108, 145–6, 260
Pakistani terrorists, 158
Paknadel, Alexis, 13–14, 105, 107, 116
Palestinian terrorists, 5, 12–13, 147–8
Pape, Robert, 203
Paradise Now (2005), 12–13
Paris terrorist attacks 2015, 165, 174
patriarchy, 31, 132–3, 144–5, 147, 151, 153–5, 160, 189, 196–7, 228–9
Patriot Games (1992), 48, 61
Pearson, Allison, 184
Pelaschiar, Laura, 56
Pennant, Cass, 70
Perešin, Anita, 192, 194
Perkins, Mitali, 245–6
Perpetrator Studies, 112, 209
Peru, 250
Petersen, Kirsten Holst, 189
Pezeu-Massabuau, Jacques, 228, 236–7
Pierce, William Luther, 272
Pinfari, Marco, 3
Pink (2016), 144
Piskurek, Cyprian, 17, 265
Pittel, Harald, 18–19, 265
Pittsburgh synagogue shooting 2018, 268
pity, 21–2
political commitment *see* artistic autonomy and political commitment
Political Warfare Executive (PWE), 31–2, 36–7

Pollard, Tom, 21
postcolonialism, 246, 250–1, 259–60
post-war revolutionary terrorists *see* left-wing terrorists
Power Man and Iron Fist (1979), 53–4, 58
Preventing and Countering Violent Extremism (PCVE), 266
propaganda, 29, 30–2, 36–7, 192–3, 226, 272
protests, 35, 116
proxy bombs, 59, 62–3
Pryluck, Calvin, 225
psychoanalysis, 37
psychological warfare, 30–2, 36–8, 43
Punjab, 145
purification, 130

Qatar, 148
Qutb, Sayyid, 109–10, 115

racial bias, 166–73, 175–80, 265, 268
racism, 20, 22, 223–4, 267, 271; *see also* Islamophobia; right-wing extremists
radicalisation, 12–13, 15, 20, 109–10, 116, 178, 214
  group belonging, 191, 223
  'jihadi brides', 183–6, 188, 193
Rai, Amit, 127–8, 131
railroads *see* trains and railroads
rape, 129–30, 155–8; *see also* gender-based violence
Rapist, The (2021), 144
Rassemblement National party, 170
recruitment of terrorists, 183–6, 191, 193; *see also* radicalisation
Red Brigades, 29, 32–3, 39
redaction, 187
refugees, 169, 172–3, 214–15
re-historicisation of terrorism, 16
relatability, 205–6

relationship of responsibility, 171–3
Reluctant Fundamentalist, The (2007), 19, 187
Remembrance Day bombing, Enniskillen, 1987, 49, 63
repentant terrorists, 15, 49, 50–5
republicanism in France, 166–8, 175–6
Resurrection Man (1994), 112
revenge, 210–12, 254–5, 258
Revill, George, 92, 96
rhetoric *see* counterterrorist terminology and rhetoric; propaganda
Rich, Adrienne, 132
right-wing extremists, 20, 22, 165–6, 169–73, 180, 210, 213, 226, 228–9, 235–6, 238–41, 268–73; *see also Chez Nous* (2017); *In the Fade* (2017); *White Right: Meeting the Enemy* (2017)
Rigouste, Mathieu, 167, 175
Riquet, Johannes, 17
Riviere, Joan, 132
Road to Rangoon, The (2015), 22–3, 246, 255–9
Rodino-Colocino, Michelle, 22
Roekel, Eva, 205
Rohingya massacre 2016–17, 247, 249, 251
Roja (1992), 146
Romper Stomper (1992), 170
Ronson, Jon, 224
Rothberg, Michael, 105, 116
Rotman, Patrick, 21, 254
Rumsfeld, Donald, 76
Russia, 32, 90
Russian terrorists, 58, 78–9
Rutherford, Anna, 189

Sadat, Anwar, 110
Sageman, Marc, 191
Said, Edward, 12, 16, 39–40
Salmi, Katya, 166–8
Saltman, Erin Marie, 193
Sampson, Kevin, 75
Sands, Bobby, 55
Sarojini Nagar bombing 2005, 106
satire, 169–70
Saxton, Libby, 225
Scanlan, Margaret, 36
Scheerer, Sebastian, 2
Schivelbusch, Wolfgang, 89
Schmitt, Carl, 159
Schmitt, Mark, 69
Schoep, Jeff, 231–3, 235
Schwartz, Lynne Sharon, 105
Schwarzenegger, Arnold, 10–11
Second World War, 30–2, 36–7
Secret Agent, The (1907), 31, 38, 112
Seedat, Zaynab, 20, 265
September 11, 2001 *see* 9/11
sexploitation, 154
sexual deviance, 14
sexual purification, 130
sexual violence *see* gender-based violence
sexualising of terrorist violence, 117
sexuality, in anti-American rhetoric, 110–11
Shah, Amit, 108
Shakespeare, William, 14, 112
Shamsie, Kamila, 14–15
Shannon, William B., 55
Shapiro, Lauren, 191
Shaw, Tony, 10–11, 13
Sidhwa, Bapsi, 260
silent threat of terrorism *see* invisible threat of terrorism
Simmba (2018), 19, 144, 147, 155–60
Singh, Jyoti, 143
Sivan, Santosh, 127, 134, 136–7; *see also Terrorist, The* (1998)
Sjoberg, Laura, 18, 196, 251, 257
skinheads, 170–1

slavery, 167–8
'sleeper' terrorists, 158
Sloterdjik, Peter, 227
Sluka, Jeffrey, 49
Smaill, Belinda, 21, 225, 234
Smith, Melanie, 193
Snowpiercer (2013), 89–90
social class, 41–3, 89
  and football, 69, 73–5, 79–81
  and right-wing extremism, 224, 232, 238–40
social inequality, 70–3, 82, 237, 240
social media, 183, 191–2, 232–4, 237, 241
song-and-dance sequences, 152–4
Soni (2018), 144
Sooryavanshi (2021), 158
Source Code (2011), 99
South Asian cinema, 18–19
Southern Rhodesia, 32
Soviet Union, 32, 90
Spark, Muriel, 16–17, 30–4, 36–7, 39, 41, 43; see also Only Problem, The (1984)
Speckhard, Anne, 217
spectacle of terrorism, 21, 74, 91, 266
Spencer, Richard, 225, 230, 238–40
Spielberg, Steven, 14
sport events as terrorist targets, 77
spy thrillers, 91
Spy Who Loved Me, The (novel, 1962), 91
Sri Lanka, 126, 128–30, 138, 145; see also Tamil separatists
Sri Lankan Mothers' Front, 138
Stampnitzky, Lisa, 205, 266
state oppression and violence, 101–2, 265–7
state terrorism, terminology of, 3
stereotypes of the terrorist see Western representations of terrorists in literature and film

Stevenson Murer, Jeffrey, 196, 214
storytelling, 186–8
Stueber, Karsten, 206–8
suicide terrorists, 5, 135
  'condemnation imperative', 203–6
  empathy for, 216–18
  female, 19, 101–2, 135, 193–6, 205, 211–12, 216–18
  motivations of, 125, 127–8, 208
  radicalisation of, 12–13
  representations of, 136
superheroes, 17
Supertrain (1979), 90
surveillance, 68, 74–5, 93, 100, 103, 266
Suu Kyi *see* Aung San Suu Kyi
symbolic targets, 38–9, 77–8, 80, 91–2
sympathy for the terrorist, 5–6, 265, 269
  ambiguous portrayals, 112–17
  'good' terrorists and 'bad' terrorists, 55–8, 169, 180, 213, 265
  hero with personal connection to terrorist, 49, 51, 53, 58–9, 61–3
  IRA, 48–50, 62–3
  reformed rebel trope, 50–1
  right-wing extremists, 170–4
  sympathy for cause, not the methods, 58–62, 63
  see also empathy
Syria, 183–4

tabooing of terrorists, 1–2, 76, 78–9, 81, 88, 93–4, 217, 265, 267, 270–1
Taking of Pelham 123, The (2009), 99
Taliban, 110
Tamil separatists, 126, 128–30, 132, 134–6
targets
  football matches, 77–82
  symbolic, 38–9, 77–8, 80, 91–2
  see also trains and railroads

INDEX

Tarr, Carrie, 168
Taylor, Ian, 72
Taylor Report, 74, 75
technology and terrorism, 17, 87–9, 91–3, 98–100, 102–3
'Tera Noor' (song), 152–4
terrorism, definition of, 23, 30; *see also* terrorist and counterterrorist, fluidity of labels
terrorism as metaphor for violence against women, 145, 147–9, 153, 155, 157–8, 160
terrorism discourse, 264
Terrorist, The (1998), 19, 147, 216, 265
  ending, 137
  feminine masquerade, 126, 131–5
  gender norms and subversions, 130–3, 135
  maternity and melodrama, 126–7, 133, 134–8
  the political and the personal, 126–8
terrorist and counterterrorist, fluidity of labels, 68, 246–9, 251–2, 259–60, 267
terrorist as the focus in terrorist fiction, 106
terrorist identity, 39–40
Thatcher, Margaret, 17, 59, 60
  stance on hooliganism, 67–72
Theidon, Kimberley, 250–1
Theroux, Louis, 224, 236
Thiruchelvam, Neelan, 128
threat of future violence, 75–7
Thwe, Pascal Khoo, 22–3, 246, 252–5
Tiger Zinda Hai (2017), 19, 144, 147, 151–5, 158, 160
Timbuktu (2014), 11
Time Bomb (1953), 90
'To Be a Somebody' (1994) *see Cracker* (1993–5)
Toros, Harmonie, 272
torture, 215–16, 266

trade unionism, 71
trains and railroads
  anxieties associated with, 90–2, 102
  in film and TV, 88–90, 95–7, 102–3
  invisibility and concealment of, 94–6
  in literature, 89–91
  technology and modernity, 87–90, 92–3, 98–100, 102
  terrorism, 88–9, 91–2, 101–3
  see also 15:17 to Paris, The (2018); *Bodyguard* (2018)
trauma
  of perpetrators of terrorism, 51–5, 209
  of victims of gender-based violence, 149
  of victims of terrorism, 53–4, 80–1
Trnka, Susanna, 257
troubled terrorist *see* reformed rebel characterisation
Troubles thrillers, 48, 54, 61
True Lies (1994), 10–11
Trujillo, Rafael, 246
Trump, Donald, 97–8, 107, 232, 238
Turner Diaries, The (1978), 272
Tutu, Desmond, 247
Twitter, 183, 233–4; *see also* social media

'ugly feelings', 71–4
UK miners' strike of 1984–85, 68–9
understanding the terrorist, 5–6, 9, 21, 80–1, 106, 216
  fictional representations as a means of, 204–6, 208–9, 215
  see also empathy; humanisation of the terrorist; sympathy for the terrorist
'ungrievable life', 6–11, 168
United States *see* America
unrepentant terrorists, 60, 63
Updike, John, 14

Urdu, 154
USSR *see* Soviet Union

Valentini, Daniele, 188
Valentini, Tiziana, 196
Vanhala, Helena, 10
veterans, 229, 233
victim as the focus in terrorist fiction, 105
victimisation of the terrorist, 20–1, 51–5, 172
victim-perpetrators, 213–15
Vidal, Frédérique, 166
vigilante justice, 156–60
violence
  against women, 143–5, 147–9, 153–7, 160, 194, 196
  and degree of sympathy for the terrorist, 50–1, 58–60, 62–3
  hierarchy of, 266–7
  intimate, 246, 248–51, 254–5, 257, 259–60
  non-political, 56
  in popular culture, 143
visual hierarchies, 173, 175, 178–80
von Knop, Katharina, 195

Walshe, Shane, 17, 264–5, 268
Walther, Rudolf, 16
War on Terror, 7, 76, 146, 268–70
Wasted Vigil, The (2008), 14
Web of Spider-Man (1986), 59–60, 62
Weber, Cynthia, 251
Western bias, 8–9
Western lifestyle, 188–90, 192–3
Western representations of terrorists in literature and film, 10–11, 15–16, 21, 48, 55, 264–8, 273

Western (film genre), 96–7
white privilege, 166–8, 170–3, 175–80, 271
  fear of losing, 229
White Right: Meeting the Enemy (2017), 22
  discomfort, notion of, 227–9
  discomfort of Khan and her subjects, 229–34
  discomforting conversations, 235–6
  emotional pull of extremism, 226
  empathy and discomfort, 240–1
  filmmaking style and process, 223–6
  ideological change, 234–5, 238, 241
  limitations of discomfort, 236–9
white supremacists *see* right-wing extremists
white terrorists, 166, 169, 212–13, 265, 268–73
Wiktorowicz, Quintan, 195
Williams, Linda, 154
Winter, Charlie, 192, 194
women in anti-American rhetoric, 111
working classes *see* social class
world cinema *see* non-Western representations of terrorists in literature and film
Writing on the Wall, The (2005), 105

Yellow Birds, The (2017), 8
YouTube, 153–4

Zakaria, Rafia, 190
Zidane, Zinedine, 175
Zimbabwe, 32
Žižek, Slavoj, 250, 254
Zola, Emile, 90
Zulaika, Joseba, 1, 38, 70, 88, 91, 93

EU representative:
Easy Access System Europe
Mustamäe tee 50, 10621 Tallinn, Estonia
Gpsr.requests@easproject.com